BY

Erna Fergusson

NEW MEXICO
A PAGEANT OF THREE PEOPLES (*1951, 1964*)

MEXICO REVISITED (*1955*)

CUBA (*1946*)

CHILE (*1943*)

OUR SOUTHWEST (*1940*)

VENEZUELA (*1939*)

GUATEMALA (*1937*)

These are Borzoi Books
Published in New York by ALFRED A. KNOPF

New Mexico

U.S. FOREST SERVICE AND THE SOIL CONSERVATION SERVICE,
ALBUQUERQUE, NEW MEXICO

New Mexico

A PAGEANT
OF THREE PEOPLES

Erna Fergusson

SECOND EDITION
with an introduction by
PAUL HORGAN

UNIVERSITY OF NEW MEXICO PRESS
Albuquerque

For LINDA MUSSER,

who helped me to know my own state,

not only because she saw it freshly as a newcomer,

but because her sympathetic appreciation of its people

has always been spiced with lively humor.

Erna Fergusson and New Mexico

An Introduction

IN HER LIFETIME, MANY PEOPLE spoke of Erna Fergusson as New Mexico's unofficial first lady, and in her memory, many still do. By this they have meant to pay tribute to a person who by her own generous activities, beauty of character, and deep study and devoted expression of the qualities of New Mexico earned for herself that title in her native state.

She was born in Albuquerque of a cultivated pioneer family. Her grandfather, Franz Huning, was a German merchant who built in Albuquerque's Old Town a miniature castle (since demolished) in the romantic style of Ludwig II. I remember it from my boyhood in Albuquerque. It was made of adobes, with wooden flourishes, and was painted white; it had turrets, fountains, *allées* of trees, a ballroom with a small pipe organ where the boys and girls of my time were dragged to dancing school; its grounds reached through fine cottonwood groves and marshes of tall grass to the Rio Grande a mile or so away. Miss Fergusson's mother was Clara Huning, daughter of Franz. She married lawyer H. B. Fergusson, who was New Mexico's territorial delegate to Congress and who, in 1912, became the state's first full-fledged congressman. Miss Fergusson's family—her sister, her two brothers, her mother, and herself—thus had experience of life in Washington, and she herself had interesting years in New York where she moved in the world of the arts and letters. When she returned afterward to Albuquerque, it was to stay; and all

New Mexico life, my own small part of it included, was enriched as a result.

I had already become a familiar of the Fergusson family through my boyhood friendship with Francis, the youngest, my contemporary, who later was to become the brilliant professor and critic. It was an event when in due course I met the novelist of the family, Harvey Fergusson, who though he did not live in Albuquerque came home for visits during the fall hunting seasons. Lina, the younger sister, was married and lived in California. Erna, the oldest, lived at home with her widowed mother, and with her made the household where of all those I knew in Albuquerque I felt most directly in touch with the graces of civilized life and the possibility of growth in those directions of the arts and ideas to which I was then aspiring as an adolescent. The years brought my own expression and its natural directions; and throughout decades Erna Fergusson gave me a great share of the wise friendship and guidance she held forth all her life to those who had the good fortune to need her sense of humanity. This was a rare and deeply empathetic quality in her which gave her immediate insight and fellow feeling for others, whether in terms of shared intellectual interests, or humor, or compassion for suffering, or courageous words and acts on her part against man's inhumanity to man. In the protracted suffering which came to her during her last years, one saw most clearly the grace and gallantry which she had long lent to others who had need of these aspects of her sustaining strength. Anyone in trouble of spirit or outward circumstance could always turn to her and receive from her the empowering fortitude which lay behind her wit, her gaiety, her enthusiasm for life's beauties, rare or common. She had a genius for casting bridges of understanding across the space of loneliness which in one or another degree every individual person feels. On taking leave of her, one always felt better than oneself.

She was a tall person who held herself beautifully and moved with energetic grace. Her eyes were a fine sky-blue which reflected her thought with piercing immediacy. Her face had marks of great humor. It was always a delight to hear her in anecdote—beautifully framed words, a voice of fine timbre, her hands held palms upward as if bearing her opinion and making gestures of circular support for her story, which was often droll and punctuated with little runs of laughter. One of her favorite comments on some egregious piece of idiocy was, "Isn't it simply gor-r-rgeous?" As her years went on, she grew more and more distinguished in mind and bearing, so that while not conventionally handsome, she ended by impressing everyone with an appearance as beautiful as it was civilized.

Her mother's modest house in Orchard Place had the elegance of complete simplicity. Mrs. Fergusson (who lived to a great age) and Erna often received friends in the late afternoons, and I remember tea in winter by the fireplace, and iced ades in summer under a great garden cottonwood tree; and usually there was some interesting guest, foreign or domestic. Albuquerque was then a small city, suited to the landscape, graced by cottonwoods, and uninterrupted views of the great Sandia range, and the still-wild shores of the accessible Rio Grande. An immigrant at the age of twelve, I came to love New Mexico very early, and the chief agents of this dedication were the Fergussons.

Too, in their conversation, and from their bookshelves, I took my earliest knowledge of another country—the literature of the twentieth century. My first adult contemporary reading stemmed from Orchard Place—*Crome Yellow* by Aldous Huxley, the early books of Willa Cather, Joseph Hergesheimer, H. L. Mencken (who published Harvey

Fergusson regularly in his magazines), D. H. Lawrence, Freud, James Branch Cabell, and the lot. All such were discussed, and in consequence, literature and life came together for me as they never had before.

Miss Fergusson helped me to see newly in other ways, too, in those days of my early youth. One such way was to see New Mexico through her experiences. On a Christmas Eve in bitter cold and starlit clarity she took me and one or two others down the river to the pueblo of Isleta to see the Indians dance at midnight. I remember the inscrutable pueblo in the dark; the bonfires playing along the roadside edge of the church to guide the Christ Child to the little clay Rio Grande town; the strange sudden eruption of the bared and decorated dancers from the kiva, and their entry into the Catholic chapel at the offertory of midnight Mass to drop their silver U.S. currency in a glass dish before the plaster infant Jesus of the crèche; and their return to the placita to dance their immemorial ballet of commemoration and propitiation of their own gods. Miss Fergusson explained to me, a Catholic northeasterner, how one culture could overlie another in that midnight ceremony in almost equal power if both agreed on a compromise which paid honor to two traditions, both of which must meaningfully survive if either was to help a people to do so. It was a prime lesson in how her power of personality could enter into contrasting expressions of life and compose harmony of differences. Her gift of social respect ripened the more she gave herself to the study of national or ethnic peoples in their disparities. She was always able to detect the common humanity as against the abstract differences imposed by nation, language, skin color, or separately derived mythology. It was this sympathetic respect which in all her books made it possible for her to enter into the spiritual localism, as it were, of the society she was interpreting for us—the Cuban, the Chilean, the Mexican, the Guatemalan, the

Hawaiian, the Pueblo Indian—to bring us the alien as if it were the most neighborly of social styles.

Miss Fergusson learned her land through the most direct experiences. Midway in her life she organized with a hearty friend named Miss Hickey a program of tours of the New Mexican Indian settlements which later was taken over by the Fred Harvey system. "Indian Detours" was what the side trips were called as they flourished in the period of the greatest prosperity, excellence, and reliability of the Santa Fe railroad during the pre-airport age of American travel. She also set out on numerous private expeditions for her own pleasure and information, and I remember seeing her off for Mexico in an early station wagon with her brilliant and lovely friend Katherine Chaves Page in the times when highways in Mexico were still better suited to oxcarts with cottonwood wheels than to modern cars with vulnerable rubber tires. I had heard of earth scratches and ruts which passed for roads as they dipped into arroyos in dry weather and halted at the brim in wet. This outset was launched only a few years after Pancho Villa's raids in Chihuahua and in New Mexico, and I anxiously asked if the two ladies were provided with weapons of defense.

"But of course," said Miss Fergusson, at the start of the overland motor voyage from Orchard Place. With every sign of reassurance, she pointed to a wall of close-meshed chicken wire between the driver's seat of the station wagon and the capacious luggage space behind; and lodged handily in the interstices behind the front seat was a Woolworth ice pick as an emergency device to repel *bandidos* or any other intruder of ill intent. The defiant comedy of this illustrated the amused absence of fear which was a deep vein of her character.

It was my fortune to see a number of her books as they grew in manuscript. She worked with newspapermen's yellow copy paper, wrote directly at the typewriter, and often asked me to read a chapter when it was in completed first draft. I could not help remarking on her system of cutting paragraphs apart and reassembling them, for instead of white paste or paper clips or staples, she kept at hand a paper of dressmaker's pins, and with these she pinned her paragraphs in place when she had their sequence firmly in mind. She laughed over my astonishment, and asked to know what was more natural to a lady writer than to use straight pins to hold her pattern together.

But what came out of this method was not something run up by a literary seamstress to meet the notions of the season. It was her knowledge of her land—its farthest history and its every earth feature—which gave substance to her text. For she had traversed all the area of New Mexico, the larger Southwest, and Mexico, often under outlandish conditions which brought to mind the travels of Archbishop Lamy alone on his burro *"sous la belle étoile"* and of Adolf Bandelier going on foot in his bowler hat, black broadcloth suit, and single pair of shoes, with his umbrella as his only weapon in a land alien in distances and community styles. In her fearlessness, humor, and sympathy, Miss Fergusson was the match of any of her forebears in the task of entering into the life and spirit of each of the Southwest's contributing cultures. You could read in her countenance a particular crinkled respect for other human beings who came from a heritage different from her own—the Indian, the Hispanic, and the Anglo-American. Her sense of all such people was so intuitively tolerant and at the same time so objectively observant that her strong feelings for them assumed shape in her work as ideas about society, first locally, and then, by strong implication, in general relation to human ways as historically significant.

Though she wrote many books about other places, it was the New Mexican country and its people which summoned forth her strongest responses. She was the first author, beyond those scientists who reported on Indian ways for the

Bureau of Ethnology in the nineteenth century and those others who kept informal records in diaries and letters of early Western experiences, to reveal to a wide public the solemn beauties and meanings of Pueblo Indian liturgical dances (*Dancing Gods*, 1932), and she returned in this, her last book, to give us *A Pageant of Three Peoples* which remains the most flavorsome and true account of her native state. It is a book of real value to that ever-widening public who have discovered New Mexico in late years, have greatly swelled both its permanent and its seasonal populations, and have brought to new dimensions the old problems which have always existed there.

In its essentials, this book is as true today as it was two decades ago when it was first published. Change has come rapidly and in some places as a mixed blessing—but this has always been true of a land of great spaces and incomparable landscape which has a laminated culture bearing marks of successive conquests through the centuries. Against a background seemingly timeless, change has been thrown into relief as the dominant theme of New Mexico. Harvey Fergusson, in his admirable novels, stated this as an artist. Miss Fergusson treats of the same vital subject as a historian and a student of human ways.

A glance at her table of contents will tell the reader how she has organized her essays. This is not a simple consecutive narrative but a gallery of views and interpretations—under the subheadings of Indian, Spanish, and Gringo—faithful to history, enlivened by the insights of an original and cultivated spirit, so that in Miss Fergusson's company we encounter familiar subject matter in many a new pattern and in strong new light. She plays the present against the past in each of her cultural surveys, and lets us see modern vestiges attached to their primal roots.

The range of her book is constantly rewarding. Chapters III and IV, for example, could enliven any discussion in comparative religion for their interpretations of Pueblo liturgy, the kachinas, and the Roman Catholic framework within which the Franciscan missionaries embraced the Indian culture. Again, since her grandfather Huning knew Kit Carson and spoke of him, Miss Fergusson is able to inform us, as no one else has, that Carson had a "thin voice"—just the sort of detail to help a historical personage spring out of his frame of the abstract into life. In Chapter XX she gives us a fine succession of capsule biographies of frontier people; and in all her pages concerned with modern life and its problems, she makes her points with anecdotal reference to actual persons, Indian, Latin, or Gringo, from whose life experience she has drawn facts and meanings. The overall result of her devoted approach to her materials is to make us see the people and actions of the past as actual gestures of life, and those of the present as beings and concerns whose reality reaches far back into tradition, chronicle, and the early source of social attitudes and technics—once again, Indian, Spanish, Gringo. A striking example of the powers which the third of these historical groups brought into our own time is given in her account of the first atomic bomb test in the Jornada del Muerto north of Alamogordo in 1945—surely the most arresting popular treatment of this cataclysmic event.

Since, as we have recognized, change is the continuing theme cast into relief by the peculiarly visible historical character of New Mexico, it is to be noted that in the two decades since this book was first published, a few of Miss Fergusson's observations have lost their factual value. We can cite examples, but against the great backdrop of her historical scope and human concern they do not seriously invalidate the general text, and she would be the first to think of the changes to be noticed—new paragraphs on yellow paper would be pinned over obsolete matter, if she were still with us to supervise this edition.

For the convenience of a new generation of readers, we may note such differences as these from statements origi-

nally set forth in Miss Fergusson's pages. In Cathedral Place
at Santa Fe, James Seligman's "notable shop" is gone, replaced by a hotel parking lot. Mesilla, New Mexico, no
longer quite drowses under its cottonwoods, having become a smart cocktail and bedroom suburb of Las Cruces.
At Albuquerque, the Alvarado Hotel is gone, that monument on the Santa Fe tracks which was for generations the
social focus of the state's metropolis. In Las Cruces a once
brilliant lupanar, later a uniquely attractive inn, is now a
bank building. If Ruidoso even twenty years ago was on the
way to commercial distortion, it is now thanks to horse racing and skiing a clamorous resort with a weekend population of forty thousand in a one-street canyon town better
suited to its original, and discreetly placed, little log cabins.
In 1951 Miss Fergusson lamented the absence of any museums worthy of the name outside Santa Fe; but today, one
feels, she would be the first to acknowledge the extraordinary growth of the Roswell Museum, which has become one of the nation's finest examples of what a small
city can achieve in developing a local cultural resource of
the first class. Elsewhere, if Miss Fergusson spoke of the
"nearest railroad town," she would now refer to the "nearest airport town," for obvious reasons. She celebrates the
Gallup Indian Ceremonial as a demonstration of what the
combined Indian peoples of New Mexico can show the
world of their ancient and beautiful arts, but in 1972 there
seemed strong likelihood that the annual event would not
continue past that year.

Such inevitable variations of historical behavior do nothing to conceal the power and sympathy, the truth and concern of Miss Fergusson's treatment of the persistent themes
of New Mexican life. These finally resolve into two main
problems—one reaching to the heart of the social spirit, the
other to the critical material issue of the availability of
water. Depending upon your view of progress and survival, both problems breed controversy.

To take the first—in all her humane descriptions and pleas in the interest of decent relationships between New Mexico's three elements of society, Miss Fergusson is always aware of the sadness implicit in acculturation under pressures which force people to change their ways. Decades ago she saw the seeds of prejudice, condescension, and intolerance in the Anglo attitudes toward the Indian and the New Mexican Latin; and today we are seeing in varying degrees of response, ranging from intelligent civil group action to mindless violence, the energy of the Chicano movement by which ancient inheritors of the land are reaching for respect, at the least, and a decent share, at the most, of their own heritage, which is now controlled by the Anglo colonizers who, with high skills and a conviction of superiority, came to the old kingdom of New Mexico and made it into a federated state among others of the same image. "Like every fight for decency," writes Miss Fergusson in these pages, "New Mexico's fight is slow, often discouraging." But she does not despair—she poses the problems in their most stark aspects, with the sense that if truly seen they can be solved, however intricate they may be. "The problem is to reconcile 'the ways of the ancients'"—this among the Pueblos—"with the concepts and needs of today: rain dances with farm machinery, inoculations with curing societies, old moralities with modern taboos—or old taboos with modern moralities." So far, Miss Fergusson observed in her time, "the outer world has been winning steadily." And she cited the self-evident idiocy of government teachers who brought to Indians the gift of pedagogic systems as if dealing with stereotypes. She quoted one teacher who exclaimed, when the system failed to settle comfortably upon all Indian pupils alike, "Oh, well, if you're going into their *psychology!* . . ."

Her sense of the needs and feelings of individuals and peoples, whether white, brown, or black, Christian or pagan, enlightened or benighted, never failed her; and it is this humane wisdom which makes her report of the multifarious society of ner native province so reliable, moving, and civilized.

As for water, the other persistent problem of New Mexico, and indeed, the whole Southwest, her voice remains eloquent in the midst of the clamor which continues to proclaim a future of progress—that is, "growth"—for New Mexico, as though there were unlimited water resources in a vast area recognized through centuries as falling within the definition of what a desert is. Since her day, New Mexico has been experiencing a development boom which looks no further than the quick profit available within the lifetime of the present generation. But Miss Fergusson quoted twenty years ago an eminent geologist and college president who said, with no reference to an increase of population but only to what then appeared in the census, "If we expect to maintain a normal increase in the standards of people already here we shall have to get more water or conserve our water better." But Miss Fergusson was never one to assume the worst. She ended her very first chapter here this way: "Altogether, New Mexico was to prove a land where men could live together well if they learned to respect water and to use it sparingly, to deal fairly with good soil, and to lay by for the inevitable years of drought. How succeeding peoples have worked these problems out over two thousand years is our story." We can only hope that, profiting by the demonstration of such wisdom as hers, future citizens will continue to seek just the bounty sufficient to good New Mexican life which continues to delight people today.

It is the many-faceted character of that life which Erna Fergusson has so sensitively described for us in these pages. She was able to do so because no one ever lived in greater harmony with the immediate environment than she. It is lovely to remember her, aside from her learning and wisdom, in the intimate image of her personal environment, which seemed to be symbolic of so much of her individual grace. One most often thinks of her presence as shaded by a great cottonwood, that most bounteous of Rio Grande trees, with its dappled light, its cool shade, its pungent leaves warmed by the sun, its great spreading silvery branches, its lovely mild rustle in the moving air.

Paul Horgan
1973

Foreword

NEW MEXICO *is the scene of the longest span of human development in the Western Hemisphere. Traces of earliest
man have been found in a mountain cave; on a high plateau
the atomic bomb was made. Much of the long drama of
human development has been only faintly reflected in New
Mexico, but the acts that have been played here have left to
the modern state vestiges of a pageant of three peoples. The
rites of prehistoric Indians and of Europeans of the Middle
Ages are still practiced here. The two frontiers—Spanish and
United States—met and fused in New Mexico. This is important for the record. It is of greater value, now that our
country has been forced into world leadership, that in New
Mexico the peoples of three cultures have successfully
worked out a life together.*

Acknowledgments

Many people—too many to name—have helped me, in conversation and in correspondence, to gather and to evaluate the material used in this book. I will only name certain authorities who have been kind enough to read chapters and to check them for factual errors. They are: archæologist Erik K. Reed of the National Park Service; anthropologists Dr. Clyde Kluckhohn, Harvard, and Dr. Anne M. Smith; William A. Brophy, former Commissioner of Indian Affairs; historians Dr. France V. Scholes and Dr. Dorothy Woodward, University of New Mexico, and Fray Angelico Chavez; sociologists Dr. Lyle Saunders and Dr. Paul A. F. Walter, Jr., University of New Mexico, and Dr. Florence Kluckhohn, Harvard; Dr. Lloyd S. Tireman, Professor of Education, University of New Mexico; Richard L. Strong, District Conservationist, and Harold B. Elmendorf, Water Division, Soil Conservation Service; Eastburn Smith, Regional Administrator, Bureau of Land Management; Frank Pooler, former Regional Director, U.S. Forest Service; Dr.

Acknowledgments

William Long, Professor, New Mexico School of Mines; Walter Connell, sheepman; and Kenneth Adams, Professor of Art, University of New Mexico.

Portions of this book appeared, in earlier and different form, in the following periodicals, whose editors I wish to thank: *Américas* (Pan American Union); *New Mexico Quarterly* (University of New Mexico Press); *Think* (International Business Machines Corporation); and *The American Indian* (Association on American Indian Affairs, Inc.).

Contents

Contents

Illustrations

PART ONE

Indian

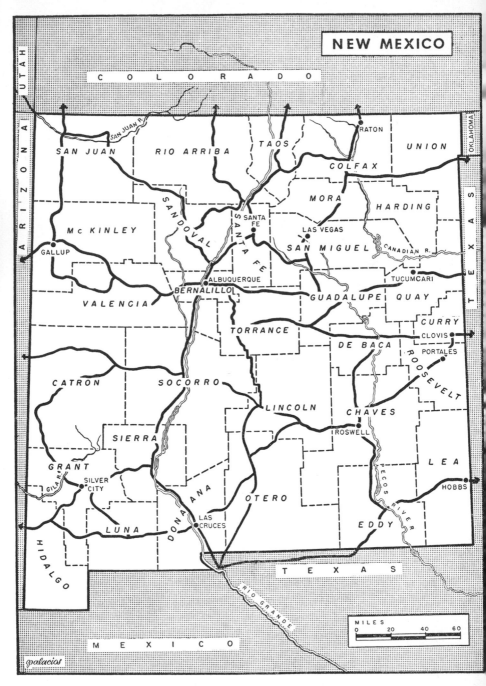

New Mexico, showing county lines and names, larger cities and towns, and principal roads.

✹ ⊂Ⱡ ✹

I

FIRST DISCOVERERS

⊂Ⱡ   So FAR as we know—though archæologists are forever digging, cowboys forever riding around, Boy Scouts
forever exploring, and anything can show up any day—the
first discoverer of New Mexico was Sandia Cave Man, so
called because all we know of him was found in a cave in
the Sandia Mountains east of Albuquerque. The first trace
of him was a claw uncovered by Boy Scouts in 1927. Any
archæologist would have recognized that claw as belonging
to the giant sloth, an animal extinct for ten thousand years
or so. But no archæologist saw it then. It was not until 1936
that an archæology student from the University of New
Mexico happened upon the same cave. He reported his discovery to his professor, Dr. Frank Hibben, and several seasons of careful excavation followed.

In a fascinating small book, *The Lost Americans*, Dr. Hibben has described how his students uncovered layer below
layer of rock and earth laid down by nature, and layers of
debris that only man could have made. Man, with his unvarying gift for leaving a mess, always bequeaths to his
heirs evidence beyond price. In this case, sure proof of
man's presence was found in two strata separated by a deposit of yellow ocher that had taken thousands of years to
accumulate. It was this irritating, powdery dust that had
discouraged the Boy Scouts; and that was fortunate because
it carried real danger of silicosis and because the boys' desertion saved the cave for investigation by trained observers.

In the layer under the yellow ocher scientists have found

3

evidences of human occupancy: scrapers and flint points, crudely worked but deadly when hurled by a strong arm. Unquestionably they were the work of man; only men make things. Sandia Man also knew how to use fire. Even before man reached America the race had produced a genius comparable to an atomic scientist, who had put fire to use. The first cooking may have resulted from clumsy fumbling, but the intelligent use of a natural force for man's good implies thinking. We know that Sandia Man cooked, for he left two hearths, as archæologists call burnt-over places. He must have been wrapped up in skins. Why else would he need scrapers? So here had been a man, skin-clad and fed on meat. This is all we know of him or of his family. No human bones were found. It was a very annoying habit of New Mexico's first discoverers that they did not leave even one tiny bone on which scientists could erect a complete and probably quite accurate skeleton.

In the stratum above that yellow ocher, and therefore indicating later occupancy of Sandia Cave, were found flint points such as had been seen before in northeastern New Mexico.

In 1925, before the Boy Scouts found Sandia Cave, a Negro cowboy, George McJunkin, riding along an arroyo near Folsom, pulled some queer-looking bones out of the cut. Along with them came flint points that looked strange to him, and he had seen many Indian arrowheads. Report of his find reached the University of Denver and started a rush of archæologists toward Folsom. For that observant cowboy had unearthed the earliest evidence then known of man in this hemisphere.

These flint points were exquisitely made. From one to three inches long, they were evenly flaked and smoothly grooved to fit a spear or dart. And with them were found the bones of mammals that had been extinct for ten thousand years. So men were here when these plains were dotted with great lakes and lush with vegetation that fed a type of bison long gone, mammoths, elephants, mastodons, four-toed horses, and giant ground sloths. With his chipped stone weapons man killed them all; and when he butchered the wide-horned bison he took the tail with the hide, as later butchers do. Many skeletons have been found, but no tail bones. Folsom Man also chased animals that we know: deer, antelope, and smaller species. He was a mighty hunter indeed, and he ranged from northeastern Colorado to the southeastern corner of New Mexico. And, like roaming men of all ages, he brought things home. In a few places odd articles have been found, things not made there. So trade had begun.

These were the ancestors of our modern Indians. But they too had ancestors. Archæologists agree that man came into the Western Hemisphere as man. This country was settled by immigrants from the start. And—if one wishes to strut a bit—by real men. It is also agreed that human beings came from Asia across Bering Strait. Maybe they crossed on the ice; maybe it was dry then and they walked across on sand. Through eons, then, they drifted southward, a slow trickle of shivering, shelterless nomads, for it was bitter cold and life was full of terrors. Man's food depended on his hand-hacked stone weapons and his skill at hurling them; he had to kill the beast or be killed by him. Archæologists will hazard no guess as to how long that slow dispersal took; certainly it was millennia before the first Americans had made their way the length of the land mass and spread over South America, where they were to attain their highest prehistoric development. We do know that they crossed New Mexico and that some of them stayed.

Sandia Cave has been studied by the late Dr. Kirk Bryan, professor of geology at Harvard. In an appendix to Frank Hibben's *Lost Americans*, Dr. Bryan maintains that the layer of yellow ocher was laid down some twenty-five thousand years ago and that Sandia Man laired there just before that era, Folsom Man just after. Some geologists think that Kirk Bryan erects too heavy a conclusion on so thin a layer of yellow ocher. Dr. Bryan was one of the world's outstanding geologists and his conclusions deserve deep respect; but the layman willingly leaves the scientists to argue about the difference between ten thousand and twenty-five thousand years.

What concerns us is that men, with a suitable complement of women, lived in New Mexico at least ten thousand years ago. And that the New Mexico we know is, in large outline, very like the land the first inhabitant knew. Dr. Eliot Blackwelder, in *The Great Basin*, writes: "The mountains and basins remain as they were in late Pleistocene times." Sandia Man, from the crest above his cave, got the view we get gazing high across the valley that seems unnaturally foreshortened from that height. Mount Taylor, then as now, rose palely blue against a bluer sky; that dead volcano would long before have spewed forth the lava that we call the *malpais* between Grants and Laguna. Perhaps plants had even then begun to break the lava apart, as the fluffy Apache plume still does. Sandia Man would have seen the azure Ladron and the purple Socorro Mountains to the southwest, and to the northwest the deep blue, corrugated Jemez range. That confused conglomeration of mountains was formed by volcanic action when several craters, still discernible, overflowed the Valle Grande with hot streams of lava. Travelers between Albuquerque and Santa Fe and farther north along the Rio Grande gorge below Taos may still trace those lava flows where they congealed.

In such places one sees how New Mexico was made; many processes of its making go on still. An occasional earth tremor suggests the vast upheavals that brought the mountains up or tilted them to form slanting cliffs like the sun-drenched face of the Sandia range above Albuquerque.

Boiling springs still bubble out of furnace-hot underground rocks. Sulphur Springs, above Jemez, with its white and yellow crusts that steam stinkingly, suggests the anteroom of Hades. The Mimbres Mountains are dotted with hot springs of undetermined therapeutic value, but prolific of legend. More immediately impressive is erosion, the dusting away of topsoil by wind and the flash floods that bring the good brown earth down arroyos while long lines of automobiles wait and drivers rage. These are minor changes; the big job of forming the land was completed before man appeared here.

Beyond Sandia Man's indifferent vision lay the pattern of the state as we know it. Trisected by two confused series of north-and-south mountain ranges, it has the Rio Grande for its lowest point and is set off east and west by the High Plains and the Colorado Plateau. New Mexico's sierras form the south end of the Rocky Mountains. Their tallest peak is Wheeler, near Taos, with an altitude of 13,151 feet. Farther south, Lake Peak and Pecos Baldy dominate the sierra that shelters Santa Fe from east winds and supplies its water from snow-fed lakes. This range divides the headwaters of New Mexico's two most useful streams, the Rio Grande and the Pecos. Doubtless magnificent brimming rivers ten thousand years ago, both now quite regularly dry up in rainless summers. But they and their tributaries have provided irrigation for many centuries of farming, and they have had long and dramatic histories in interstate and international affairs.

South of Santa Fe the mighty Rockies peter out, as indicated by the name Cerrillos, Little Hills; the Sandias come on like an afterthought. But there are elevations on southward to keep the Rio Grande and the Rio Pecos quite distinct, even above-timberline peaks, not so tall as Wheeler Peak, but quite as impressive, especially under snow. The sierras of Manzano, Los Pinos, Oscura, and San Andres show quite well who named them. Only the Organs, rising like serried pipes east of Las Cruces, have adopted a newer speech. All these mountains now start hopeful streams eastward toward the Pecos, making its absent-minded way to join the Rio Grande and thus go on to the Gulf of Mexico. Some of these little hopefuls get lost in sand before reaching the river, but they all offer incontrovertible evidence that this was once a well-watered land.

East of the Pecos there are no mountains, just the high plains that break down in steep escarpments, known for a hundred miles or more as Cap Rock. Men marked their trails across those grasslands with stakes, which gave them the name of Llano Estacado (Staked Plains). Buffalo, and later cattle, grazed there. Deep under the high plains the slow seepage of ages had been storing water in vast beds of sand long before Sandia Man. Those sands held petroleum too, in deep dark pools where water sometimes floated on the oil. Both oil and water are making history now. In the Pecos valley, underground water had chiseled out those miraculous caves we know as the Carlsbad Caverns, and doubtless others still undiscovered but made manifest by the Bottomless Lakes near Roswell, the Blue Hole near Santa Rosa, and other unnamed holes reported by cowboys who always just save themselves from falling in.

Northeastern New Mexico is drained by the Canadian River, which rises not far from the Rio Grande's headwaters under Colorado's peaks. It collects lesser streams whose names appear and reappear in our history: the Cimarron, the Mora, Ute Creek, the Tucumcari, and the Conchas. Where they rise, near the Sangre de Cristo Mountains, these creeks have for many ages irrigated soft green valleys. But the Canadian's longest course is through cattle country, and its most dramatic history belongs to the Staked Plains and even to Oklahoma and to Arkansas, where it flows into the Mississippi.

Between the headwaters of the Canadian and Rio Grande and those of the San Juan runs the Continental Divide, that wavering ridge which divides waters between the Gulf of Mexico and the Gulf of California. The Pacific drainage in New Mexico begins with the San Juan River, which rises in Colorado but swings so wide and generous a loop into New Mexico that it brings in more water than all the state's other streams. Its bright green course is weirdly vivid in the Navajo's rolling desert, where the only peaks are as lordly remote and unscalable as Shiprock, and sand colors are even more startling than the river's green. Heading north again, the San Juan almost touches Four Corners, the only spot in the United States where four states meet. In Utah it joins the Colorado above the Grand Canyon. Fed by the streams of seven states, the Colorado now supplies southern California with water from Hoover Dam and causes more interstate and international disputes than the Rio Grande and the Pecos combined.

Near the border between Colorado and New Mexico the Continental Divide swings slightly west of south, crosses the highway near Thoreau, and follows the crest of the Zuni range to pass over the Lava Fields and meet the tourist again at Pie Town in the Datils. Tipping New Mexico definitely eastward, the Divide runs west along the ridges of the Tularosa, the Black, and the Mogollon ranges, and on to the Mexican border through the Burro and the Pyramid mountains. All these sierras send what water they have to the Colorado, but north of the Lava Fields it is very little. The southern ranges do better, pouring down hundreds of tiny rills that unite in ever larger streams to form the San Francisco and the Gila rivers, which join before they enter the Colorado.

Dr. Ross Calvin has given the Gila its best name in the title of his book, *River of the Sun*. Knowing its every foot and all that lives there, Dr. Calvin has described from personal intimacy the entire valley's flora and fauna, from the springs where icy driblets water subarctic lichens to the splendid blossoming desert where the Gila enters the Colorado. Prehistoric man, with his Stone Age weapons, fished and hunted in so many of those canyons that the Mogollon and the Mimbres mountains are among the archæologists' most fertile fields.

The river that most fully exemplifies New Mexico and all the peoples who have made it is the fabled, historic, and forever undependable Rio Grande. Coming too from that mother of rivers, Colorado, the Rio Grande flows almost due south through the very heart of New Mexico. A strong, clear current in its upper section, the stream has cut through layers of basalt and sandstone to make the Cañon del Norte. The new road to Taos avoids that splendid gorge, leaving it to fishermen who flip big speckled trout out of pools under foaming rapids. Geologists think that the entire prehistoric stream was of this character, clear and swift in its graveled channel before man-made erosion filled it with silt. Now it is never clear again after its confluence with the muddy Chama River.

Starting limpidly up under the snowy peaks of southern Colorado, the Chama, reinforced by rushing mountain brooks, has soon cut through red sandstone in Apache Canyon and become heavy with reddish silt. Below the village of Abiquiu, sitting aloof on its hill, the Chama is roiled with mud that it dumps into the main stream at Española.

The Rio Grande then flows along a meandering channel through a widening valley cut by numberless arroyos that are either desert dry or running in flash floods from the mountains. The principal silt-bearers are the Galisteo from the east and the Jemez and Rio Puerco from the west. The Jemez comes sparkling from the center of the Jemez range and slices its way through strata of sandstone and volcanic deposits colored like the rainbow. But when it enters the

Rio Grande it is foul with mud. In its middle course the Rio Grande lives up to the name the Spanish gave it: Rio Bravo (Fierce River). Although it is reduced to a trickle in dry weather, melting snows or heavy rains may swell it into a raging torrent that inundates farms and towns. Even Albuquerque has seen cloudbursts that reduced shining real estate developments to soggy ruin. Run-off is slow because silt has aggraded the river bed and waterlogged it for a hundred miles. Towns in the lower valley have their own enemy in the Rio Puerco, Dirty River, whose name pictures well the load of silt it brings from the western slopes of the Jemez range.

A distinctive feature of New Mexico's landscape is the *bolson*. This Spanish word means money-bag, and geologists have adopted it to describe an enclosed valley, dead as the Dead Sea, with no tributary streams and no outlet. In some cases, as on the San Augustine Plains south of the Datil Mountains, there is a fine stand of grass in good years. In others, the drying waters have left basins of salt or gypsum where nothing will grow. There are salt lakes east of the Manzano range. And farther south lies the Jornada del Muerto, Journey of the Dead, where many Spaniards perished. Another bolson, the Tularosa Basin, cradles the White Sands, gypsum beds whose deadly glitter, snow-white but bone-dry, was a fitting background for the first atomic explosion.

Such basins have been true wastelands. But New Mexico, newly eager to turn her liabilities into assets as tourist attractions, advertises the White Sands widely. Dr. Calvin has suggested that the entire Tularosa Basin might be set aside as an outdoor museum for the study of the panorama of Southwestern flora and fauna with a bit of archæology thrown in.

Many of these features of the New Mexico landscape may be traced to an age-long drought after Sandia Man's time. The climate may have cooled off then. Geologists estimate that snow and timberlines were a thousand feet or so lower then than now. Pine and cedar then grew on the mountain's lower slopes, and many of our bare mesas were wooded. It is likely that the line, now near Socorro, where the typical northern piñon and juniper yield to mesquite and creosote bush was farther south. And when precipitation was heavier the rivers were certainly longer and deeper. Creeks that now run only in flood or disappear in sand were then permanent rivers. Only so could the land have supported the huge herds of herbivorous beasts that Sandia Man and Folsom Man killed with their flint points.

Then everything changed. Over the ages rainfall lessened; rivers narrowed, shortened, or dried up altogether. The prehistoric beasts disappeared. It has been suggested that man, always a greedy hunter, slaughtered so many tender calves that he eliminated whole breeds. But any New Mexican knows that a prolonged drought can kill off anything. The only large animal to survive was the bison, but he persisted only as a smaller type and with less hornspread. The horse, that long-haired, four-toed racer, was seen no more until the Spaniards brought in his distant relative, also an Asiatic original. Some Navajos say their people knew the prehistoric horse, but this myth finds no scientific endorsement.

Through those long ages of drought, man, always tougher than animals, survived. Such earlier types as archæologists guess Sandia Man and Folsom Man to have been had interbred with later arrivals from the north, and so evolved a human being not unlike the modern Pueblo. These people lived all over New Mexico as the Spaniards knew it in their most grandiose period. From northern Colorado and Utah south into Chihuahua and Sonora, from the Gulf of Mexico to the Gulf of California, we find traces of people who were learning to make things. Everything they left, show-

ing steady improvement from good to better to best, indicates people of intelligence, inventiveness, and adaptability.
Above all, they had phenomenal endurance. The land they
roamed did not make for an easy life.

Their New Mexico was the semi-arid mountain and desert country we know. Below timberline the mountains bear
a fine stand of conifers, dark and ever green, set off by
patches of evanescent quaking aspens whose color follows
the seasons from the spring's pale green to the golden yellow of autumn and winter's silver gray. Where water is
scarce, piñon and juniper grow sturdy though not tall.
These are New Mexico's colors: dark and light green, varied by gray in chamiso and cactus and set against rocks
more vivid than the plants. And over-all, of course, and un-
forgettably, the unexcelled blueness of the sky.

In all the sierras some canyons carry water. Most of them
are dry except in flood time, when they bring down rocks
that the waters deposit as waterworn stones, coarse gravel,
and fine, soft sands. Broken slopes that roll down to the
rivers are commonly called mesas in New Mexico, though
the true mesa, as its name implies, is flat on top and has steep
sides.

Where the streams form permanent rivers, the valleys
have fed many tribes of men fairly well on native plants;
have fed them even better when men learned to irrigate.
Wherever the soil accumulates, it is rich. Mountain canyons
are leafy with alder, willow, and mountain cottonwood,
and are starred with exquisite flowers and ferns. Deer disappear into thickets, squirrels chatter, bluebirds flash. On
the lower terraces quail whirr in the aromatic chamiso and
take on all the colors of the land. The river bottoms are
shaded by stately cottonwoods and come alive, twice a year,
with migrating water fowl. In the hottest areas mesquite
grows into a tree giving a lacelike shade, and yucca holds
up its tall candlelike white blooms. Such soil produces ev-

erything that a temperate climate can, but only where water can be put upon the land.

Altogether, New Mexico was to prove a land where men could live well if they learned to respect water and to use it sparingly, to deal fairly with good soil, and to lay by for the inevitable years of drought. How succeeding peoples have worked out these problems over two thousand years is our story.

II

FIRST SETTLERS

⊂╞   For ages impossible to calculate accurately, men roamed the wide Southwest, living on roots and berries, seeds and nuts. They were hunters too, but their flint points were cruder than those made by their progenitor, Folsom Man. In time some genius thought of grinding seeds on rough stones. Perhaps a man invented the metate and mano, grinders that have kept the Indian woman in stooping servitude ever since. But more likely a woman thought of saving seeds for next year's planting: only dauntless women could have held off hungry mates and squalling brats from edible hoards. Stone-lined storage cists have been found, especially in the Cochise Mountains of southeastern Arizona, and their builders have been called Seed Gatherers.

The most important seed was maize. It was long believed that corn came north from Mexico about A.D. 700. But in 1949 two Harvard students excavating in the Bat Cave near the San Augustine Plains in New Mexico came upon tiny cobs. No thicker than a pencil and less than two inches long, they were unmistakably corn; up to 1950, 766 examples had been studied and dated. It is now believed that the Indian's sacred plant was known in New Mexico as early as 2000 B.C., by when it was probably being planted, tended, and garnered.

When they had corn to hoe, men began to build permanent homes. The prehistoric farmers, like many today, built a granary before they built a house, but by the time the Southwesterner was really settled he had dug and roofed another circular pit and had a home. The mounds that have grown up over these pit houses are found all over the area from south of Utah's Great Salt Lake, across southern Colorado, in the San Juan and Rio Grande drainages in New Mexico, along Arizona's Gila and Little Colorado and their tributaries, as far as the Colorado to the west, and southward into Chihuahua.

The growth of pines varies so much between wet and dry years that cut trees may be dated by their rings, and beams have been found that were cut as early as A.D. 217. The dry air of the Southwest has preserved other evidences of man's slow but sure conquest of his environment. The ancients provided well for their dead, and burials reveal and help to date developing techniques. Basketry led to pottery; the first pots were mud-daubed baskets; then pots were built up of coils of mud; and finally they were refined into polished, painted bowls and ladles. Weapons changed and grew tougher and more accurate through the years; and ornaments of stone and bone were enhanced by the turquoise so typical of New Mexico and so like the sky's blue.

Dr. Marie Wormington, whose *Prehistoric Indians of the Southwest* gives many fascinating data, believes that the men wore the jewels. She draws a depressing picture of the women, who went unadorned and cut off their hair to weave with while the men kept theirs long and well-combed —we see the comb beside male skeletons. Dr. Wormington also suggests that the greatest advance was owing not to corn, but to the humbler though more exacting bean. You cannot go off and leave a bean patch as you can a corn field. And beans yield even more than corn of the protein on which civilizations are built. The bean ranks as one of the sacred plants along with corn, squash, and tobacco. But it is ceremonially celebrated only by the Hopis, in an archaic rite of extraordinary beauty.

Archæologists have studied and dated every find and

written a whole library on the details of pre-Pueblo life. For the casual observer, the arresting fact is that more than one thousand years of human development have been preserved in artifacts buried in the dry dust of New Mexico's ruins, but most miraculously in the customs of twentieth-century Indians who, in scores of ways, live and think and worship as their remote ancestors did.

The forebears of the Pueblo farmer of today scratched the ground with a stick and planted. Some prehistoric Indians dug little ditches near the streams, but the first remarkable irrigation systems were those of the Hohokam, a Pima word meaning Those Who Have Vanished. In the Salt River valley of Arizona, students have uncovered 150 miles of well-platted canals indicating superior intelligence and stability. Dating the work of the Hohokam is difficult because they built with mesquite and cottonwood, whose rings are not reliable guides as are pine rings. But their pottery seems contemporary with pre-Pueblo work of about A.D. 700.

The Hohokam made an interesting fusion with a people from the north, called Salado because they lived by that river whose name means salty. They had moved out of cliff houses and into the valley because of a dire drought between 1277 and 1299; niggardly growth of tree rings proves this clearly. There the two peoples lived side by side for centuries, keeping their customs distinct. The Hohokam cremated their dead; the Salado buried theirs. Hohokam pots are not large; a Salado jar has been found with a capacity of thirty gallons.

The Salado built with adobe poured in layers and then plastered with caliche, a hard native lime. This technique produced the magnificent structure first described by Father Eusebio Kino, a seventeenth-century Jesuit, who called it La Casa Grande, The Big House. Even in ruins its four-storied bulk looms out of the desert so grandly that it should have been spared the hideous wooden shed the Park Service has built to protect it. Some archæologists venture to guess that the Casa Grande may have been the center of an autocracy such as ruled the Aztecs, Toltecs, and Maya of Mexico. If so, it is the only indication of dictatorship uncovered in Southwestern archæology. All other evidences indicate a life in which no man was better fed than another and in which superiority was an individual attainment and never hereditary.

It has been guessed that a Salado group may have wandered far enough from the Salt River valley to settle on the Galisteo in New Mexico. For this there is no material evidence, but excavations in the Mogollon Mountains have uncovered a kiva that may link the Arizona folk with pre-Pueblo people developing farther north.

It would be hard to imagine a more delightful place to seek a missing link than a University of Chicago site at Pine Lawn, near Reserve, New Mexico, where the digs are shaded by aromatic conifers and one can catch a trout for supper. The few roads across the Mogollon range are snow-bound in winter and subject to summer washouts. But between times a well-graded highway offers stupendous vistas as a car swoops around hairpin turns revealing wide green slopes, craggy primeval canyons, and sky-high blue peaks. This is the mountain wilderness whose streams drain finally into the Gila, Ross Calvin's "River of the Sun."

On one of the Gila's tributaries, the Mimbres, lived a mysterious people whose pottery—thin, balanced, and exquisitely colored and decorated—is so fine that it has been compared to the best Greek work. Douglas and d'Harnoncourt, in *Indian Art of the United States*, find it individual enough to be the work of one man. Archæologists say it is too widespread for that, but certainly Mimbres pottery is the work of one school. Its conventionalized bugs, birds, animals, and imaginative monsters show not only perfec-

tion of craft but also very sophisticated humor. Mary Jane
Colter of the Harvey System has copied them on dishes
where all may see them.

Peoples easier to trace into the modern world were called
the Anasazi (The Ancient Ones) by the Navajos, who
knew their ruins well and speculated about them. At Mesa
Verde, Aztec, and Chaco Canyon archæologists have traced
their whole course from pit houses to great apartment
dwellings, from nomadic clans to urban dwellers. By A.D.
1000 these pre-Pueblo peoples were living in true cities.

With city life came civilization. Agriculture produced
enough for all and winter leisure gave time for artistic expression. The best work of the great prehistoric period is
equal to that of any Stone Age people. As populations grew,
government became more centralized and priesthoods may
have forced an almost theocratic state. But life was basically
democratic, as may be deduced from the modern pueblos,
where customs still observed and rites still practiced indicate an unbroken line of descent from the ancients. This
unique situation makes New Mexico a paradise for both
archæologist and ethnologist and provides material for the
accurate dioramas that are so helpful a feature of the Park
Service museums at Mesa Verde, Aztec, and Chaco Canyon.

These three great centers of pre-Pueblo living were occupied concurrently and abandoned, in the order given,
during the thirteenth century. Chaco Canyon was the last
to be deserted. Its people apparently drifted westward onto
the Pajarito (Little Bird) Plateau, and on into the Rio
Grande valley. Visitors may readily visit these splendid
ruins in the order of their desertion.

Mesa Verde, as its name states, is a green tableland forested with piñon and juniper varied by the taller ponderosa
pine and Douglas fir. Good cover for mule deer, foxes, coyotes, and bobcats. During the tourist season few wild creatures appear near the roads, but the traveler may glimpse a

deer and can always see the flicker of sun and shadow and patches of brilliance in Indian paintbrush, pentstemon, and lupine. The mesa is slashed deep by numberless canyons, some with water, more without, all of the soft sandstone and limestone that wind has eroded into caves. Here are the dwellings, pale ghosts of cities four stories high with watch-towers, retaining walls, and many round kivas. Seen across a green canyon, Balcony House, Spruce Tree House, and the noblest, Cliff Palace, seem lived in or only just deserted.

Thousands of people lived here, farming in the canyons, lugging food and water up the cliffs in baskets or jars slung on tumplines; the men weaving, the women making pottery; all invoking good and fending off evil by kiva ceremonies. Their best pottery, with black designs on gray, is excel-lent; they used dyes in their weaving, and they left a pro-fusion of jewelry. People with so much time for adornment were living well.

In 1276, as tree rings have proved, drought began. For twenty-four years each year's rings are tighter and nar-rower. Even a modern farmer would be put out of business by such a drought. People dependent upon flash floods and underground water were starved out. So they left Mesa Verde. Probably a few at a time, carrying burdens and babies, they moved off seeking water. Some may have be-come the ancestors of the modern Hopi. Others—judging by pottery remains—joined related Anasazi in the San Juan valley of New Mexico.

There they built a city that was miscalled Aztec by some reader of Prescott's *Conquest of Mexico* who did not know that these were a different people. The misnomer has stuck. These ruins center in an apartment house of five hundred rooms, largely excavated. Its solid outer wall and inner rooms, arranged in steplike tiers, are built of stone that had been carried fifteen or twenty miles; beams came from farther away. But the workers were not only burden-bearers; they were also architects who planned well, first-rate stonemasons, and decorators with a sense of form and design. Some walls still show colored stones laid in decorative courses, and some inner doors are fitted with reed curtains like split-bamboo shades.

Aztec's most impressive building is a kiva so huge that it must have been a center of elaborate ceremonialism. It is unique in having small rooms around the main chamber, which has a platform at its north end. Altogether that big kiva inspired a young archæologist to an unfortunate job of remodeling it into something resembling an Elks Lodge room. But aside from this monstrosity the ruin is vivid with a sense of lives lived there. These people, too, cultivated the soil, and they had a good water supply from the San Juan River. They were good craftsmen and traders. Their jewelry includes California shell, Utah and New Mexico turquoise, and even bronze bells from Mexico. But like Mesa Verde, this center was abandoned because of drought.

Early in the thirteenth century, Aztec's inhabitants began to drift westward; they may have joined related clans in Chaco Canyon. These centers had been in contact: Chaco Canyon types of material underlie Mesa Verde ware at Aztec. So Chaco Canyon was the first site to be settled as well as the last to be deserted; rings in the beams indicate that the last inhabitants moved away about 1300. Because they turned up finally in the Rio Grande valley there is a clear connection between the Anasazi culture and that of the modern Pueblos.

The first drifters into Chaco Canyon saw, as we see today, a wide shallow valley cut into the polychrome desert. In spots it is streaked with rose and ocher and with green too pale to be quite real; in others it is marked by left-over cones of darker, harder stuff. The Chaco was then, as it is now, a river flowing only with windblown sand, but under hard rains it can roar with a rush of waters that have dug deep tributary canyons. Before the white man's flocks and herds overgrazed and eroded the land, many underground pools were retained for the corn to reach. As the Hopis still do, those prehistoric farmers twirled holes in the sand with pointed sticks, dropped in the corn, and held the moisture by constant hoeing, using hoes with stone blades.

The Chaco Canyon people lived in small houses strung along the canyon for thirty miles, as well as in the splendid communal dwellings in the canyon. These could have housed ten thousand people; probably no more than five or six thousand lived there at any one time. The safest method of computing population fails at Chaco Canyon, where few burials and no evidence of cremation have been found. What the Southwestern ancients did with their dead remains an unsolved mystery, though Dr. Gerhardt von Bonin, professor of anatomy at the University of Illinois, suggests that bones of people as ill-fed as the pre-Pueblos would have disintegrated completely. Dr. Bonin bases this tentative theory on one summer's work at Pine Lawn.

Chaco Canyon's largest ruin is Pueblo Bonito, with eight-hundred rooms and thirty kivas, the largest apartment house constructed up to then or until New York arrived independently at the same idea in 1882. D-shaped Pueblo Bonito offers a blank outer face and is terraced down to the inner court. This fortresslike style is still hinted at by modern pueblos.

The overwhelming wonder of Chaco Canyon is its stonework, comparable at its best to the work of modern masons with stone tools. It shows artistry, too, as though the builder had stepped back to consider what would look best as well as be most durable. Most provocative in every way is Chetro Ketl, a super kiva like the one at Aztec and as inexplicable. The University of New Mexico, in excavating, has happily left it unrestored. Kivas and living rooms have yielded a mass of material now on view at the University in

Albuquerque and the State Museum in Santa Fe. This includes cotton blankets colored with vegetable dyes, pottery, basketry, and jewelry. Some of the finest bits have been found in wall crypts so cleverly plastered over that only chance has uncovered them. Among them are ceremonial objects like those in use today, notably *tablitas,* headdresses worn by women in the dances.

All the finds at Chaco Canyon reflect a life probably as good as men of any age could have achieved without metal. It is easy to think of prehistoric Indians as primitive, but they created a centralized government that did not preclude democracy and that lasted more than twice as long as the United States has endured to date.

The likeliest reason for the evacuation of Chaco Canyon is, as usual, drought, though imaginative theorizers have guessed at boredom or a mass scare induced by a plague of witches. The people left their homes in the broad Chaco Canyon, and after many years and many settlements came onto a forested plateau on the east flank of the Jemez Mountains, which Dr. Edgar L. Hewitt, who directed the first excavations there, called the Pajarito Plateau.

Driving along the wide highway from Santa Fe to the atomic city of Los Alamos, one can see how the plateau lies. In sublime quietude the peaks lift their deeper blue against the sky's clarity. The patches of bright green, like lawns, are aspen groves, and those rough, rocky knuckles thrusting toward the Rio Grande divide leafy canyons wherein tiny streams live as long as they can before they are buried in sand. Between peaks and valley the plateau of eight-thousand-foot altitude is studded with lime and sandstone mesas. It offered excellent living: water for irrigation in the canyons, conifers and aspens for building, and many caves already hollowed out in the friable volcanic tuff, which could be readily shaped and dressed to build rooms in front of the caves.

All around the Jemez range's roughly circular perimeter are such cliffs, stratified in terra cotta red, sulphur yellow, and dusty white often topped by dark basalt. It is the archæologists' exhaustless laboratory, and they have located hundreds of ruins ranging in style from the simplest single-room houses to the apartment dwellings at Puyé and Rito de los Frjioles (Creek of the Beans).

The Puyé ruins are owned by the Pueblo of Santa Clara, whose people speak Tewa, probably the tongue their ancestors spoke at Puyé. Santa Clara Indians often recognize artifacts discovered at those ruins, but dislike to talk about things that may have been sacred to their ancestors. South of Puyé are other towns with musical Tewa names: Tsankowí, Otowí, Tsheregé. Then the mesa is rent by a deep canyon wherein lie the most famous and most studied cliff dwellings of the Pajarito Plateau. The Rito de los Frijoles flows in the canyon. The ruins—guarded and expounded by the National Park Service—are called the Bandelier National Monument after their first student, Adolph Bandelier, a Swiss archæologist who visited them in the 1880's.

This canyon, not more than half a mile wide, never less than two hundred feet deep, and only six miles long, was a perfect homesite. The stream, fed by springs near the Jemez crest, sparkles in sunny spots, quiets itself in pools where trout glint against shining pebbles, and carries an ample flow for small-scale irrigation. Tall dark pines stand stately above thickets of willow, alder, and chokecherry. Raspberry and gooseberry bushes grow underneath, and strawberry plants carpet the ground. Deer and rabbits like such thickets, and birds nest there. The ancient people overlooked no useful plant or animal. They knew all the edible leaves and roots, as well as mint and watercress for flavor and many plants for conjuring or curing.

The canyon's south wall is a steep slope on which trees

grow. The north wall is as sheer as though a knife had cut
through the yellow and white tuff, and as smooth as finished
masonry. In places tuff cones, like tents, stand away from the
cliff; in others the wall has fallen in a long talus slope. The
cliff itself is potted with caves that the people had dug out
and walled in to make homes. The whole settlement, strung
along the cliff, was called Tyounyi. Petroglyphs scratched
into the stone indicate the homes of clans, many of which
persist in the modern pueblos—Bear, Sun, Water, Snake. On
the canyon's floor is the ruin of an unfinished three-story
circular dwelling. Many kivas indicate an elaborate ceremonial life. The largest and most interesting kiva is set into
a wide arched recess, the Ceremonial Cave, two hundred
feet above the canyon's floor. It can be reached only by
modern pole-ladders and steps cut in the rock. The aboriginal
approach has been lost.

Many other trails are known. Shallow hand and foot holes
in the sheer cliff, barely negotiable by a shod modern, lead
to the mesa above. The mesa itself is crossed by miles of
trails—sometimes worn hip-deep by padding moccasins—that
connected this tribe with the rest of the Indian world. From
Colorado to Mexico and east and west, these trade routes
can be traced one thousand miles or more.

We know well the ancient life of the Rito de los Frijoles
from Bandelier's novel, *The Delight Makers*. First published
in 1890, this is an absorbing romance accounting for the
pueblo's desertion by a combination of feuds and witches
at home and enemies without. Frijoles Canyon, like the
other great prehistoric centers, was abandoned before
historic times; but here, drought does not seem a likely
cause.

The migration from the Pajarito Plateau into the Rio
Grande valley was marked by a general decline. Building
became poorer, pottery more careless in form and design;
all standards appear to have been lowered. No reasons for

this decline have been established. Perhaps old women or jittery leaders were fleeing haunted spots; the people may have had rows, as modern pueblos do, and split up in a huff. The occupied area was gradually narrowed to the Rio Grande drainage, with offshoots—by way of Laguna, Acoma, and Zuni—to the Hopi villages. These were the pueblos the Spaniards found inhabited in 1540.

All Pueblo people are of common ancestry, but they speak different languages or dialects that seem oddly related. The Hopis, that most peaceful folk, speak the Shoshonean language, as do the warlike Comanches; the Zunis' speech is theirs alone. In the Rio Grande area a basic tongue was diversified into several languages and dialects, much as Latin into the Romance languages. Tewa is spoken by the pueblos north of Santa Fe; Keres by those south of it along the Jemez River and—by a curious leap—in distant Acoma and Laguna. Taos and Isleta, separated by Keres and Tewa, speak a different tongue, Tiwa. People the Spanish knew as Tanos, living on the Santa Fe and Galisteo rivers, and the Piros of the Manzanos and the Socorro area have disappeared. So have the inhabitants of Pecos, except as their descendants are found among their relatives at Jemez.

Pecos—or Cicuyé, its native name—is a dull red adobe ruin set on the dull red banks of an arroyo that empties into the Pecos River. To the traveler along the highway, it looms up like a ruined castle among shrubbery. The valley is well watered; the mountains and plains offer good hunting. But anciently Pecos was easily accessible to the Pueblos' most feared enemies, the Comanches of the plains. This fact caused its final abandonment within the historic period.

Cicuyé offers the archæologist a key to the whole pre-Pueblo period. In 1916, when Alfred Vincent Kidder was excavating there for Phillips Academy at Andover, he realized that he could date all pueblo pottery by comparing it with Pecos ceramics. The harried pueblo had fallen and been rebuilt so many times that its trash heaps and crumbled rooms preserved layer under layer of potsherds in perfect order. They also yielded an unusually large number of skulls and skeletons buried in the trash heaps where digging was easiest. This custom is a boon to archæologists because pots, broken to let the spirit out, were buried with the bodies, and dating was thus made doubly sure.

Among villages, now lost, which the Spaniards knew were the Tiguez pueblos near modern Bernalillo. Of twelve named by the conquerors, one—Kuaua—has been unearthed and restored as the Coronado State Monument. Like Cicuyé, it marks a spot where archæology and history meet, but here the interest centers in certain frescoes.

In 1935, Gordon Vivian, a University of New Mexico student, was digging out a kiva. Suddenly he uncovered the painted fingers of an upraised hand and part of a ceremonial mask! It was an archæological thriller. After slow and painstaking work, excavators found that the four walls of a room eighteen feet square had been painted in earth colors: black, white, red, yellow, brown, and green. Only the east wall was too eroded to save. The other frescoes, though damaged, could be peeled off in sheets of plaster no thicker than wrapping-paper. Wesley Bliss worked out the technique that removed thirty-five layers, seventeen of them painted. These were remounted on fresh plaster, glue, and burlap. One set has been reproduced on the walls of the Hall of Ethnology in the State Museum at Santa Fe, where many Indians see it and silently nod their recognition of masks and symbols.

Even more provocative are reports of a lost fresco. In 1582, the Spaniard Espejo recorded that he had seen in one of the Tiguez pueblos a picture of the martyrdom of two Franciscans he had been searching for. In 1598, Oñate saw the same paintings and described their horrors fully. But there has been no further record. Perhaps Christianized Indians destroyed them; perhaps some still-buried ruin in the area will give up that unique painting.

More interesting as ruins are three pueblos on the slopes of the Manzano range. Officially called the Saline Pueblos because of the nearby salt lakes, they were more picturesquely named by Charles F. Lummis about 1890 as The Cities that Were Forgotten. The ruins that so impressed him were not prehistoric buildings, but seventeenth-century missions. The church towers at Quarai, rising solidly above the piñon wood, were lookouts too, from which sentinels could command the wide Estancia plain, where raiding bands of Comanches or Apaches might appear. Lummis, fresh from the green East, wrote: "Mid-ocean is not more lonesome than the plains, nor night so gloomy as that dumb sunlight." The Western eye, inured to the way that midday sunlight washes all color out, can distinguish many tones in those palely golden grasslands where in the hollows blue shadows deepen into plum-color.

Abó, in a sheltered canyon on the Manzano Mountains' south flank, may prove the most interesting as excavations go on. The mission is of handsome proportions, and its former size is attested by the numbers of cut stones that have been used to build small homes and sheep corrals in the vicinity.

Tabirá, out on the plain, is not only a ruined pueblo and a mission, but a legendary treasure-house as well. This place somehow became confused in popular imagination with the Gran Quivira that lured the Spanish conquerors off on a fruitless gold hunt. The legend has never died. Even today the Park Service superintendent at Tabirá is pestered by treasure-seekers who come with maps and deathbed confessions and—most lately—Geiger counters.

Paul A. F. Walter, in a report for the Museum of New Mexico, gave these pueblos another unforgettable name, that of his book, *The Cities that Died of Fear*. This phrase summarizes more than the fate of the Saline Pueblos. The whole pueblo world was declining; fear of the nomads was certainly one cause of their shrinking closer together. There may have been other reasons. Perhaps we shall never know. We can only guess that the last prehistoric period had prepared the way for an easy Spanish conquest; the conquered were subdued before the conquerors arrived.

III

THE WAY OF THE KACHINAS

⊂⊇ THE PREHISTORIC Pueblos, like all peoples, based their religious beliefs on what they saw about them. According to their myths, they came not from the sea like the Greeks, nor from vast forests like the Norsemen. They imagined themselves as coming from an underworld, dark, damp, unlovely. Many Pueblos know the spot where their ancestors emerged. The tales are varied, but the Pueblos all came from below and suffered many vicissitudes on their long climb to the light. In some cases they lost children, who became the supernatural beings, *kachinas;* in others, the people's own evil led to such deformities as the Mud-Heads, masked figures who appear in the Shalako dance at Zuni, and who typify the offspring of incest. Always, after long wanderings, they reached the "middle." Many pueblos have such centers. At Zuni the Shalako begin their superb dance drama every year at the earth's very center.

As the people emerged blinking into light, they were guided by the kachinas, who taught them the true way. They were divided into clans related through the mother, or into moieties, divisions of the people known as North and South People among the Tewa; Turquoise and Squash People among the Keres. Each person had his appointed place in the scheme, and all relationships were so clearly defined that to this day relatives are greeted by special kinship terms.

The kachinas gave practical advice too: how to plant and harvest according to the moon and stars, how best to trap animals. Societies were formed for all purposes: war, hunting, growth, production, and healing. All life needed the help of everyone. The least child knew that he must keep his heart right for the people's good. Some men—and women too—who had special powers, became priests to direct the ceremonies and pray in secret.

The people's religion was founded in their origin myths and in what they had to cope with in their sunny, arid land. The best summary of the subject is Elsie Clews Parsons's *Pueblo Indian Religion*. She disproves the old idea that Indians were sun-worshippers. The sun was no deity, but it was watched and kept in its appointed track by ceremonies. The beautiful relay races at Taos in the early morning of May 3, and again on September 30, have to do with the sun's course. Visitors note how little the racers care to win as they speed back and forth from the aspen bower—delicate green in May, golden yellow in September. Stern competition is a white man's notion; Indians work together for the good of all. Stick-kick races at Taos and Zuni have a similar intent.

All Pueblos named the directions: sometimes five, counting the middle; sometimes six, including up and down. Zenith and nadir are personified in the Zuni Shalako and other dances, making six, but the number four figures importantly in the tales. As the heroes of our fairy tales fail twice and win on the third try, the Pueblo has four to go. Each direction has a special color, but these differ from pueblo to pueblo.

In a country of such impressive mountains and mesas, it was inevitable that the tribes should build legends around them as the Greeks did around Olympus, and the Jews around Ararat.

Pueblo Peak, rising so regally robed in purple above Taos, has been fiercely guarded by the people through the ages and even into the United States courts. The little Fire God of the Shalako comes from Zuni's sacred Corn Mountain. The Hopis go to San Francisco Peaks, where their kachinas live. The Tewas look toward Lake Peak in the Sangre de Cristo range, or toward summits in the Jemez Mountains; and the Keres are drawn—as who is not who lives in the Rio Grande valley?—to the oblique profile of the ever changing blue Sandias. As water is prayed for, it is held sacred too. Pueblo Peak guards the mystical waters of Blue Lake, and every August all of Indian Taos goes there for rites few white men have ever seen. Many Pueblos revere crystal springs that bubble out of rocks and run away to hide in sand. The Hopis' Shaded Water does that; and the Zunis' Shalako Spring moves so softly that it is called the Lake of Whispering Water. Indians never lack the poetic word or descriptive phrase.

Every winter certain kachinas come down from the San Francisco Peaks to dance in the Hopi villages. In midsummer they return to the sacred peaks. They are costumed with great beauty, and their symbolical appearance and withdrawal give point and significance to all life. Equally spectacular and complicated is the masked ceremony of the Shalako at Zuni. Its date, mystically determined by certain chiefs, is generally between Thanksgiving and Christmas. Houses are newly built or renovated to receive the kachinas, who vary from the slim, almost naked little Fire God to the four or five Shalakos whose eagle-feather crowns and monumental masks tower fifteen feet above their dancing feet. These, the pueblo's best dancers, have prepared themselves by prayer, fasting, ceremonial cleansing, and continence. They bear the responsibility of assuring good for all by their correct performance. Children certainly accept them as supernaturals; doubtless adults take them symbolically as Christians take many of their observances. But of reverent attention and careful observance of every detail there is no lack.

All kachina masks are sacred. Made of deerskin, buffalo hide, or cowhide, they are shaped and decorated under rigid conditions, guarded in certain homes, and "fed" with smoke, sacred meal, or the scent of food. Their number is legion. Dr. Parsons counted sixty-seven in Zuni. Doubtless there are as many in the eastern pueblos, where no outsider sees the masked dances. When a polite Indian turns back a car outside a Rio Grande pueblo or miles away from the rock of Acoma, the visitor may be sure that a masked ceremony is going on. This exclusion is due to the ban put upon all Indian ceremonies by the sixteenth-century missionaries. The Pueblos conformed outwardly, but continued the ceremonies in secret. In some cases masks are used in public dances. Buffalo- and deer-heads are worn like masks; eagle dancers are masked, as is the amusing Pecos Bull, at Jemez on August 2. The dancer with bobbing horse's head and tailed rump represents the mounted Santiago, the patron saint of medieval Spain. He, of course, appears freely anywhere. But this was miming the monks could understand. Those monstrous forms with massive beaks, horns, and fearsome rolling eyes smacked too much of devilishness.

Masked dances were not suppressed among the Hopis and Zunis because the Spaniards did not conquer them in any lasting way. When overcome, the peoples soon ejected their conquerors and went back to their heathen ways. Or to the ways of the kachinas, according to the point of view. The happy result is that we may see these marvelous masked dances, the finest in our hemisphere, perhaps the finest anywhere, in choreography, costume, steps, and especially in ritual significance.

These ceremonies are based on the legends, and their exact meanings are often obscure even to the Indians. But in general the Pueblos think of all life as interrelated and good, and of all forms of worship as right. Proselyting is inconceivable to the Pueblo, who accepts every man's faith as best for him; he will even adopt and add to his own what he likes of the proselyter's offering. Perhaps the Corn Mother, who figures in many myths, comes closest to our Jewish-Christian conception of an individualized creator.

Corn is the most sacred plant; even stripped cobs are handled reverently, and dried husks tied to the Koshare's head add their color of death to his skeletonlike ensemble. Corn, as pollen or as once-ground coarse meal, is used as Catholics use holy water. It is strewn over prayer sticks and feathers, tossed toward the sun at dawn, dropped on dead faces, rubbed on the newborn.

Birds and animals have their sacred as well as their practical uses. Buffalo- and deer-dances are prayers for good hunting, but they also explain to the game the need for their sacrifice that the people may have food. Needless slaughter is foreign to the Pueblos: they kill only for food or for ceremonial use. In such cases the killing is a rite, as when the deer is smothered with sacred meal.

The lowly, ubiquitous coyote was a legendary clown, the kind who always wins with a grin, and his swishing tail is worn in many dances. So is the tail of his cousin, the fox. The turtle's shell makes rattles, and the turtle, who likes water, is entrusted with prayers for water as in the Turtle Dance at Zia and other pueblos. The snake plays many roles, though never as a tempting devil. Its sinuous movements suggest water, and the most striking prayer for rain is the Hopi Snake Dance in August. Snake symbols are easy to identify on pottery and in decoration generally.

Birds, who fly skyward and are so beautiful and gay, give their names to many clans and provide feathers. Every dance costume includes feathers for both color and meaning. Many feathers used ceremonially are easy to identify. Turkey and eagle tails ray stiffly out; bluebird, duck, and hawk are familiar. Much of the cloudy white is the down of eagles kept in cages. Many a tiny tip set in a headdress or tied to a prayer stick may be understood only by the shaman who uses it. The value of feathers may be linked with the little-known habits of certain birds or their part in legend; but it must be obvious that they lend fleetness to a runner or waft a prayer to the home of the gods.

Throughout the pueblo world prayer sticks are used, except at Taos where only loose feathers appear in ritual. Three or four inches long and only a bit thicker than a pencil, the prayer stick must be made from the prescribed wood taken in the right way, often only by the shaman. Each quill or downy tuft tied to the stick or floating from it on a cord, every bit of paint, even the twisting of the yucca string, must be meticulously right, just as the kachina taught. Prayer sticks have many uses. They may represent pleas for future good, appreciation for good received, or an out-and-out bargain. "I plant the prayer stick; you bring on the rain." Perhaps they serve all these purposes. Like sacred meal and pollen, prayer sticks are found in sacred spots, are thrown into holy springs, hidden in house rafters, planted in the corn field, buried with the dead.

Prayer sticks adorn the altars, and altars are of infinite variety. The most elaborate are set up for ceremonies, usually in kivas or society rooms where the outsider may not go. But correct altars are sometimes shown in the Harvey hotels at Albuquerque, Santa Fe, or the Grand Canyon. One easily recognizes the medicine bowl filled with water for asperging, the painted kachinas, the sun, lightning, cloud, or rain symbols. Often there is a sand-painting on the floor and a path of sacred meal to lead or lure the kachina to the place. Indians making paths of sacred meal and sprinkling it may be noted by any watchful visitor. Shalako are sprinkled as they pass the rows of spectators; paths are clearly marked at the Snake Dance; the game killed in the Deer Dance is sprinkled. Often fetiches stand by the altar: little clay or stone figurines of birds or beasts tied up with feathers and turquoise and shell beads. The stone lions of Cochiti, now almost worn away by weather, still serve as fetiches for the hunt. In the Hopi and Zuni villages, known as the West, fetiches are generally considered most potent. They are worn as charms and are placed on the altars, which are also adorned with kachina dolls made to represent the gods as the masked dancers do. These dolls are carved by men from waterborne cottonwood roots, and they serve as children's toys as well as altar ornaments. All these things are highly conventionalized and must be made precisely as the kachina taught. Only so can they bring the good.

A Jemez Indian told Dr. Parsons: "If our customs and medicine are good, they have power. If we have power we bring rains, good crops, and health." All is postulated on good: having a good heart with no ugly thought, as well as a body cleansed both inside and out. The medicine may be medication, but it is also the form, the correctness. The power comes—as in other highly developed faiths—from making and keeping contact with supernatural good. The ancient Pueblo had no sense of sin; the Catholic missionaries labored valiantly to give him that. Modern psychologists are more inclined to approve the effect of his ancient beliefs.

The making of the altar and other preliminary ceremonies may take days; they are secretly performed in the kiva or the society chamber. They include ceremonial smoking, relating of suitable legends, chanting, and the asperging and dressing of dancers for their public appearance. This is the dance to which visitors flock. When it is due, the correct standard is raised above the kiva: a tall pole topped with a ball painted white, black, and turquoise, and adorned with parrot and eagle feathers, embroidered sash, or coyote skin.

With the dancers comes their chorus; men who chant to drum accompaniment and make gestures suggestive of falling rain. The music seems simple, though it is often complicated with three or even four rhythms carried at once by chanters, drummers, dancers, and in gesture. Trained musicians faint before this feat. Different dances require different music, often mimetic. Bull-roarers swung by a strong man make the sound of wind; thunder-stones struck together should start a rolling in the clouds; lightning-frames shoot in and out in colored zigzags; bone whistles, flutes, and rattles produce suggestive sounds. Instead of beating on drums, the musician may beat on a rolled sheepskin or inverted basket or rub one notched stick over another. Everything is to inform the supernaturals that rain is wanted. Most rituals include prayers for rain, from which all good comes: food, health, and the tribe's increase.

The ancient Pueblos' calendar was worked out by the shamans and adjusted at need. Most ceremonials are still dated thus, to the utter confusion of tourists. Each season had its appointed ritual. Between times, or when war, disease, or other evil threatened, shamans or societies made retreats to pray and fast. The societies varied from pueblo to pueblo, but there were few men who did not belong to one. Many belonged to several, and in some places women were society members.

The Pueblo's personal life was standardized as rigidly as the year. No room for individual vagary, none for genius or revolt. This way of thinking is breaking down, but so slowly that use of the present tense is still correct in discussing it.

The child is born into his mother's clan or becomes a member of his father's moiety. In the West, where clan predominates, he is named by his mother's sister, and her brothers are more important to him than his own father. This system weakens toward the East, where European customs have strengthened the father's position and the boy takes his father's name. In every pueblo the baby learns songs and dance rhythms as grandfather jounces him and tells stories to explain why the crow is black, how the rabbit turned white, and how the old coyote fooled everybody. These tales are infused with Pueblo humor, ranging from subtle allusion to vulgar slapstick.

At puberty, boys go into the kiva for training. All boys must learn ritual: only so will they be able to do their share in society or moiety. They must also prove their manhood. Girls learn from their mothers, especially corn-grinding, which is a ceremonial as well as practical accomplishment. Beautiful songs accompany the swing of the woman's body over the metate. Women may serve in societies, especially in the West; they take part in most dances, their slow shuffle, without raising the feet, symbolizing woman's contact with mother earth. This makes a fine contrast to the man's insistent pounding. Children learn to dance by dancing. Tiny ones, fresh from modern schools, but correctly accoutered and serious, keep the perfect rhythm all day, untiring.

As they grow, children take part in old rites of exorcism before planting, in ceremonial rabbit drives, and in kick-stick races. They learn dances to bring success in the hunt or in war.

In all Pueblo life and thought the most pervasive and persistent conception is that of group good. Morality consists in conformity to custom and correctness in performance. Neglect or error will bring evil to the people. The idea of individual sin or reward for individual good does not enter into Pueblo thought. A man's worth is computed not by what he has amassed for himself, but by what good he has done his group.

These customs and beliefs—the ways of the ancients—have survived into the middle of the twentieth century to give the individual Pueblo personal integration and security within his group. Certainly all have not been true to their best ethic, any more than all Christians have. But the Pueblo's confidence in what the kachinas taught has given him notable dignity, spiced with humor, and the strength to adjust to many changes without losing his inner verities.

IV

CHANGING PUEBLO LIFE

AT FIRST glance, the fascination of pueblo life lies in its seeming changelessness. In a sense, of course, this is true. But the oldest ruins show that life was in a state of flux even when they were occupied. Elsie Clews Parsons takes two hundred pages of text to describe interpueblo borrowings owing to travel, trade, intermarriage, and imitation. The Pueblos are a flexible people; they often show themselves more realistic about inevitable change than their white friends do.

One young student, determined that pottery types must be kept pure, scolded a Santa Clara potter for using a design that belonged to another pueblo. She answered: "This is too my design. My sister-in-law from over there in Zia, she gave it to me." John Adair, collecting data for his excellent study, *Navajo and Pueblo Silversmiths*, traced designs and methods from whites to Pueblo to Navajo and back again.

Even religious rites, the least alterable element in any culture, have been freely exchanged. Zunis perform a Navajo Yeibechai dance better, many think, than the Navajos do it. Pueblos exposed to Comanche raids learned the Comanche War Dance as the best medicine against their enemies. Dr. Parsons relates that Taos once sold its Elk Dance to a Nambe chief for ten turquoise, five red beads, twelve dance-blankets, twelve deerskins, and the promise that the dance would always be correctly performed. But even correct performance has been subject to modifications, most noticeably in dance costumes. Originally garments of daily

40

wear, these naturally were a mélange of many tribes' dress; and now they are heavy with manufactured bells, buckles, and beads taken over from whites during four hundred years.

In the westernmost pueblos Hopi and Zuni remain much alike; they have influenced the Keres pueblos of Acoma and Laguna, and to a lesser degree Tiwa Isleta. Taos, farthest north, shows so many Apache, Comanche, and Ute traits that Taoseños have been called Plains Indians living in a pueblo. They show, however, the influence of the Tewas to the south, and Tewas and Keres have affected each other. The best example of this interinfluence is in the curing societies and the priestly functions. Curing, everywhere important, is a group function in the West and pretty well into the Keres pueblos. But in Taos the shaman may cure through his individual dreams and powers, as the Plains Indians cured. The intervening Keres and Tewas partake of both systems.

The extreme test of Pueblo adaptability came with the Spanish conquerors, who brought a new government, a new religion, and a whole set of new superstitions. A less pliant people might have been overwhelmed. But not the supple, subtle Pueblos. They accepted what fitted into their preconceptions and sidestepped what did not. With essential and mystical practices they retreated into the kivas, to undisclosed shrines, and especially into a secretiveness that persists to this day. The youngest Pueblo child has learned not to tell a white person anything. A supervisor, visiting a schoolroom in Santo Domingo, inquired gaily: "And what did you children have for breakfast this morning?" The class leader, a bright-eyed imp, hissed a swift incomprehensible phrase, undoubtedly the Keres for "Clam up!" Not one word could be got out of any of them. What would have been merely an adult's stupid condescension to white children was inexcusable prying to the little Pueblos. Ethnologists report that many intelligent informers, even college graduates, show fear of divulging sacred matters. Talk lessens power; revealing a rite may destroy its force. It is not surprising that lacunæ exist in our knowledge; what is amazing is that we know so much.

The Spanish thought they had converted the Pueblos; they got them to build churches, attend services, and bring their children for baptism and even confirmation. But the Pueblos were accepting the new faith with discrimination. They rejected the conception of a personalized, omnipotent God; the idea of sin punishable by torment in an after life; and especially belief in vicarious atonement. Christ the Redeemer does not enter strongly into Catholicism as practiced in the pueblos. Few gory crucifixes appear in their churches. And such self-torture as they saw Spanish flagellantes inflict struck them as silly. Saints, however, offered no jolt to the Pueblo mind. Like kachinas, saints had been human and were now transfigured into supernaturals with special powers. Carrying the saint's statue out to bless the fields was in the kachina tradition.

The ancient Pueblo calendar was easily adjusted to that of the Christians, which was based, after all, on the same seasonal changes. Solstice ceremonies and hunting dances belong to midwinter, just as Christmas does: they turn the solar system back toward light and life. At Taos, after Christmas Eve vespers in the pueblo, the priest returns to town and the pueblo to its old ways. Tall bonfires, flaming skyward from the terraced roofs, redden the snow where brown bodies stamp and shake their bells in the dance. In the Keres pueblos and at Isleta, wise Catholic priests permit buffalo- and deer-dances in the churches. Nothing in New Mexico is more dramatic than the painted figures wrapping themselves in blankets and approaching the crèche with bowed heads and offerings ready. Twelfth Night is inauguration day for the newly elected pueblo governors, and the people observe the ancient custom of throwing gifts from the housetops to the dancers below. Easter, Christian season of rebirth, is celebrated by many pueblos with their corn dances which also honor the patron saint on his holy day. This tolerance of pagan rites is one of the most gracious of Spanish concessions to an alien expression of the religious spirit.

In practical matters the Pueblos accepted Spanish ways without much difficulty. After a few battles they were allowed to stay in their towns, theirs now by the mercy of His Most Catholic Majesty of Spain. They built churches, as they had built their homes, with stone and adobe; but they painted pictures and carved wood as the padres directed. They cut doors in their house walls and learned to make chimneys. And they gratefully accepted domestic animals. Moccasins were more durable with cowhide soles, sheep pelts were soft to sleep on, and wool was easy to weave. The black wool dresses Pueblo women still wear in the dances replaced deerskin or cotton slips, and wool blankets were quite as warm as, and easier to make than, the old robes of twisted rabbit skin. Here enters the "blanket Indian" in the white man's blanket! Above all, the Pueblo found glass beads and shiny bells much gaudier and noisier than the old wampum, turquoise, and bones.

To facilitate gathering tribute and enlisting workers from the pueblos, Governor Castaño de Sosa ordered each pueblo to elect a governor. We like to think that manhood suffrage is an Anglo-Saxon gift to the Americas. But here it was, thirty years before the Pilgrims landed, and from imperial Spain. The Pueblos accepted the new officer as a link with the white man's government, and added ex-governors to their governing council. The Spaniards, recognizing the ancient religious leaders, called them caciques, an Arawakan word meaning chief which is still generally used.

Problems were discussed and rules made in council.

There was never any hurry; every man was given time to express his opinion fully while every other man listened respectfully. Unanimity was the desideratum; the concern of all was to avoid a sharp division or an open break. However acrimonious the feeling, no decision was final until all were convinced that a right solution had been reached. White people are always irked by these interminable council meetings and the way they leave an important matter unresolved for the moment—or the year. But this was the way of the ancients.

The Spanish governor presented each pueblo governor with a silver-headed cane. This was an acceptable badge of office because it was similar to the ritual wands of society chiefs. In 1863, when twenty pueblo governors called upon President Lincoln he gave them each another cane with his name and the date inscribed on it. These two canes are now the required badge of office; no governor is considered properly installed or empowered to act unless he has them in his possession.

So the Spaniards brought much that was good and not too hard to take. But they also brought diseases devastating to people who had no inherited immunity against them. Smallpox, which killed off five thousand Indians in the epidemic of 1780, receded only after the Indian Service enforced vaccination. Tuberculosis is still far too prevalent, as are trachoma and syphilis. Children die from measles and whooping cough, and—lacking still enough screens, sanitary privies, and clean water—dysentery kills babies every summer. Many of these afflictions are still blamed on witchcraft, not yet eradicated.

When it came to witches, the Pueblos and the Spanish understood each other well. Indians had long blamed sickness on ghosts or wrong thoughts; as a shaman could cure evil, he could cause it. The notion that any person might be a witch was European, but the Pueblos were ready to agree that evil thoughts might come from a malicious neighbor. Sticking dolls full of cactus spines in order to hurt an enemy, heeding the owl's hoot, and covering the baby's head to ward off the evil eye were quickly adopted. The monks and their converts differed only when the Inquisition tried as witches shamans who were performing ancestral rites for the general good.

So with all their changes in Pueblo living, the Spanish did not change Pueblo thinking much. The monks did their best. They established some schools. The priest at Jemez won special commendation for teaching a few of the boys to read. But the monks taught mostly doctrine; a boy knew enough if he could serve Mass and grow up to be a fiscal and collect the tithes. The Pueblos went on living as the kachinas had taught. The deep currents of life were unaffected. Group solidarity was maintained, and in it the individual found his strength.

It took the United States, with its Nordic rigidity, to begin to break down this power-giving integration. The United States, for over half a century, tried deliberately to eradicate the old customs and ways of thinking. It was an unsuccessful undertaking as planned, but it has resulted in some curious confusions and paradoxes and has made life harder for many Pueblo people.

The United States, taking over in 1846, declared the Indians citizens, confirmed them in the communal ownership of their lands, and put the Army in charge of them. The Army used Pueblos in wars against Navajos and Apaches, but did nothing to educate them. Then, in the eighties, a new policy assigned all Indians in the United States to various religious bodies, and Protestant missionaries appeared in New Mexico.

Protestants were no less convinced than Catholics that their faith, and only theirs, was God's, but they were less experienced with Indian converts and less patient with slow or partial conversions. Precipitately they invaded every phase of Indian life and demanded conformity in every particular. Thus they broke up families, divided village groups, and caused many personal problems not primarily religious. Dr. Parsons relates that a Baptist missionary, who settled in Laguna in 1851, caused a split that has never healed. Elected governor by his converts, the Reverend Samuel Gorman so alienated the unconverted that they left their village. What he left undone was finished off by a Presbyterian who arrived in 1875. Between them these pious gentlemen stirred up such dissension that the Lagunas now live in six pueblos, and many Laguna families are found in Isleta. Dr. Parsons also quotes a Hopi on missionaries. "Why," he asked, "do they come into our plazas? The plazas are for kachinas. The chapel is for Jesus." Granting that there is more than one way, the Hopi asked to be allowed to follow his way in peace. But freedom of religion had not then been construed as applying to the Indians, who were offered only the freedom to choose among Christian faiths.

This widespread invasion of privacies had consequences that might seem funny if one did not know how hurtful may be a tug of war between respected mentors. White administrators insisted upon cutting the boys' hair and required all children to wear white man's clothes. As a cropped Pueblo was not allowed to appear in certain ceremonies, this barbering might deprive a man of his right and his duty to serve his people. Most pueblos have been forced to yield on this point of hair. But in Taos, where G-string, leggings, and moccasins are orthodox male attire, dress poses a problem to this day. In his sensitive novel, *The Man Who Killed the Deer*, Frank Waters shows how trousers and heeled shoes may symbolize the struggle between old and new in Taos.

Long before the Pueblo baby can talk, he is subjected to contradictory pulls. Born into clan or moiety, he is named according to tribal custom and sprinkled with holy meal; he may then be baptized and sprinkled with holy water. As late as 1949, an infant was buried with Christian rites, but clothes, food, and toys were cast into the grave. The growing child acquires manners, learns to be quiet, uncomplaining, respectful to the old, and is taught his duty to the group. He is seldom punished, but may be shamed or ridiculed into doing right. But in the government-run Indian School he learns new myths, other morals, and a new series of shames. White teachers are often appalled at sexual knowledge shown by Pueblo children, to whom the facts of nature and the forms of the body may be interesting but are never evil. Such teachers are doubly shocked when Indian parents, appealed to, find the protest funny.

Very small children are faced with decisions that would test an adult. At the Christmas dance in Jemez in 1948, Santa Claus appeared along with the masked buffalo, deer, and antelope dancers. This was in the tradition of adding a new figure to the pantheon. But something was troubling a fourteen-year-old girl from the Catholic school. Watching her younger brother she was nervous, biting her fingers.

"I do hope," she kept saying, "he won't take a feather."

"Take a feather? Why?"

"Yes. See the old men giving the boys feathers? If a boy takes one he has to go to the kiva with the old man and join his healing society. . . . But we don't want any more of that! That's old savage stuff!"

Not many old men did well with their feathers. Three or four, stately in their blankets, left the plaza with one little boy tagging behind, but most of them, six or seven, left alone. Another day, in another pueblo, the tale might be different.

Kiva training for boys continues in the face of government schools and truant officers. Some Pueblos, like the British, believe that at adolescence a boy should be trained for a man's life by men. This means months out of school, longer for those selected for priestly discipline. Up to now most boys submit willingly. Even their mothers do not complain at having to prepare orthodox food for their sons in kiva instead of the canned meals they serve at home. Protests come from white teachers, who invoke attendance rules. But federal courts have held that the Pueblo is entitled to religious training without interference. At last the Indian is allowed freedom to choose his own ancient religion.

This attitude, long advocated by individuals and by associations for protection of Indians, became official policy when President Hoover, himself a Friend, appointed two Friends, Charles J. Rhoads and Henry Scattergood, as Commissioner and Assistant Commissioner of Indian Affairs. Military discipline was replaced by modern educational methods, uniforms were abandoned, girls were issued bright ginghams and taught to make their own dresses in any style they chose. Jails were turned into workshops or washhouses; children were allowed to speak their own languages; and their religion was not scorned. Owing to pressure from the New Mexico Association on Indian Affairs and the Association on American Indian Affairs, Indian arts and crafts were introduced in the schools. Pottery-making was not a success; Pueblo women did not wish other pueblos to learn their techniques. Weaving, silversmithing, and woodcarving have remained regular courses and are generally taught by Indians.

Then came John Collier. Appointed Commissioner in 1932, he came from years of work for Indians and as a scathing critic of government policy. A student of anthropology, he undertook sweeping reforms. Inevitably they encountered opposition from white people who did not understand, and from Indians who always distrusted Uncle Sam's erratic caprices and who thought that these reforms might soon pass away.

A successful policy has been that of raising boarding schools to the status of high schools and of keeping small children in schools near home, where motherly Pueblo housekeepers can help with the new language. A few textbooks were prepared for Pueblo children, and pamphlets such as *Respect for Indian Culture and Religious Freedom* were issued and presumably read. But teachers firmly rooted in our folkways are not too capable of helping children across a gap between cultures, often being unaware that such a gap exists. A modern teacher said: "Oh, well, if you're going into their *psychology!*"

Indian Service teachers' salaries are too low to attract many people willing or able to understand the Pueblo child. Many complain that their pupils are dull, sullen, unco-operative. They refuse to enter into the spirit of a game or to compete for high grades. Most baffling of all, they never jeer at a lagger; they are more likely to wait for him or to offer help. The Pueblo child has learned long before school age that the individual must act for the group. The will to win, with our traditional "and the devil take the hindmost," is hard to inculcate.

Most Pueblos finish only the six grades offered in the day school. They do as well as other children with a language handicap. Attendance sometimes as high as ninety per cent suggests that even conservative Pueblos value education, if only as protection against the outer world.

But the outer world has been winning steadily. What teachers and missionaries, backed by the full force of the United States, could not do is being gradually done by gadgets, jobs, and youthful desire to conform. Children, home from school, prefer shoes, pants, and dresses. Girls who have learned to open cans buy store goods. Kerosene lamps light the whitewashed rooms, and buckets replace *ollas*. It has got so a photographer has to bring his own moccasins and painted jar to get a picturesque shot of an Acoma woman reflected in the water hole or of a Taoseña dipping water from Taos Creek. Farmers have bought wagons and then automobiles.

The individual is taking on comforts and conveniences at a great rate. But communal ways change by slower transition. A century ago the War Chief's duties were implicit in his title. When the Spaniards gave the Pueblos horses, his function was readily extended to their care. That led to control of grazing lands and of all flocks and herds. Without a bobble, the War Chief has now taken over irrigation ditches, and it is his musical yodel that calls men out to clean them in the spring. Only his duties have changed, not the War Chief's title or dignity.

Changes are of the outer life that all can see. But there is no lack of evidence of a hidden constancy that lies deep. Taos Creek, from which young women dip their water in tin pails, flows from the sacred lake. Jemez, dominated by a shining metal watertower, keeps captive eagles on its roofs. Acomas live near their fields at Acomita, leaving only old people on their rocky mesa as guards, but on holy days they all go home. So do the progressive Santa Anas. Only an aged sentinel lives in their old pueblo; young men operate a tractor co-operatively on their rich valley lands. And all pueblos bar visitors on the days of their most sacred dances.

Any pueblo on a dance day presents a panorama of this changing pueblo life, especially in the Rio Grande pueblos, where the Catholic church is strongest. The many corn dances, held to celebrate the day of the patron saint, are typical. Mass in the mission church is conducted by friars in the habit of a medieval order, though their ways, like the Indians', are affected by modern life. Franciscans come in motor cars and wear well-shined shoes. The sermon may be in English followed by a Spanish translation. The congregation's garb reflects every prehistoric and modern age, from shell ornaments to Army issue and the permanent wave stylish in the nearest railroad town.

The day of the Indian begins when the saint has been reverently borne by a chanting procession from the church to a shrine in the plaza. Then the priests retire and interest shifts to the kivas. Above each one rises the feathered standard, brilliantly outlined against the sky. And there a man sits, immobile, patiently biding the end of the Catholic stir below. When the dancers emerge it is clear that they are the day's real meaning. Even the saint's leafy shrine, guarded by men with guns and visited at intervals by worshippers, becomes only a background for rites hallowed for the Pueblo by observance much longer than that of any Christian ceremony.

The Pueblo, humanly wise and often with a mystic wisdom too, is not overly impressed with the white man's religion as he practices it. And he suffers to see how the white man violates nature. The Pueblo has lived long in this difficult country. Deep down he knows that this spring's warm brown water depends upon rainfall and that rainfall depends upon certain rites. Young men must learn those ritual observances lest both land and people perish. He loves his land and he believes in the kachinas who have taught him to use it harmoniously. Should he, then, give up the ways of the ancients for untried ways that do not seem to work as well for their practitioners? On the whole, he thinks not.

So the Pueblo, while tolerantly practicing alien ceremonies, continues to perform the rites the kachinas taught. Not only the rain and hunting dances that outsiders are welcome to see, but many others of even deeper power. His images and myths are as vital to his thinking as the Biblical myths are to ours. We accept facts established by geologists with-

out losing the story of Adam and Eve in the Garden. So
to this mid-twentieth century the Pueblo brings old beliefs
that may light his life with beauty or shadow it with fear,
but that surely pervade his daily thinking. His problem is
to reconcile "the ways of the ancients" with the concepts
and needs of today: rain dances with farm machinery, in-
noculations with curing societies, old moralities with modern taboos—or old taboos with modern moralities. The
dance that may impress the white onlooker as a triumph of
art in step, costume, music, and choreography is to the Indian—observer as well as performer—the renewal of an ancient faith and the bulwark of his security.

V

THE MODERN PUEBLO

⊂⊋ THE PUEBLO INDIAN won the right to vote in 1948, a belated recognition of the citizen status granted him by the United States a century ago. In theory he has been as free as any American to speak his mind, worship as he prefers, go where he likes, and learn what he can. But problems that have bedeviled these village Indians for centuries have been intensified, at midcentury, by the increasing need for speedier adjustment and have been complicated by the returned veteran with his rights, needs, and desires.

Pueblo Indians have served in all our wars since they were recruited about 1850 to fight Navajos and Apaches. In World War I Indians were not drafted, but a few Pueblos volunteered and brought home excited tales of the world beyond the great water. In World War II Indians were subject to the draft, and most Pueblos accepted it readily. The United States was their country; they were willing to fight for it. A few individuals tried to get exemption; some claimed religious obligations. This pleased and amused aging caciques who had feared the loss of old rites for lack of learners, and who now had novices under vow. But such cases were few. The Pueblo record, on the whole, was as good as any.

The villages sent their young men off with what protection they could, probably a dance. In Isleta such a dance could be called only by the full council, and the draft board had precipitately removed one councilman to boot camp thousands of miles away. The Indian Service, informed of the case, presented it to the proper commanding officer, who allowed the young councilman to return. The dance was held, and we won the war.

Meanwhile old men had been praying and seeing visions. A very dependable Isleta, whose son was fighting in the South Pacific, remembered that a clan headman had called on him in May 1945. The old man said nothing for a long time. Then he spoke. "I know how troubled you are. We are all troubled. For your son. For all our sons. It is bad over there, very bad. But it will soon be over. Something will come from the clouds. Maybe our old thunder gods. I don't know. But from the clouds it will come, and the fighting will end. This I know." And so it came. From the clouds.

In World War II, 1,065 Pueblo men and women served in all theaters and in all services. Twenty-five were lost; many were wounded. Those at home did well in buying bonds and in factories where their dexterity, quick eyes, and ability to learn were invaluable. A few have stayed on in factories and in cities. Most of them returned to the pueblo with its securities, practical as well as mystical.

Most of these young Indians had finished the pueblo day school before the war. A few had gone on to high school; fewer to college. But there has been a notable lack of trained technicians and professional people. The Indian Service's answer to such criticisms is that funds are inadequate.

But young Indians are being forced into modern life by the same pressures that affect young white people. Their lands are inadequate to support a growing population; they can earn more in industry than as farmers; they long to better their living conditions and to see their children advance. But they also feel the pull of their inherited traditions and tribal customs.

This paradox is sharply evident among Pueblos whose

young men are working in Albuquerque and Santa Fe as mechanics, at Los Alamos as trained technicians in many lines; quite a few have gone into selling Indian artifacts and even making a business of Indian songs and dances. But a majority retain their status in the pueblo, where they enjoy the advantages of inalienable landownership of tax-free lands, a situation not wholly enviable.

There are nineteen pueblos in New Mexico and naturally they differ in many ways, as people always differ even in fairly homogeneous groups. But they have enough similarities to allow us to consider the Pueblo people as a whole. Traditionally their governments are sacerdotal in character, dominated by shamans, generally old men who understand the ways of men and of nature and the importance of keeping men and nature in harmony. This idea underlies the Pueblo saying: "If our hearts are right, the rain will come." Such leaders are naturally influential even in the selection of elected officials as well as in every detail of daily life. The extent of this priestly control and of the younger people's struggle against it largely determines whether a pueblo is considered conservative or progressive.

Pueblo youngsters who go to college maintain a fair average. A few do notably well; several have gone on to advanced degrees and professional or technical training. But the government has been woefully slow to help the Indian of superior capabilities. Great as is the need for trained people to work with their own groups, the Pueblos have produced no doctors, dentists, or lawyers, though a few surveyors, engineers, and agronomists have graduated from agricultural colleges. In 1959 the Indian Service invested $145,000 in Indian scholarships. The tribes in New Mexico have done much better since the discovery of oil, gas, and uranium on their reservations; Navajos, Apaches, and some Pueblos have established really handsome scholarships for their young people.

Pueblo Indians, with few exceptions, are not happy in town. Though they are invited to municipal and church activities, few really throw themselves into YM or YWCA's, Scouts, Epworth Leagues, or the Youth Center. On their evenings off, they are more likely to be found strolling the streets, eating at the hamburger joints, attending the movies, dancing—always with Indians. Perhaps the other ways are too alien. Perhaps it is because few Pueblos have yet entered the white-collar jobs that lead to their being enough at ease for social acceptance. It is sadly true that Pueblos living in Albuquerque or in Santa Fe can meet the rents only in slum or near-slum areas. Naturally they prefer life in the pueblo and on their tax-free lands.

To most of us freedom from a land tax would seem wholly enviable. But both New Mexico and Arizona long denied the vote to "Indians not taxed." In fact the Indians pay all taxes except those on the communally owned lands granted them by the King of Spain and confirmed to them by the United States in 1846. This anomalous situation of U.S. citizens and inalienable lands lies at the root of the Pueblo's dilemma.

Few pueblos ever owned enough land to support the people in what we consider decency, and for generations white settlers continually encroached on both land and water rights without hindrance. Indians had no vote; nobody cared. Then New Mexico's Senator Bursum introduced into the Congress in 1922 a bill that would have confirmed the intruders in their holdings. That stirred up a public furor led by Santa Fe's artists and writers, who foresaw the doom of much beauty in craft, dance, and living, as well as a people's starvation. Ten years of struggle brought two results: the pueblo lands were saved or just compensation paid for those not deemed recoverable; and associations for the protection of Indians became unremittingly vigilant.

Plenty in the Pueblo's situation still taxes the ingenuity

and patience of his wisest and most sympathetic friends. Pueblo lands are still inadequate to meet rising standards of living or increasing populations. The Pueblo farmer has to seek seasonal work on ranches or a job in town and permit his women and children to sell pottery and turquoise along the highways. But it is never just a question of finding outside jobs. What has baffled generations of lawyers is the Pueblo's position as landowner.

Pueblo lands are inalienable, but the federal government reserves the right to supervise their management, to lease them to outsiders, and to buy or lease additional acreage for the pueblo. Each pueblo is an autonomy within New Mexico, but not subject to the state's laws. It is self-governing through a council chosen by varied forms of manhood suffrage, and with ex-governors as members. The individual Pueblo man is subject to council rulings unless he breaks a federal law. This does not make him a ward of the government, but, like any citizen who uses the federal domain, he must obey regulations governing land use. Through the years the adaptable Pueblo has managed well enough between pueblo council and federal government. But his quandary is deepened by the vote and the veteran. Politicians have come into the peaceful pueblo scene. And some veterans have acquired the white man's desire for a sharp division and a quick decision. It would be a paradox indeed if the Indian's way of long talk ending in general agreement were to be lost just as the United Nations are trying to learn the method.

In several cases Pueblos egged on by white advisers have gone into the federal courts to protest what they considered violations of their rights as citizens. The courts have held that with Indians as with whites the local government's authority must be recognized. Disgruntled Pueblos, Judge Colin Neblett reminded them in deciding a Taos case in 1949, have the same right to change their government as have citizens anywhere—in New Jersey, say, or Louisiana, or Boston.

Pueblo people, as a rule, bow without demur to council authority. Even veterans have submitted to whipping for drunkenness (the lash in such cases may be laid onto a man's blanket rather than his backside). Pueblo law, like our common law, has its presumptions: courts have ruled that a Pueblo council is as entitled to whip a drunk as the State of Delaware is to flog a wife-beater.

Drink has caused many a conflict between pueblo elders and the returned veteran. According to a federal law passed when all our frontiers were harried by savages inflamed with firewater, it is a penitentiary offense to give or sell liquor to Indians. This law has never been repealed, but in 1953 New Mexico and in 1954 Arizona legalized the sale of liquor to Indians. Since then the Navajo Tribal Council has prohibited the sale of liquor on the reservation; arrests for drunkenness had markedly declined, though it is still a problem.

The liquor problem may underlie council opposition to on-the-job training. Veterans of one pueblo had signed up for work in a garage in town when councilmen, in blanketed dignity, called on the garage owner and declared the deal off. In that case the veterans slipped away to the garage at night; technical training became an underground activity. Pueblo veterans, applying for on-the-farm training, encountered a triple difficulty. Bankers, ready to treat all GI's alike, found that the Pueblo could not mortgage his house, though he had built it, owned it unquestionably, and was a good credit risk. Nor could he show title to the land he tilled. And councilmen feared that veterans might claim ownership to pueblo lands to which they had only the right of use. Such objections were overcome finally by special written agreements with pueblo councils. In Zuni, where old men feared that the old societies would be disrupted by on-the-farm training, a wise administrator suggested organizing classes along the lines of the ancient pueblo societies, and the old men agreed. Deeper fears were that modern farming methods might interfere with the ancient ceremonial calendar. But as the kachinas seem to have been good farmers with sound ideas about planting and harvesting, these difficulties too were surmounted—after long discussion.

Over two hundred veterans have taken technical training and as many more have studied agriculture. The matter-of-fact men who train Indians find that they are just like anybody else: they range from poor to good to super. Not a few have been called first-rate, and several have gone on to technical and agricultural colleges. All this should lead to more productive farms and, in time, to men who can qualify as supervisors and directors not in the pueblos only, but in state and county in general. This will provide a true bridge between cultures.

The real tug for the trained Pueblo comes when he must decide between two standards of value. As a good Pueblo he should take part in certain kiva rites and respond when called to serve as a pueblo official. As a worker in town he should not leave his job. Adjustments are made on all sides. A substitute may be hired to perform the appointed task in the pueblo. Many employers in town grant time off, accepting the Pueblo's religious obligations as they do those of the Catholic or the Jew. Sometimes practical considerations are baffling, as in Taos, where nobody may stay out of the pueblo overnight. Reconciling this rule with the demands of a waitress's job in town would tax a diplomat.

The extreme test is that of a man earning twenty dollars a day at Los Alamos who is summoned to an unpaid honor in San Ildefonso or Santa Clara. Years ago no cash consideration would have outweighed the Pueblo's obligation to serve or the prestige his service would bring him. But our money standards are affecting the Pueblo even at religious depths. Some Pueblos give up a good job for the unpaid dignity; a few deliberately begin to live like white men, though one who stays away too long may lose the right to land. This situation may mark the beginning of capitalism in the ancient pueblo communes. The man who stays at home farms more land than his share; he is using the city worker's portion. So the rich grow richer and the poor poorer. The class consciousness that often follows such a trend has not yet invaded the pueblos. But some day a matron whose husband runs large herds is going to hire a neighbor to help in the house. Then the democratic pueblo will begin to go the way New England went.

Pueblo people do not like to see the beginning of inequalities. An Isleta man, himself running more stock on pueblo land than he thinks fair, is studying a plan to protect the town workers by some system of rental payments for land use. The Pueblo still thinks first of the general good. And many of the most modern, preferring life with family, friends, and the old ways, are making smooth personal adjustments.

An Isleta veteran, who is a draftsman with the Army Engineers in Albuquerque, commutes thirteen miles daily in order to live at home and bring his child up as a good Pueblo. His wife, a nurse, agrees fully. Their adobe house has a screened porch, an electrical kitchen, and a neon-lighted workbench for the man. Such young men and women may manage a workable fusion of modern conveniences and ancient values. This would be a triumph of true civilization; but the hazards are many, for while pueblo life is being assailed from without, its internal affairs are often in confusion because old customs do not meet modern conditions. This Isleta veteran is typical of many now employed at atomic centers.

An Acoma who had been living with his Laguna wife in

her pueblo got the Acoma cacique's permission to move his 250 sheep back home. When he arrived with family and goods in a truck and his teen-age son driving the sheep, the governor stopped him. The Grazing Service had ruled that the Acoma lands could not support additional sheep; moreover, the cacique had no right to act in a civil matter. At a conference suggested by the Indian Service, the old cacique yielded gracefully and the claimant returned to his wife's pueblo, where land was available. This ruling, incidentally, drew the line between religious and civil authority within the pueblo. It is more difficult to define pueblo jurisdiction when it conflicts with that of the state or nation.

Marriage and divorce, long considered the pueblo's own affairs, produce both comedy and tragedy. A Laguna pair had been married according to Laguna custom for thirty years. Then the husband, an employee of the Santa Fe railroad, reached retirement age. As his pension would be figured on the number of his dependents, the Santa Fe asked to see his marriage certificate. The Laguna couple had no proof of marriage; just the children. Not acceptable. So the long-wed couple, highly amused, had a wedding with license, children, grandchildren, and a party.

It does not always work out so pleasantly. In another pueblo, a man married by tribal rites went to war, leaving a wife and three children. On his return he was married to another woman by a justice of the peace and went to a priest for the religious ceremony. The padre, making a routine check, learned of the former marriage and refused to officiate. The Indian Service attorney, William Brophy, held that the pueblo marriage was valid. The wife filed suit for divorce in the state court, thus marking a break with old custom.

Any individual Pueblo is free to employ counsel and bring suit. But the pueblo as a unit must be represented by the Indian Service attorney or one approved by him. This rule was designed to protect Indians from shysters; but the people have not forgotten that the Indian Service failed to guard their land and water rights. Even today they complain that the government closes deals in their interest without consulting them. Men of the caliber of councilmen naturally resent such tutelage and often consult private attorneys, though any lawyer who advises them must act as a friend, without fee or other emolument.

Some pueblos have large business deals with outsiders. Santa Clara and San Ildefonso have contracts with Los Alamos for sand and gravel sales and for land rents that run into five figures annually. And Isleta, given a small herd of cattle during the depression, did not butcher it but bred up the stock and used the income for the general good. This income has put in a water system and a sewer is proposed. In 1949 the pueblo herd brought in about ninety thousand dollars, which was used for electrification of the pueblo.

In such matters the council acts. In 1849 New Mexico's first legislature ruled that each pueblo was a body corporate. Isleta is organized as a corporation. But in operation most councils proceed by the old Indian way of long talk, no matter how long it takes to reach a decision. Isleta once suffered a split in the council that tied up business important to white men, who urged forcing the issue. But the majority leader demurred. "Give me time and I'll get an agreement." In time he did. The minority leader resigned in order to make the decision unanimous, saying: "God has forgiven us all. Let us forgive each other."

In affairs of wider concern the pueblos are united in the All Pueblo Council, organized in 1922 to fight the Bursum Bill. It meets on call, preferably with no non-Indian observers. Even if white advisers are invited, they are bowed politely out at the end of the matter in hand. Santo Domingo has been the traditional meeting place since Spanish days. Once a council officer, a Baptist and an Indian Service employee, called a meeting at a Baptist church in Albuquerque. Not a pueblo representative appeared. Many Indians dislike seeing an "agency Indian" in a position of power; others did not wish to convene in a church.

Unhappily, missionaries, devoted preachers of the religion of peace, produce divisiveness and bad feeling among the Pueblos. They not only oppose the ancient beliefs, but also, lacking the Indian's tolerance, often openly combat one another. Missionaries of eight or ten churches proselyte among the Pueblos, furnishing that humorous folk with amusement, but also with concern. When the children of a Holiness Pilgrim complained that Catholic children had stoned them, the people were aroused; children should not be taught to hate. But when a couple of Latter-day Saints were ordered out by elders who thought they were preaching polygamy, laughter ran through the Pueblo world. "What sort of a religion is that?" snorted the anciently monogamous Pueblos.

Among the faiths that the Pueblos know is the peyote cult, which involves the taking of peyote, a stimulant drug from mescal buttons. It has been taken since time immemorial by Mexican Indians, but it entered New Mexico from the Plains tribes. John Collier, when he was Indian Commissioner, welcomed it as a possible means of uniting the Indian population; Indians often call it "the Indian Church." In New Mexico the peyote cult has taken root only among the Navajos and in Taos pueblo, where the conservatives opposed it because it emphasized the individual rather than any group. Some whites have opposed it as immoral: a New Mexico statute makes the possession of peyote a crime. But by federal ruling peyote is not a narcotic. This confusion needs further court action. The question remains: is the taking of peyote a silly custom, a vicious habit, nobody's business, or the Indians' true religion?

Despite all outside pressures, the Pueblos seem most at ease with the Catholic Church. But they are capable of taking issue with it. When an archbishop asked Santo Domingo for land on which to build a convent, the council politely refused, explaining that on certain days no outsider might enter the pueblo. No defiance was intended; they were all Catholics, but no land would be given. His Grace, unaccustomed to opposition, reminded the council that, as Catholics, they could be excommunicated; denied the Church's sacraments they might go to hell. Here he was on the caciques' own ground. "Tell him," one directed the interpreter, "that God does not care how we express our reverence, with holy water or holy meal. And if it comes to a future life, we know as much as he does about that. . . . You talk a lot about heaven," he concluded, "but you can't produce one single angel, not even a little one." This exchange was delightedly quoted by a visitor from another pueblo.

The Church withdrew its clergy, and for some years Santo Domingo was without Catholic Mass. Then, urged by a white friend, the council recanted in a public statement: ". . . fully realizing that the Catholic religion is the true one . . . the only faith practiced among its people since the time of the Spanish Franciscians, [the council] do hereby pledge themselves to keep their people practicing the said religion." This, as the Indian Service attorney, himself a Catholic, was quick to point out, was contrary to the Constitution. Even the council could not deny religious freedom to any person who might prefer a faith not Catholic. So, though the Catholic mission was reopened, other faiths were not barred.

There remained the question of the caciques' right to require certain duties of Christian Indians. Where does civic duty end and enforced support of religion begin? A federal court has ruled that "no tax . . . may be levied to support any religious activities . . . whatever they may be called." How does this affect the Pueblo required to sweep out the plaza before a dance? Such services have been construed as civic duties and, for refusing them, men have been deprived of their land rights. The United States Supreme Court has not yet ruled on any specific case.

The Pueblos, as usual, make their own adjustments. A baby baptized by the Catholic priest was presented to the cacique for the clan naming. Lifting it toward the sun, the old man said: "May this child grow into a man who will learn the white man's ways and use what is good; may he also learn the Pueblo way, respect it, and cherish its best too."

A veteran home from the European theater described his solution. "When I was little," he said, "I used to worry because my teachers told me my people would go to hell because they were pagans. That was hard for a little boy of ten. I used to look at my family and wonder. They looked so nice; they laughed so much at home. I really suffered. . . . Now, of course, I know better. I go to Mass, but I don't worry about my family any more."

Thus the Pueblo's age-old sublety still finds ways to hold fast the traditional verities, often so quietly that the outsider suspects nothing. The traditional September fiesta in the progressive pueblo of Laguna seemed to have become a county fair where the most blatant modernity had smothered both the pueblo dance and the Catholic saint's day observance. Mass was said in the pale old adobe church and a shrine for San Jose was set up in the dance plaza. But the day's big event was the baseball game.

On a diamond ringed with cars and trucks, the Winslow Redskins and the Lagunas were playing off the final of an eighteen-pueblo series. The Laguna governor and the president of the All Pueblo Council, both Protestants and "agency Indians," were there. Indian rooters from two states yelled defiance at the umpire and swarmed among booths where cones, Cokes, and hot dogs were sold. Across the din of the merry-go-round came the sound of Indian music; Manuel Archuleta of San Juan and his Laguna wife were doing a brisk business selling records of Indian songs.

The dancing, when it came, was a sorry travesty of the ancient ceremonies. Two young dancers attired in black velvet Eton jackets and knee-breeches cut to show their fine musculature performed the Hoop Dance with professional skill and aplomb. But it had no meaning whatever: it was a vaudeville turn, no more. The old dance, correct for the day, came on raggedly with a few old men and women shuffling aimlessly, untrained, poorly costumed, the dying remnant of a vigorous religious expression.

On such a day Laguna seems to offer sad proof that the splendid old ceremonies with their deep meaning are forever gone. But in many pueblos they exist in gorgeous correctness. Even World War II and Korean veterans with their squared military shoulders appear stripped and painted, conventionally accoutered for the dance. One, between figures at Zia, came to greet a friend. "Yes," he said, "we dance. While we were gone the old folks kept these things going for our protection. Now we must do our part."

Even the fiesta at Laguna is not the proof of degeneration that it seems. It is rather evidence that the Pueblo has again found his way to evade the intruder. A Laguna woman said: "Don't you worry about the Lagunas. Our private dances, the ones white people never see, are still the most beautiful anywhere. Everything is perfect, everybody watches and is absolutely quiet. Nobody cares about what white people see."

So the Pueblo, having absorbed Catholicism, American education, and a cash economy, may be able to preserve his ancient ceremonies in secret societies, as other esoteric rites have been preserved. If these fine ceremonies are hidden from the outsider, it will be our loss, not the Indian's.

VI

THE TRADITIONAL NAVAJO

THE NAVAJOS, known to themselves as Diné (the People), have been the most widely and seriously studied of all our tribes. Volumes have been written about their ceremonies. More volumes are in the making as students continue to delve into this curious culture, which seems ever more mature in the light of modern thinking. The best examples of Navajo handiwork win respect everywhere. Musicians and choreographers record their songs and study their dance techniques. Literary critics consider Navajo legends equal to the world's most poetic mythologies. And students of comparative religion find in Navajo ceremonies "splendid symbols of abstract ideas." The Diné may not be dismissed as a primitive tribe; they are a highly developed people worthy of respectful study.

The related Navajo and Apache tribes were latecomers into New Mexico, appearing from the north about one thousand years ago. Both brought many Plains Indian traits, some of which persist as proof of their common origin. The Spanish, more correctly than they knew, lumped the two groups as Apaches de Navajo or Navajo-Apache. The word *Navajo* has been translated as "planted fields," and also as "knife." Both translations have applicability.

Long before the Spanish came, Navajo and Apache cultures had begun to differ as the people drifted apart and borrowed from others. The Navajo developed further and more elaborately because he could always improve on what he learned. As a trader he roamed widely, swapping buckskin, buffalo hides, and baskets for Ute beadwork and elk skins in the north, for Hopi cotton mantles and ceremonial articles in the west, and for fruits and maize and the sacred turquoise along the Rio Grande. Always he learned the ceremony that went with the article he bought, or the story that explained it.

A Navajo trade trip, like all their life, proceeded with ceremony. A smart trader—one who had performed the rites correctly or who had supernatural powers—was chosen leader. During the journey prayers were chanted at every stop. In his *Ancient Navajo*, Dr. Willard Williams Hill quotes an invocation. "The beautiful thing is starting toward me, I being the son of the sun." That song ends: "The beautiful one is come to me, I being the son of the sun." Riding to trade with the Pueblos, the song might be: "Dwellers in the earth, may I have success in dealing with them." Utes they called Dwellers in the Cedar-bark, and with them the approach was quite different. Each Navajo had a Ute friend with whom he exchanged gifts; no price was mentioned. But with the Pueblos hard commercialism was the rule. Clyde Kluckhohn quotes a modern Navajo as saying that you must watch the Pueblos: "They may give you only food." There were rites on the return journey too, and back at home every trader was purified of alien contact by the Blessing Chant. Trade articles also must be freed of malignancy: turquoise was "cooked" in a heated yucca root, a treatment that had the added advantage of deepening the prized sky color.

According to scattered Spanish records, the Navajos ranged over the northern and eastern portions of their present reservation. Dr. Hill has found a report dated 1744 that estimates their numbers at from two to four thousand. Many lived in stone huts such as are still found, and raised corn, beans, squash, and melons. By that time they had a few sheep and goats—got by trade or theft—and even a few horses. Plains Indians valued horses more highly than the sturdy boys and likely girls they also carried off. They cared little for saddles, but bid high for bridles, iron tools, and the brass and copper they hammered into jewelry before they acquired silver. They also swapped for *bayeta*, the bright scarlet English baize that lined Spanish officers' capes. Navajo women raveled this out and used it in their blankets, adding a rich red note to the natural colors of their wool. Navajo blankets soon became the most highly prized article of trade from the plains to Mexico.

The great annual fairs at Taos and Pecos brought together throngs of Indians of all tribes to barter their wares among themselves and to exchange them for Spanish manufactured goods. In spite of Spain's just laws and severe penalties for the protection of Indians, cheating was as general as trade, and bad feeling grew. Plains Indians, having made much peace talk at the fair, might stop on the way home to raid a pueblo or a Spanish hamlet. The Spanish could neither conquer nor convert them.

Henry Kelly, in a published thesis entitled *Franciscan Missions of New Mexico*, honors several intrepid and hopeful friars who tried to establish missions among the Navajos. One, who had settled a group of converts at Cebolleta, found on his next visit that they had all abjured the faith. They had, he was told, allowed "water to be thrown on their children" because of the presents. But presents were not enough to keep them, "who had been raised like the deer," in one place. They offered to be friends, but not Christians.

So the haughty Navajo did not even pretend conversion as the smoother and more easily subdued Pueblo did. The Navajo, mounted and armed and with a wide wilderness to roam, needed no faith other than his own, which was deeply integrated with his life and thought. Even his adopted Pueblo customs were Navajo now. He had fully incorporated the clan system, based on matrilineal descent, which came from the Hopi and the Zuni—as did the kachina cults. As with the Pueblo kachina, the Yei is both the dancer masked to represent a supernatural being and a carved doll. With the kachinas came the painted altar, the sacred meal, the prayer sticks, rattles, and fetiches, and the bull-roarer to chase evil away. Though these religious objects are as a rule more elaborately and more skillfully made by the Pueblos, the Navajos excelled in the imaginative development of the Pueblo myths and in the lofty spiritual content they gave them.

The Navajo twin heroes were born of Changing Woman at the behest of Begodchiddy, who comes close to the Jewish-Christian idea of God as Creator. Christianized Navajos sometimes use the words interchangeably. Changing Woman, also called Turquoise Woman, is the only altogether beneficent force in the Navajo cosmogony—a hint perhaps of woman's power and importance in Navajo life. All the tales of the wanderings, trials, and triumphs of the twins are infused with the beauty of color and light, of mountain and canyon forms, of cloud shapes and of the marvel of storms, as well as of the spiritual beauty of growth through meeting adversity strongly.

Like the Pueblo's mythical ancestors, the Navajo's climbed laboriously upward through successive worlds of greater light and understanding. Haniel Long, the poet, finds here the all-human "not-yet-finished emergence." This is the matter of the Navajo creation myth, one version of which has been translated into English of classic simplicity by Mary Cabot Wheelwright with the aid of the Navajo chanter Hasteen Klah. This myth may be traced from Mexico to the Great Lakes region; it may have wider connections. To the Navajo it is the basis of legends that explain his colored desert, gashed canyons, and towering peaks that became sacred to the supernaturals. On these tales are based the Navajo's ethic and his religious ceremonies.

Knowledge of the ceremonies is the vocation of the medicine man or chanter, who, like his Athapascan ancestor, may be and often is a mystic guided by visions. His priestly function and prescribed offices stem from the Pueblo culture and require rigid training. Learning even one ceremony may take years of extraordinary concentration. The chanter must know every word of hundreds of songs, each with its correct gestures, and must memorize every line and color of the sand paintings that illustrate the rite. A chant is as intricate as the Catholic Mass, and its symbolism dramatizes the myth as the Mass does the Passion, and no more obviously. Every "sing" is also a healing ceremony. Not only are physical ailments cured, but fears are eradicated and psychic disturbances resolved. The Navajo believes that every evil is the result of disharmony with spiritual forces; curing is bringing the patient back into right relationship with all life.

Right relationship is basic to the Navajo ethic. Even today the child learns how to enter the hogan (the Navajo house), where to sit, how to address each person, and how to manage his personal needs and to care for his belongings. Even small children own things, and their ownership is respected as they respect the right of others. Once beyond babyhood, they begin to share in the work. As most Navajos still live in the octagonal wattled log hogans, with a fire in the center, tasks have changed little through the ages. The floor must be kept clean, clothes and gear neatly hung around the walls, firewood and water fetched, and ashes carried out.

From infancy the child drops to sleep to the telling of his clan myth and many other myths. So when he goes out with his sheep he knows a legend for every mountain and curious red sandstone formation, for every plant and animal. He knows the why of the bushy tail, the stripe, the chatter, the quick flirt of a wing. And he can sing.

> Lo, the light brown one!
> Truly in the distant glade
> Below, through the opening
> In the far, green trees
> Wanders the antelope.

Or watching a ground squirrel scolding, he may chant:

> Slender and striped
> Slender and striped
> Look at him standing up there!
> He stands up there
> So slender in his stripes,
> The squirrel in his little, white shirt!

These translations are from Margaret Erwin Schevill's *Beautiful on the Earth*, a sympathetic appreciation of Navajo mysticism in the light of Jung's psychology.

For the Navajo child, every act has its simple ritual. Each day he greets the sunrise. Seasonally he helps with planting and harvesting, lambing and shearing. All life is rhythmic; for every important event there is a prescribed observance, as for the baby's naming and in the puberty ceremony, when boys and girls sit hooded under blankets and shivering to hear the Yei's eerie hoot. Boys are then lightly struck with yucca, and girls are touched with corn cobs. Unblinded, the children see that the Yei are men in masks; achieving adulthood consists in learning that masked figures are only symbols of the supernaturals. There are marriage rites and cleansing ceremonies, the most important having to do with curing and the eradication of sickness.

Although Navajo myths do not emphasize fear, and hell is not taught, Navajos have an obsessive dread of the dead.

Even modern Navajos shrink from touching a corpse; men in military service devised cleansing rites for themselves. They have a related fear of ghosts, and few Navajos will walk alone at night when the dark unquiet dead may pull the living into their shadowy dwelling-place. Witches, who may be anybody, deal with such spirits and cause ills and evils. Dr. Kluckhohn's studies of individuals reveal that fear of being called a witch holds many a Navajo in the paths of rectitude. It also militates against our get-ahead ethic. A Diné who prospers may be doing so with unsanctified aid. Some students believe that work on the irrigated farms under the Fruitland Dam on the San Juan River lagged because men were afraid of being accused of witchcraft.

The individual Navajo protects himself against the spells of witches by observing taboos and by interpreting his dreams, if he can. If he cannot, he seeks a medicine man. Dreams are never meaningless. Some psychiatrists believe that unlettered shamans often use great wisdom in freeing their patients from conflicts reflected in dreams.

The Navajo's religion is individual. Like the Christian rather than the group-minded Pueblo, he is concerned with his personal relationship to the supernatural. But unlike Christian prayers, his chants are not supplications; they are invocations of universal power which even the supernaturals must obey. It is only necessary to do everything correctly; right thoughts, acts, and syllables bring good by inevitable law. Illness, a symptom of failure to do right, may be cured by a ceremony properly performed. Navajo sings—those marvelous combinations of prayer, chant, sand-painting, and dance—are held for the benefit of an individual.

The patient's family, which bears all the expenses, selects the medicine man and erects a large new hogan on a spot uncontaminated by human life, but near water and firewood. The chanter and his assistants come first, bringing their ceremonial bundles of sacred articles: long eagle-feathers, holy plants, pollen, and materials for the sand-paintings. The family meanwhile is building its camp and readying piles of fragrant piñon and juniper for the fires.

Word has spread by mysterious channels, and a great concourse gathers, often from many miles away. By wagon and horseback they come, women carrying babies on cradleboards, small children with bright quick eyes peering over a wagon's side. There are trucks, too, and cars of every type. Everybody is in his best velvet jacket to display his wealth in turquoise, silver, jet, and shell. Hundreds, even thousands, of Navajos come to help the cure by their good thoughts. But they gather also for gossip, trade, racing, and gambling. Often tribal business is transacted; old men stand to intone long speeches in their guttural phrases. A Navajo sing, like a Christian camp-meeting, is not religion undefiled.

Throughout the day people drift into the medicine hogan, where the chanter sits with his patient. The medicine man is usually past middle age; few young men have either memory or patience to learn the ritual; many chants have been lost for lack of neophytes. Others seem doomed to extinction. Oliver La Farge's sensitive novel, *Enemy Gods*, presents well the confusion of the young Navajo astray between faiths. For these reasons five-day sings are more common now than the nine-day ceremonies. The procedure is similar. The patient and all participants undergo bodily cleansing through light diet and daily emetics, and by continence; mental cleansing by right thoughts. Sometimes the patient is given a sweat bath or massage. Mostly the healing is through ritual touching of the body and by prayer and suggestion. The earlier parts of the ceremony free the patient from evil; then the powers are called upon to flood him with good.

On the last days, the medicine man directs the so-called sand-painting, which Dr. Kluckhohn prefers to call "dry painting" because many other materials are used with the sand. Sometimes a bowl of water is sunk in the painting's center. Charcoal mixed with white sand makes blue; ground rocks provide red and yellow; pollen and petals may be used, even twigs and cones. Beginning at the center of the area to be covered, the medicine man lets his color flow in a thin trickle through thumb and finger, making lines as accurately and as fast as an artist could make them with pencil or brush. As the painting grows, other painters join, to work under the quick eye of the medicine man, who corrects every error. No variation is permitted except in the decoration of the Yei's kirtle or bag.

The completed painting illustrates the myth. Begodchiddy is never pictured, and Changing Woman appears only in the most used Blessing Chant. Yei frequently appear as elongated full-faced figures; mountains, clouds, streams, and many animals are drawn symbolically, but recognizably too. Often the rainbow surrounds all as a protection. The finished work is exquisite in its soft clarity of color, its balanced composition. Other peoples in many parts of the world have made such dry paintings; none has ever equaled the Navajo for sheer beauty and high artistry.

Before sunset every painting must be destroyed; the hallowed sand is applied to the patient's body for healing. What then remains is carried reverently away.

To the average onlooker the night's dancing may be even more memorable than the day's quiet observances. As night comes, the rich red of sandstone cliffs has merged into purplish black, and the sharp sun and shadow of mesa and canyon have dulled into looming shapes and bottomless gulfs. Hard bright stars come out, or a frosty moon spreads silveriness over gray-green sage and green juniper. Then fires glow for supper and tall bonfires pierce the night. Always it is cold, for the great Navajo sings occur only in winter.

Unlike the Pueblo ceremonies, most Navajo dances are not accompanied by chorus or drummer. Dancers chant their own accompaniment in the harsh syllables and jerky rhythms so difficult for the white ear to catch. But by the time one has sat muffled in blankets through a long cold night, the falsetto wailing has created a spell in which the high-stepping masked figures making their angular gestures seem as natural as the wheeling planets in a starry sky. By the coming of the blue dawn in the white east the hypnosis is complete and no translation of the Blue Bird Song is needed to make the onlooker feel the beauty and the glory of the Navajo world.

Such a religion is a true contribution to universal culture. Wherever the Navajo got his legends and forms, his genuis has made of them a humanly wise and highly spiritual religion. One is impressed with the maturity of certain concepts. The hero must wander far and alone, facing dangers that test his integrity as well as his courage; he must even be brave enough to violate certain taboos. In one tale, when the hero's steadiness had dissolved the fearful whirlwind, its spirit says: "It was not so bad when you faced it. Was it?" The result of the typical hero's ordeal is a person fully in command of himself, spiritually mature. That all Navajos are not spiritually mature is no more remarkable than that all Christians are not Christlike. Many medicine men do seem to incarnate their ideals and to be philosophical, steadfast, and wise guides.

The first comprehending student of Navajo ceremonies was Dr. Washington Matthews, a U.S. Army surgeon who was also a musician and sensitive to beauty in any form. His *Mountain Chant* (1887) and his *Night Chant* (1902) were long the only source books for students of Navajo religion. There were not many students. Soldiers, missionaries, and Indian Service people, like the Spanish before them, had no preparation for understanding alien beliefs; they were never students, just critics. Only some traders accepted Navajo ways as valid. They learned enough Navajo to do business easily; some of them married Navajo women and adopted many traditions and customs. But few achieved real understanding of the culture they shared.

A few traders became legends in their own right. Lorenzo Hubbell, son of a Spanish New Mexican and a Connecticut Yankee, established the first trading-post at Ganado, Arizona, where life was baronial and patriarchal. His sons grew up speaking English, Spanish, and Navajo interchangeably and lived long fruitful lives among people never alien to them. Louisa Wade, born among the Utes in Colorado, spoke both Ute and Navajo as a child, and when she married John Wetherill and went to live at Kayenta, Arizona, she became trusted adviser to that part of the Navajo reservation. She collected vast lore; much of it was used by Frances Gilmor in *Traders to the Navajo*. The Day family of St. Michaels, like the Wetherills, lived close to their Navajo neighbors as friends and married partners. Such people accepted Navajo ways as children accept the familiar. Often they sang and danced and were healed, initiated, and included in tribal councils. Most of them neither made records of what they knew nor tried to evaluate it.

In 1912 there appeared *An Ethnologic Vocabulary of the Navajo Language*. Credited to the Franciscan Fathers of St. Michaels, this was the work of Father Berard Haile, a person so sympathetic that he could not serve people without studying them or teach them his faith without understanding theirs. So he learned to speak Navajo fluently and studied the ceremonies. He has published a translation of the *Star Chant* and a study of the war ceremony, *Enemy Way*.

The dance that ends this ceremony is known to many visitors as the Squaw Dance, a misnomer, as the Algonquin word "squaw" is never used by western Indians. It is properly called the Girl Dance. Each maiden chooses a man and dances him around until he buys her off. Originally the couple did not touch, but nowadays they link right arms and circle stolidly. The watching white is entertained to see how long they swing before the man pays. The watching Navajo knows that this ancient rite, borrowed from the Utes, is part of a war dance. But it is far from the frenzied rousing of the fighting spirit associated with Indian war dances. It is indeed never held before men go to war, but on their return; and it is a promise that the earth, blood-soaked from fighting, will again produce vegetation and that maidens will control the rain.

Naturally, Enemy Way was not held for recruits going off to World War II; for them a medicine man chanted the Blessing Way "that all might be beautiful before them." On their return, Enemy Way was necessary to purify the fighters of blood shed and death witnessed. Part of this cere-mony is "killing the ghost of the scalp." A real scalp is de-sirable. Old men used to cherish a dusty one buried some-where in a tin can; nowadays "the equivalent" will serve. It has been noted that even nowadays a Navajo murder gen-erally involves a crushed head that might have yielded enough skin and hair to serve as a scalp. In any case, the re-turned warrior, with face blackened to conceal him from the enemy, must shoot the scalp to kill it; thus its evil power becomes beneficent and is transferred to him. This ancient Navajo rite may be as sound a way as any to rid a battle-shocked veteran of the horrors he has seen. In modern life, Enemy Way is sometimes performed to cleanse a man of contact with such civilian enemies as policemen or prosti-tutes in town.

Every penetrating study of Navajo ritual attracted more students to the reservation, many of them for an initiatory talk with Father Berard in his austere study at St. Michaels. Among these was Clyde Kluckhohn, who, in his teens, went to visit relatives near Ramah, New Mexico, and was soon on a horse and away with the Navajos. That summer gave him command of their language and resulted in a book of youthful vim, *To the Foot of the Rainbow*. It has led to years of detailed and intimate study of Navajo life, and has brought many students to the reservation.

The Navajo reservation has thus become one of the most popular laboratories for the study of a fully developed culture. Out of numerous scholarly treatises some books of general interest have come. Gladys Reichard, who learned one summer the techniques of living in a hogan and weaving a blanket, wrote *Spider Woman*. As her knowledge widened and deepened, she produced *Compulsive Prayer*, the best short statement of the Navajo's sense of oneness with the universe and of his belief that good must come from right acts and thoughts. It paints a telling portrait of the dignified Navajo, standing erect and calling on universal law.

Then came Mary Cabot Wheelwright, a proper Bostonian, whose interest was aroused and her life work determined when she saw her first Yeibechai, the splendid nine-day ceremony in which the Yei appear in masked dance. Distressed because nobody could tell her in detail what underlay such refined and elaborate ritual, Miss Wheelwright began to study, to seek.

Soon she met Arthur and Frances Newcomb at Nava near Two Grey Hills, New Mexico. Arthur was a trader who spoke Navajo. Franc was that rare Indian Service teacher who did not pity herself as marooned on a desolate desert, but congratulated herself on the discovery of a new art. Enthralled with the sand-paintings, she saw as many as she could. As she was not permitted to draw inside the medicine hogan, Franc Newcomb began to memorize the paintings; in time she developed a visual memory of amazing accuracy. Watching the medicine man, following each line as the sand dribbled, she soon mastered the basic conventions of the art: the placing of the sacred plants—corn, beans, tobacco, and squash; that black is north, white east, blue south, and yellow west. Also how the colors sometimes varied. Many things. Finally when she saw a new painting, Franc Newcomb had only to memorize its distinctive features.

The chanter who was Mrs. Newcomb's teacher was Hasteen Klah, whom she was to introduce to Miss Wheelwright. He had chosen the Newcombs' home for his after his friend Dick Wetherill was killed at Pueblo Bonito and Mrs. Wetherill had moved her children to town. At Nava, Klah lived alone in a hogan, using his gifts as requested, and weaving. A wise man in mundane as well as in spiritual things, Klah knew that his knowledge was doomed to disappear; every year he saw fewer singers trained, more chants lost. So he began to weave his paintings into blankets with sand-colored backgrounds and other colors of soft vegetable dyes. Weaving was woman's work, but it was the only way he had to preserve his paintings. But when he saw Franc Newcomb's work, Klah knew that there was another way. He began to correct her drawings and to tell her the legends they illustrated. It was the beginning of a remarkable collection, part of which has been published. In 1937, working with Gladys Reichard, Mrs. Newcomb produced *The Navajo Shooting Chant;* later she published *The Mountain Chant* and *Navajo Omens and Taboos.*

It is difficult and expensive to get such work published or properly displayed. Miss Wheelwright, gratefully appreciative of what the trader's wife and the shaman were doing, undertook that task. She had a broad knowledge of comparative religions, especially oriental mysticisms, and she constantly added to that lore while she collected Navajo chants. Working with Hasteen Klah and an interpreter, Miss Wheelwright published several important chants with text and sand-paintings. She has, besides, twelve ceremonies

"more or less complete" with both myths and sand-paintings. It is pitifully few. Nobody knows how many there
may have been; as each ceremony requires possibly fifty
chants and at least four sand-paintings, and as only thirty-
five complete chants are now known, the loss has already
been great.

To house her collections and to provide a repository
where the work of others might be preserved and studied,
Miss Wheelwright endowed the Museum of Navajo Ceremonial Art. Built with Klah's approval and blessed by him,
this is a hogan-like structure among the piñons near Santa
Fe. Klah died in 1937, but Miss Wheelwright, until her
death in 1958, continued to work with the few remaining
chanters on the reservation; her peerless collections continue to grow. In 1950, the Bollingen Foundation of New
York presented the Museum with fifty-two sand-paintings
meticulously copied by Maude Oakes.

These are the records of a dying art, a vanishing faith.
Many important sings have already disappeared. Students
agree that few chanters know more than one complete ceremony; as each old medicine man dies, his knowledge dies
with him. This is a loss to universal culture. Our civilization has destroyed most, if not all, of the ancient mystical
world in which the Navajo lived, the ancient ethic he practiced. Only time will tell how well he is compensated for
this loss by industrial and scientific wonders and assorted
faiths.

❦ ⊂⊒ ❦

VII

THE MODERN NAVAJO

⊂⊒ THE NAVAJO tribe, the largest and now the richest in the United States, has grown in less than a century from 15,000 to over 90,000 people living on a reservation about the size of West Virginia. The largest part of the reservation is in Arizona, but there are small areas in Utah and Colorado, and a larger area in New Mexico, which counts about 30,000 people. Most of the Navajos live outside the reservation in an area west of Albuquerque, which has its own problems because it is policed by county sheriffs, States Highway patrolmen, and Navajo police, known as Law and Order men. A lawbreaker has only to slip from one jurisdiction to another to escape arrest; bootleggers have flourished and drunkenness remains a major problem in this area.

The Navajo diet still averages about 1,200 calories daily, as contrasted with our national minimum of 2,500. Infant deaths from diarrhea and enteritis are many times the national percentage, and epidemics of children's diseases are frequent and devastating. In 1950 infant mortality was 318 per 100,000; but by 1959 it had decreased to 236 per 100,000. The spreading of information about birth control, the humane way to limit children to the number that might survive, is impossible because of certain minority beliefs. The Navajo death rate is 74.7 per cent, as compared with a 26.3 per cent national death rate. That this is a national problem became apparent in 1942, when draft boards rejected 65 per cent of Navajo draftees as physically unfit.

Tuberculosis was the most frequent ailment; then followed venereal disease, undernourishment, and congenital diseases. So few Navajo recruits could write or even speak English that a special training center was established for them. There they learned with alacrity. Over two thousand Navajos served in all the services and many others worked in war plants. But these were a minority of the tribe, and few of them really mastered English.

The United States has dealt with the Navajo since 1846, when the Navajos, having refused to make peace with Mexico, welcomed the American occupation of New Mexico. So an expedition under Colonel Doniphan was dispatched to the Navajo country to "require of the Navajos security for their future conduct."

Colonel Doniphan's Missourians were appalled to see Isleta Indians dancing around a pole topped by "the scalps of three warriors, the long straight black hair sweeping the wind."

Going on over "craggy mountains of stupendous height . . . steep and rugged acclivities, precipices and yawning chasms," the lowlanders finally came upon Navajos. At first they made friends. But at Ojo del Oso (Bear Spring) Doniphan heard a young chief state the Navajo position. Sarcillo Largo said: "You have a strange cause of war against the Diné. We have waged war against the Mexicans for years. You have lately . . . conquered them. . . . Now you turn upon us for attempting what you have done yourselves."

But they signed a treaty, the first of many that were violated by the Indians. Navajos who signed treaties said that Navajos who broke them were not of their people. Maybe they were not; the tribe was, as it still is, loosely knit.

In 1848, President Taylor appointed James S. Calhoun Indian Agent in New Mexico. Calhoun sent another expedition against the Navajos under Lt. Colonel John M. Washington, whose unlikely name adorns a pass in the Chuska Mountains. Out of this foray came a New Mexico classic. *Journal of a Military Reconnaisance,* by James H. Simpson, contains some of the best descriptions ever written of the stupendous Navajo country, and his illustrator Kern's drawings are more accurate than any photograph. Both young men were much taken with the peaceful domestic life of the Navajos. In Canyon de Chelly's wide valley of golden sands with the mysterious White House set like a cameo in the pinkish canyon wall, they found women weaving under the piñon trees while men coaxed corn and peaches to grow. Canyon de Chelly was to be the last refuge of the Diné in their final despair.

Colonel Washington's treaties fared no better than earlier ones or those which followed. Navajo bands continued to raid peaceful settlements while the white man's rage mounted. The Army built forts. In the very heart of the Navajo country they erected Fort Defiance, whose remaining stone buildings are eloquent of its name.

Then came the Civil War, and Indians got out of hand. In 1862, Brigadier General James H. Carleton, new Commander of the Department of New Mexico, declared an end to treating with Navajos. They must be defeated. As colonel, the general named Christopher Carson, the redoubtable Kit, who could not write but whose dictated autobiography bristles with the phrase "Done it."

Carson's orders were to round up all Navajos, peaceably if possible, and move them to the Bosque Redondo (Round Wood) near Fort Sumner. The Navajos refused to budge. So on the deadline date, July 20, 1863, Colonel Carson moved against them with a regiment of New Mexico volunteers, men with generations of depredations to avenge. Fighting like Indians—hard-riding, light-eating, unresting— Carson's troop flushed Navajos out of canyons, pursued them across deserts in sandy heat and over mountains in snowy cold, killed three hundred of them in 1863, and finally, in February of 1864, trapped the last of them in lovely Canyon de Chelly. Then started what the Navajos called their "long walk," which brought them to Fort Sumner, where they were to be held in exile. Carson could report "Done it."

History knows no more tragic displaced persons than the Navajos at Bosque Redondo, where three thousand of them were penned in with a band of Apaches who were their bitter foes. General Carleton installed a few brush dams along the Pecos, dug a ditch six or seven miles long, issued seeds to his captives, and asked Archbishop Lamy to send over some padres to open a school. But the general failed to count upon human nature, Indian nature, and nature.

Worms ate acres of corn, drought caused three crop failures in succession, smallpox decimated the people. Meanwhile unprincipled storekeepers were selling liquor and firearms to Indians and supplying them with tainted and even maggoty beef. One agent was indicted for fraud.

The tribe made one break for freedom, but was rounded up by Apache Scouts, a new and trusted arm of the Army. By this time the Diné were defeated, sullen, embittered, and ready to agree to anything if only they might go back to their homeland, where the four sacred mountains stood guard and the supernaturals could hear them. In 1868 their chiefs signed a treaty agreeing to keep the peace. The United States agreed to restore the people to their ancient range and to supply each family with a few animals, tools, seeds, and cash for a couple of years. This was done, and the pattern of modern Navajo life emerged. The people became good sheep-folk, with children herding and women shearing, washing, carding, and weaving. Men remained the hunters and chanters. They had brought home from their dire exile the new art of silversmithing, and Navajo jewelry became an article of trade, first with Indians and later with white traders. None of this altered the old life much. The Diné continued to live in groups scattered over their vast domain, looking to medicine men for spiritual guidance and to headmen for practical advice.

The one possible way to bring such a people into the current of our country's life—by education—the government bungled badly. In 1868 the United States had promised schooling for every Navajo child between six and sixteen, with compulsory attendance and a teacher for every thirty pupils. This promise has never been kept. Even at the middle of the twentieth century, Congressional appropriations for Indian education would leave some nine thousand Navajo children without schooling. Apologists for the Indian Service state that Navajos fought against education. As indeed they did.

Those old-time Indian schools were even more terrifying to Navajos than to Pueblos. Naturally people hid their children from the government man who came to take them to some dreadful place. Those who were taken often did not return for years; by that time they had forgotten their language and certainly had missed training in the ways taught by the supernaturals. Life in those schools was grim; success seemed to be measured by clothing. Get an Indian into trousers and you were civilizing him. The best Indian was the one who did not "go back to the blanket." There was no idea of helping the Indian to live better at home or to reconcile his ancient ways with the needs of his status as a citizen.

To a tragic extent this thinking still prevails. Mission schools naturally set out first to destroy the ancient religion regardless of its importance as an integrating force in the personality. And many Indian Service people show little understanding of the new teaching methods, though they promised even more for Navajos than for Pueblos. On the reservation, day schools could minimize the barbarous disruption of family life caused by snatching six-year-olds away from home; and each might serve as a community center where adults could use such equipment as lathes, sewing-machines, and washtubs. Such a program's success would depend upon teachers capable of understanding it.

A few understanding teachers appeared; some continue to serve out of pure devotion. Salaries which in 1950 began at $2,498.28 per year have risen to $4,345 per year with annual increments of $165. For this honorarium a college degree is required, with courses in "education," but no special preparation for dealing with people of an alien culture.

A manual training instructor proudly exhibited flowerpots from the dime store that his pupils had turned upside down and hung with cords—as birdcages. "Do Navajos keep birds?" "Oh no, these go to Indian Service people." Primary arithmetic charts showed pictures of Scottie dogs, elephants, and oranges. Granting that future voters should be able to count elephants, sheep would seem a more suitable symbol for little herders who have learned to tally their flocks long before reaching school age. A primer is illustrated with pink-cheeked children running out of clapboard houses onto green lawns, or indoors at properly laid tables. The end story presents Mother's pink ruffled dressing-table with powderbox! Navajo children are brown. Their homes are hogans, and lawns are unknown. Tables are rare; the dressing-table seems the ultimate insult to the Navajo way of life.

Some teachers pitch out all such books and charts and make their own. Margot Astrov, an anthropologist, increased the attendance at a day school some children rode forty miles to attend. Her pupils learned words needed daily and made their own charts. Recognizing the traditional mobility of the Navajo, Mrs. Astrov took her classes out to gather edible and medicinal plants and to fetch shrubs and bright stones to beautify the school yard. Talking and writing about their finds and illustrating them with crayon and clay made the children eager to learn. When the class found good potter's clay, a boy brought in his grandmother, who had almost forgotten the potter's art, but was willing to teach. As an interpreter was needed, Mrs. Astrov proposed barter: for every Navajo word she learned she offered two English words, written as well as spoken.

Clyde Kluckhohn has suggested a study of the mental habits of white people associated with Navajos, an idea that merits serious consideration. Their training might well begin with *The Navaho Door,* by Alexander and Dorothea Leighton, whose basic idea seems too sensible to need stating. "In helping people adjust themselves one must be sure he is not attacking beliefs and practices vital to their welfare." As physicians primarily concerned with health, the Leightons enlisted the interest of medicine men. "You burn down a hogan in which a death has occurred? So do we use fire or boiling water to destroy the evil of disease."

If every Indian Service employee had understood such ideas, much dull covert opposition might have been avoided. Teachers resisted what they did not understand; traders backed them up; and missionaries decried any respect for the Navajo's ancient beliefs. Among them they incited some old Navajos to demand a return to the hickory-stick education that had beaten some English into them.

Despite its critics, the new education might have succeeded if it had not suffered collapse along with the rest of Collier's well-conceived program. The cornerstone of that program was stock-reduction, and here speed was most essential. An illiterate generation may be succeeded by literate children. People as recuperative as the Navajos might improve their health in a decade of sanitation and decent care. But land once rendered desert does not come back.

While the tribe increased, its land steadily deteriorated.

Photographs taken in the 1870's show knee-high grass, clear pools, and permanent streams where now there is only desolation. Then eight thousand Navajos ran thirty-four thousand sheep. Through the years the government expanded the reservation and issued more sheep; Indian agents as well as Indians believed that the more stock a man had the richer he was. But flocks were not improved. "Navajo sheep" were long-legged scrubs. By 1933, one and a half million superannuated ewes, rams long past their vigor, and puny lambs were vying for the scant grass with thousands of bony horses and a few scrawny cows. Their hoofs had so loosened the topsoil that every storm was flushing tons of silt down the Colorado River; when it threatened to choke Hoover Dam Californians began to take notice. A stock-reduction program won Congressional approval, and the Soil Conservation Service took charge. They decided what animals must be sacrificed, beginning with nonproductive stock. And they decreed how many animals a family might graze, and where.

This new policy, a complete reversal of former ideas, was accepted by the Navajos in council. But many a man changed his mind when he reported to his wife: Navajo women own the sheep. Overlooking them was a major error. Another was failing to propitiate the traders, who damned stock-reduction almost to a man. Some feared a lessening of profits in wool. All knew of families left without enough sheep to live on, or whose only saddlehorse or wagon team was taken. Navajos asked them: "What shall we leave our children?"

The administration's program, which included the building of roads, dams, and schoolhouses, would have employed many men at good wages and compensated them for the loss of their sheep. But the outbreak of war put an end to that, and the Navajo's failure to understand the whole situation left a residue of bad feeling and distrust of government.

When Navajos and their mentors are observed in meeting, the wonder grows that anything is ever understood. Government directives phrased in Washington's legalistic language are presented to the Navajo council in bureaucratese. "In setting up this machinery we plan to tie it in with your experience. . . . We must iron out some problematical points . . . before testing the reactions of your people." How incomprehensible is such talk—quoted from the transcript of an actual meeting—is proved by the hours of elucidation that follow it. "I meant to say. . . . Let me clarify." But "in the event that," is still not "if"; and "testing the reactions of" has not become "ask." The Leightons have drawn up some suggested speeches-to-Navajos which might well serve as models for administrators.

The Navajo Council, where such deliberations occur, was set up in 1923 as an elective, representative body. It has worked fairly well; experienced students of the Navajos, including Father Berard Haile, believe it would work better if it recognized the Navajo's natural leaders. Headmen are still powerful. Many of them belong to the forty or fifty thousand "long hairs" who speak no English and may live one hundred miles from a highway. But council action often waits on their judgment.

Headmen from distant places ride days to attend such a gathering as the annual fair at Shiprock. On one such occasion, where hamburgers tainted the air and cars and trucks lighted the circle where the Yeibechai would dance, thousands of Navajos had gathered to hear their problems discussed in their own tongue. Man after man spoke, long speeches in the harsh gutturals, with dramatic pauses; few gestures. None of the audience wearied; even young people in modern dress attended closely, grunting approval or laughing at a humorous sally. How shrewd are the judgments of such leaders appears when Washington's best ideas come back tattered by the Navajo's criticism.

To reach these leaders who had no English, a linguist on the Superintendent's staff, aided by bilingual Navajos, issued a Navajo-language paper. It was discontinued in 1958 because it was no longer needed. Schoolchildren learned to read it aloud, older people were eager listeners; the little sheets were worn out by handling. It was a good bridge to the many Diné still living in lonely hogans, miles beyond communication.

Stop where a motor can go no farther. Sky-piercing peaks inclose a silent land, sage- or piñon-scented, scarred into deep red gashes by seasonal storms. Not a house. No road, but just a wagon track discernible only to the accustomed eyes. Then a moving mass colored like the plain. A band of sheep followed by a little girl shy as a squirrel and with shining, inquisitive black eyes. Or a distant puff of dust approaches slowly to reveal a creaking wagon. A man sitting leanly erect. A woman in a fringed shawl bunched beside him. The box swarming with children and the aged. The family is going to the trading-post.

For many Diné the trading-post remains almost the only contact with the outside world. Traders believe that they are the Navajo's best and only realistic friends. Good men or bad, sensible or erratic, stayers for generations or flitters-by who make a trading-post the scene of a picturesque interlude, they have always been useful. Shirtsleeved and suspendered, with sweater frayed at the elbows, the trader stands all day behind his counter. Day begins at dawn and ends when he pushes the last Navajo out at dark. He may have a helper or two, often his wife or son. There is little light, and the air is pungent with the odor of unwashed Navajo, laced with the scents of piñon and tobacco smoke, an unforgettable smell. A fat stove stands in a sand-box that serves as spittoon. No chairs; sometimes a bench. Mostly the customers stand, saying nothing, moving little. Trading is done by gestures. A woman will point with her chin at what she wants. Coffee, sugar, and lard. Canned goods, especially tomatoes and green chile. Beans. Plush for blouses, and for skirts the transparent velvet in luscious fruit-colors which has replaced the old-fashioned calico. Levis. Sturdy high shoes for the sheep-herder; otherwise oxfords. Candy for the child who has stood patiently with begging eyes but no coaxing. When all is in a pile the woman points to the pelts she has dumped on the floor or unwraps her latest blanket from a flour sack.

Then the dickering begins. It ends when the Navajo says: "Put it on the paper." This means more credit from the trader, who takes in pawn silver belts, bracelets, and rings or strings of turquoise and shell. That pawned jewelry, hung in picturesque masses above the groceries, is not a tourist lure; it is sound security.

Progressive Indian Service people advocate "giving the Indian responsibility, letting him make his own mistakes, but helping him to adjust to the modern world." The trader, if he condescends so far, reminds us that this is precisely what traders do. For seventy years they have done business with the Navajo, giving him credit. They issue silver and turquoise to the smiths and guarantee to take the women's blankets. And long before Indian associations were formed, the trader was demanding the Navajo's best work and marketing it.

Lorenzo Hubbell at Ganado urged Navajo women to copy the best old designs and accepted only their finest work. C. N. Cotton, a wholesaler in Gallup, first put Navajo blankets on the eastern market and suggested their use as rugs. At that time, about 1890, there were nine licensed traders to the Navajos; their numbers increased as eastern markets were developed. Mike Kirk at Manuelito and Bertram Staples at Coolidge made heavy old Navajo silver a jewelry fad, and Staples developed flat table-silver in true Navajo feeling. Rugs became known by the names of traders who insisted upon old designs and vegetable dyes. J. B. Moore's rugs from Crystal and Two Grey Hills; Cozy McSparron's Chin Lee rug with its soft yellow stripes; and a similar one developed by the Lippincotts at Wide Ruins. By 1940 there was a Navajo Traders Association of dealers who exacted good work and who were paying some $1,865,000 annually for Navajo products.

Traders tend to regard government doings as unrealistic, at worst even vicious, at best a damned nuisance. Paper promises pile up, but the trader still prescribes patent medicines off the shelf, aids the woman in labor or the child strangling with diphtheria, and makes bone-breaking drives to doctor or hospital. Education is promised, but the trader must still speak Navajo all day. Irrigation is discussed, but young men still have no lands to till. Worst of all, the returned veteran faced a future of disillusionment and frustration.

He had stormed ashore at Anzio, marched across Germany, sailed the Pacific as a pharmacist's mate, or been one of the Navajo Marines who outwitted Japanese intelligence by inventing a Navajo vocabulary to convey military information over walkie-talkies. The war over, he, like all soldiers, wanted to go home. Stepping off the train at Winslow or Gallup, he was welcomed by a patriotic committee. But his chances of achieving the American way of life he had been fighting for were meager indeed.

Back on the reservation, he found that the stock-reduction program had proved itself; even the most recalcitrant traders had stopped their grousing. Grass was beginning to come back along the draws; in fenced demonstration-areas it now stood as tall as it did in the eighties. And fewer sheep were producing more wool and meat. Fleeces now average six and seven pounds instead of four and a half; lambs weigh in at sixty-five instead of forty pounds. Navajo stockmen—and women—take pride in breeding up their herds; the canniest of them are buying up nonreservation lands and competing with their white neighbors. Navajo women in bright plush blouses appear at wool-growers' conventions, fingering the prize fleeces and nodding their chignons over a speaker's points.

But for the returned veteran there are no sheep; there is no way that he can get any. Under the stock-reduction program only stockowners were awarded grazing permits; no provision was made for young people growing up. This has tended to establish a moneyed aristocracy and to leave a majority of the tribe in poverty. A man who is a silversmith may make a living, but only some three hundred families work at the ancient crafts of smithing and weaving. Markets fall off as factory goods supplant handwork and ruin the taste for it.

Farming, then? But land under the Fruitland Dam on the San Juan River had been allotted while the soldier was away. At best, five acres will not support a family, and the veteran was not a good farmer. On-the-farm and on-the-job training lagged, and the Navajo veteran, like the Pueblo, found loans hard to get. The tribe's revolving credit fund has done better: in 1949 such loans set up thirty families in trading-posts, coal mines, log-hauling, trucking. Qualified veterans found jobs with the missions, the traders, and at the superintendency at Window Rock. Several supervisors and a score of range riders are Navajos. But few GI's had the necessary qualifications for such work. Like the rest of the tribe, they had to seek manual labor.

The individual Navajo remained poor and ill equipped to better himself until oil and uranium came along to change his life and orientation. The Navajo reservation, assigned to the Indians as hopelessly arid land, began to spout oil about a generation ago, and in 1953 the discovery of uranium by the Navajo Paddy Martinez on Santa Fe Railway land was followed by the discovery of vast amounts of uranium on the reservation. In 1948 the average family income was $400.00 a year; but by 1958 it had increased to $2,335.00. The tribe received in 1958 approximately $16,000,000 from leases for uranium, oil, and gas and also from forests.

Some advanced ideas have been put into effect at Window Rock, a great red-sandstone-windowed butte which is the Navajo capital. There the Navajo Tribal Council meets, and the Chairman of the Council, presently Raymond Nakai, has his office. The Remington Rand Company was hired to set up the tribal offices with all the necessary equipment, and there trained Navajo stenographers, filing clerks, and bookkeepers handle banks of filing cases and card catalogues. A record is kept of every Navajo who has applied for any service in health, education, welfare, employment, recreation, or management in marketing his herds, flocks, or handicrafts. An annual fair is held at Window Rock which brings together not only thousands of Navajos but almost as many whites and Indians of other tribes. They come to do business with this tribe which now owns and operates lumber mills and a coal mine. The tribe is encouraging industry to settle on the edge of Navajo country.

Before the great uranium development, programs of industrial development were begun with money borrowed from the federal government, but now the tribe is affluent enough to finance its own industries, which include several trading posts, tribal motels, and several housing developments that have survived a period of experimentation. Generally more successful have been the efforts to cooperate with industry in towns that can hire Navajo labor and the programs to train and place Navajo workers.

Such people naturally have a broad and well-financed educational plan with the ultimate goal of producing Navajos fully adapted to modern life, including their own professionals to lead and direct the tribal business. The tribal budget for fiscal 1958 called for the expenditure of twelve million dollars, of which five million was for education. The purpose is to keep every Navajo child in school, well fed, well clothed, and fully supplied with all he needs in order to absorb all the education he can. For those who can progress beyond grade school the tribe offers a series of high school, college, and professional scholarships. Navajo children average well in school; their only handicap —lack of English—is being overcome by the special language training being offered in the public schools.

Health, so closely tied in with education, is being rapidly improved on the reservation, where modern medicine is reducing the incidence of tuberculosis and trachoma.

An important factor in the improvement of health conditions is a Navajo woman, Anna Wauneka, a Council member who heads the Health Committee and serves on the U.S. Public Health Advisory Committee. She goes on the radio to spread useful information in both Navajo and English. Many Navajos have radios—if not in the hogan, then in the pickup truck—and those who do not can easily get to listen to one in the nearest trading post or clinic. People who once distrusted white doctors and were terrified of hospitals as places where people died, are now quite willing to go to a clinic for examination or treatment and to a hospital to have their babies delivered or even for surgery.

The Navajo's readiness to go along with whatever seems good became evident when Salk anti-polio vaccine was suddenly available in sufficient quantities to protect most of the population. Doctors all over the United States found it difficult to get people to bring their children in for inoculation. But on the Navajo reservation it was different. Anna Wauneka, as chairman of the Health Committee, got on the radio and in both English and Navajo explained that here was real protection against a hideous and crippling disease. She urged the people to take their children at once to the nearest center, at a trading post or a clinic. The Navajos, even those who did not understand English, responded promptly and in such numbers that the doctors ran out of vaccine. They consider the outlook for continuing immunization very good indeed.

Part of this happy result is due also to the government's policy of inviting medicine men to participate in the health program. Most medicine men now refer patients to hospitals and clinics.

The reservation's resources, including the human, could stand a lot of developing. Though only some twenty thousand acres of land are deemed irrigable, better farming could make them more productive. A fine stand of ponderosa pine, handled by the Forest Service, is an inexhaustible resource. But the tribal sawmill, employing 350 Navajos, is managed by white men; Navajos do not qualify for technical or managerial jobs. This is true also of a flour mill at Round Rock. Small coal-mines employ about two hundred men, owners and their families. Other minerals include oil, gas, and such more precious substances as uranium. The tribe get about $445,500 in royalties and leases, but the vast potential wealth from such sources remains untapped.

The Indian Service hopes to inaugurate a processing economy. Navajos did well in war factories. Why should they not manufacture their own raw materials: wood, leather, wool, and metals? Here one runs into outside hostility. Capitalists hesitate to invest where government supervision may be implied, especially where government policies change as rapidly as they do in the Indian Service. But chambers of commerce in towns like Gallup, Winslow, and Farmington are beginning to take an interest.

To develop that prime resource, the people, the government has established agricultural and vocational schools, and likely youngsters who have missed schooling are being taught English in special classes. Their progress is phenomenal. The Navajos' opposition to education is no more—now they demand it. But until a generation has been trained, most Diné must move away from their reservation and the sacred mountains that guard it.

The Indian Service's vigorous employment service has placed as many as 15,000 men in one summer. They find all-year work on railroads and sawmills, seasonal jobs in the sugar-beet fields of Colorado, the orange groves of California, the carrot farms of New Mexico. Such workers are hired in groups of twenty men including one who speaks English. The Indian Service insists upon the minimum decency of houses with roofs that do not leak, water spigots not too far away, and sanitary privies.

Such measures, and the fact that a man can have his family with him, are lessening the employer's plaint that Navajos are undependable. The sawmill manager complained: "Come word of a Squaw Dance or let a man get worrying about his wife and off he goes. Navajos have no sense of responsibility." This carping manager has a home at the mill where his family lives with him; Navajo workers have not.

The rare English-speaking Navajo who tries to make his way outside often meets conditions too hard to take. Men who met no discrimination in service find lack of protection and even vicious mistreatment in town. At best, they encounter indifference. It must appear that the only white men concerned with Navajos are the operators of speakeasies and brothels. Police in the towns that ring the reservation readily pick up any Navajo as a vagrant or a drunk; many have been denied legal advice or medical care; a few have been beaten; at least one died unattended in jail. Town police and county sheriffs complain that they have too few officers to handle the Navajo problem; the reservation police number only a dozen. All around the reservation lies a no man's land of lawlessness comparable with the West at its wildest.

Drunkenness is rife among young Navajos, a symptom

of personal dislocations and social evils. The few Diné who could return to the faith of their fathers have done best. Many families held an Enemy Way for the returned soldier, to cleanse him of the touch of death. One who had been bombarded in an abandoned tomb on a Pacific Island talked it out with the medicine man and was at ease. But those who could not accept the old ways have suffered grievously. One, a WAVE, tried to escape by expressing scorn for the old ways, and then through drink; finally her fine mind gave way.

To relieve the reservation's overpopulation, Navajos must be induced to migrate. In 1943 a resettlement project was undertaken to establish more than one thousand Navajos, Hopis, and Mojaves under the Parker Dam on the Colorado River in Arizona. Starting with forty acres and a government loan, many of these new farmers paid out within three or four years and were living nicely in screened homes with water piped in and electricity. Veterans are quick to unite in buying machinery, in making cement, and in farming cooperatively.

Yet this project, well conceived and administered, has encountered the same difficulties as the Bosque Redondo scheme in 1863. Mojaves resent seeing Navajos and Hopis on lands that were theirs. Hopis traditionally distrust Navajos. Navajos react normally, with both dislike and distrust. And missionaries of various faiths add religious tensions to those already existing among the tribes.

Many veterans, more articulate or freer than their elders, express bitter resentment against the missionaries. The reservation is a mission field where eleven churches maintain 134 missionaries, 69 missionary teachers, and 1 unaffiliated missionary. At St. Michaels the Catholics support a school in which children are taught, indoctrinated with the faith, directed in scrubbing and window-washing by exacting nuns, and proudly turned out quite unable to readjust to family or home. A Methodist school at Farmington is similarly successful and boastful. Indian Service people remind us that mission schools choose their pupils, skipping the backward children and the obstructionist parents. It seems true that these schools will be more successful in training Navajos to leave the reservation than in teaching them to cope with life at home.

What Navajos make of this varied religious experience is indicated by the rapid growth of the peyote cult. Navajos first adopted it from Taos, but it has also entered the reservation from other tribes, especially the Colorado Utes. Unlike some earlier students of peyote-taking, students of the Navajos find no evidence that it is habit-forming or that it breaks down the moral fiber or leads to sexual orgies. They find a peyote ceremony marked by reverence, and unadorned to bareness. In an ordinary hogan men and women sit solemnly around an earth mound that bears crescent marks, but not the colors of a sand-painting. A fire burns, and drums accompany songs that go on all night or are stilled for reports of experiences. Peyote buttons may be eaten or taken in smoke; two, three, or four, are the usual dose. The effect varies. Sometimes the drug blocks the motor nerves, and the eater or smoker cannot walk. Others see greatly enhanced visions in color. The sorriest result seems to be nausea. The meeting ends at daybreak with a ceremonial taking of food. Later there is a large meal including the four "goods": meat, water, corn, and fruit.

No ill effects follow a peyote session. In contrast to a cocktail party or some camp-meetings, its evil sequelæ are nil. Among peyote's good effects is an aversion to alcohol. Abstention from liquor is required of peyotists; this odd cult seems to be the best, if not the only hope of curing the tribe of increasing alcoholism.

Students watch hopefully for evidence that the Navajos will deepen and enrich this faith as they did the Pueblo myths so long ago. But so far peyote rites are kept unified by supervisors who travel from tribe to tribe. Songs are sung in many languages—Ute, Kiowa, Comanche. Navajos have begun to make songs. Observances are based on the Mexican myth of a sufferer who journeys, seeks, and finally finds surcease in peyote. But, like all new religions, peyotism has been deeply marked by what it supplants. The influence of Christianity is especially strong. Jesus is invoked in many songs; one begins "J, E, S, U, S." Catholic derivation is clear in a song that calls on "God, Jesus, Mary, and the Heavenly Angels." But among Navajo peyotists the mark of Christianity is deepest in their attitude toward prayer. The ancient Navajo compulsive prayer has been supplanted by the Christian prayer of humble supplication.

Christian exclusiveness has not yet prevailed over the ancient Indian tolerance. Both peyotists and adherents of the old religion hope to keep them separate. But conversions to the peyote cult are on the increase. Even a few chanters have been converted, producing confusion rather than modification. One chanter carries a peyote button in his medicine bag; a peyote priest also puts on sings as a medicine man. So far only one trivial innovation has appeared on the reservation. Near Shiprock peyotists practice the *V-Way* that they invented to protect their soldiers going to war in 1942. The usual peyote rite is called the *Moon-Way*. The *V-Way* includes speech as well as song, and speech that suggests the soul-cleansing of the prayer-meeting sinner who confesses all.

The hold of peyotism on the Navajo is probably best explained by one of them. "The old Navajo religion," he said, "gave us curing and religion. Christianity gave us religion and salvation, but no curing. The white doctor gives us curing, but no religion and no salvation. Only peyotism gives us everything."

VIII

THE WARLIKE APACHE

APACHES have long been thought of as the most ferocious of savages, viciously cruel and unconquerable because they were treacherous and untrustworthy: they broke treaties. It is worth remembering that this reputation comes from their enemies, Spanish and American officers whom they outsmarted or settlers who suffered hideously at their hands. Later writers parrot the phrases. A modern Christian gentleman writes: "to the red man's untutored sense the distinction between *meum* and *tuum* is nowhere important," and "Kindness was for them not even weakness. To their benighted intelligence it was an unexperienced emotion hardly to be comprehended." But soldiers who fought him respected the Apache as a fighting man and for the skill of his leaders. When paratroopers sought a war cry expressive of invincible defiance they chose *Geronimo!* That they hit upon the least admirable of Apache chiefs is only another proof of the white man's lack of perspicuity about Apaches.

Fortunately for the final record, some white men got on well with Apaches. They did this by treating them like human beings, not like untamable savages, and by distinguishing between good and bad Apaches. Such men might have accomplished without warfare our national purpose of despoiling the Indian of his lands. But their advice was consistently disregarded by an Army bent on war and by a distant government guided by the counsel of officers in the field. This resulted in thirty years of warfare and unnumbered horrors perpetrated by both sides. Not all the atrocities were Apaches'.

The Apache has been little studied, probably because the culture of the related Navajo developed so much more richly. Both spoke an Athapascan tongue, but the Apache culture shows more traits of the Plains Indians and fewer of the Pueblos. They packed their goods on travois, hauled by dogs or women; lived in pointed tepees or flattened them down into the thatched wickiups still used in Arizona. The best account of Apache mores is in the studies of Edward Morris Opler, especially *The Apache Life Way*. Here we get the impartial view of the anthropologist, whose concern is to know rather than to decry or to change other people's ways.

When white men first knew them, the Apaches were emerging from the seed-gathering era, though men hunted and women scratched the ground and raised what corn they could between moves. The most useful wild plant was the maguey, whose fibers served as strong thread, its thorns as needles, its broad leaves as waterproof thatch, and its crown as a succulent roasted dish. The women cooked, fermented corn into the potent tiswin, wove baskets, and tanned buckskin and the tougher buffalo-hides into silky suppleness. They made the men's long-sleeved buckskin shirts and knee-high boots, and their own modest garments. These straight slips of buckskin, elaborately adorned with beaded yokes, may still be seen at the girls' puberty rites. Girls were trained in all these crafts, as well as in racing. An Apache woman might have to make a long run with her baby hung on its cradleboard from her brow. And she had to be brave and enduring. Britton Davis, in *The Truth About Geronimo*, tells of a young mother whose leg had been shattered by a shot. The surgeon, busy with soldiers, left her for hours and finally amputated the leg without anæsthetic or even a drink of whisky. The Apache girl uttered no cry.

Girls worked and played apart from boys, but premarital unions were not unusual. Two caught in the sex act were made to marry. Rape was considered bad, but might be settled by the gift of a couple of horses. Incest was unforgivable because it partook of sorcery. An unfaithful wife might be punished by having her nose cut off. An Apache chief was highly indignant when asked by a U.S. Army officer to forego this husbandly prerogative.

Chastity was esteemed, largely because a virgin might have mystical experiences valuable to the tribe. A modern Jicarilla girl was told by a prairie dog that the drought was caused by poisoning its kind. Another Jicarilla girl, walking among flowers, heard a voice warning her that evil impended because medicine men were neglecting the use of flower pollen. Both girls warned the old men, who mended their ways. People were expected to have such experiences; men or women who developed unusual powers became shamans.

Power might be used for either good or evil. Witchcraft is still widely accepted among Apaches, and the uneasy dead, wandering as dark ghosts, are feared. Shamans were called upon to make cures by removing spells and exorcising spirits. Moral training came from the family. Opler quotes some precepts. "Do not use a bad word you wouldn't like used to you. Do not feel that you are anyone's enemy. Do not take anything from another child, just because you are bigger. [If the United States had heard this one, the Apache Wars might have been avoided.] Don't steal from your friends. [Stealing from enemies was approved. Ask any hero of World War II.] Don't fight a girl; girls are weaker. Don't laugh at feeble old men and women." Before such axioms the notion of the benighted savage is hard to maintain.

Boys were trained as hunters and fighters. They were tossed into cold water to toughen them, made to run to a mountain top to improve their wind, punished by smothering if they cried, taught to fight other boys. The child was loved and knew it; so he accepted training, however severe, as necessary to make the tough, resilient, self-reliant man he wished to be. His arms were good; the Apache bow was the strongest ever made, his flint-tipped arrows could pierce a man to the heart; his sling, lance, and clubs were balanced and true. When he acquired the white man's gun the Apache became a fair shot. Mounted, he became one with the horse, which he trained to follow his voice and to respond to the lightest pressure of his bare thigh against its flank.

In their mountains these trained fighters were all but invincible. Where the Apache had cover and could reach water or carry it in an animal's entrails, he could live for days without food. When he had food he gorged; provision for the future was impossible. Critics of the modern Apache's improvidence might think of this.

Family groups, related through the mother, united at need into bands, but there was no tribal solidarity. White men came to call Apaches by the names of territories they ranged—Chiricahua, Mimbreño, White Mountain; by the names of their leaders—Cochise, Geronimo, Mangas Coloradas; or by some peculiarity. Mescaleros were addicted to mescal; Jicarillas wove *jicaras*, watertight little baskets.

These were the people the Spanish explorers met. Coronado found them friendly in 1540 when he crossed those widely magnificent borderlands between present-day Mexico and the United States. And he spoke well of buffalo-hunting people on the plains, who may have been Apaches. This word the Spanish adopted from the Zunis; it meant *enemy*.

Like the Navajos, the Apaches came to the fairs at Taos

and Pecos, where they exchanged their buffalo jerky, tanned skins, and captured slaves for white man's goods, especially metal. Here also they rested between raids and got a big feed and perhaps tips for the next raid. Often they detoured on the way home to strip some helpless *paisano's* harvest or to carry off his children as slaves.

Opler suggests that Apaches were not primarily warriors, but fought when they thought they had to. Men were expected to volunteer as proof of manliness; Opler quotes one who refused to go because he had nothing against the enemy. He was scorned as a pacifist is in our society. War fever was worked up in a big circle dance, and each man was provided with amulet and powder. During his absence his wife had to be true to him and to keep the woodpile tidy: if sticks got scattered her man might be lost. On the return, the warrior who had killed must pause outside the camp for purification. Booty was distributed among the poor.

The Spanish never succeeded in "reducing" the Apaches by either warfare or conversion. After the Mexican Republic had been established, Apache warfare became too hideous to contemplate; both sides committed horrors. Mexican governors tricked Apache bands into towns and slaughtered them; scalps were all but legal tender. When the U.S. Army marched in, in 1846, Apaches welcomed the Americans as allies against the common enemy, the Mexicans. They may have thought too that the bluecoats could control United States citizens. Apaches had known two kinds of men from the States. In 1826 Sylvester Pattie, leasing the Santa Rita mines, recognized Apaches as interested and held a council with them. All smoked, spat into a hole, filled it with earth and danced on the spot in token of burying all hatred. This treaty was scrupulously observed by both parties.

The other kind of United States citizen was James Johnson, a trader and friend of Juan José, an honorable and influential Apache chief. In 1835, when a captured Mexican spy told Juan José that the governor of Sonora had agreed to give Johnson one hundred pesos for every warrior of his band, the Apache did not believe it: his friend would not betray him. So Johnson found his work easy. He came as a friend into the camp where Juan José's three wives, many children, and others were going about their peaceful pursuits. As he dickered with Juan José for a mule, Johnson touched a lighted cigar to a powder keg and blew the whole place into a shambles, the while he shot his friend in the back. Johnson got away on a fast horse.

In no time two hundred Apaches were on the warpath, led by Mangas Coloradas, Red Sleeves, recognized chief of the eastern Chiricahuas, as Cochise was of the western. Mangas's first act was to fall on an innocent party of fur trappers and massacre them all. It was the first of half a century of "Apache atrocities." United States citizens were not told, of course, what had brought it about.

Mangas Coloradas had a huge head that held a good brain. He had attended Father Font's mission school at Santa Rita, and he knew that the United States could outnumber if not outfight Apaches. So when the Army came along he was ready to make treaties and to keep them, taking revenge only for evil committed. The Apache could distinguish between good and bad men, even under an alien skin.

In 1851 John Russel Bartlett surveyed the boundary between Mexico and the United States. Like the clumsiest tenderfeet, his men went advertising their whereabouts by large clouds of dust by day and huge campfires at night. Yet Bartlett, believing his party alone in unpeopled wilderness, was startled when an enormous, red-sleeved Apache silently appeared in his camp. Mangas Coloradas had come to warn him against "bad Apaches." Bartlett described this episode in his *Personal Narrative* and told how Mangas continued to protect the party's horses from marauders.

The two gentlemen, Apache and white, misunderstood each other only in relation to two captured Mexican boys whom Bartlett wished to restore to their families. Their Apache owner protested that he had made good Apaches of them, loved them as his own. Besides they were property worth money. Perhaps this point appealed to Bartlett, whose entourage included several Negro slaves. The affair was settled by cash.

U.S. Army officers, like the Spanish, ran into touble when they tried to protect their new citizens. The Apache saw no reason for ending his centuries-old warfare with Mexicans; nor did he grant Mexico's right to cede to the United States lands that had always been his. In formal parleys between bluecoated West Pointers and their bargaining peers in G-strings, the Apache always reserved the right to do as he pleased about Mexicans. Nor did he recognize any international boundary; his domain still included northern Mexico as well as much that was now United States territory. The stage was set for the Apache wars.

Kit Carson, who had been Indian Agent at Ute Park and at Abiquiu, had an Indian policy of his own. He wrote: "This country will always remain in its impoverished state as long as them [sic] mountain Indians are allowed to run at large; and the only remedy is to compel them to live in settlements, cultivate the soil, and learn to gain their maintenance independent of the general government." He disapproved of rations because the usual issue of a blanket, a knife or hatchet, some vermilion, and a length of cloth was less than the Indian could earn in one day's hunt and because bringing Indians into the towns was bad.

When it came to fighting Indians, Carson put his trust in experienced New Mexicans and in their leader, Colonel Ceran St. Vrain. "If," he wrote, "the volunteers had been under the . . . sole direction of Colonel St. Vrain there would have been no need for troops in this country."

An example of what he meant was "the White massacre" near Wagon Mound. Called from his home on the Rayado, Carson swiftly led a detachment of soldiers to the still-smoking camp where the men of Mr. White's party had been killed. Mrs. White and their six-year-old daughter had been carried off. Carson set off in hot pursuit, but the commanding officer, who outranked him, ordered him back. The next day, following the trail, Carson kept coming on bits of Mrs. White's clothing; perhaps she was trying to guide her rescuers. But they were too late. Her body, when they found it, was in such condition that Carson thought her better dead. The Indians were gone, and so was the child.

Years later there lived among the Jicarillas a woman named Inez in whose dark face bright blue eyes burned. She was all Apache, refused to speak English, told of no childish memories. Her son was called *Huero* (Blond); such a name might have been given the son of a blonde mother.

Between 1862 and 1871, the United States spent thirty-eight million dollars in its Apache wars, but it exterminated less than one hundred Apaches, including women, children, and men too old to fight. That made Apaches come pretty high.

Much of this fighting was in New Mexico, especially in its southwestern Grant County, whose widely scattered ranches and mines were easy targets for Apaches who knew every peak and crevice, every hidden vale, every box canyon. They struck like lightning, faded away like smoke, each man for himself, to gather again in a prearranged spot. Settlers grew alert to the owl's hoot, often the Apache's signal for attack, and to the thin line of smoke on a mountain top. The Army improved on this method with one using mirrors, flashing the sun's rays in readable dots and dashes.

The United States was learning that the Apaches were

not one people with a responsible leader. The lot you caught was never the one that had committed the outrage. It became routine to avenge every attack on a lonely ranch house or unprotected wagon train on the next Apache sighted. Silver City citizens offered $250 for every Apache scalp. Neither the Army nor civil authorities tried to find and punish the guilty individual Apache; nor did they proceed against white men who committed crimes against Apaches. Men were getting rich by selling arms, ammunition, and whisky to Indians, to say nothing of scalp bounties. The Army was good business too. Some men wanted no end to the wars. This was the wild west at its worst, when bad men dominated and decency had not arrived.

Fortunately for our national self-respect, there were always a few men, both military and civilian, who dealt honorably with Apaches, and whose neglected records prove that honorable dealing brought results. Notable among these forgotten men was John P. Clum, whose name does not appear in military accounts, perhaps because his methods might have made the military quite unnecessary.

Clum was twenty-two in 1871 when he was appointed Civilian Agent of the San Carlos Indian Reservation in Arizona. His qualifications were that he was already in Santa Fe, operating the first meteorological station in the Southwest, and that he was a member of the Dutch Reformed Church. The government had inaugurated its policy of making Indians the charge of churches.

Of the last two agents one had been killed and the other had escaped just in time. But Clum decided to accept the appointment. He spent some time in Washington, where he may have learned how not to handle Apaches. In any case, he reversed all previous policies, declined military protection, and established himself at San Carlos with one physician and one clerk as his sole support. By 1874, forty-five hundred Apaches had moved onto the reservation, which

was just their kind of country: lofty, timbered, with brac-
ing air, streams that swelled each spring with melting snows,
plenty of game, and tiny flats where crops could be raised.
The amazing tale of what Clum did and how he did it
may be read in *Apache Agent*, written from John Clum's
notes by his son. It is a book to be read with reverence for
the man's courage and decency and with sadness because we
had so few John Clums.

Clum was sensible and no weakling, and he believed in
the American system. He proposed to make his charges self-
supporting and respectful of the law. He soon had four
stout Apache policemen bringing in malefactors, who were
tried in a court of Apaches sitting with Clum. And he put
men to work as fast as he could, laying stone foundations
and making adobes for agency buildings. By 1875 he was
issuing scrip for work and making the Apaches buy their
own supplies. Agriculture was flourishing, with 200 acres
under cultivation, and the tribe had 4,200 sheep, 200 cows,
and 200 goats and burros combined. Clum reported: "The
troops were gone, consequently morale was excellent."

The soldiers were gone, but certain officers were finding
it intolerable that this civilian stripling in fringed shirt and
sombrero should be making them superfluous. Clum's efforts were repeatedly nullified by unprovoked attacks on
peaceful Apaches. Many reports to Washington were
doubtless designed to undermine his authority. But Clum's
Apaches stuck to him. They trusted his fairness, feared his
toughness, knew that his courage never failed. Clum, for his
part, had perfect confidence in his Apache police, who
served not only to arrest transgressors, but also to propa-
gandize newcomers to the reservation. Many Apaches came
voluntarily seeking peace; other bands were sent there as
they were conquered. This was the measure of Clum's success; that the government was always giving him more and
more difficult assignments. But his policy of punishing crim-

inal Apaches as criminals was never adopted: over and over again, evil individual Indians were given a chance to rest a while at U.S. expense and then go on the rampage again.

The highlight of Clum's career was his capture of the most vicious of these unconquerables, Geronimo. The only time that slippery savage was captured was by Clum and his Apache police.

Geronimo was a master of guerrilla warfare and a shrewd negotiator. He was also a medicine man with mystical knowledge of his enemy's whereabouts, strength, and plans. Opler quotes an Apache: "On the warpath Geronimo fixed it so . . . morning would break after we had climbed a mountain. So Geronimo sang, and the night remained for two or three hours longer. I saw this myself." To make his medicine, Geronimo smoked in the four directions, using a downy feather, an abalone shell, and a bag of pollen. Then he sang about his "power," which was most appropriately the coyote, a wily trickster, sly, and with the gift of disappearance. Geronimo too could make himself invisible, and he had a gun ceremony that made him invulnerable. He was never wounded. Singing, Geronimo accompanied himself on a drum; at the end he howled like a coyote. This was the supernatural power the U.S. Army faced, all unknowing.

Geronimo liked to bathe at Ojo Caliente in Monticello Canyon, where there had been an Indian agency. Learning that Geronimo and his band would be there, the Indian Commissioner in Washington wired Clum at San Carlos: "If practicable, take your Indian police and arrest renegades at Ojo Caliente, New Mexico. Seize stolen horses in their possession; restore property to rightful owners. Remove renegades to San Carlos and hold them in confinement for murder and robbery. Call on military for aid, if needed. (signed) Smith, Commissioner."

Clum got this order on March 20, 1877. By this time

Clum's Apache police force consisted of fifty-four men who had been drilled by his assistant, ex-Army sergeant Sweeney, into a body of men who could take orders like white men, as well as see, hear, endure, and disappear like Apaches. This was the nucleus of the famous Apache Scouts, without whose special gifts the Army might still be chasing Apaches. And this was their first military assignment.

As soon as possible, Clum started, on foot, the four-hundred-mile march across those cactus-maguey deserts which so appall the motorist even with his thermos bottles, his air-conditioning, and his speed. John Clum set twenty-five miles as the day's march, though the Indians, saying that they could easily do forty, put on a dance one night to show how unwearied they were. Clum wrote: "If some of you white he-men challenge my judgment, I suggest you try it for yourself. The route is still there. . . . The trail distance still remains four hundred miles; the sand storms still blow, and the sun still broils." His challenge remains unanswered.

Clum, with his footsoldiers, crossed the Black Range much as the motor road now crosses it. It is superb country, with thick timber, tall grass studded with brilliant wild-flowers, and glimpses of wild creatures in the thickets. They dropped into Ojo Caliente knowing that Geronimo had seen them come. But Geronimo did not know that eighty reserves, commanded by Lieutenant Beauford, had slipped in the night before. Apache scouts had outwitted Apache renegades. Major Wade, ordered by General Hatch to meet Clum on April 21, had not appeared. So Clum proceeded without benefit of the military.

On the morning of April 21 the slight and boyish Clum stood on the agency porch to face sour-visaged Geronimo and his most scowling chiefs. Clum, who could be stern and autocratic at need, gave the Apache no chance to parley. He did the talking, charging Geronimo with breaking treaties, with violating agreements, with many specific robberies and murders. He promised peace to the people who would come peacefully to San Carlos. He must have looked the innocent, easy to handle. But Clum had arranged a series of signals. When he put his hand to his hat, Beauford and his eighty trained Apaches ran out of the agency building. In a trice they had surrounded Geronimo's band. In another they had disarmed the mighty Geronimo and placed his band under guard.

Geronimo, who had outwitted the U.S. Army for years, had been captured by one young man with a steady eye, a cool nerve, and one hundred Apaches he could trust. The Army, represented by three troops of cavalry under Major Wade, arrived the next morning just in time to see Victorio, the other unconquerable, make his surrender.

Clum made his victory secure. He humiliated Geronimo by putting him and other chiefs in irons and by hauling them in wagons to San Carlos, where he put them in the guardhouse. He then notified the sheriff that he held prisoners charged with murder. He had reduced the doughty warrior, enemy of the United States, to the status of a sordid criminal answerable to a county sheriff. He wired the Commissioner of Indian Affairs that his instructions had been carried out to the letter.

But the Army could not let Clum alone. General Kautz, commanding the department of Arizona, ordered Lieutenant Abbott to take over as military inspector at San Carlos. Geronimo was released.

Clum informed the officer that any show of military would send hundreds of Apaches out on the warpath again. At the same time he wired the Commissioner: "If your department will increase my salary sufficiently and equip two more companies of Indian police for me, I will volunteer to take care of all Apaches in Arizona—and the troops can be removed. (Signed) John P. Clum, U.S. Indian Agent."

The result might have been expected. Newspapers throughout the country excoriated the young upstart who would boast that he could do better than the Army. Arizona citizens especially demanded that the Army stay. One said to Clum: "What are you trying to do? Ruin my business? . . . Most of our profit comes from feeding soldiers and army mules."

So Clum resigned; he had repeatedly proffered his resignation.

Not until 1886 did General Nelson A. Miles take Geronimo, and then he did it by a bit of double-dealing. Geronimo, needing a change of scene and a rest from constant fighting, sent a courier to General Miles at San Carlos with an offer to come in and surrender. General Miles accepted, but instead of giving the renegades the freedom of the reservation, as usual, he imprisoned them. Within one week he had some 350 Apaches on a train rolling off toward Florida.

The hideous feature of this affair is that neither Miles nor his officers discriminated between men who had been hostile and men who had been scouts; many of Clum's police, who had really made possible the captures, were shipped off with the real enemies, imprisoned like them, and, like them, separated from their families.

Clum was not alone in believing that the Army was often ruthlessly and stupidly wrong in dealing with Apaches. Britton Davis, a United States Army officer, wrote: "We have heard much talk of the treachery of the Indian. In treachery, broken pledges on the part of high officials, lies, thievery, slaughter of defenseless women and children, and every crime in the catalogue of man's inhumanity to man, the Indian was a mere amateur compared to the 'noble white man.' His crimes were retail, ours wholesale." Sergeant Neil Erickson, Swedish-born, quoted by Colonel C. B. Benton in *The Westerners Brand Book,* said: "I can tell you now though that if I had known as much about Indians then as I do today . . . I think I would have deserted the U.S. Army and gone with the Apaches. Those Indians got a raw deal."

So the Apache wars came to an end with most of the Apaches, good and bad alike, imprisoned in muggy Florida, where, being mountain people, they suffered extremely. The protests of Herbert Welsh, secretary of the Indian Rights Association, got them moved to Fort Sill in the Indian Territory, where some of their descendants are today. But most of them, given a chance to choose, made their final trek by train back to the mountains of New Mexico. Geronimo died in Oklahoma in 1909, his wife on the Mescalero reservation in 1950.

Modern Apaches know their history, but scouts and the sons of scouts seem to have forgotten the painful injustice of their removal to Florida. A few wizened old men still appear at G.A.R. meetings, some wearing the close-fitting cap that only a medicine man may wear and that may be the only Apache item in a heterogeneous uniform. Younger men are proud of descent from U.S. Apache Scouts. Nor have they reason not to be proud of descent from other Apaches who fought as brave men have done in all times and places for their own homes and way of life. It may be that time will teach us that these fearful Apaches were more warred against than warring.

IX

THE MODERN APACHE

Mescalero

⌨ IN 1949 Albuquerque suffered what may have been the last Apache raid—or the first one indicating the completeness of this aborigine's adjustment to modern methods. The Mescaleros, sponsored by the Chamber of Commerce and an American Legion Post, were presenting their Devil Dance in the baseball park to raise funds for a community center on their reservation.

These Mescaleros are descendants of Lipans from Texas and the last of Geronimo's eastern Chiricahuas. Their reservation contains some of the best land in New Mexico, with fine grazing on the slope toward the Tularosa Basin and superb forested uplands in the White Mountains. It supports one thousand people fairly well; properly developed, it could do better. Some Mescaleros boast of ancestors who were Apache Scouts; others take pride in their descent from Geronimo. A bad enough forebear is a good ancestor.

These commercially-minded Mescaleros are cashing in on their good location as a stopover for tourists traveling between the Carlsbad Caverns and Santa Fe. They engaged the Stanford Research Institute, and on their advice have set up a civic center to accommodate tourists as well as for conducting tribal affairs. Handsome buildings house administrative offices, along with a motel, a restaurant, and a shop for the sale of traditional bead- and leatherwork.

The Mescaleros are cattlemen with a thriving lumber business too. Their forests have been well managed and produce an average annual income of about twenty-five thousand dollars. But lumbering is secondary to the cattle business, for which the reservation is singularly well fitted. Rising from plain to peak, its wide meadows permit grazing in the upper levels during the summer; the lower pastures grow heavy grass for winter feeding. Cattle sales have grossed some fifty thousand dollars annually. Of an average ten thosuand head, ninety per cent are owned by individuals, some of whom live well and hire Texas "hands" to work their herds.

Non-Indian cattlemen complain that the Mescaleros, who pay no taxes, offer unfair competition with those who do. But the average Mescalero family income is less than two thousand dollars a year, and many of the people are poor. None lives so well as the complaining stockman. These Mescaleros are one of the few tribes in the country whose conditions are improving.

That life is not better for the Mescaleros is partly their "own fault"—or the fault of human aversion to change. Few men flex their muscles to chop trees, raise ridgepoles, build good houses. After the Reorganization Act of 1934, in the first fervor of self-government, the tribal council borrowed $350,000 to build homes. These loans, plus interest, were promptly paid off from sale of the tribal timber; the tribe still owns the houses, which are occupied on a perpetual-use assignment. But the excellent plan went no farther. Most people live contentedly in wickiups, tents, or half-roofed shelters, and drink from the clear ditch that gurgles by. In that salubrious climate and for people generally unacquainted with modern conveniences, such homes are comfortable enough. Typhoid is rare. Home-building and water development would be logical and practicable next steps, as would be windmills and spreader dams for watering cattle, diversion dams for irrigation, and wells for domestic use. But eager superintendents have so far been unable to stir the council out of its age-old lethargy.

This is a prime example of the real Indian trouble. How long should Indians be protected while they learn to govern themselves and to manage their own affairs? Mescalero also has enlightening political implications.

The council, discovering a surplus in 1949, figured out that funds in hand could give each individual, infants and all, fifty dollars in cash. The Superintendent forwarded their proposal to Washington with his recommendation against it. It came to the attention of a Congressional committee. An election was due, the first at which New Mexico Indians could vote. Certain lawmakers, doubtless inspired by the truest American principles, supported the Indians. Here is a true test of the expressed determination of Indian Service administrators to "let the Indians make their own mistakes," as the only way to true self-reliance and self-control. Fifty dollars in the pocket of each Mescalero would be gone within the month; fifty thousand dollars invested in water development would put the reservation into practically perfect shape and result in more cash and better living for all. Such are the problems of Indian Service administrators. How it looks to the Indian was wryly expressed by an old Apache. "When the Reorganization Act came we were proud to be like other Americans; to be elected to serve our people. We had always sat in the back of the wagon like children while a white man drove. Now we thought we could take the reins, while the Superintendent went ahead pointing the way. But now we see the Superintendent in the driver's seat while we still sit in the back. Sometimes we can't even see where our wagon is going."

Even a passing visit to the reservation demonstrates that Mescaleros are fast adopting our customs, if not our cannier virtues. Women no longer flounce about in the long ruffled skirts and loose overblouses that supplanted their ancient buckskin dresses; only smart town shops now make Apache skirts and pleat them wet on broomsticks. Mescalero women wear clean prints and saddle shoes. Few men still wear the long pigtails under tall black hats; they affect Hawaiian shirts and blue jeans. Many Apaches drive cars, even if they live in huts and drink ditch water. They attend Mass in the Catholic church or the service of the Reformed Church in America. A few heed the itinerant Latter-day Saints who visit them occasionally. That medicine men still operate is, of course, no incongruity to Indians. Ghosts still walk, bad people still conjure up evil spells. But these are the things that white people know nothing about.

Sadly, the old ways pass; too often what is forgotten would fit well into the new life or carry the old moralities onto the modern scene. Crafts are practically lost. Youngsters will not learn the old songs; they will dance all night in a cheap place in town, but are reluctant to enter the circle dance that old people still find important. Only the dark underside of life remains Apache, kept alive by silly fears and hatreds.

Even young men who served in World War II have not wrought notable changes on their people or in their own lives. More than one hundred served with credit to the United States and to their tribal reputation for courage. But only ten have taken any training under the GI Bill. Most of them live at home as before.

One notable exception is a descendant of Geronimo who replaced his progenitor's faith in his medicine with trust in instruments. As a navigator in the Air Force it was the young Apache's responsibility to take a plane from a point in Florida to a certain spot in England. "They guyed me a good deal. A poor ignorant Indian! I had to prove my race as well as hit that spot. So I checked and checked again. I was nervous, all right. But when we landed I had hit it right on the nose!"

Most Mescaleros move along together, adopting what they see, fending off what they do not comprehend, appearing in public as Apaches only on the Fourth of July when the ancient puberty ceremony for girls is held. The general scene is like a camp-meeting. Cars stir the heavy dust that makes noses painfully sensitive to the acrid smell of frying fat. El Paso, Roswell, and Alamogordo have sent ice cream trucks and every sort of legal bottled drink. Every stand has a radio. Happily, Manuel Archuleta's Indian records compete with be-bop. Illegal drink is also available; its traces are clear in wavering foot-trails and mad driving on mountainsides.

The Apache policeman said: "It is not Indian, it is a white man problem, this drinking. If white men would control their sales we could control our young men." A sage older man thought beer halls with music and dancing on the reservation would help to cut down dangerous drinking.

Only at dead center of the whirling, noisy, dusty show was there a hint of old Apache. It was a canvas tent, not a skin tepee, but it was cooled with leafy boughs. Within, old women sat on their heels chanting hour after hour. It was as though their wailing and their persistence might keep alive some old flame as well as prepare these maidens for maturity. The little girls stood shuffling in the dance, soft faces serious, eyes downcast, their costumes the fine buckskin dresses newly made for the ceremony, with deep fringe and wide yokes trimmed with beads.

Outdoors the long hot day wore slowly on. Steaming people went from the rodeo to the food, perched talking on woodpiles, bought silly gewgaws. No Apache baskets were offered for sale, but only bits of beadwork made for the cheapest white taste. A photographer from El Paso had been commissioned by the Council to take pictures for postcards. He caught a girl on her way to the tepee with an aged aunt in attendance; an old scout lifted his hat to show his twisted pigtails; a careful young matron removed the mosquito netting from the cradleboard that held her flat-faced baby. But it was hard to find anything typically Apache. The cameraman hoped for some night scenes with fires.

At evening cool there was a shift in the audience. Tourists were on their way. The games had ended and the grandstand crowd had left. Old Indian Service people and townfolk who come every year drove up to see the dance. They were quieter; knew what they would see. First there was the circle dance that everyone should have joined, but from which young Apaches held aloof, leaving its mystic generation of power to old folk and a few loyal Indian Service employees who helped to enlarge the ring. Finally a score of old Apache women, soberly stamping, and more and more younger folk joined in, in self-conscious groups. At the end girls ran giggling and young men pursued, but it was all done in the light of the neon glows from food stands. No real capture nowadays, so far as anybody knows or will say.

Very late, when the moon had sunk lopsidedly over the divide, leaving the sky to a thick misty coating of stars, the dying fire was rebuilt and the Crown Dancers appeared. Scents came from burning piñon and night dampness; radios were muted; the ignorant and irreverent had gone; drunks and babies had toppled over asleep. To rattle and chant, to tiny beaten drum, the weird figures came in their squatting pose, seeming quite properly attired in shawls instead of skins. The crowns, which give the dance its name, are tall painted structures made of thin withes and adorned with feathers. Each one jerks with the dancer's movement. There was seriousness now. Apache had replaced white man. But it was the disappearing Indian moving in a rhythm remembered mostly for show purposes in support of a faith all but outgrown.

Jicarilla

Life on New Mexico's other Apache reservation is

harsher. A reservation that straddles the continental divide between the Colorado-New Mexico boundary and the Albuquerque-Farmington highway, it is cold; often its winter temperatures are the lowest in the nation. Its tallest peaks rise above timberline, but lower down fine forests are slowly recovering from years of bad lumbering practices. In 1949 its timber brought the tribe ten thousand dollars. The reservation also supports eleven thousand cow units (an estimate based on the amount one cow eats), including sheep and goats as well as cattle, owned by the tribe and by individuals. No increase seems presently possible here; the range is stocked to capacity. Nor does farming seem a likely way out. There are few streams fit for irrigation; here and there tiny plots of dry farming give a dubious yield, but the growing season is too short for profitable agriculture. The Jicarillas must be stockmen, and are considered fairly good at it. But as the tribe increased between 1944 and 1950 from 799 to over 900 people, these Apaches were soon in as bad a fix as the Navajos, but their position is gradually improving.

Headquarters is at Dulce, a white clapboard town with well-built modern houses for Civil Service people, a store, post office, and government offices. Few Indians except government employees live here. Up the hill is the Dutch Reformed Mission: church, clubhouse, and homes for missionaries. And over the hill are the school buildings, with homes for the doctor and teachers.

The Apaches live in widely scattered, weathered frame shacks and dusty tents. The picturesque pointed tepees of their ancestors appear now only on ceremonial occasions; civilization seems to have brought ugliness with no greater comfort except that supplied by sheet-iron cookstoves. Other furniture consists of piles of dirty sheepskins and a few pots and pans. Flies, filth, and unwashed children abound. Water is scarce; often it must be hauled miles from the nearest lake. Dulce Lake, Horse Lake, Stinking Lake are set in grassy hollows like ultramarine jewels in plush, but their waters are often brackish and alkaline. Most homes are not permanent; sheep people drift with the flocks.

Teachers and missionaries, laboring devotedly for what they consider good for Apaches, seem doubtful of their success. A gentle mission worker carries a bunch of keys heavy enough to brain an ox, and unlocks and relocks every door as she shows the clubhouse for Indians. "They all steal; they even bring us their things to lock up." Missionaries find immorality on the increase: more illegitimate babies, more drunkenness. "They have lost the old taboos that kept boys and girls apart; they have not yet learned morality."

Teachers express the conviction that little Apaches are better off in the boarding school than in their homes. "Immorality and filth! Bickering and broken marriages!" They admit that most youngsters return home as soon as they can. Each year a few more enter the Indian High School at Santa Fe, but even those return home after graduation.

An Apache, middle-aged and learned in tribal lore, said: "The legends can only be told in winter. But the children are in school in winter, so they cannot learn what is right to do. They have no morals now." This is the measure and perhaps the reason for what fifty years of civilized training has done to an Indian tribe.

That training has not been long, and the best of it has been highly irregular and personal. A dictatorial triumvirate, representing business, government, and religion, wrought the greatest changes in the Jicarillas' ways. One thoughtful Apache, admitting its beneficence, blames this dictatorship for the self-distrust and lack of initiative of today's Jicarillas.

Emmet Wirt represented business. Coming west in the 1890's he had a butcher shop in which he sold the Army meat for Indians. Then he became a licensed trader at

Dulce. The Jicarillas were miserably poor. They earned only a pittance with basket and beadwork. Years of the dole had reduced strong fighting men and mighty hunters to dirty outcasts huddled in filthy hovels. They still hunted sporadically: mule deer, turkey, quail, and grouse for food; muskrat, beaver, mink, and weasel for hats and for fur to weave into their long braids. Wirt found markets for them; gave them credit at his store, even in defiance of the Indian Service; fed those who could not pay, but taught fair dealing his own way. Once he rode twenty miles after an Apache who tried to cash a government check off the reservation instead of paying a bit on Emmet's bill. When the man refused to stop, Wirt lassoed his horse, brought him down, and got the endorsed check. Such forthrightness, combined with fairness and friendliness, won the Apaches so completely that Wirt was the most powerful man on the reservation until his death in 1938. He was a man of his era: tough, just literate, but a reader; profane to a legendary degree; a shrewd trader; and an honest man whose morals were his own.

When the Jicarillas returned from a sojourn among the Mescaleros, a little girl came with them, riding behind her sister. She was extraordinarily lovely, with long-lashed eyes, delicate brown skin, and grace in every motion. Her beauty grew with her, and when she was still very young, tiny Tonita became a member of Wirt's household. She had several children by him. One son still living on the reservation talks quite unaffectedly of her, of his father, Wirt, and of his "Apache father" (his mother's Apache husband) and full-Apache half brothers and sisters. As a father, Emmet Wirt recognized and educated his illegitimate children equally with his legitimate daughter; as a friend, he willed his store to the tribe; it is still their main dependence.

Government was best represented by two men—an agent and a doctor. Chester Faris, as agent, believed in building manhood. He persuaded the government to issue sheep to

the Apaches in 1921. Emmet Wirt heartily approved; the
two men worked together to improve the breed. Four years
later the average family still had only twelve sheep, but the
Apache was regaining a measure of his manhood. He was
killing predatory bears, bobcats, and coyotes instead of being a predator himself, and outdoor life with the flocks was
arresting the tuberculosis that had reduced the tribe from
1100 in 1900 to 580 by 1921.

Children still died like flies, and parents feared and
dreaded the school. Once, in 1921, after the bathing and
delousing which was the preliminary scholastic exercise,
two youngsters died in the school. Nobody remembers
why; there was no doctor there. But the Apaches came,
several hundred strong, to rescue their children; they were
ready to burn down the school. While the principal escaped,
hidden in a load of hay, Wirt held the mob. Speaking
Apache with ease, he flailed his coatless arms, bullied, threatened, promised, persuaded them to wait on a council meeting to be held the next day. There Chester Faris presented
to the six councilmen Dr. Howard M. Cornell, then serving
as physician to a lumber company near by. With Emmet
Wirt as interpreter, the doctor explained how those deaths
might have occurred, how modern medicine might help
the children. After the Council had sent the rioting parents
home, Dr. Cornell was inclined to preen a bit. "Hell," said
Wirt, "I had that all done before they ever met."

Dr. Cornell was persuaded to give up his lucrative post
for the poor salary of a reservation doctor. On first examination, he found eighty per cent of the children tubercu-
lous. So the triumvirate, Faris, Wirt, and Cornell, turned
the school house into a sanitarium and sent the handful of
healthy children to the mission school.

Dr. Cornell built up a staff of seven nurses, mostly from
the Dutch Reformed Mission. One of them, Miss Hendrina
Hospers, as visiting nurse, found a family of five down with

flu. She stayed for three days, chopping wood, carrying water, sleeping on sheepskins alive with lice, and saved the family. Dr. Cornell, finding a woman in labor in the midst of a big fair, could persuade her to go to the hospital only if her Apache midwife went along. "Sure," said Dr. Cornell, "she can help me." He wrapped the midwife in a large white gown, showed her how to scrub her hands, explained the techniques as he delivered the baby. "Now," said the midwife to the doctor, "I know how. You get up on that table and I'll take down your big tummy."

The third influence, religion, is largely represented by the Dutch Reformed Mission manned by Hollanders. Spreading missionary ideas is a disappointing labor. Even the Jicarilla convert, mouthing the taught phrases—"Of course I don't believe any of that; Jesus is my Saviour"— seem to be dangling between beliefs, uprooted and convictionless. Perhaps only a student of comparative religions and of how myths grow could make the Christian faith comprehensible to an Apache. As it is, the pagan, not the Christian, seems to find harmony between the faiths. One Apache, having listened all afternoon to an exposition of redemption through the blood of Christ, said: "Yes, that's all true. There are many trails to the mountain."

Not surprisingly, the Jicarillas have lost their more elevated trails to the mountain while retaining many old-time phobias and exorcisms. One still hears of the burning of houses in which someone has died. Young people dread the dark where black ghosts roam and believe that if a child cries out in its sleep it is beset by bad spirits. Only painting an intended victim's face with red ochre will prevent the witch from recognizing him. Bobby-soxers from the school may be so adorned.

Even veterans of World War II cling to the old beliefs. One who broke his leg falling off a truck went as soon as he could to Taos. A medicine man there guaranteed to show the face of the guilty witch for ten dollars. The young GI sat enthralled while the shaman chanted and gesticulated over a black bowl of water. When the veil was withdrawn, sure enough he saw a face reflected. Satisfied that he knew who his tormentor was, he returned home and doubtless spent another ten dollars to counteract the spell.

The far-away doctor is often most revered. A Jicarilla who enjoyed no great fame at home made a good living among the Navajos, who found his invocations most effective in relieving pain. An inquirer learned that the storekeeper in Cuba had been wondering why that old Apache bought so much aspirin.

Even English-speaking Apaches who have been to school have curious experiences. One of them explained why some Apaches hesitate to kill coyotes; a typical white sheep-man's complaint is that their Indian neighbors will not co-operate in exterminating the lamb's most vicious enemy. Once, the Apache said, two of his nephews who were herding his sheep did not come home when expected. He went to investigate and found their bodies in La Jara Lake. "But my sheep, they weren't scattered like would be natural. They were just grazing, like with a good sheep-herder. Then I saw who was herding them. A coyote was there, just at the edge of the piñon wood, with his tail out all fluffy. When he saw me, I said: 'Thank you for taking care of my sheep.' Then he went away. . . . Yes, they were all right. Maybe he ate one or two, but that was for pay." He paused. "I belong to the coyote people."

The new culture's roots are not yet firm enough to displace the old culture. And distrust of the white man takes many forms. Once Emmet Wirt, who as Deputy U.S. Marshal had made enemies, saw an ex-convict coming at him with a knife. Just in time Wirt shot and the man fell dead. Wirt sent for the sheriff and was quietly awaiting arrest in a saloon when horses were heard outdoors. In no time the place was full of Apaches, who in those days still wore the tall black hats, pigtails wrapped in fur, and blankets. "Come," said the leader, "let's go. We brought you a good horse." Wirt's determination to stay, to stand trial, filled them with amazed distress. "Don't trust those white men, they'll hang you sure." Perhaps Wirt's acquittal on a well-sustained plea of self-defense had more educational value than many precepts.

The Jicarillas, like the Mescaleros, wonder how much self-government they really enjoy. Tribal funds are controlled by the Council, but their hired clerk, a Civil Service white employee approved by the Indian Service, disburses sums to maintain fences, windmills, and roads. The store Emmet Wirt left them is managed by a white man. More than once the Superintendent has overruled the Council to dismiss a man they liked or to appoint one they did not.

Like the Mescaleros', the Jicarillas' council wants to distribute a part of the tribal fund, in this case some third of a million dollars. People, they say, need wagons and horses to haul timber for better houses; cash to buy improvements; windmills to water vegetable gardens "so we can feed our children better." They name individuals whose tribal dole is inadequate for a minimum diet. "A good sheep-herder," said one councilman, "looks after the weak lambs. The government will not let us do that. They put in a storekeeper who will not give credit. What is a poor man to do until he sells his lambs? All stock business is done on credit."

Indian Service people aver that the Apaches have no money sense, their acquaintance with money being very recent. They doubt the Apaches' sincere desire for the better living they prate of. They name eight or ten families with annual incomes of ten thousand dollars or better. A few live in well-built houses with screened windows and porches, weatherproof barns, and a water supply. Others in that income bracket live like their poorer neighbors. Even those with access to piped water at Dulce make no gardens. A mature Apache, half white and the product of white schools, said: "I work for a good government salary; yet I owe $3,800 at the store. I ought to have that much in the bank. I could pay that off tomorrow; I have enough assets. But I won't. I'm just too Apache. No Jicarilla ever has a bank account."

Something must be wrong with educational and Christianizing methods that show no better results after forty years of school, church, government tutelage. The answer may lie in the present situation.

All Jicarilla children attend a boarding school at Dulce. The younger ones and some teachers are housed in a rickety old frame building; it is contrary to government policy to repair a condemned building. One only hopes that appropriations for a new structure will come before somebody drops a match. The older children occupy a newer and more solid building. Those who finish the eighth grade must go to the Indian School at Santa Fe for further training. There the Apache child has no chance to associate with white children, to learn their ways, or to adopt their standards. Naturally they return to the reservation—an island dominated by aliens, but home. Only three have ventured on to college; two half-whites, one adopted by whites. One has stayed away in a Civil Service job in Washington.

Back on the reservation the young Apache who has learned about movies and liquor finds both in the squalid villages that surround him. Police control is nil. One Apache policeman patrols the entire reservation and deplores the free selling of liquor to Indians. But the Apache may not arrest a white man, the U.S. marshal is far away, the state police are uninterested. If a deputy sheriff were reached, his brother-in-law, cousin, or his very self might turn out to be the liquor dealer. Drinking is increasing. One hears of young men, even high school graduates, veterans, even young women, who drink. The accent is on youth. For youth has lost the old taboos without taking on the missionaries' morals.

Perhaps these Apaches are the most instructive example of what our government has done with, or to, its conquered dependents.

1 *The White Sands gypsum dunes*

CAPLIN AND
THOMPSON, OLD
ALBUQUERQUE

2   *Wheeler Peak rises regally above Taos Pueblo*

NEW MEXICO STATE TOURIST BUREAU

3 The ruins at Aztec, vivid reminders of the life of the ancients

4 *Modern Pueblos still make drums*

5 The mission church at Santo Domingo, standing apart from the village

6 *Apache Crown dancers' costumes retain only a few ancient items*

CAPLIN AND THOMPSON, OLD ALBUQUERQUE

7 *Taos
pueblo looks
much as it did
when the Span-
iards first saw it
in 1540*

CAPLIN AND
THOMPSON, OLD
ALBUQUERQUE

8   *A Navajo who remembered the exile to Fort Sumner in 1864*

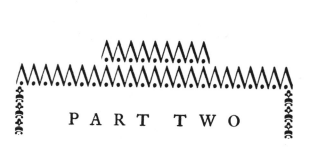

PART TWO

Spanish

X

SPANISH DISCOVERERS

Cᴇ Nᴇᴡ Mᴇxɪᴄᴏ's second discoverers were soldiers. Although Europeans with white skins, they often had the flashing black eyes and blue-black hair and beard of their Moorish ancestors. Some showed traces of aboriginal American heritage, for Spaniards entered New Mexico fifty years after Columbus had first set foot on a Caribbean island; early enough so that sons of Indian women could have grown into Spanish soldiers. They were conquerors, just out of the age of knighthood, infused with the conviction that the world was theirs, that their right and mission was to take and hold it for the glory of the vast Spanish empire rapidly expanding throughout the Americas and across the Pacific. Clanking in armor, superbly mounted, these men represented the highest civilization of their time, and they brought unquestioning belief in their civilization and their religion.

With the soldiers came their men of religion. Franciscan friars walked in sandaled feet, meek and unarmed, but as determined as any soldier to conquer in the name of the cross they bore. They too brought mediæval ways of thinking. The Spanish discoverers had begun to leave Europe before the Protestant Revolt. They came from a unified, rigidly controlled world believing that only one way was acceptable to a just, a beneficent deity—an idea inconceivable to the tolerant Indian then, as it is now.

The conqueror was Francisco Vásquez de Coronado, whose conquest was celebrated in a Cuarto Centennial in

1940, and whose history has been many times retold. Its definitive telling may be in *Coronado and the Turquoise Trail* by Herbert E. Bolton, though Dr. Bolton modestly admits that more material may come to light. Archives in Mexico and in Seville are a bottomless mine of reports, letters, depositions, and trial records.

Coronado was not the first white man to know the vast stretches of mountain and desert that soon became known as Nuevo Mexico. Alvar Núñez Cabeza de Vaca, shipwrecked in 1528 at an unidentified spot in the Gulf of Mexico, and washed ashore at a place thought by some to be near the present site of Galveston, Texas, had walked across the continent with three companions. They were sometimes the slaves of Indians; sometimes they were revered for an unaccountable gift for healing. Historians think that they crossed the Rio Grande a few miles north of El Paso, and so touched New Mexico. There they saw Indians living in permanent houses and raising corn, beans, and squash. When they finally reached Mexico City after eight years of toilsome wandering, Cabeza de Vaca's tale roused that capital to a furor. Perhaps those towns farther north were the Seven Cities of ancient legend; they might be the center of an empire more splendid than that of Moctezuma, richer than that of the Incas.

Antonio de Mendoza, then Viceroy of New Spain, decided on further exploration. He needed a stupendous achievement to outclass Cortés; moreover, Mexico was filling up with roistering younger sons from Spain, trained as soldiers, but otherwise a nuisance. An impressive and profitable enterprise would enhance Mendoza's prestige and incidentally relieve his domestic problem.

Neither Cabeza de Vaca nor his two white companions cared for further faring into that fabulous northland. There remained only the fourth, a Moorish Negro slave named Estevan, who could be "acquired" without consulting his wishes. But Estevan probably welcomed the opportunity to go along. He had proved his ability to deal with Indians, he knew several of their dialects, and he had a feathered gourd given him somewhere north of the Rio Grande. Estevan was the man for guide.

The responsibility was given Fray Marcos de Niza, described by his Franciscan superior as "skilled in cosmography and the arts of the sea, as well as in theology." He was an experienced explorer who had been with Pizarro in Peru. His orders were to check on Cabeza de Vaca's tales, to report on the land and peoples he saw, to win converts, and by peaceful means to take possession of everything for His Most Christian Majesty, the Emperor Charles V. The good gray friar and the Negro went on alone, attended by Indians from the north as servants and burden-bearers.

The route they took seems roundabout to us, but they were retracing Cabeza de Vaca's trail west to Culiacán and north across modern Sinaloa and Sonora, hoping always for sight of the "South Sea." On his return, Friar Marcos reported a triumphant advance among Indians who welcomed him, received the faith, and told of other people up ahead who had gold. Gold was already the retreating mirage.

In northern Sinaloa, the friar sent Estevan ahead with orders to send back a cross one palm long if he had good news, larger if he had better news, very large if it were something grand. Estevan, pushing ahead with his Indian escort and shaking his gourd rattle as token of authority, soon sent back a cross as big as a man. Estevan had heard of Seven Cities of Cíbola (the first use of that name), but he had not seen them. Estevan's messenger said the Cíbolans lived in turquoise-studded houses and had much gold. This tale was enough to enable Friar Marcos, remembering Peru, to build up quite a gorgeous empire. So he kept on following the Negro, who left larger and larger crosses along the way, but kept elusively ahead.

As the friar came toiling along he heard more and more about the fabulous Seven Cities of Cíbola and saw natives wearing turquoise, cotton *mantas*, and well-tanned hides. The feeblest signs seemed proof of what he wanted to believe. His route was taking him down the Sonora River and over a divide near the present international boundary. There he touched the San Pedro River and swung northeastward across El Gran Despoblado, still a great unpeopled area of magnificent pine forest. Across the Gila River the friar's Indian guides angled sharply eastward, promising sight very soon of the Seven Cities.

Exact routes are hard to trace, but Agnes Morley Cleaveland points out, on her ranch in the Datil Mountains, three old oak trees that may prove that the expedition passed that way. Perhaps the crosses carved on the trees record the dramatic end of Estevan. That dashing Negro had been killed by the Cíbolan Indians. The tale long accepted is that he had been too free with women, but Elsie Clews Parsons suggests that the famous feathered gourd was bad medicine in Zuni, and that Estevan was killed as a witch, not as a philanderer.

When this sad news reached Friar Marcos, he soon turned back toward Mexico. Whether he had gone far enough to see Háwikuh, the first of the seven cities, is disputed. Even the friar reported seeing it only from a hilltop. Only distance could have invested those adobe walls with the shining glory they came to have in the telling. Certainly the friar's account lost nothing in the versions of it that sped through Mexico.

Viceroy Mendoza was overwhelmed by aspirants to lead an expedition to the new land of gold and glory, among them the richest, most experienced, most powerful officers in the Americas. He chose Francisco Vásquez de Coronado, who stands up well as the ideal Spanish conqueror. Son of a good family of Salamanca, he was a gallant officer.

We hope he was both fair-haired and handsome, though no portraits remain. He had married Beatriz, daughter of a wealthy noble family, had made a friend of the viceroy, and had been successful in various civil posts, including the governorship of Sinaloa. His capital, Culiacán, was well along on Friar Marcos's route.

Coronado was appointed commander of the expedition and captain-general of all the places mentioned by Friar Marcos, as well as of any others he might discover. In Mexico unattached young men rushed to volunteer; over three hundred men were quickly recruited, many of them on horseback; many were rich enough to equip themselves magnificently and to invest in the undertaking. The Spanish empire was enlarged at the expense of the explorers.

So the great expedition was as we like to think of it. Dr. Bolton estimates its cost, in today's figures, at one million dollars. It had officers in glittering armor with floating plumes and brilliant capes, mounted on fine horses, and followed by well-trained men, to say nothing of the hundreds of burden-bearing, working Indians. Spain's great gift for organization had, within twenty years, brought enormous Indian populations into servitude, though the fiction was that they entered it voluntarily.

The army rendezvoused at Compostela, five hundred miles northwest of Mexico City, where Mendoza came to see them off. Students have dug out detailed information of men, horses—stallions and mares—equipment, and arms; of coats of mail, buckskin jackets, and the padded cotton armor of the Mexican Indians. Arms varied from the Indian's clubs, javelins, and slings to European crossbows, lances, arquebuses, and even a few cannons. The muster roll reveals how this Spanish army came not from peninsular Spain alone, but also from Charles V's empire. There were five Portuguese, two Italians, one Frenchman, one Scotsman, and one German. Among them were three women, not high-born ladies, but the first of the stout pioneer women who were to have so much to do with New Mexico's long history. One of them has character for us: Francisca de Hozes, wife of Alonso Sánchez, was a good nurse, a great gossip, and a loquacious witness in Mexico years later.

This was a young man's army. Coronado was only thirty years old; most of his officers were younger. They were adventurous, daring, full of fun and horseplay, deeply religious, medievally superstitious, and hard to discipline. Above all, they were articulate and they revealed themselves and each other fully in their accounts and letters, and in testimony taken in investigations after they got back. Perhaps the best, certainly the most dramatic, firsthand story is Pedro Castañeda de Nájera's *Account of the Journey to Cíbola*. Of the start from Compostela he wrote: "Such a noble body was never assembled in the Indies, nor so many men of quality in so small a body." With them went Fray Marcos, heading a band of missionaries, just how many is not known.

Coronado was also supported by a naval arm. Hernando de Alarcón had sailed from Acapulco with two ships loaded with provisions for the army and gewgaws for Indians. Fray Marcos had implied that the sea was not far from his line of march. Alarcón also had orders to explore the island of California, already known and named.

Mendoza formally reviewed the troops, accepted each officer's oath of allegiance, and gave an inspiring address. All were confessed; Mass was said. On February 22, 1540, Coronado's army rode splendidly off, led by Fray Marcos along the route he had traveled.

This magnificent army had much to learn. Caballeros found that packsaddles slip, horses founder, and men eat unwisely and get sick. But they learned. Gentlemen on horseback were toughening into pioneers. The story is a marvelous one, full of amusing and thrilling adventure. Its significance for us today is not in what happened on the trail, but in what Coronado's men did in New Mexico.

It was to be many weary months before they reached Cíbola. Long before that, Coronado had begun to doubt Friar Marcos's geography. He did not get in touch with Alarcón as expected, and Indians told him that the sea was very far away. Crossing the Despoblado, he lost horses. Food became scarce. Curiously, these armed Spaniards did not kill game. Two men died from eating poisonous plants. The mountains were difficult; pack animals slipped and fell. But in time they descended to a stream they called the *Río Bermejo* (Red River), later called the Colorado, and followed it to its junction with the Zuñi River. An advance guard under García López de Cárdenas had a brush with some Cíbolans, who scared off the horses. But Coronado, hoping for a peaceful conquest, disregarded this inhospitable greeting. So he came within sight of the famed and fabulous city of Cíbola.

This was probably Háwikuh. It was not a shining city with turquoise set in the doorways, but an adobe pueblo "all crumpled together." Cárdenas wrote that the soldiers hurled such curses at Fray Marcos "that I prayed God to protect him from them." Coronado had met his first disappointment. And here he fought Spain's first battle against New Mexico's Pueblos.

The Cíbolans had no idea of surrendering to King and Church despite Coronado's most mellifluous promises of the King's pardon and the Church's grace. Smoke signals had brought up fighting men. Women and children had been removed to the sacred mountain. Zunis' characteristic intransigence was making its first appearance. Even Coronado's best suit of armor and plumed helmet did not impress them. Their terraced mud houses became a fortress; their stones and arrows made it impossible for horsemen to approach. But Spaniards on foot were equal to embattled Indians, and within an hour the pueblo surrendered. Coronado had been wounded, but not seriously. He was able to treat with the chiefs. He was not a bloodthirsty man, and he agreed to leave them in their homes. Food for his starving and bedraggled men was most important; at the moment, maize, turkeys, and good salt were more important than fine gold.

In a letter to Mendoza dated August 3, 1540, Coronado described the pueblo, noting exactly what strikes modern travelers—terraced houses, flat dry country, wind, and strong, sudden rains. He thought the Indians worshipped water, not a bad guess. He mentioned wild animals, including the cattle (buffalo) whose well-tanned hides he had seen. Coronado sent back a Zuni painting of these buffalo, along with some cotton cloth, bows and arrows, and a few turquoises. No wealth of the Indies here.

This episode followed the over-all pattern of the Spanish conquest of the Americas. Indians were called upon to submit to Emperor and God on promise of peace in this world, eternal bliss in the world to come. If they yielded they were baptized, introduced to tithes and taxes, and counted as Christianized and civilized. If they demurred, they were fought until they capitulated.

Coronado, recovering from his wounds at Zuñi, had heard of other "kingdoms." Any one of them might have gold; certainly all had souls to save. So he despatched Hernando de Alvarado eastward and Pedro de Tovar to the west, where lay the province of Tusayán, and where he might come upon the South Sea and meet Alarcón. Tovar had several footsoldiers and seventeen mounted men who slowed him down; the Zunis, even loaded, could out-trot the horses. With Tovar went Fray Juan de Padilla, a veteran of Cortés's conquest of southern Mexico. It was he who shouted for the advance when the Hopis drew a line of sacred meal to indicate "thus far and no farther." They, like the Zunis, would have none of King and Church. Like the Zunis, they were forced to give in. They supplied a few cotton mantas, some maize and piñones. Tovar had no orders to go farther, so he returned to Cíbola. He had heard of a great river, though no mention was made, it seems, of the canyon it had dug. But he heard that there were giants there. So Coronado sent off another detachment under García López de Cárdenas, a dashing soldier and already so adept in the Indian sign language that he refused to take an interpreter with him. The people of Tusayán, whom we know as Hopis, gave him food and guides, and he went on. So Cárdenas was the first white man to see the Grand Canyon of the Colorado. Dr. Bolton thinks he stood near the Grand View, the point from which tourists usually get their first view of that stupendous gorge.

Naturally those adventurous youngsters wanted to get to the bottom of the canyon, and three of the lightest and most daring tried it. They did not get to the river, but they slid, dropped, and helped each other down far enough to report that the river was as wide as the Indians had said, and that rocks that appeared man-size were "taller than the tallest towers of Castile." These were Castañeda's words. He had been left behind with the main army in Sonora, but his second-hand reports always enriched the style of any tale.

Here was no South Sea, no word of Alarcón—above all, no gold. Coronado had written Mendoza: "It does not appear to me there is any hope of finding either gold or silver, but I trust in God that if there is any to be had we shall get our share of it." This pious hope he sent with Juan Gallego, a horseman sturdy enough for a three-thousand-mile journey, and Melchior Díaz, one of his most dependable aides. With them went Fray Marcos, New Mexico's first promoter, by then discredited, old, and perhaps ill.

Díaz went south as far as San Gerónimo and then struck

westward toward the sea, seeking Alarcón. All he found of him was a wooden cross at the junction of two rivers, the Gila and the Colorado. Alarcón had buried letters stating that he had turned back there. His cruise as far up the Colorado as Yuma had established that California was a peninsula and not an island, but he and Coronado never joined forces.

Coronado now turned his hopes eastward. He had heard of Acús, Acoma, and "other small kingdoms . . . on a river." This information came from two visitors from Cicuyé—Cacique and "a tall young man, well-built and robust," whom he called *Bigotes* because of his fine mustache. The visit was marked by a formal exchange of gifts—dressed skins, shields, and headpieces from the Indians; glassware, beads, and bells from the Spanish. Coronado then named the brilliant young captain Alvarado to take a score of soldiers and the bellicose Fray Juan Padilla and follow the visitors toward that river on the east.

Alvarado traveled an Indian trail across the malpais to Acoma, seventy-five miles east of Háwikuh, thus missing El Morro, the famous Inscription Rock, and hurting his horses' hooves very badly. One of his soldiers described Acoma as "the greatest stronghold ever seen," adding that if the Indians had not come hospitably down "we would not have been able to disturb them in the least." Alvarado and his men noted the peaceful lake that has given its name to Laguna, and in three days' travel reached a river they named Nuestra Señora because the date was September 7, eve of the Feast of Our Lady. It was probably near Isleta that white men first looked across our Rio Grande valley's maize fields and cottonwood groves and to the deep blue of the Manzanos. At that season they surely noted how silvery white the clouds were, with shadows not dark but blue.

The first pueblos Alvarado mentions were those of Tiguex, near Bernalillo, where he camped for a few days.

Alvarado was traveling fast with his guide Bigotes and
with Fray Juan de Padilla, who was making converts at a
great rate. Indians "even climbed on the backs of others to
reach the arms of crosses and decorate them with feathers
and roses." Alvarado visited all the pueblos along the river
at the foot of the purply-black buttes that mark the end of
the Jemez lava flow. He even made his way through the
Cañon del Norte and across the plain fragrant with sage to
Taos, which he called Braba. From Tiguex he wrote Coronado, advising him to winter there; this valley was much
better than Cíbola. Then he set out for Cicuyé and the
plains where the big cattle were.

Bigotes led the Spaniards along a trail he knew well: from
the Rio Grande up the Galisteo, skirting the Cerrillos range
where the turquoise mines were, through Lamy Pass and
Glorieta Canyon, the route the railroad follows now. At
Cicuyé, now so noble as the Pecos ruins, Alvarado found
the people friendly, though they guarded their women as
was their custom. Bigotes now declined to go farther, offering as guides two plains Indians, his slaves: Ysopete and another called El Turco because he looked like a Turk. This
may have been intended as a trick to lead off and lose the
intruders, but it resulted in greatly enlarging the Spanish
empire.

From Cicuyé the trail went south along the Pecos, purl-
ing sweetly along between alders and willows, perhaps as
far as modern Anton Chico, and then struck eastward and
so down the Canadian to the plains. There white man first
met the buffalo; herds of animals so multitudinous that they
could only be compared with the fish in the sea. When an-
gered, the bulls were fierce "with wicked horns," the meat
was good, the hunt thrilling.

El Turco now tried to lead them on to Quivira, a land where there was much gold and where Bigotes had acquired a gold bracelet. That did it. Alvarado decided to go back to get that bracelet and some honest information out of the tricky Bigotes. But back in Cicuyé both Cacique and Bigotes denied all knowledge of any gold or any bracelet. Maybe El Turco was the liar. The Spaniard, gold-hungry and impatient, put both in chains and started back to Tiguex.

There he found Cárdenas, who had come on as an advance guard for Coronado and was already making his men comfortable in a pueblo that the Indians had evacuated for them. Alvarado and Cárdenas—young, high-handed, and impetuous—were preparing not only winter quarters, but also trouble aplenty for their more diplomatic and humane commander.

When Coronado arrived, he approved Cárdenas's arrangements, but more supplies were needed and soldiers were sent in all directions to requisition food, blankets, living space.

Coronado's own mind was preoccupied with El Turco's ever gaudier tales of Quivira's opulence. Bigotes's bracelet would have offered final proof of their truth, but that obdurate Indian persistently denied knowledge of it, even when Tovar's dogs were set on him. Perhaps Coronado knew nothing of this or of the reported rape of an Indian woman. His lust for gold was aroused, and he had to see this Quivira for himself. But first he had a battle to fight.

The Indians had been getting restive, especially because the hasty Spaniards allowed no time for the democratic Pueblos to consult everybody. Even their pious hospitality wore thin as these demanding guests became more grasping. Many Indians had been robbed of their winter supplies, others had seen the baiting of Bigotes. Runners sped from pueblo to pueblo. Finally a Spanish soldier, snatching a blanket, was struck. A savage had laid hand on an inviolable white man! The battle was joined at Arenal, where Alameda now stands.

By the end of December 1541 the Indians in all the Tiguex pueblos had been fought to a standstill. Those taken in battle were burned at the stake. These two atrocities—the baiting of Bigotes and the burning of captives—were of great importance in the later trials because Spain's humane Laws of the Indies had already been promulgated. Coronado, whom Bolton rates as one of the most humane of the conquerors, was cleared of guilt at his trial, and the impetuous Cárdenas held guilty.

By spring Coronado was ready to set out for Quivira with El Turco as guide. Following Alvarado's trail, he went farther onto the plains, where the Spaniards were overwhelmed by the vast flatness of those grasslands, trackless as the sea. The Indians they met were friendly, probably Apaches. The soldiers were amused at the funny prairie dog and its villages, and learned to relish its meat. They hunted buffalo. They were held up by the great Barrancas, those deep gorges that redly slash the Texas Panhandle.

Thence Coronado sent the main army back. He was beginning to distrust El Turco, but he pushed on with thirty men picked for courage, stamina, and good mounts. This party followed El Turco along the Red and Arkansas rivers, and came at last upon a huddle of Indian lodges. Tabás, they called it; it was probably near present-day Lyons, Kansas. There El Turco was finally proved an arrant liar; even he could think of no more promises to make. Pushed by his enraged officers, Coronado reluctantly consented to have the man garroted. Then he prepared to return to Mexico.

However disappointing to him personally, Coronado's quest had immense historical importance. For at the very time he reached that point in Kansas, De Soto had touched the Mississippi. Those two Spaniards had spanned the continent in 1541, and Spain could claim about one third of the present United States. Curiously, the final link in that human chain was supplied by an Indian woman, a slave of one of Coronado's captains, who ran away at the Barrancas and was seen by one of De Soto's men near the Mississippi.

Coronado knew nothing of this. When he was on trial in Mexico later, charged with having defrauded the Crown of incalculable wealth by going no farther, he could only admit that he had found no splendid cities, no gold or silver mines, but only vast lands that seemed poor, sterile, worthless. Coronado was cleared, but he died a few years later, probably about 1549. Others might try again for the riches of what they were calling La Tierra Nueva.

When Coronado had left Tiguex, three friars in his command had elected to stay on in that New Land; the wealth they sought was there in plenty: souls to be saved. But no word of them had come back from the mysterious north.

Fray Luis de Escalona, a saintly man, had settled with his Negro slave boy, Cristóbal, in Cicuyé, where he hoped for success with children. Later writers presumed that he was killed there. Of Fray Juan de la Cruz even less is known, though a later Franciscan chronicler listed him as a martyr too. The third was that intrepid Fray Juan de Padilla, as fierce in the faith as he was in battle. He made the long trek back to Quivira attended by two Indian lay brothers from Mexico; a Negro, Sebastián, with his family; and a Portuguese, Andrés do Campo, a gardener who had three horses and a buckskin coat. This was the man who came back after five years to report that Fray Juan had got on well with the Indians of Quivira, but had been killed by enemies of theirs farther east.

These martyrdoms naturally aroused the Franciscan Order throughout the Spanish world. But for forty years

La Tierra Nueva was not again invaded. Then Fray Agustín Rodríguez got permission to go north with two companions, Fray Francisco López and Fray Juan de Santa María. For their protection went Captain Francisco Sánchez Chamuscado with a dozen soldiers. Doubtless the soldiery had mines as well as martyrs in mind. By this time Spanish settlements had been pushed into the northern states of modern Mexico, where mines of silver and gold had greatly enriched the explorers. There was always hope of new and better diggings. Our greatest interest in this expedition is that it traced a new route. Taking off from a settlement in southern Chihuahua, Rodríguez and Chamuscado descended the Conchos River to one they called Guadalquivir, a new name for the Rio Grande, which they followed westward and through El Paso, the pass whose name has never been changed. From El Paso they traveled north into the country of the Piros Indians, and perhaps as far north as Tiguex. These friars, too, remained in La Tierra Nueva while Chamuscado returned to report no mines found. But he died on the way to Mexico City.

Then, in 1582, came Friar Bernardino Beltrán, accompanied by Don Antonio de Espejo, whom Hammond and Rey, in the introduction to their translation of *The Espejo Expedition into New Mexico*, describe as a gentleman under a cloud and eager to restore his good name by doughty deeds. Like Chamuscado, Espejo found no mines, though he journeyed well beyond the Hopi mesas on a false clue. But he made two notable contributions to our New Mexico.

Espejo, leaving Cicuyé, followed the Pecos River south until it met the Rio Grande and Chamuscado's trail. He had discovered the valley that was to produce such wealth in oil as Spain never dreamed of. And, in reporting on his travels, Espejo first used the words Nuevo Mexico, thus giving the state its historic name before the end of the sixteenth century.

For sixteenth-century Spaniards, New Mexico had produced only failure. What they sought was not there. But
with Mexico and Peru still in his imagination, no viceroy
would admit that rich mines would not be found in those
arid northern lands. It only needed more expeditions with
more daring or more persistent leaders. In any case the new
lands must be colonized and held for Church and Crown.

XI

SPANISH SETTLERS

◘ To HEAD the first colonizing expedition into New Mexico the Viceroy of New Spain chose Don Juan de Oñate, son of a rich mining man of Zacatecas. He was wealthy and had wealthy friends, and his wife, Doña Isabel, was a granddaughter of Hernán Cortés and of the lovely, mysterious Marina, or Malinche. In the New World there was no prouder heritage.

On Oñate's muster roll of 1595 appears the name of Gaspar Pérez de Villagrá, gentleman of Puebla, graduate of the University of Salamanca, and poet. At forty-three he was described as of medium stature and gray-haired—aging in that era when life did not begin at forty. Villagrá's *Historia de la Nueva Mexico*, published in Madrid in 1610, makes New Mexico the first state with a written history. Written with Homeric magnificence, replete with classical allusions, and fulsomely addressed to King Philip II, the *Historia* is not very good poetry, but it is useful as a first-hand account of stirring times. Gilberto Espinosa, recognizing its values, has made a readable translation in prose.

It took General Oñate two years to assemble and supply forces, and by then his commission had expired and his money was running low. His friends presented his case to the Viceroy, raised additional funds, and went on his bond for the rest. Finally, on January 26, 1598, Oñate, heavy and magnificent in his armor, could with spur and rein make his stallion curvet, order the bugle to call the advance, and see his splendid train begin to move. Doña Isabel had chosen to remain behind, but in the forefront rode their twelve-year-old son, Don Cristóbal, quite as elegantly got up as any hidalgo and as good a man on a horse.

It was a "colony" of 400 men, 130 with wives and children, and Indians to bear the burdens and to serve as interpreters when they could. There were also "eight seraphic, apostolic, preaching priests," as Benavides described them, with two lay brothers and friars, including Friar Alonzo Martínez as *comisario*. A large herd of animals was driven along to provide meat, and oxen pulled the eighty-three carts loaded with necessities and with the general's indispensable wardrobe of satin, velvet, and fine English cloth, his plumed hats and extra suits of armor. He had, of course, a tent to be set up each night with its bedsteads and *prie-dieu*.

Seen in a museum today, a *carreta* looks too frail to go ten miles; it is only a basket of saplings mounted on solid wooden wheels of cottonwood sections and put together with wooden pins and leather thongs. A *carreta* could not carry much of a load, and it was forever getting stuck in sand or mired in mud and having to be unloaded and freed. At worst the cause of its nerve-shattering creaking ignited the wheels and the whole cargo went up in smoke. But it took some load off human backs.

When an advance guard reached the Rio Grande at a point twenty-five miles below El Paso, they had suffered four fatiguing days without water. Horses plunged into the stream and drank until they burst. Men, too, drank until they lay waterlogged, "more like toads than men." The waters teemed with fish, which they caught and cooked and feasted upon, sitting in the shade of cottonwoods on the damp sand. But the slow-moving colony was still struggling through dry sand, and the sky remained a cloudless, hard, unrelenting blue. So they prayed. And it rained. This was known thereafter as "the Day of the Miraculous Shower."

The first colony entered New Mexico with austere religious rites, a miracle, and a play. At the pass, near modern El Paso, its members observed Holy Thursday. Villagrá writes: "Don Juan ordered a large chapel built. . . . That night was one of prayer and penance for all. The women and children came barefoot to pray. . . . The soldiers, with cruel scourges, beat their [own] backs unmercifully until the camp ran crimson with their blood. The humble Franciscan friars, barefoot and clothed in cruel thorny girdles, devoutly chanted their doleful hymns. . . . Don Juan, unknown to anyone except me, went to a secluded spot where he cruelly scourged himself, mingling bitter tears with the blood which flowed from his many wounds." These are the rites of the Penitentes, still practiced in New Mexico in Holy Week.

At El Paso, Oñate met friendly Indians and ordered the building of a leafy chapel where Mass was said and Friar Martínez preached. There, with the army "in their most gala attire with splendid accoutrements and glistening arms," the general took possession of the new land "and all contiguous territory." The day ended with a fiesta and a play written by Captain Marcos Farfán. This first drama, meant to edify the Indians, showed the natives welcoming the first priests joyfully and begging for baptism.

So Spain set her mark on New Mexico in a religion of blood and tears, a miracle bringing rain, and a play with a moral purpose.

Following the Rio Grande's brown stream and its shady *bosques* was pleasant enough, but cliffs closed in a few miles above modern Rincon and the route led up onto the hills. This was that waterless ninety miles of the Jornada del Muerto. Oñate made it without a death, but the carretas were so slowed down by the heavy sand that he left them in charge of his nephew and lieutenant, Vicente de Zaldívar

Mendoza, and pushed on with the troops. Now they would have to live on the country.

Oñate sighted his first pueblo at a spot that has since been drowned out by Elephant Butte Lake, his second near Socorro. The Indians were timid and fled at the sight of armored men on horseback, but trinkets lured them back, and the strangers were invited into the kiva. Villagrá's description of this visit is a prime example of how preconceptions color first impressions. He reports that the people greeted them in "a most hospitable manner . . . acting most friendly toward us and showing great reverence for the crucifix." But when they presented blankets he assumed that "they were hoping to entice with them the Castilian women whom they . . . coveted." And he repeated the old untruth that the natives held their women in common before marriage and that a man was allowed as many wives as he could support.

Villagrá was horrified at paintings he saw in the kiva; kachinas looked to him like demons with fierce and terrible features. And in a Tiguex pueblo he reported a more hideously shocking fresco: "Pictured upon the wall we saw the details of the martyrdom of those saintly men, Fray Agustín, Fray Juan, and Fray Francisco. The paintings showed us exactly how they had met their death, stoned and beaten by the savage Indians." These murals have never been found. The Governor decided to take no note of those martyrdoms then. So in the dead of night the Spaniards slipped out and went on.

They visited San Felipe and Santo Domingo. Neither was quite where the modern pueblo stands, but Oñate probably followed the damp sand road we know along the river under the black lava buttes. At Santo Domingo, on July 7, Oñate summoned a meeting of seven leaders from other pueblos and offered them the usual Spanish alternatives: peace and love as tribute-paying vassals of His Most Catholic Majesty, Philip II of Spain; or hellfire forever. The caciques chose Philip II.

Like his predecessors, Oñate followed the Rio Grande north, swinging eastward to miss White Rock Canyon. Thus he by-passed the site of Santa Fe and chose for his capital the pueblo of San Juan, where the fertile valley is wide and the views most splendid, with the Taos Mountains to the north, lava cliffs crowned by the Jemez range to the west, and to the south the Sangre de Cristo, looking more massive than peaked from this point. Oñate named his capital San Juan de los Caballeros, perhaps to honor both his officers and the saint on whose day he took it.

From there Oñate went or sent his lieutenants to look over his new domain. They went east to Picurís in the pretty Santa Barbara valley and over the divide to Taos. They went southeast past San Marcos and Galisteo to Pecos. They saw the nearby Tewa villages. So they were well traveled and could boast to the laggards when Zaldívar came in with the carts at the end of July. He had abandoned two thirds of them as the provisions were used up, but it had been an agonizingly slow trek for a young man, and Don Vicente was ready for something sprightlier.

In September a fiesta was celebrated. Friar Martínez had laid out a chapel, and it had been run up so fast that it was ready for dedication after two weeks of work. On September 8 "the Governor ordered a holiday to celebrate the occasion. The horsemen, gathered for a sham battle . . . skillfully clashed in combat, showing great dexterity in the handling of their arms." This drama, unlike Captain Farfán's lost play, is still performed in many places, usually on San Juan's day, June 24. It presents the defeat of the Moors at Granada in 1492, and is known as *Los Moros y los Cristianos*.

The chapel at San Juan, New Mexico's first church, is quite lost. But from that center the Franciscans began their task of civilizing the Pueblos. They visited all the Tewa villages and built a *convento* in one they called San Ildefonso. They reported "indoctrinating" the Keres and established a mission at Santo Domingo; perhaps they made a few converts among the Rio Grande Tiwa at Isleta and Sandia. On this basis they claimed sixty thousand converts, three times the number of the estimated total Indian population. George Kubler, whose *Religious Architecture in New Mexico* is based on the latest research, avers that not one church built before 1600 endures. So New Mexico's claim to sixteenth-century missions, the boast of earlier writers, disintegrates in the light of modern scholarship.

The seventeenth century was to be the century of missions. But Oñate was more interested in mines than in missions. As a mining man from rich Zacatecas, he doubtless hoped to find a silver lode over every hill. But he did not go over the right hills. Nor did his lieutenants, though they reported many adventures.

Young Vicente de Zaldívar was sent eastward, unhampered this time by *carretas*. With sixty mounted men he quickly reached the Pecos River and stopped to fish, as everybody still does. He pushed on across the rolling land that would have been all silver and gold in September, with grass taller than we know now, and a fine larder of leaping jackrabbits and antelope and of doves and quail on the wing. He saw Indians dressed and tented in finely tanned skins. But the big excitement was those woolly cattle, "so amusing . . . that there is not an individual so melancholy who, if he were to see them a hundred times a day, would not laugh heartily as many times. All agreed that one need only corral them to have a domestic herd that would be an unending source of wealth in meat, hides, and wool."

Juan de Montoya, writing to the king, relates that Zaldívar's men spent three days building a corral where they expected to trap ten thousand buffalo; they thought they saw that many near their camp. As these clumsy animals, "when they run seem to jump as if they were crippled," they considered the prey very easy. But when driven gently toward the trap those stubborn beasts "stampeded in the direction of the people with such violence that they broke through everything . . . and there was no way of stopping them. . . . Of the most terrible tenacity and courage . . . they are so tricky that if the one who is rounding them up stops, they go slowly and stop and roll like mules, and with this rest they renew their running." Zaldívar then tried roping calves, hoping that sucking domestic cows would gentle them. But the pesky little things just died. Even the native wildlife of New Mexico refused to co-operate. Zaldívar was forced to settle for killing buffalo for meat, as his successors were to do until the breed was eradicated. Montoya found the meat good; and both hides and wool were to prove valuable as exports to the mines in Chihuahua.

Montoya was apparently a learned priest who undertook to bound New Mexico correctly once and for all. "New Mexico," he wrote, "extends from the north to the strait located between Nombre de Dios and Panama, turning west within sight of the continent of China, with a narrow strait of ocean . . . which the geographers . . . locate on the maps by guesswork for we do not know the true facts." So Montoya was cautious; but he had no doubt that New Mexico was a peninsula extending northward between Newfoundland and China.

Oñate had been having trouble at San Juan. Disgusted with this poverty-stricken land, forty-five captains and soldiers had planned to desert. Oñate was lenient this time but when a similar plot was revealed later, Villagrá and Márquez were sent after the malcontents. The young officers summarily hanged the two they caught, and so stored up serious charges against themselves and their general for later investigation. But Oñate judged things settled enough to permit more exploring. He set out for the west, where lay the sea full of pearls.

Acoma was the scene of the most dramatic episodes of New Mexico's settling, and Villagrá raised them to melodramatic heights. They were the highlights of his life too. His drama opens at San Juan with an Acoma spy, Zutacapan, listening in. If he had overheard one of Oñate's exhortations to the Tewas he might well have decided that Acomas never never should be slaves. The general's assurance that all he did was for love always wound up with the threat of hellfire forever if his words were not heeded. When the Spaniards reached Acoma the trap was set.

Oñate, seasoned soldier, scented trouble and politely declined a cordial invitation to enter the kiva. But both Spaniards and Acomas had been impressed. The Spaniards had seen nothing like that towering rock island, whose only approach was over a trail of toe- and hand-holes in a crevasse. It looked impregnable to assault, and it was too high to demolish with such cannon as the general had. After a display of horsemanship on the plain, with a great clashing of armor and firing of arquebuses, he thought it best to go on peaceably. It must have occurred to the Acomas that the armor and arquebuses would be hard to beat.

At Zuñi, luckily for Villagrá, a heavy snow fell and horses strayed away. No Spaniard ever lost a horse if he could help it, so the soldiers rode back toward Acoma, searching. There, on a lonely plain, they came upon the poet chronicler who, setting out alone to overtake the general, had become suspicious of Zutacapan at Acoma, and had continued on his way. But his horse fell into a brush-covered hole. Was it a man-trap set by the wily Zutacapan or just a standard deer-trap? Villagrá knew, of course, that it was Acoma perfidy. So he went on afoot with his boots on backward to confuse his pursuers. This might be difficult to do, but it has passed in Villagrá's account for all these years. So the soldiers found him. It seems likely that they supplied him at once with paper and quills. He had much to write: imagined, wordy interchanges between Zutacapan, urging war, and more peaceably inclined Acomas.

Oñate pushed on as far as the Hopi villages. Walpi at least was as unscalable as Acoma, but the people there received him well, and he could add them to his list of peaceful conquests. By then it was December, cold and snowy, and the South Sea far away. The expedition decided to return to San Juan for Christmas. This too was just as well. Before he reached Acoma the general was met by a captain and six men come to report that Juan de Zaldívar, brother of Vicente of the *carretas* and the buffalo, had been ambushed and killed at Acoma. It seems that the kindly disposed Acoma leaders had left the village and Zutacapan was in command.

Grief-stricken over the death of his nephew and worried over the loss of twelve men out of his limited force, Oñate by-passed treacherous Acoma and went sadly on to San Juan. Here his son Don Cristóbal appears briefly as the messenger sent on ahead to notify the capital of the Governor's approach. Oñate appealed to the clergy and received their assurance that the punishment of Acoma would be a justified act of war. He named Vicente de Zaldívar to command the force sent to avenge his brother's murder.

Villagrá is at his best in describing this violent and bloody battle for Acoma. Beginning with the Indians howling derisively from the summit and the Spaniards confessing and being absolved below, it mounts through three days of vicious hand-to-hand fighting. The Spaniards, feinting on the north, had found another trail on the south. They gained the top and dropped a beam across a crevasse, only to be checked by a batch of yelling savages. But Villagrá, old as he was, leaped the gap and replaced the beam. The Spaniards had entered the pueblo.

Fighting on from about where the church now stands, they won the pueblo street by street, house by house, man by man. It was a mighty battle, up there under the clear January sky. At its height the Spaniards' battle cry was heeded. Even as they shouted *"Dios y Santiago!"* fighting Indians saw among them an apparition of Santiago mounted on a white horse and wielding a terrible swift sword. Villagrá's estimate that six hundred Indians were killed has been allowed to stand by serious historians. Steel and the saint had won again. Acoma, the impregnable, was altogether destroyed.

In that January of 1599, Oñate needed reinforcements badly. So he begged them of the Viceroy, reporting that great wealth lay just over the hill. Meanwhile Indians and colonists were starving, and dissatisfaction was mounting. The clergy ruled that, though Indians might be dying of starvation, Spaniards had to live. More and more Spaniards were talking more and more openly about deserting and heading south. Oñate was later accused of conniving at the killing of malcontents. He left loyal men in charge and set out for Quivira, reaching the Arkansas River. Near modern Wichita he had a brush with the Kaw Indians, but he found no wealth and he came home to find his colony in open rebellion.

During the general's absence, citizens of San Juan had again plotted to desert; the clergy permitted the dissidents to meet in the church. George P. Hammond, whose *Don Juan de Oñate* is authoritative, states: "It is clear that both the religious and military authorities were responsible for the flight of the colony." Each, of course, accused the other of pusillanimity in the inevitable trial years later. But they left in October 1601, and Oñate, back from that disappointing Kansas, found only a rump colony. He sent the ever faithful Vicente de Zaldívar to present his claims to the Viceroy and prepared to hold on.

It took months to get to Mexico City, months to return. By the time a ruling got back circumstances had changed. But the basic problem remained unaltered and was earnestly and responsibly debated: what to do with the Christianized Indians if the colony were abandoned? Would it be better to leave them to revert to heathenism or to remove them by force and save their souls?

Meanwhile Oñate was struggling to hold his colony together and to keep the Indians under control. He put down one revolt among the Jumanos, and the friars built a few churches. Then the general, a stubborn man, decided to make one more try for treasure. New Mexico was sterile and the Kansas plains were empty. But there might still be pearls in California. Late in 1604 he set out to see. Beyond the end of his former journey he followed the Colorado River to the Gulf of California. Friar Alonzo de Benavides, in his *Memorial on New Mexico*, pictures it: "Fully dressed and armed with a shield on his arm and sword in hand, he gallantly waded into water up to his waist, slashing the water with his sword and declaring: 'I take possession of this sea and harbor in the name of the King of Spain our lord.'" Oñate had found no pearls, but he had restated Spain's claim to the continent from gulf to gulf if not from sea to sea.

On his way back to San Juan, Oñate opened New Mexico's great stone autograph album. Midway between Zuñi and Acoma rises a stupendous mesa sheared off in a flat face of pale sandstone. The Spanish saw its steep walls and towering cliffs as a castle and called it El Morro. Because of its uses it is now commonly called Inscription Rock. On top are the ruins of an aboriginal village and at its foot there are fresh springs and plenty of firewood. That broad smooth sheet of stone is an invitation to carve; no boy of any age or any people could resist scratching there his name, his boast, or a picture. Most of the earliest inscriptions are undated, stone-hacked petroglyphs. Oñate's is the earliest carved in letters and dated. Its first phrase, repeated by all later Spaniards, has added a picturesque figure of speech to New Mexico's bilingual language: *"Pasó por aquí"* (there passed by here); it goes on: "Don Juan de Oñate from the discovery of the South Sea in 1605." There are many other Spanish names, incised with dagger points; the carefully blocked names and dates of U.S. Army engineers; and a scattering of less well-known names. The Park Service guards it now: New Mexico's autograph album is closed.

We do not know that Don Cristóbal accompanied his father on this successful effort to reach the South Sea; perhaps if he had he would have left his name on El Morro too. He was twenty-two now, and in 1608 the colony's *Cabildo*, dissatisfied with an officer sent to replace Don Juan de Oñate, named Don Cristóbal governor. But the Viceroy overruled the appointment. Oñate's son was too young and inexperienced, and "they say he scarcely knows how to read and write." New Mexico might make a good soldier out of a man, but it was no place to get an academic education.

As was customary, Oñate underwent a rigorous investigation. He was found guilty on various counts and was exiled from both New Mexico and New Spain. Several of his officers were tried with him, among them Villagrá and Zaldívar. Villagrá, was accused of, among other crimes, writing "beautiful but untrue accounts" of New Mexico. By chance, good or bad, this activity is no longer considered criminally actionable.

To inaugurate the new program, the Viceroy appointed as governor Don Pedro de Peralta, adjuring him to protect and support the missions and to move the capital to a better place. One of Don Pedro's first acts was to transport the seat of government and the colonists to the pleasant valley of the little Santa Fe River. This was in 1610, the established and certain date of our capital's founding. With Peralta, as *custodio* of the eight friars who accompanied him, went Friar Isidro Ordóñez. These two, Peralta and Ordóñez, were to make a deal of history in New Mexico and to set its tone for a century or so.

XII

CHURCH AND STATE

⊂∃ AFTER Oñate's fiasco it had been decided that New Mexico, so disappointing as a producer of wealth, should be continued as a missionary province. The Crown granted the Franciscan Order an annuity of sixty thousand pesos to support the missions and, with its genius for organization, clearly defined the Order's ecclesiastical and military powers. The missionaries were to have control of their Indian converts; military and civil officials would serve primarily for their protection: it was so stated in every governor's instructions. Certainly the hope of finding mines, if not gold already minted, was never lost. So the two groups had divergent aims. The friars sought to Christianize the Indians; the governors probably always sought both gold and glory. Both brought to this distant frontier echoes of the ceaseless warring between Church and State which was disrupting seventeenth-century Europe. The century of missions was far from peaceful in New Mexico.

Establishing missions was of first importance. The friars set out at once to revive the Indians' fading Christianity, to rebuild the churches, and to found new missions. Men of faith and courage, they were often sent alone among savages who were outright hostile or who had been aroused against all white men by some one man's cupidity or lust. They learned enough Indian words to expound simple doctrine and explain the sacraments. They attended the dying; often they knew enough medicine to aid the ill. If one of them died a martyr, there were always others to take his place.

It was slow work and hard. These early missionaries often suffered cold and hunger, for they depended upon what their converts gave them until a regular mission supply service began in 1631. Meanwhile occasional caravans brought to each mission ten axes, three adzes, three spades, ten hoes, one medium-sized saw, one chisel, two augers, and one plane; a large latch for the church door and some smaller ones; and two small locks, a dozen hinges, and six thousand nails. Anything else the friar needed, such as pulleys or hoists, he was left to fabricate on the spot.

Building was perforce of the simplest. The friar just marked a cruciform outline on the ground, tucked up his skirts, rolled up his sleeves, and led his neophytes in building. Adobe was commonly used, and the bricklayers were Indian women and children who also plastered the walls and floors with mud and whitened the sanctuary inside with yeso or tinted it with colored earth. Men scorned this labor, but they cut, hauled, and worked logs. Walls three or four feet thick upheld pine logs overlaid with split cedar or aspen branches and a heavy dirt roof. With all this the Indians were familiar. The friars introduced such European ideas as high windows to light the altar like a clerestory and taught the best carpenters to carve designs remembered from New Spain or Spain across the sea and to prick out the patterns in color. As final touches of beauty and ceremonial necessity, the friars often taught some primitive artist to trace European scrolls in colored earth on walls or altars, to carve statues of the saints in wood, or to paint their pictures on wooden slabs or buffalo hides. Often, as in the churches at Laguna and Acoma, the painter's aboriginal ideas come charmingly through.

It was crude work at best, but often the floor plan the friar stepped off, the ceiling's height, and the placement of windows, altar, choir loft, and pulpit made a balanced perfection more beautiful than any modern church in New

Mexico can show. And the adzed surfaces, carved corbels, spiral pulpits, and simple frescoes are finer in their poverty than anything bought since factory-made articles have become available.

Each mission included workshops and barns, tilled fields, vegetable gardens and orchards. Many Franciscans were learned men, but their practical knowledge, ingenuity, and plain horse-sense were surely more useful than all their erudition. They were not only preaching Christianity; they were also trying to eradicate the old customs and to replace them with European folkways. So the friars taught the care and breeding of domestic animals and the uses of new crops. They introduced European vegetables, including such unlikely ones as artichokes and cucumbers. Peach and apricot trees began to flush the spring along the ditches, and one friar introduced wine grapes. Among the amenities were the *rosas de Castilla* that still throw their fragrant golden blankets of bloom over walls and fences.

Early seventeenth-century mission architecture may be studied in its purity only in ruins, but they are noble ruins. Every traveler between Las Vegas and Santa Fe may see the earth-colored bulk of the Pecos mission church, built before 1635. Also of that era is the mission church of San Diego on the Jemez River. Built with massive stone bastions and a belfry that served as a watchtower too, it is a marvel of symmetry and dignity standing among the junipers above the shaded stream.

On a day's drive out of Albuquerque one may visit the missions of the Tiwas of the Manzano Mountains, the Piros farther south, and the Jumanos of the saline plains. Ruins now, they retain a dreamlike quality that was first described by Charles Fletcher Lummis in his *Land of Poco Tiempo*. He wrote of these pueblos as the "Cities that Were Forgotten," and sharply scolded the American traveler for visiting castles on the Rhine instead of in New Mexico's mountains. These cities were not only forgotten, but also deserted when Apache raids had reduced their life to sheer horror and dread. A later writer, Paul A. F. Walter, has named them *The Cities that Died of Fear*, as in truth they did. That fear is reflected in a crumbling stone and adobe watchtower that stands near an ancient apple orchard. One gnarled antiquated tree was, according to tradition, planted by the friars who named the range Manzano, which means apple tree. The tree has never been cut to date it by counting its rings. Farther south is Cuarai on a giant spring known as Punto de Agua (Point of Water).

This spring is a joyous thing in an arid land. Its wide basin collects the spring-fresh and filtered water from the whole southeastern slope of the Manzanos. And it is so clear that watercress seems to drag its silver roots in air. Its fragrance is of wild mint, and for much of the summer wild verbena runs all over the place in a violet carpet. Alders, sycamores, and willows help to make bright green this sheltered cup on the edge of the pine forest.

Lummis, fresh from the verdant East, saw the rolling saline plain as ashen desolation, ghastly, weird. The Salt Lakes struck him as accursed, though he knew that they had always given freely of their salt and baking soda. And the ruined mission church at Los Jumanos he described as "a wraith in pallid stone . . . above dead grass . . . a spectral city." Perhaps only a New Mexican's eye can catch the subtle gradations of metal colors and gem colors in this scene: the gold and silver of grasses, the copper of certain shrubs, and the soft tones of amethyst, sapphire, and watery beryl where the plain dips into shadow. The walls do rise palely; the stones are gray, gray-blue, and yellow-gray.

Nobody remembers by what curious quirk the name Gran Quivira was applied to Los Jumanos pueblo, protected now as the Gran Quivira National Monument. Protection is necessary because the legend of treasure is still linked to the name. The Park Service ranger, who is developing a little museum, is often asked for permits to dig. Somebody has found a new map; has heard an old tale. No treasure has been found to date.

The last of these dreamlike mission ruins is that of Abó in a southern canyon of the Manzanos. The way to it may be traced from the highway by the homes and corrals built of heavy squared stones and timber plundered from the church. After the Apache raids had ceased, simple people came back to where there were good water and ready wood and stone to build with.

Other seventeenth-century missions were destroyed in the Indian uprising of 1680 and later rebuilt in a different place or so "restored" that little of the original remains. Thus Isleta's sturdy San Agustín was rebuilt with its magnificent buttresses in the eighteenth century. It took nineteenth-century taste to top it with silly steeples that mar its dignity as a tipsy hat would mar a noble face. Zia had a convent early in the century and probably a chapel. The present exquisite adobe structure dates from the early eighteenth century, but embodies seventeenth-century features in its beautifully balanced façade with a bell hung in the center and a balcony over the door.

Our most sympathetic picture of seventeenth-century missionarying in New Mexico comes from Friar Alonzo de Benavides, who came north in 1625 as *custodio* and first *comisario* of the Holy Office. He remained four years, traveled widely, and wrote a report so remarkable that he was sent to Spain to present it personally to the King, and perhaps to get more money for missions. He did both.

In his *Memorial*, Benavides could name fifty churches served by twenty-six friars. Among them was Santa Fe's first church for non-Indians, on the site of the present cathedral. Altogether Benavides's work did much to warm and enliven the fervor of the missionaries. It also led to great

improvement in the caravans due every two years. Bene-
vides complained that "five and six years are wont to pass
without royal officials bethinking themselves about us—and
God knows what it costs to remind them." Dr. France
Scholes, in *New Mexico Mission Supply Service*, shows that
dependable regularity was not established until Friar Tomas
Manso took over in 1631.

This friar, whom Dr. Scholes considers one of New Mexico's greatest men, organized an overland service longer
than, and quite as hazardous as, the later Santa Fe Trail; it
too crossed deserts and mountains and was menaced by hostile Indians. For twenty-five years, Manso directed the caravans as efficiently as a modern railroader handles trains, and
maintained his schedules. His trains consisted of thirty-two
wagons hauled by mules or oxen, and the necessary mule-
teers, herdsmen, servants, and military escort.

Dr. Scholes has printed full cargo lists containing such
items as sacramental wine, prepared candlewax, altar cloths
and rugs, choir robes of Chinese damask, paintings and images of holy figures, a silver chalice, and copper and brass
vessels for holy water. More mundane were hats for the
friars, woolen stockings, sackcloth, linen, sheets, and blankets. For the infirmaries came medicines, soap, pins, syringe,
lancet, barber's scissors, copper cupping instruments, and a
grindstone. To spice and sweeten the diet came honey in
jugs, conserves, raisins and almonds, pepper, cinnamon, and
saffron. Even now lucky people dig up ancient copper,
brass, and iron pots and basins that came in the caravans.
There were, besides, food for the journey and as much luggage as enterprising civilians could get aboard.

Benavides found New Mexico large, and both too cold
and too hot. "At a latitude of 40 degrees, north winds always predominate, and snow remains on the ground most
of the year . . . rivers freeze; iron-bound wagons cannot
cross. To prevent sacred wine from freezing in the chalice,

the padres keep braziers burning." In summer, on the other hand, "tallow candles and salt pork melt," and he found a total lack of breeze. But this dreadful land abounded in myriads of souls to save, and the friars had found hordes of them clamoring for baptism.

This marvelous aboriginal eagerness for conversion was owing to a miracle. Missionaries newly come from Spain brought word of a Franciscan nun, María de Jesús de la Concepción, who had been appearing to the Indians in New Mexico. Although Sister María had never been to the New World, her knowledge of New Mexico's Indians seemed great. Several padres told Benavides that Jumanos Indians had come in for four summers begging baptism and saying that a lady in blue had been visiting them. Shown a portrait of the Spanish nun, they recognized it, though they said that she was young and not old like the painting. Missionaries sent to the Jumano country met a procession of people bearing a flower-decked cross they said the nun had directed them to make.

When Benavides went to Spain to report to the King, he sought out the nun in her convent. She confirmed all the tales, adding that she had often appeared to Indians three or four times in twenty-four hours. She had flown fifteen or twenty thousand miles on her errands of conversion. Benavides wrote: "She has a beautiful face, very white although rosy, with large black eyes. . . . Her habit is the same as our habit, coarse gray sackcloth . . . and the cord of St. Francis." Later he mentioned that her cloak was blue; the Indians had always described her as garbed in blue. In writing to his "paternities in New Mexico," the friar ended by saying that he had obtained the very habit in which she made her flights and that "the veil radiates such a fragrance that it is a comfort to the spirit."

Benavides's report glowed not only with miracles, but also with good tidings of all sorts. He found the Indians wearing clothes and shoes. They were excellent farmers. Houses were of stone, strong and beautiful, and the work of the friars was beyond compare. At Picurís he praised a school "of all the arts"; at Taos, "a marvelous choir of wonderful boy musicians"; Friar Cristóbal de Quiros at San Felipe "has taught and trained these Indians well, not only in the things pertaining to our Holy Catholic faith, but in the ways of civilization, such as reading, writing, and singing, as well as playing all kinds of musical instruments." At Pecos he found all baptized and well instructed; the friars had brought in craftsmen to teach the Indians carpentry. Even in recalcitrant Zuñi some boys had been taught to chant. But those Indians kept their sacred fire glowing; Benavides thought they worshipped it. The Church had hard going in Zuñi.

Benavides also found troublous matters. In Taos an old woman inspired by the Devil urged women to live in concubinage. She was killed by a bolt of lightning on a clear day and everybody got married. The friars constantly complained of concubinage; perhaps they meant marriages not blessed by the Church. Monogamy was the rule among the Pueblos, though one sober historian notes that it was "a rather brittle monogamy."

The Jemez, like the Zunis, were hard to keep "reduced." Benavides found them "indomitable and belligerent; above all, great idolators." But they were "gay by nature, always talking of dances and games." More than once they burned out a padre and retired to the mountains, but finally Friar Martín Arvide got them to sow and garner crops, to learn crafts, to attend school. Even the cacique, who had proudly worn a necklace of Christian ears, turned docile. This was the same Friar Martín who had been almost killed at Picurís because he scolded an old Indian for resisting the baptizing of his son.

In 1612 Friar Isidro Ordóñez arrived as *comisario*; Dr.

Scholes believes his commission was forged. At once he entered upon a struggle with Governor Peralta which was to mar the century of missions with unworthy wrangling between Church and State.

Governor Peralta had set about building his new capital, La Villa Real de San Francisco de Santa Fe. He had laid it out with the Casa Real, known now as the Palace of the Governors, facing the plaza where the whipping-post and gibbet stood. It is noteworthy that a separate chapel was built *analco*, across the river, to serve the Tlaxcala Indians who had come from Mexico. This was San Miguel, later ambitiously labeled the oldest church in the United States. It is not even the oldest in New Mexico, and it has been often destroyed and rebuilt. But it has its charms, including the lay brother who recites all the baseless legends about it.

The first open break between Peralta and Ordóñez came when Ordóñez announced that any colonists who wished might return to New Spain. A clear infringement on the Governor's prerogatives, this act was also dangerous, as many desertions would weaken the colony. Some settlers did go.

The second break came when Ordóñez intercepted troops on the road to Taos and ordered them back to Santa Fe to celebrate the Pentecost. When the Governor countermanded the order, Ordóñez excommunicated him, demanding a fine and sentencing the Governor to appear before the church, barefooted and bearing a lighted candle, to receive absolution. Ordóñez declared himself an agent of the Holy Office and threatened to excommunicate anybody who even spoke to the Governor. What a day for the gossips, whispering indoors! Friar Tirado, the gentle guardian of Santa Fe, urged the Governor to comply and suggested a nice quiet absolution before dawn with only a few friends at hand. But the Governor demanded written orders before he would submit, and Ordóñez evidently preferred not to put himself on paper.

Dr. Scholes, whose *Church and State in New Mexico* is the authority for this long-drawn conflict, finds Ordóñez wrong in this case. Dr. Scholes's scholarly account, based on research in government and Holy Office records in Mexico, has given us a series of lively portraits of seventeenth-century men and women. As each accused was reported upon by himself, his friends, his bitterest enemies, and his official investigator, the amount of unsavory gossip and amusing incident brought into open court is amazing.

We know, for instance, that when Ordóñez demanded an escort for a journey to New Spain to report in person, Governor Peralta—one can almost see the sardonic gleam in his eye—offered to go himself, "that your fathership may be the better protected and served." This was not just what his fathership desired, and while he was in a rage he had the Governor's chair removed from its honored place near the altar and set outside. Peralta seated himself among the Indians. From that lowly station he heard Fray Ordóñez declaim: "Let no one persuade you that I do not have the same power and authority that the Pope in Rome has. . . . I can punish any person who is not obedient to the commandments of the Church and mine."

The Governor then set out for distant Mexico City to plead his own cause. But the implacable Ordóñez pursued and captured him more than once and jailed him in various pueblos, notably Santo Domingo, which had been declared the Franciscan center and ecclesiastical capital of New Mexico.

Dr. Scholes warns us that our only authority for this case is Friar Francisco Pérez Guerta, who was strongly pro-Peralta. But uncontroverted evidence shows Ordóñez as a man with an overweening will to power and extraordinary daring. He was not, as he claimed, an agent of the Holy Office. In due course he was tried by the Provincial of his Order; he was even sent to Rome. No record of his trial is known. Likewise the *residencia* of Peralta by his successor has been lost. So final judgment of these two powerful antagonists awaits some novelist or dramatist with a Freudian slant. We know only that they set the tone for another fifty years of bitter bickering.

The underlying disagreement never changed, but there was superficial variety aplenty. Governor Eulate was accused of approving the Pueblos' ancient ceremonies, but also of treating cruelly Indians who worked for him. This case resulted in the Viceroy's ruling that no outsiders should attend the Pueblos' elections; that feast days should be celebrated in the pueblos, so that the Indians would not have to travel to Santa Fe; that only a limited number of Indians should be called to leave their own fields to work for either governor or mission; that Indian women should work in Spanish homes "only with their husbands, and voluntarily"; and that no Indian's hair should be cut as punishment for a slight offense. Spain kept trying to enforce decent treatment of Indians.

Dr. Scholes's book is replete with rich human material that loses neither drama nor humor in his restrained, scholarly treatment. The tale that best reflects the century's mediæval style is that of Governor Bernardo López de Mendizábal and his high-born lady, Doña Teresa. They arrived in the state we like to associate with our Spanish governors, bringing a carriage, a bed with velvet hangings, a gilded desk, silver plate, expensive clothes, and boots of finest Cordovan leather. Many of these luxuries the Governor bartered for slaves, herds, and other goods to ship out. Governors were forbidden to enter trade, but Dr. Scholes finds that they commonly did.

The new Governor also brought books; among them a

copy of Ariosto's *Orlando Furioso* belonging to Doña Teresa, who had lived in Italy with her father, a Spanish diplomat. She had a few familiar belongings to offset the forlornness of that adobe Casa Real, with its dirt floors and leaky dirt roofs. There was not much mitigation for her outside her home: her husband was constantly embroiled in quarrels that surrounded her with enemies and brought spying eyes even into her bedroom.

Against López de Mendizábal all the usual accusations were brought, and some most unusual ones. It was reported that when the Cabildo asked for better quarters, the Governor replied that he rated those elected councilmen on a par with his Negress and his mule and that their meeting place was good enough. More serious were the charges of heresy brought against both the Governor and his wife. Prying servants testified that they had been seen at night in their bedroom performing acts that were sure proof of Judaism. Both had been observed, so deponents swore, bathing and washing their hair on Friday nights. Obviously only Jews could so violate the proper Christian rite of the Saturday night bath. The Governor's defense was that he did not bathe on Fridays and sometimes did not wash his hair for weeks on end.

Doña Teresa was charged by servants with reading a book in a foreign tongue, even with laughing as she read. So the lady's one solace in her loneliness was cited as proof of heresy. Both were cleared of these charges, but López de Mendizábal had died poor in the Holy Office prison before the verdict. One may hope that Doña Teresa was able to return to Spain. So disappears from history New Mexico's first woman with a book.

Throughout the century, governors' charges against the clergy were equally harsh. A friar was accused of beating a Hopi shaman into a bloody mass and burning him with turpentine. One in Taos was charged by women and boys with immoral practices. These were flagrantly unusual cases, and the offenders were brought to trial. Lesser charges were that the friars used Indian lands to raise their crops and pasture their herds, as laymen were not allowed to do; that they employed Indians without pay while laymen had to pay wages; that they imported too many luxuries. The religious countered by stating that their bulging granaries fed all the people in times of famine; that they were teaching proper farming and herding; that they needed fine churches and rich furnishings to impress their Indian neophytes. They were always jealous of their immunity from civil law and their right to govern all Indians except those living in Santa Fe.

What the Indians made of this ceaseless quarreling is not hard to imagine. It could not be hidden from them; often they were involved in it. The wonder is not that the Pueblos revolted in 1680, but that they had not revolted long before.

The decade preceding 1680 was full of horror. In 1670 a drought reduced the people to eating hides boiled with herbs and roots. Epidemic followed. The Apaches rose up and their hordes rolled over the exposed pueblos. In 1672 the missions in the Manzano Mountains and on the plains were abandoned; the cities died of fear. The friars might have held the Pueblos, many of whom had fully accepted Catholicism, if they had had food to give. But the missions, too, were famine-stricken. Friar Francisco de Ayeta arrived with the mission caravan in 1674, but what he brought was too little and too late.

In 1675, in the midst of the Indians' distress, Governor Treviño decided to suppress all "superstitious practices" for good. Forty-seven medicine men were tried for sorcery and three were hanged. Among those released was a man of the sort best treated fairly or killed. This was Popé, a powerful shaman of San Juan. Affronted by the trial and by a close watch kept on him at home, Popé moved to Taos, where he was revered as having supernatural powers. He named his ghostly guides, but his best allies were the Pueblos' utter disillusionment with the Spaniards and their religion, and the deep underlying faith in the kachinas. The new gods had not saved them; perhaps the old gods could.

Popé proved himself a great leader, astute, far-seeing, and ruthless at need. In a Taos kiva he met a few leaders and worked out a plan. Messengers were sent to all the pueblos, even as far as Hopiland. Few knew what was going on; it was New Mexico's best-kept secret until the making of the atomic bomb. Leaders in every pueblo received a knotted cord, one knot to be untied each day. When all the knots were undone it would be the time to kill every Spaniard: friars, women and children—everybody. The date set was August 11, 1680.

Then something went wrong. On August 9 several Indians reported to Governor Otermín in Santa Fe. Governors from Tanos pueblos corroborated the rumor, adding that only two knots were still untied. The Governor acted, but not quickly enough. Charles Wilson Hackett, in his authoritative *Revolt of the Pueblo Indians*, says that Otermín did not realize the seriousness of the uprising. He sent word to the nearby villages to be on the alert "in order that the churches might not be profaned and that a force of men might be put under arms upon the shortest possible notice."

Popé moved much faster. At once he sent runners speeding over the ancient trails, light in moccasins and G-strings, doubtless winged with feathers. Hackett does not mention horses; men go faster anyhow. So the date was changed, and before sunset on August 10 all the Pueblos knew. All had begun to kill. It was a hideous day of slaughter, with priests killed at the altars; women and children massacred; men cut down with their own stolen weapons.

One of Popé's cleverest moves was to assure the Governor in Santa Fe that the colonists in Rio Abajo, down river, had all been killed, and the Rio Abajo people that the Governor and all residents of the Villa were gone. As a matter of fact, both groups were carrying on pluckily.

Otermín, slow to believe the truth, delayed until the thirteenth, when he ordered the inhabitants of La Cañada and Los Cerrillos into the Villa Real. There he crowded into barricaded patios about a thousand refugees and their animals. Only about a hundred men were able and armed. Indians swarmed in from all sides. One leader, Juan from Galisteo, wrapped in red taffeta plundered from the church, offered a choice: all Spaniards to leave peacefully, or war. Otermín chose to fight. Sallying out, he drove off the Tanos, who destroyed San Miguel as they went. But Pueblo reinforcements were coming from the north, and Otermín was forced back to the Casa Real, which he held until the Indians cut off the water supply. Finally, in a council of officers, the Spaniards agreed to abandon the Villa Real and retire to Isleta, where they hoped to find any Rio Abajo survivors.

Meanwhile the Lieutenant Governor of the Rio Abajo, Alonso García, had gathered in the fleeing, horror-stricken people from as far west as Jemez, from the mountain settlements to the east and Santo Domingo to the north, and had brought them to Isleta. That pueblo had not revolted; it was the Spaniards' refuge. About fifteen hundred of them huddled there, believing that all the Rio Arriba folk had been killed. García's letters to Otermín were not answered. Finally he decided to go south to meet Friar Ayeta with the mission caravan. But he had found time to fill thirteen folio pages with notarized statements from his officers and the religious. No Spanish officer ever forgot that future and inevitable investigation.

So García was ready for Otermín, who arrived in a fury at what he took to be his lieutenant's dereliction. Together they went south. The religious were reverently bearing what they had been able to save from the churches. The people had very little. But Ayeta met them in time to save them from starvation.

This retreat was the abandonment of Spain's northernmost colony; the worst setback that powerful empire had ever known. The desolate survivors, established at El Paso, were so disheartened that when volunteers were called for a reconquest, only six former colonists stepped up. But others, mostly very young and raw recruits from villages farther south, responded. By November 5, 1681, the indomitable Otermín was armed, provisioned, and at the head of 130 soldiers ready to ride north.

This effort at reconquest was a sad and confused failure. Otermín bivouacked with his main troop at Isleta, sending Juan Domínguez de Mendoza ahead to learn how many Indian apostates were ready to surrender. Amnesty was offered; the friars stood by to hear confessions and to absolve all penitents. Many Indians, beginning with Isleta, abjured their error and wept as they begged absolution. Weeping, the friars granted it, and, weeping, the soldiery looked on. But this was a gigantic ruse.

The Indians' leader, one Luis Tupatú of Picurís, was scheming to trap the Spanish at Cochití; he had even baited the trap with pretty maidens bathed for the occasion. But, as always, there was a leak. This time one Alonso Catití warned his Spanish half-brother. Mendoza retreated to Isleta, where Otermín called a council of war. It had been a snowy December, the Manzanos were powdered down onto the skirts of the mesa, the dry grass was scanty, the horses were weakening. Afoot, the Spanish would be at the mercy of the Indians, who were counting on that. They decided to get out while they still could. The friars' great concern was to save the faithful Isletas; they took with them 385, who were settled at El Paso.

New Mexico was Indian again, but many man-made

beauties had been destroyed. After Otermín's retreat, the Pueblos had set about cleansing their homes of every reminder of their serfdom and oppression. All along his march Otermín found the pueblos deserted; the people had joined their Apache allies in the mountains. The churches had been demolished, the altars desecrated in ways too vile to name, and in the plazas were piled the charred remnants of burned crosses, crucifixes, sacred statues, and paintings. Everywhere they found kachinas, those "heathen idols," prayer sticks, sacred meal, and dance regalia. The friars reverently burned the holy articles that had been profaned; the soldiery made an orgy of destroying every pueblo as they retreated. So New Mexico suffered two destructive orgies.

In 1682 the Pueblos seemed to have won. Spain had lost her colony. But the Spanish Empire was still the greatest in the world, and the Church, in spite of Protestantism marching on in Europe and beginning to invade the New World, was still the most potent force in Christendom. Neither Empire nor Church could admit final defeat in New Mexico. So a strong man was chosen, and in 1692 the reconquest began.

XIII

RECONQUERED PROVINCE

⊂⊃ To RECONQUER that lost province, the Viceroy of New Spain chose Don Diego de Vargas Zapata y Luján Ponce de León y Contreras, more handily known as De Vargas. Born in Madrid of illustrious lineage, Don Diego was a soldier, a proved administrator, a deeply religious man, and a man rich enough to reconquer the lost province "at his own expense." The only authentic portrait of him, which hangs in Madrid, shows the true Spanish aristocrat, slender to narrowness, with long head, aquiline nose, and sallow face framed in long black hair. He wore a hairline mustache and a minute goatee.

Appointed Governor General of New Mexico in 1691, De Vargas was delayed in getting started, but once past El Paso, he made a swift and easy march up the Rio del Norte, finding the pueblos deserted. From hills and mesas bright black eyes doubtless watched that armored advance led by flags and the cross. But the people stayed hidden. On the night of September 12, 1692, De Vargas camped within sight of the Villa Real, which was occupied by Tanos Indians. The army spent the night in prayer, the priests giving absolution to all, and at dawn advanced, crossing the Santa Fe River at Agua Fria and approaching the town from the northwest.

The Indians were howling imprecations from the house-tops, but making no sally. The Spaniards cut off the water, as the Indians had done before. De Vargas then sent in his trumpeter offering peace and pardon to all who would surrender. Pueblo allies were coming in, but the Spanish easily made them prisoners without violence. One among them, Domingo, became convinced of De Vargas's fair intentions and, after long parley, persuaded the Tanos to yield. Always cunning bargainers, the besieged demanded that De Vargas enter the walled enclosure accompanied only by the *custodio* and six soldiers, all without sidearms. The General then proved his courage by walking unarmed through a gangway between high walls and into a fortified place. "Who," he said, "will not risk himself to secure perpetual glory and an illustrious name?" Those he did indeed secure.

The Indians recanted, begging absolution of the priests and forgiveness of the General. In the plaza, the soldiers erected a leafy arbor where Mass was said. It looked like a peaceful occupation rather than a conquest. De Vargas then set out for the northern pueblos.

At San Juan, Luis Tapatú, he who had tried to trap Otermín's lieutenant at Cochití, stood upon his dignity, refusing to surrender unless given a welcome suitable to his rank as ruler of all the pueblos. De Vargas agreed and the Indian approached, dressed in skins and crowned with a heart-shaped shell. De Vargas greeted him with the formal embrace and the two exchanged gifts—animal pelts from the Indian, a horse from the white man.

Tapatú, having bowed the knee, begged for help against the Apaches, who had been a constant nuisance. Tapatú, the potentate, shrank considerably on closer view. De Vargas rode on, offering peace, forgiveness, and protection. With promises he won all the pueblos, from Taos, Pecos, and Jemez, to Zuni and distant Hopiland, known then and for many years thereafter as Moqui, a Zuni word applied to them in derogation.

On his return from the west, De Vargas left his sprawling inscription on El Morro. It reads: "Here was General Don Diego de Vargas who conquered for our Holy Faith and

the royal crown all New Mexico at his own expense in the
year 1692."

Then he returned to Mexico to report the peaceful occupation of the lost province. This conquest was so salving to
Spanish pride—the loss of New Mexico had been the Empire's greatest setback—that a special leaflet was issued in
De Vargas's honor: *El Mercurio Volante* (the Flying Mercury), which Irving Leonard has translated into such easy
English that it reads like today's newspaper. De Vargas was
extolled as *El Reconquistador,* who had restored the lost
province once and for all. But the appearance of finality
was false.

After months of rest and recruiting, De Vargas started
north again with eight hundred colonists, women and children in *carretas,* domestic animals in dusty droves, dogs underfoot. This was a colonizing expedition. Danger was past.
De Vargas, finding the Indians friendly all along the way,
soon left his slow-moving caravan and pushed on to prepare
the Royal City.

On December 16, a cold, bright day, the Governor General rode into Santa Fe, still occupied by the Tanos. Almost
at once the Spaniards called upon the Indians for corn. The
shivering friars asked permission to move into the Casa Real.
The Cabildo, too, wished to occupy its old quarters. De
Vargas had promised the Indians that nothing would be
taken from them, but the old pattern was coming through.
Indians must feed and house their betters. The Tanos, refusing to go into the snowy mountains to cut timbers to rebuild the chapel, offered a kiva as a good place for worship.
When they were ordered to move back to their ancient
pueblo of Galisteo, leaving Santa Fe to the intruders, a war
was on.

This time there was little talk; hundreds of colonists were
demanding shelter. De Vargas moved quickly to the assault,
with Santiago on a banner and his name on every soldier's

lips. By nightfall the Tanos had surrendered. De Vargas ordered seventy of them executed. Four hundred others, including women and children, were given to the Spaniards as "servants." Enslaved. It was the end of the Tano group. Only a few families in Santo Domingo still recognize their descent from the Tano.

This time it would be *conquista*. Civilized man, with fire and sword, would "reduce" the savage to Christianity. The ensuing months were filled with hideous, blood-soaked warfare. The histories and the legends relate dramatic tales of fights at the Black Mesa above San Ildefonso, at the old pueblo of Jemez, and at Acoma. The true conquest was not done until 1696. De Vargas, like governors before him, was tried, imprisoned, and dishonored; but he was cleared. He served a second term as Governor General and died in Bernalillo in 1704. His remains were later removed to the parish church in Santa Fe, which was rebuilt into the Cathedral, where they still lie. But De Vargas's most venerated monument is the chapel of El Rosario.

It was long believed that De Vargas carried on his horse a statue of the Virgin, and that before the battle for Santa Fe he prayed to her for victory, promising to erect a chapel in her honor. But Fra Angelico Chavez, Franciscan, poet, painter, World War II veteran, and historian, has uncovered new evidence. In *La Conquistadora, Our Lady of the Conquest*, loving in tone and sound in scholarship, he states that the statue was in Santa Fe long before De Vargas's day. It may have been brought by Benavides in 1625; its title may refer to the original conquest. It was not mentioned in church or civil records because it was owned by a *cofradía* (lay fraternity) to which De Vargas belonged. In any case he built the chapel of El Rosario where his camp stood by the river, and every June the faithful of the ancient villa carry La Conquistadora from the cathedral to the chapel one Sunday and back again the next. The processions are most impressive, with hundreds of marchers and the elegant little image, richly garbed in brocades and jewels, borne on the shoulders of four reverently proud young girls. The statue had suffered during the ages, but in 1933 Gustave Baumann's delicate artist's hands brought back its original grace and beauty; and modern taste has decreed a style of wardrobe that must be followed by donors of its adornment.

De Vargas was succeeded by a century of governors whose chronicles are monotonous in the similarity of their problems: to hold what had been retaken, rebuild what had been destroyed, expand Spain's reach, and make new converts. Only a few left names or deeds memorable today.

In 1706 Governor Cuervo ordered settlers to move south from Bernalillo to a shady ford on the Rio del Norte. The town they built he named in honor of the Viceroy, el Duque de Alburquerque. Later and lazier spellers have dropped an r from this name, but the town's unique name is still a publicity asset.

In 1716, the Governor, the Marqués de Peñuela, decreed a fiesta in Santa Fe to honor De Vargas and his Reconquistadores. If this annual September observance does not come to us with quite unbroken continuity, it was certainly inaugurated by Governor Peñuela nearly two hundred and fifty years ago.

Peñuela's successor, Don Juan Ignacio Flores Mogollón, gave his name to a mountain range that might better have honored the Apaches who held it so long against so many. The Spanish were forever unable to conquer the Apaches, but the desert tribes were more amenable. The Austrian Jesuit, Padre Eusebio Francisco Kino, converted the gentle Pimas and Papagos, traveling on foot or burro-back across the deserts as far as the Colorado River. This was to be the western boundary of New Mexico until 1863, when Arizona was cut off as a separate territory.

To the north neither Padre Kino nor his successors succeeded with the Hopis. Even today's motorist, driving comfortably from Tucson or from the Rio Grande, must gain a deep respect for the devout friars who toiled on foot over that sand and rock to carry their faith to people whose land promised the invader nothing.

But one feels an equal respect for the Hopis on those gray and craggy mesas where sturdy, industrious, and weatherwise men with stone-age tools managed to raise crops and live. They had also developed fine weaving, basketry, pottery, and a religion that infused all life. Yearly they welcomed kachinas with dance; at intervals they performed rites to keep the life forces active and beneficent. This was the deep conviction that made the friars' efforts forever futile.

Both Jesuits and Franciscans tried to convert the Hopis; four military expeditions were sent against them. When missionaries came, the Hopis talked; they even built churches. When the military showed fight, they fought. Like diplomats of the first rank, the aborigines yielded many points, but held to their main proviso: that they be left free to worship in their own way. This stipulation was of course unthinkable to the seventeenth-century Spanish Catholic.

Friars thought that the people desired conversion; they even persuaded a few of them to move into settlements on the Rio Grande. But their shamans, whom the Franciscans called *caciques demoniados*, held out to the bitter end. And it was bitter. Even when drought and starvation had more than decimated the tribe, they remained obdurate. So they saved for a more tolerant age some of the most exquisite ceremonial dances in the world. And they left also an amazing example of slow martyrdom for the principle of religious freedom.

Eastward, the problem was that the plains Indians simply

did not stay converted. Henry W. Kelly, in *Franciscan Missions of New Mexico*, reports that the Navajos told Fray Miguel Menchero that they "were grown up and could not become Christians because they had been raised like the deer." They were willing to "give some of the children to have water thrown upon them" . . . but the elders would not become Christians. They had, they coolly stated, submitted to the water because the missionaries rewarded them with picks and hoes. No presents, no baptism.

One point on which Indians and Spaniards agreed was the importance of business. Indians liked to swap tanned hides for manufactured articles, especially weapons and ammunition. Both sides had captives to trade. The Spanish settled recaptured whites and Christian Indians in certain villages—a plaza of Belén, the hamlets of Abiquiu and Tomé. Captives taken in war were bought and sold in open market, especially at the huge annual fair at Taos, which brought together Pueblo and Plains Indians and every Spaniard who was not in jail or sick in bed. In good years all went well. In bad years fighting might result, or Indians returning home might detour to raid a settlement. Governors never had enough soldiers to defend the people assailed by Utes from the north, Comanches and Navajos from the east, Apaches from north and west. Bancroft describes New Mexico at that time as a habitable island surrounded by impenetrable wilderness. The vast empty terra incognita to the north could be disregarded. But east and west, Spain's precarious hold was threatened.

The eighteenth century was a century of world wars centering in Europe, some faint repercussion of which was always felt in far New Mexico. As other countries continued to expand, Spain had to look to her empire's remotest boundaries. She claimed vastly more than she could possibly patrol. In North America her explorers had covered the lands from Florida to California, and as far north as the sixtieth parallel. She had even made some effort to connect these far-flung settlements. As early as 1650, Spanish expeditions had pushed north from Mexico into the land of the Tejas Indians, which seemed too remote to be worth settling. But before the end of the century France was threatening Spain there, thanks to a highly picturesque traitor.

This was Don Diego de Peñalosa, a Spaniard who had thrilled the court of Louis XIV with tales of rich lands beyond the River Michipi. Peñalosa certainly had wrongs to avenge. He had been governor of New Mexico from 1661 to 1665, after which he had been tried by the Holy Office, stripped of his wealth, and humiliated beyond bearing. But his pride was not broken. For his penitential walk through the streets of Mexico City bearing the green candle he appeared arrayed in velvet and lace. He then tried to reach Spain to present his defense, but was denied permission to enter that country. When he tried to sell out to the English, the Spanish ambassador in London blocked him. But at the French court Peñalosa aroused a lively interest, especially in the ambitious mind of young Robert Cavalier, Sieur de La Salle. In 1684 La Salle landed at Matagorda Bay on the Texas coast of the Gulf of Mexico.

When that news reached Mexico it threw that viceregal city into a ferment. After that there was no doubt that Spain would hold the lands along the Gulf, distant as they were. Several presidios were established and abandoned, missions were begun and deserted. The first one to take root was built on the San Antonio River in 1718; this was to become famous as the Alamo.

With the establishment of the California missions about the middle of the century, Spain had some show of settlement from ocean to ocean. But the tiny hamlets and lonely missions were so far apart that their administration was a growing problem. In 1776, as part of a general reorganization of Spain's colonial administration, the wide empty spaces that were to become Texas, New Mexico, Arizona, and the northern states of Mexico were united as Las Provincias Internas. But paper changes made government no easier.

In that same fateful year of 1776, on the fourth of July, two friars, Silvestre Vélez de Escalante and Francisco Atanacio Domínguez, left Santa Fe to try to find a route beyond the land of the Moquis to the settlements on San Francisco Bay. They reached only some spot in southern Utah or northern Arizona—a ford on the turbulent Colorado is named the Padres' Ford—but they had covered eighteen hundred miles of what was to become the famous Spanish Trail from New Mexico to California.

Spain was struggling to hold the vastest empire the world had ever seen, but it was a losing fight. Other vigorous peoples were exploring all the continents. Above all, what had happened on the Atlantic seaboard in that fateful year of 1776 was going to determine New Mexico's political fate. But these world-shaking events were little noted by the simple people who were the ancestors of modern New Mexicans.

XIV

SPANISH COLONIAL LIFE

▣   COLONIAL New Mexico has been pictured as the scene of a luxurious life among the *ricos*, with a happy peasantry dancing, singing, and fiestaing—and all of pure Spanish blood. But none of these notions holds up upon investigation. Even the myth of pure Spanish blood evaporates before facts, as all pure-blood myths do. As we have seen, every expedition drew from the whole Spanish empire and was accompanied by hundreds of Mexican Indians to do the heavy work; even an occasional Negro is cited: Father Chavez found that De Vargas's drummer was a Negro.

From Oñate's time on, there was also an embryo middle class of farmers and artisans who peddled their produce and worked for wages. On the whole they were steady folk, but among them were such drifters as infest any frontier—offscourings of the mines in northern Mexico, and even fugitives from justice. Good people and bad were ignorant, superstitious, largely illiterate. In 1681 only three out of 147 recruits for the reconquest of New Mexico could sign the muster roll. Of New Mexico women appearing before the Inquisition in Mexico, none could write her name.

This middle class, as always, produced men of force and talent who rose to power. There were not enough hidalgos, who owned the best lands, to fill all the offices. The entire non-Indian population seldom exceeded one thousand, of whom eighty per cent were of mixed blood, as church records prove. Father Chavez, studying the church archives, found that even some haughty families have forgotten a lovely Pocahontas or Malinche of an ancestress. He also found that tracing any family tree beyond 1700 involves guesswork, all records having been destroyed in 1680. But from the reconquest on, the record is clear. No yearner for membership in something-or-other can show a better documented lineage than can any New Mexico villager.

The life these people lived was grim, what with the hazards of weather, the menace of Indian attack, isolation, and utter neglect by a weakening government. By happy chance, we have an excellent account of the colony by a hidalgo of the early nineteenth century. *La Exposición sucinta y sencilla de la provincia del Nuevo Mexico*, a succinct and simple report published in Cadiz in 1812, was the work of New Mexico's only delegate to the Spanish *cortés*.

This delegate, elected by the mayors and prominent men, was Don Pedro Pino, a wealthy and distinguished descendant of one of De Vargas's captains. His report is available in an excellent translation by Carroll and Haggard in a volume that also contains notes made in 1832 by Don Antonio Barreiro, a lawyer representing the Republic of Mexico. This gives a fascinating picture of the last days of the Spanish colony, with sidelights from the Mexican era.

Don Pedro left Santa Fe in October 1811. The inspired priest, Hidalgo, had already cried out against Spanish oppression in his *grito de Dolores*, thus setting off the revolution that was to establish Mexico as an independent republic. Don Pedro knew nothing of this as he journeyed nine hundred leagues from Santa Fe to Vera Cruz. No wonder Don Pedro reached Spain too late to sit in the *cortés*. Out of this disappointment came a couplet, meaner than the facts warrant:

> *Don Pedro fué*
> *Don Pedro vino.*

New Mexico's representative did more than go and come —if not for king and *cortés*, certainly for posterity. His report gives us a detailed picture of a life that had probably changed little in over one hundred years.

The function of any representative, then as now, is to extol his district, blame its backwardness on governmental neglect, and, of course, to ask for money. In performing these duties Don Pedro was pre-eminent. In praise he wrote: "In 118 years, New Mexico has maintained a state of warfare with thirty-three wild tribes and . . . has not lost one span within its old boundaries." This he thinks proves loyalty to Spain and the desire to continue as "part of the Crown of Castile." The people, Don Pedro wrote, were "poor and harmless with no defense whatever, with no soldiers, with no formal treasury, with no constitution, and with no laws to protect the settlements, agriculture, or industry." Settlers who volunteered to fight against the Indians provided their own arms—rifles, pistols, bows, arrows, and shields. "Likewise they must pay for their own ammunition and supplies." Many men, he adds, were ruined by a single campaign and were forced to sell their children into peonage to supply their own needs. Don Pedro did not mention that rich men often paid or supplied the men who served under them; he himself did so.

Don Pedro found his Indian neighbors "hardly different from us." His description of the Pueblos suggests that the friars had done their work well. "Many Indians can read and write . . . all speak Spanish . . . have good reasoning power, keen judgment, and a natural persuasive eloquence. They are slow to deliberate; they act in everything in common accord; and in their dealings they are extremely honest and truthful. . . . They rarely suffer from hunger because their foresight leads them to act with caution."

Don Pedro foresaw the Indians' early end. "Ancient Americans, now you belong to history alone and your remains will shortly perish!" He was, perhaps, the first of a long line of mourners who still grieve at the passing of the Indian, who will probably outlast us all.

Don Pedro recommended the establishment of five presidios at strategic points and a military academy to train officers. The Santa Fe presidio he thought useless, and he advised selling its adobe wall and moving the troops. Doubtless Don Pedro aroused some citizens to indignant protest against tearing down the fine old wall in the name of progress, as similar proposals still arouse Santa Feans. Anyhow, this recommendation was disregarded as were his others. When *Licenciado* Barreiro knew Santa Fe twenty years later, a crumbling remnant of the old wall still stood.

Otherwise Santa Fe had changed little. Barreiro found El Palacio "substantial, but in the worst condition imaginable." It was faced by the Castrense, the military chapel, of which no trace remains. On the west side of the plaza stood "a clean and beautiful oratorio" that the finest ladies of the city delighted in cleaning and adorning. The rest of the plaza was enclosed by private dwellings and it had "frame porticos all around." In the center stood a sundial, the only timepiece in town, with the maxim: *Vita fugit sicut umbra* (Life flees like a shadow). Barreiro found the rest of Santa Fe disordered and disagreeable. Only the private homes "although constructed of adobe and very low, are quite comfortable and very clean." He, a Mexican from a chimneyless land, was much impressed by fireplaces. He also found several clothing stores and a brisk commerce.

Santa Fe's population, according to the ubiquitous Baron Humboldt, was about five thousand in Don Pedro's day. Besides being capital of the province, Santa Fe was the administrative center of settlements from El Bado de San Miguel, near Las Vegas, to Jemez. Albuquerque headed the Rio Abajo—six towns including Socorro and Laguna. The largest district, taking in all the northern settlements, was Santa Cruz de la Cañada.

Santa Cruz with its handsome church seems the gateway to a dreamlike vision of old New Mexico. Now as then, people graze their flocks on the pale gold hills and farm along the bosky Santa Cruz stream. In Chimayó, weavers still make striped blankets on their ancestors' heavy wooden looms. The Santuario still attracts pilgrims to pray or to carry off the miraculously healing sand. Farther up the mountain, in Cundiyó and Córdova, woodcarvers carry on the family tradition. And at the apex, where tiny Truchas sits just under the blue-green peaks, one gets a daily pageant of light and shadow across hundreds of miles of valley and plain and the yearly modulations from golden yellow of aspen in the fall through the silvery snows of winter to spring's tender green and summer's lushness.

Don Pedro Pino, Spanish colonial, showed himself amazingly modern at times. He noted that as the Pueblos had enough land to make a living, "they do not have [the] vagrants or beggars that swarm like lice in . . . Mexico." He commended "the good discipline and cleanliness which contribute so much to public health." And he warned: "Let the nation be fully informed: the means of establishing peace in New Spain lies in giving every one an interest in the property of the territory as is being done in my province." If Spain had heeded, if Mexico had heeded, these wise words from New Mexico in 1812, how many revolutions might have been avoided!

Don Pedro also warned his sovereign against the United States. Its citizens, he wrote, "knowing that by possessing this province, they would be masters from the North Sea to the South Sea . . . have tried with . . . lucrative commerce and promises of . . . protective laws to unite this territory to Louisiana." Even in 1812, Don Pedro could see destiny marching westward.

But Don Pedro, the hidalgo, could not see an evil that was to make the United States occupation easier. This was peonage; it marked New Mexico deeply until yesterday, if not today. The *patrón* had more lands and grazed more sheep than his poor village neighbors, and commanded the work of many others held in debt. He considered himself, of course, the protector of them all. How it really was is best presented by later arrivals. John Ayers, in *A Soldier's Experiences in New Mexico*, called emancipation "a greater boon to these enslaved Mexicans than even to the Negroes. . . . By their laws, peons could be brought back if they ran away. They could punish them in any way; it was worse than slavery, for slaves had a mercantile value while if a peon died his place was filled with no loss but the small debt he was working out." At best, when the *patrón* was kind and looked after his people in old age or illness, the peon's attitude of dependence and subservience was going to prove a poor basis for American citizenship. And for both villager and peon there was no way out.

There were few schools, and Barreiro found those deplorable owing to "neglect, carelessness, the ignorance of teachers, and the lack of interest of the authorities." There were, of course, no college, no lawyers, no physician. The one surgeon was paid by the soldiers. A few hidalgos were taught by the priests, but there was no educated class. Like English county squires of the same period, hidalgos held themselves high and maintained strict standards of morals and manners; their very derelictions were according to rule. A gentleman fought at need, entertained lavishly, guarded his women and kept them ignorant, and had no truck with books or thought. Few books are among the treasures of our old Spanish families. Thought was taboo throughout the Spanish empire, a ban heartily endorsed by the Church. Even Republican Mexico, in 1823, limited its guarantee to protect "the life, liberty, property, and civil rights" of foreigners to those "who profess the Roman Catholic Apostolic Religion."

Barreiro, the Mexican lawyer, reported that crime was never punished because "no one knows how to conduct an examining trial, to prepare a defense, or to prosecute a case." Jails, he wrote, were "only a few filthy rooms in the capital." But Don Pedro Pino found that prisoners were "rewarded rather than punished . . . since they spend their time in noisy revelry . . . and at night they escape and go to dances."

Life's monotony was broken by the annual buffalo-hunt on the plains and by the winter caravan to Chihuahua. At La Joya, south of Socorro, as many as five hundred merchants might gather with their loaded *carretas* and their retainers. A captain would be elected and sentries assigned to guard the van and rear; there was always danger of Apache attack.

Hidalgos were such a vision as no movie could better. Riding small wiry horses descended from Arabians, they sat hand-tooled and silver-studded saddles, handled ornate bridles with vicious bits, and with huge roweled spurs roused their steeds to spectacular curvetings. Their sombreros were flat-topped, black, and held on by a chin strap. Woolen pantaloons with leather jackets and leggings were eminently practical, and the finely woven serape was warm and rainproof. But it also lent color and swank. The peon, also mounted, emulated as well as he could his *patrón's* elegance, but he wore high moccasins instead of hand-made boots, and settled for silverless saddle and bridle. But the wide hat and the swinging serape were his, and he rode with as much skill and dash as any aristocrat.

Often *trobadores* rode with the caravan to sing in camp at night and to enter contests in Mexico. Rubén Cobos found that one singer, Martín Chicoria, was claimed a hundred years later by a score of hamlets. According to legend, Chicoria had been forced to go to stand up for New Mexico against a famed singer of Chihuahua. There the *trobador*

Gracia poked fun at the New Mexicans as buffalo hunters and unfit to sing among gentlemen. Chicoria was held to have won with a neat pun on Gracia's name, which means grace. Such verses translate poorly, but many old people still remember the skill and wit of those impromptu singers.

New Mexico's trade went east and west as well as south. Eastward, Mexican citizens first traced the route that would be known as the Santa Fe Trail. Tempted by the "lucrative commerce" that Don Pedro mentioned, they went even beyond the plains, where they captured slaves, and as far as the Missouri settlements.

Antonio Armijo, in 1829, followed the trail of Escalante and Domínguez even beyond their ford, and extended the Old Spanish Trail to the Pacific. LeRoy Hafen, who has made the most exhaustive study of Armijo's journey, believes that he followed Jedediah Smith's route from the Great Salt Lake to California. But Armijo was the first to make it through from Santa Fe to San Diego. He also visited El Pueblo de los Angeles, known for many years only as El Pueblo. Armijo reported that his party was hospitably received by Californians, "who were very surprised to see them arrive from a direction that until then was unknown; and they traded the products they brought with them for mules, horses, and stock." Mexicans often thereafter traded mules to Missourians. Enter the Missouri mule, via Santa Fe!

Armijo apologized that "the empresarios, although . . . courageous, rugged, and eager to discover new lands, are lacking in instruction and literature . . . to note the various products of the territory the Mexican Republic possessed in this region; and they are able only to say that there exist suitable locations for establishing new villages and that in the hills there appear variously colored rocks or veins. . . ."

Armijo had opened a trade route that was to see twenty years of heavy use before the U.S. Army broke new trails.

He did not mention its most hideous activity, the running down of desert Indian children to be sold as slaves. This was an evil not only of Mexican trade expeditions, but also of many of the earlier expeditions from the States.

Colonial life in New Mexico was narrow and hard, seemingly without a future. But even in the 1820's strong, rough, tough men were already on their way. They would demolish much that was pleasant, but they would in time give the people a chance to make their own future. The old ways persisted in spite of superficial changes, and life in New Mexico is still much modified by the life of the Spanish colony.

XV

OUR SPANISH HERITAGE

LIFE in modern New Mexico is deeply marked by the life Don Pedro Pino knew, perhaps most deeply by what was so familiar to him that he did not mention it: things like houses and clothing, food, and ways of thought. Above all, who would ever have thought that the Spanish language would greatly modify the talk of those incoming heretics, or that spoken Spanish would be corrupted by a new vocabulary?

The speediest and most thoughtless tourist must perforce learn some Spanish words. How else will he be warned when an *arroyo* is up, follow a ditch when an *acequia* is mentioned, know when he is told to turn at a tank in the desert that the word is a mispronunciation of the Spanish *estanque* (watering pool)? In town how will he find the *plaza;* know that a *portal* is not a gate but a porch; that a *patio,* like a *placita,* is inside a house; that a *cantina* is the place to seek liquid refreshment; and that food may be looked for in *la cocina* (the kitchen)? Faced with a menu he may not recognize *tortillas* and *sopaipillas* as breadstuffs, and he may learn only with tears that *chile* is far from chilly. Spanish place names dot our map even where they are most heinously mispronounced by people least appreciative of our Spanish heritage.

This patrimony of ours is not an unmixed blessing. In so far as we enjoy the benefits of a second tongue and an outlook on two cultures, it is enriching and good. Much of New Mexico's charm and grace of living are owing to our

Spanish background, as appears in many a remote hamlet where life is closer to the Spanish colony than to the modern state.

An old gentleman sits on a backless chair on the sunny side of the house. The dooryard is damp and hard from watering and sweeping. His garden of beans, chile, squash, and corn is moist from the ditch gurgling against a wooden gate. A dog suns himself. A chicken pecks around. A visitor is welcomed with an ease suggestive of a castle, not a mud hut. The señora, emerging for a greeting, may be wiping wet hands on an apron, and her hair may be tied in a towel, but she offers no apology as she sets another chair. Poverty is evident, but the dignity of people comfortable with themselves is dominant.

Life in such a village is hard. If water fails, there may not be enough to eat. Every summer men go off to work on ranches, the beet fields of Colorado, or the sheep camps of Wyoming, leaving a village of widows. But it is a village firmly centered in the Church, in family, and in neighborliness. The priest has immense influence. Simple faith is expressed in regular attendance at Mass, in the care of the old carved *santos* or in modern plaster images, and in processions on the saint's day.

Many of the old people do not speak English, though they may understand more than they pretend. Younger people can speak it, but prefer not to. Children are called upon to act as interpreters. They speak English at school, Spanish everywhere else. If the old people become confiding they will protest that the old ways were better. The Church is losing its power. Young people go off to town where they learn nothing good. Women vote. The government is taking our land away to sell to rich gringos. The word *gringo* and the tone of its use reveal resentment against people still regarded as interlopers. These villagers are an unadjusted people—citizens, but outside the current of the state's life, and easily dominated politically. Hatred of the gringo is the undercurrent of many a politician's campaign; bossism, certainly no New Mexico invention, is easily founded on the traditional respect for the old Spanish *patrón*. Today he may be a descendant of the old hidalgo or a son of the sheep-herder or small farmer. He may even be a gringo. In any case the step from *patrón* to political boss was no step at all. And freedom from the *patrón*-boss is clearly related to a knowledge of English.

In so far, then, as half our population has been handicapped by lack of English, our Spanish patrimony—misused —has made New Mexico a backward state by any national standards. In literacy, individual income, and health we lag. After one hundred years as citizens of the United States, many New Mexicans do not speak English and are therefore unable to appreciate the best of our country or to protect themselves from its worst elements. This backwardness is not the fault of the Spanish-speaking villager. The really backward elements have always been, and still are, the powerful in politics, government, and even education.

Thoughtful educators admit that we have the teachers, the skills, and the will to learn that could give every New Mexican citizen a mastery of English within one school generation, twelve years. Yet this question is never brought before the legislature or mentioned in a political campaign. Most amazingly, it gets little attention from teachers, whose powerful lobby is most concerned with teachers' welfare. So education in New Mexico, where half the population is rural, Spanish-speaking, and Catholic, follows lines laid down long ago in New England. The child gets little that bears on his life at home. And the parent, too realistic to share the Nordic's blind faith in book learning, judges by results. Nina Otero, in *Old Spain in Our Southwest,* tells a charming tale of a boatman who was shamed by an educated traveler for not being schooled. Next day—as is the way of tales—the boat upset and the educated traveler, who could not swim, was sinking fast when the ignorant boatman rescued him.

Parents who, like the boatman, distrust schooling keep children out of school to work, to attend a fiesta or a funeral, or because the children do not want to go. The child's indifference is often due to sheer boredom. In many schools one teacher handles six or even eight grades. She may have half an hour a day, then, in which to give the pre-firsts a little English. For long hours they sit squirming under the assault of strange and incomprehensible words. No wonder they quit. As many as five thousand a year fall out before the third grade, the language of their country forever an unknown tongue. Of those who stay, many fall behind one grade, two grades, three grades. Then they are older than other children in their class. Frustrated, they leave school, still with no workable English, or they enter the ranks of pachucos—juvenile knife-fighters.

Equally short-sighted is our failure to teach Spanish in the lower grades, where the Spanish-speaking child should learn to read and write his parent's tongue and gain a respect for it. The English-speaking child might gain even more—a breadth of thought and appreciation sadly lacking now. So we throw away our state's truest distinction—that it is the only state in the union truly bilingual and bicultural—and make instead a state with a split personality and many unnecessary problems. This is our heritage not from the Spanish, but from the ignorant invaders from the States. Ralph Emerson Twitchell, in his *Leading Facts of New Mexico History*, tells us that Missouri troops tossed out of the government buildings official papers that they could not have read even in English. William A. Pile, Governor from 1869 to 1870, had his servants haul off old papers that offended his Protestantism by reference to "His Most Catholic Majesty." This tale is suggestive, though it may be apochryphal. But irreplaceable papers blew about Santa Fe's dusty streets or were used to wrap meat or chewing tobacco. Later Governors pleaded with Congress for as little as $15,000 to translate documents that were piled in dusty heaps or sinking into sodden masses under leaky roofs, and were refused. Don Donaciano Vigil, custodian of land records, managed to salvage enough to make property records fairly complete. And W. H. H. Davis, first U.S. Attorney, and later acting Governor, saved what he could. He later produced one of New Mexico's classics, *El Gringo*. But such educated and appreciative men were rare on our frontier.

Yet thanks to a few people of good taste, largely writers and artists, many features of the old Spanish life have been brought back to enrich our lives. In architecture, decoration, and dress, as well as in speech and food, the modern state is the colony's heir. This is especially true of building.

Transients may overlook really luxurious homes on the hills outside Taos, Santa Fe, or Albuquerque because they sit close to earth instead of looming grandly above it. These copy the houses that had to be fortresses as well as homes. This long, low adobe structure, simple to the point of poverty, but in line with the current taste for the functional and unadorned, promises to become a stereotype as unalterable as the mid-Victorian house.

Stern necessity determined this architecture. Adobe was the only material at hand, and Indians knew how to make sun-dried bricks with straw and lay them up with mud. For protection, they made walls too thick for an arrow to pierce, and inner courtyards where women could work in safety and animals could be loaded. This patio was entered through a *zaguan* wide enough for *carretas* and carriages, but well protected by a ten-foot gate of thick boards held together by iron bars. Windows, even after glass came in, were closed by solid barred shutters. Before the railroad came there was little glass: small sheets of mica let some light through. Floors were of adobe; Spaniards learned from the Pueblos how to harden them with oxblood. Indian, too, was the corner fireplace, made to take upright sticks, and perfect on the draw.

The gentleman's house differed from the peasant's only in size and decoration. The peon's hut, like the Indian's, was only as wide as the length of the piñon or cedar beams growing near by, but the rich hidalgo could send his peons to the mountains for tall trees to roof rooms fifteen or twenty feet wide. Often they were adorned with carving on exposed beams and corbels, and painted with the earth colors so hard to reproduce with modern paint. Such houses graciously adjust to different ways. Walls too thick for arrows are now pierced by French doors and picture windows that seem suitable enough; the *zaguan* is now a heated entrance-hall, floored with hardwood, waxed tile, or brick; and the patio is still completely right for a climate of strong sun and stiff winds.

Set among the modern furnishings are a few wobbly, hand-hewn cupboards and benches, and Navajo rugs or Chimayo blankets bought in curio shops, looted from old houses and churches, or copied by enterprising merchants. All reflect the dire poverty of the Spanish frontier, but also the people's overmastering desire to retain the amenities of a life known elsewhere.

The *rico* brought from Mexico as much as he could load on a burro or a *carreta*. That amounted to a few painted chests, pictures of the saints which could be rolled, sacred statues, and mirrors. Imagine the excitement when the family saw these treasures unwrapped from blankets and skins! For the ladies came lace mantillas, the Chinese embroidered shawls that we call "Spanish," delicate embroideries from Manila, jewels—gold filigree from Mexican craftsmen and whatever had come from Paris, London, or Madrid—and clothes.

In Santa Fe, a week or two before the annual Fiesta, descendants of those ladies parade in elegant costumes brought a century and more ago from Europe capitals. Nothing of lady's, gentleman's, or child's wardrobe failed to reach New Mexico. If its style was a year or two late, that mattered to nobody.

On the whole life was austere, and most of its appurtenances home-made. Lewis Garrard, who wrote *Wah-to-Yah* at the age of nineteen, described the Taos home of Ceran St. Vrain, who, as a rich merchant on the Santa Fe Trail, probably had more than most. "A handsomely furnished room with a fireplace in one corner and walls hung with portraits of holy characters and crosses. . . . At supper I sat at table and ate potatoes for the first time in several months. . . . A mattress was unrolled from the wall where in daytime it served as a seat, and I turned in between sheets. Yes, sheets! A house, a table, vegetables, and sheets!" But there was no bedstead and probably no chair. Chests, benches, and stools would have served. They serve now as coffee tables or occasionals.

Women working in the patio made sheets of home-grown cotton and stuffed mattresses with wool kept fresh and fluffy by many washings and sunnings. Weaving was man's work, but women did the long-stitch wool embroidery we call *colcha* because it was used on bedspreads. Illiterate women with quick eyes for color and form copied Chinese or East Indian designs on chests, and their skilled fingers turned out pieces of true artistry.

Other specialists made clothes. Women wore the full, short cotton skirts that New Mexico scorned until they were imported from Mexico and sold in shops to Eastern women. They were topped by the low-necked blouse that shocked newcomers. Both Garrard and W. H. H. Davis protested that more concealment would be more seductive. But the dark cotton rebozo provided concealment as desired, as well as shade, some warmth, and coquetry ad lib. This was the peasant woman's dress. The lady, who may have dressed so at home, went abroad wrapped in a *tápalo*, a fine black cashmere shawl with heavy knotted silk fringe. The *tápalo* has disappeared only within the last generation. Even now one may see an old lady so muffled slipping into a church. For feast days the *patrona* wore her imported finery, as she does now.

Smoking was another feminine grace. Ladies carried their tobacco, *punche*, and cornhusk wrappings in tiny silver bottles and boxes, and rolled their own. The puritanical Davis was shocked, but young Garrard found that "smoking certainly does enhance the charms of the Mexican señoritas who, with neatly rolled up shucks between their coral lips, perpetrate winning smiles." Newcomers were staggered too by the general habit of protecting the complexion by smearing it with red clay. Mr. Davis found this "no less than disgusting." But before the *baile* the red was washed off and replaced by a heavy white powder made of ground bones.

Men's serapes and trousers were home-made, as were the white drawers emerging from the plantaloons' side split. Leatherworkers on the ranches made high boots that served as chaps. They even made saddles, though the hidalgo's finest boots and saddles came from Mexico, as did his flat Spanish hat with chin strap. Resident silversmiths made buttons for the hidalgo's clothes and heavy ornaments for the horse's trappings, as well as household ware.

Table service consisted of bowls, plates, and platters; cups, goblets, and ewers; spoons, forks, and ladles. Knives did not appear; food was served in pieces that could be managed with fork and spoon. Much of this fine silverware has been lost, traded for china when the Yankee came in, melted down, or abandoned as worthless. One of the finest bowls known was found outdoors with chickens drinking from it. But the silver gleam caught Mrs. Field's eye through the blackened filth, and she bought it. This was Mary Lester Field, who in 1886 brought from her Tennessee home an unerring eye for the beautiful and, as a young matron in Albuquerque, began a collection that has few equals. She found goblets that had long served in kitchens, spoons and forks rubbed sideways by scraping on iron pots, cups marked by babies' teeth, and beakers that had been banged on heavy tables. When it became known that she was buying, many pieces were smuggled to her under heavy *tápalos* at night by impoverished old ladies.

This fine collection now belongs to the University of New Mexico, where visitors may see it. While hallmarks are hard to read, some appear to be Spanish; others are easily identified as Mexican because Mexican work was severely plain and quite unlike the ornate Spanish styles of the time.

The meals served in rich homes on silver pieced out by pottery, and in poor homes on pottery without silver, were the original of today's "Mexican food." It was better then because it was made more slowly. Corn softened in lye, hand-ground, and patted into tortillas to serve fresh from the hot stone has a richer taste than mill-ground meal. Beans simmered all day and all night in a pot set deep in hot ashes have a savor worthy of the spicy sauce. Meat dressed with many lesser herbs as well as the ubiquitous chile, and cooked until all is well blended has flavor no electric stove can impart. And wheaten loaves baked in outdoor ovens come out with a thick crust you can still crunch in a pueblo where Indian women prefer to bake that way.

This was the diet: mutton, beef, poultry, varied by game; corn, and beans. A little wheat was raised and some rice was shipped in. Vegetables were mostly used as flavoring, but fruits appeared fresh in season and dried the rest of the year.

Although the diet was limited, provision was lavish; families were large and hospitality was boundless. Any passerby was welcomed as an honored guest. The beautiful Spanish phrase "this is your house" was certainly true as long as a guest stayed in it. Such a home was the hacienda of Colonel Manuel Chaves at San Mateo. Frances Douglas de Kalb, who visited there in the 1890's with her husband, Charles Fletcher Lummis, remembered "spaciousness, vast acreage, and a great house, always immaculate and with many guests there. The kitchen was filled with happy and willing servants." One was called La Cautiva (the captive) because she had been taken in a raid on Indians and had become loved as a member of the family. "The mother Doña Vicenta was as fine a woman as I ever met. She was deeply religious, prayers in the house were frequent." Like all such ladies, Doña Vicenta was supreme in her home. Her children stood until given permission to sit, kissed her hand at greeting and parting, never smoked in her presence. As *patrona* she commanded all the serving women and men about the house. Keys hung at her belt, and she unlocked storerooms and cupboards.

Lummis, himself, was struck by less housewifely matters. In letters to the *Chillicothe* (Ohio) *Leader* in 1885, he described the house as having a wide central hallway. The influence of the States was shown, too, in flowered wallpaper on adobe walls, Brussels carpets, lace curtains at long windows, paintings, mirrors, and heavy walnut furniture. This was the typical rich home after trade with the States was safe. Young Lummis grew most lyrical over the charms of the Chaves daughters "with orbs of jet . . . wherein a little devil lurked" and their skill at the piano and in song. With evenings and firelight, songs in English and Spanish, gay games and dances, crisp cakes and wine, no wonder the youth thought he could have stayed a lifetime.

Such scenes marked the end of the old, the beginning of

the new. But much of the old was to linger long. The two sons of this family, Amado and Ireneo, law graduates of George Washington University and quite of the modern world, were still stately Spanish gentlemen whose backs never relaxed even in old age. The daughters, educated in feminine arts by mother and nuns, stayed in the traditional life.

That life was gay enough. Even in Don Pedro Pino's day, heavy coaches lumbered over wheel-cut tracks, carrying ladies from hacienda to hacienda. Marriages arranged in family council led to extensive entertaining. Festivals in celebration of Christmas, Mardi Gras, Easter, and saints' days often lasted for weeks. Fiestas illustrated the democracy-with-aristocracy that is Spain's great gift to civilized living. However autocratic the *patrón*, however meekly the peon kissed his hand and took his orders, there was an easy camaraderie between them. The Don and Doña attended the village church or invited the villagers to their private chapel. They all danced at the *bailes*, and the singers, caroling impromptu verses, freely poked fun at the greatest and grandest.

The *bailes*, or fandangoes, are by no means gone, just changed. Hardwood floors have replaced hard earth or boards rubbed with tallow; electric lights, the tallow dips; and name-orchestras, the old *música*: fiddler, guitarist, and accordionist. But the smooth, swift grace of the dancers is unchanged. And many of the old dances are college favorites now, not only in New Mexico, but as far away as Massachusetts, where a couple of Harvard students from Santa Fe made them popular. Prime favorite is *La Varsoviana*, a coquettish sort of schottische said to have been taken from Warsaw to Spain by Napoleon's troops, and so to Mexico. But college students quickly learn others too, and many are popular.

Among the losses we deplore is the *trobador*. The impromptu singer is rare nowadays, but *corridos*, ballads, are a natural folk-expression still. A crime, an accidental killing, the virtues of a political candidate, especially the fate of soldiers, are occasions for a song. One *corrido* popular near Albuquerque recites in sixteen verses the tale of Lieutenant Eloy Baca, who was killed in Germany. Another rather sadly reflects the need of the Spanish-speaking citizen to prove himself.

> *Me voy de soldado razo*
> *Y cuando me halle en compañía*
> *Muy lejos ya de mi tierra*
> *Les probaré que mi raza*
> *Sabe morir donde quiera.*

> I go as a soldier of my race
> And when I find myself with others
> Far from my homeland
> I shall prove to them that my race
> Knows how to die anywhere.

Still unnoticed by our English-speaking population, these folksongs attract students to a wealth of music and verse, sometimes related to mediæval European songs, but a truly indigenous art too. They are secular, religious, ribald, sentimental, and occasional.

Equally unappreciated are the old morality plays, written long ago by missionaries to instruct their Indian converts. *Los Moros y Los Cristianos*, which opened in San Juan in 1598, still runs in many places, but most dramatically in San Juan. A swashbuckling version of the defeat of the Moors in Spain, it is often played on horseback with Moors in miters and floating ribbons, Spaniards in helmets and armor, all bearing lances and equally proficient in handling their quick ponies. A fresco of this spirited encounter, painted by

Dorothy Stewart, suitably adorns Albuquerque's Little Theatre.

Many villages present favorite plays annually. *Adán y Eva* is performed during Lent in Atrisco near Albuquerque. *El Niño Perdido*, about the Christ Child disputing with the elders, has kept many a bright boy out of school in Cañón de Taos to learn the long actionless role of the Child.

The play of plays widely performed at Christmas time is *Los Pastores*, a simple tale of the shepherds following the star to Bethlehem. As Mary sings a tender lullaby, gifts are brought not by kings bearing frankincense and myrrh, but by ragged shepherds offering the new baby blankets and other warm things for his comfort. New Mexico villagers understand a poor mother and child in a stable. But they can also burlesque human indolence in Bartolo, a shepherd just too sleepy to go see the miraculous Child.

From such poor but reverent people comes New Mexico's beautiful custom of holiday lights. Long ago flat roofs glowed on Christmas Eve with rows of rosy lanterns, paper sacks holding candles set in sand. Before the people had paper sacks, they built tiny fires on the roofs or in front of the houses, as the Indians still do in Taos, to light the Christ Child on his way. These were the *luminarias*. Purists prefer to call the lighted sacks *faroles* (lanterns). But so many people have learned to say *luminarias* that the word has become part of our common speech. The custom has been generally adopted not only for Christmas, but for other holidays as well.

A curious survival not yet fully understood is the dance drama *Los Matachines*. Given in both Spanish villages and Indian pueblos, it seems to reflect the struggle between good, in the person of a white veiled child, and evil, amusingly portrayed by a man with horns and a tail. Features of its costuming suggest Morocco; it may be related to the morris dancing of old England. *Los Matachines* is widely known throughout the Spanish world; it is danced in the Philippines, from where laborers have brought it to Hawaii. Perhaps in time it will return to the mainland on its long trail back to its source in Spain.

Los Matachines is danced every year in the Sandia Mountain village of San Antonio in fulfillment of a vow. Once, the villagers say, in an Apache raid the savages came in such hordes that not all the men in the village seemed able to stop them. Then suddenly San Antonio appeared among them as a child dressed in blue, and with his miraculous aid they drove off the attackers. After that the villagers built a chapel just were the saint had appeared, and promised to honor him with *Los Matachines* every year. Once, so village tradition tells, they neglected the dance, and the spring dried up. They have never neglected it since.

Modern life is not destroying this lovely legend. During World War II a San Antonio mother vowed that if her sons came home safely they would dance *Los Matachines*. In time they both returned from the European theater, safe and well. The pious mother had not lived to see the fulfillment of her vow, though the dutiful sons did, of course, take part in the dance on the next San Antonio day.

Persistent old superstitions are less gracious relics of Spain in New Mexico. As to witches and omens, it is hard to tell how much of our Spanish heritage is Indian. The two groups interchanged their phobias and their herb remedies as they mingled their habits and their bloodstreams. *Brujo* (witch) and *curandero* (curer) are common words in pueblo and town. An Albuquerque woman, blaming her pains on the bad offices of her sister-in-law, called on a *curandero* from Santo Domingo. An old *curandero* in Los Lunas makes a good living with herbs and spells; many of his patients are Isleta Indians. Owls are considered bad omens by both whites and Indians, and all tell tales of people malevolently turned into animals or birds. Fear of the evil eye is widespread: even a kindly gaze, too long or too intent, may cause a woman to cover her child's head and turn away.

This dark tide of fear rises even into educated classes and comes into courts of law. In the 1930's a man was tried for the murder of his wife. His defense was that only by killing her body could he save her soul from dark spells put upon her. Another man, a highly competent technician, paid a quack fifty dollars to prove that his bride's illness was caused by witchcraft, and another fifty to point out the witch. This the *curandero* did by showing the old woman's face in a broken egg. The man swore he saw it! They caught the witch by beating a black dog that ran along just ahead of the wagon. When they reached home, sure enough, the suspect was badly bruised! Knowledge of the evil's origin, as in our best psychiatric clinics, brought relief.

Strangers are often struck by the New Mexican's preference for suffering and horror, especially in his religion. It is as though a hard life in a harsh land had made violence natural. Old saints carved in wood, the *bultos*, or painted, the *santos*, realistically portray agonies and are plentifully bedecked with blood. This preoccupation, whatever its source, reaches its maximum in the observances of the Penitentes, properly called Los Hermanos de Luz (The Brothers of Light), which has been important in New Mexico since Oñate's day. Their self-flagellations are personal penance, but also penance offered as remission for the sins of the world. Such an Order naturally gained power when priests were few and their visits rare, and the *Hermano Mayor* read prayers from little notebooks that are still cherished. Naturally too, such an Order extended its influence into politics and the courts. It is still a common claim that no Penitente can be convicted of a crime where the Order is strong.

Approved by the Church for centuries, the Penitentes lost their clerical support in 1828, when most of the Franciscans, as loyal Spaniards, left the Mexican Republic.

Bishop Salpointe, successor to Archbishop Lamy, prohibited their appearances in the churches; later clerics condemned them altogether. But the Penitentes kept right on with their observances. Finally, in 1948, Archbishop Edwin V. Byrne extended to them the blessing and protection of the Catholic Church, provided the order "proceeds with moderation" under the Church's supervision.

In "the Penitente counties," the minor wailing of their flute, the *pito*, may be heard at intervals throughout the year. On visits to sick or dying brothers, the members shuffle along chanting to the *pito*'s plaint, one of the saddest, lonesomest sounds imaginable. During Lent men go often to the *morada*, set always away from the village.

This two-roomed adobe chapel may be recognized by its lack of windows and by heavy crosses leaning near. Hidden ceremonies within culminate in Holy Week, when the Brothers re-enact the Passion. Accompanied by the *pito*, flagellants move in slow procession, their heads hidden in black sacks, their bare backs bleeding under the yucca lash and redly soaking their white cotton drawers. Bare feet are tortured on stones and thorns. No man cries out. One bears the heavy cross, falling as Jesus did, and often taking lashes from his fellows. Within memory, the *Cristo* was tied to the cross and left hanging there for minutes. Our grandfathers remembered seeing men nailed to the cross. There are reports of deaths and the tradition that a man's shoes, left on his doorstep, were the family's notice that he had died in holy penance.

Penitentes are religious men, performing rites full of meaning for them. Much has been written about them. The best account, factual and sympathetic at once, is *Brothers of Light* by Alice Corbin Henderson. Her husband, William Penhallow Henderson, enhanced the text with drawings that convey well the poignance of simple men in a stern land, seeking. A recurrent phrase in one of their chants is

"*Dénos, Señor, buena muerte*" (Give us, Lord, a good death), as though only death could compensate for a life so hard. But the final note is one of joyous hope. After a midnight ceremony of black terror, noise of chains and rattles, groans, and the slapping of wet whips, there comes suddenly a knocking on the door. "Who knocks?" On the answer "*Jesu Cristo!*" the door is opened, candles are lit, and the hours and days of torment yield to the glory of holy Saturday and the promise of Easter.

These ceremonies may be seen. Visitors who come with reverence and good manners are not turned away. Real friends may be invited in; prayers are offered for them.

So our Spanish heritage offers enrichment to those who have eyes to see, wit to use. Even those who have no Spanish blood nor any claim to conquering ancestors may enjoy the widening view of another language popularly spoken and the culture that made it. Much beauty comes to us from our Spanish heritage, not only in material things we can use and in mediæval folkways we can enjoy, but also in manners we could adopt with profit. New Mexico is, too, the sensitive point at which the two American cultures meet, overlap, and amalgamate. But often the effort at amalgamation is rough and ugly. Human beings are not yet civilized enough to let this union develop as beautifully as it should. Too often we have let our Spanish heritage hamper rather than help us.

XVI

THE NEW NEW MEXICAN

New Mexico's most pressing problem is that faced by our citizens whose mother tongue is Spanish. In a sense it is a problem of Americanization, but in this case the foreign of language and custom were here first and in large majority, a lead they retained for a century; it is estimated that in 1950 the Spanish-speaking citizens formed about forty per cent of the population. A century ago, when the United States took New Mexico over from Mexico, it honorably declared all the inhabitants citizens with the right to vote, to freedom of religion, and to property. No provision was made to teach English to the new citizens, and English was the basic need—the tool for building a new life, the weapon and shield against dishonorable men who followed the honorable government. The only excuse is that it was fifty years too soon. At the end of the century, Puerto Rico and the Philippines were given opportunities that would have put New Mexico fifty years ahead of where it is now.

In the twentieth century the Spanish-speaking people are themselves beginning to solve their own problem of adjusting to new ways of life and thought and of realizing themselves as American citizens without either humility or arrogance. The touchiness of the matter—and of some people —is indicated by New Mexico's nervousness about names and hyphens. Only here nobody rests quite securely as an "American." If you are not a Spanish-American or "Hispano," you are an Anglo-American or "Anglo." This latter group includes Irish, Italians, Germans, Eastern Europeans,

Scandinavians, Asiatics, and, most aptly after all, Negroes.
A Negro bootblack, asked what was being paid for votes
this year, answered: "I dunno, boss, they ain't got round to
us Anglos yet."

The word *Mexican*, so proudly borne by a great people,
is taboo in New Mexico. Only a young man, highly educated, rich, and related to distinguished families in Mexico,
can say: "Don't call me Spanish-American. I'm American,
and I'm Mexican, and proud of both!" The word *Mexican*
is commonly held to imply the disrespect or condescension
accorded to inferiors. It was countered by the derogatory
word *gringo*. Originally probably it meant only "for-
eigner"; the manner of its expression could make it a fighting word. But nowadays the unfitness of Anglo is so apparent that gringo is used quite easily.

When the Americans first came into New Mexico—and a
heterogeneous lot they were—there was no doubt what they
were, nor any doubt that the people they found here, even
while New Mexico was still a Spanish colony, were Mexicans. No problem of nomenclature arose—unless some New
Mexicans, understanding Mexico's revolt from Spain, dis-
liked being called Spanish, as Mexicans, Cubans, and many
other Americans still do. In 1898 the uninformed wondered
if people of Spanish heritage would fight against Spain.
They were eager to, volunteered in numbers, and made a
fine record as Rough Riders. Teddy Roosevelt delighted to
honor them, often visited New Mexico, appointed Miguel
Antonio Otero governor of the state, and stood sponsor for
Theodore Roosevelt Armijo.

So far Mexican was a name no man need be ashamed of.
Old newspaper files contain the most adulatory obituaries
of Mexican gentlemen. But by 1918 the whole country was
hyphenized. German-American was not desirable; many
weaklings changed their German names. French-American,
on the other hand, was fine. And Spanish-American was in-

vented when Four Minute Men, lauding the readiness of Mexican boys to go off to fight, were reminded that they were not Mexican nationals, but Americans like anybody else. So the Four Minute Men agreed and the newspapers concurred that Spanish-American it should be. And so it is

This naming is awkward; it becomes paradoxical when it is applied to Mexican nationals coming into New Mexico. How depressing for a Mexican citizen to be assured that his former nation is unworthy, that he must refuse to be called by its name.

Other problems are more pressing as young people learn English and take on new ways. The old dependence upon the *patrón* and the old fatalism are weakening. The phrase *"Dios lo quiere,"* God wills it, is being superseded by "I'll not let that happen again," as up-and-coming young people are developing by their own efforts into citizens any state could be proud of.

This new New Mexican may be the son of an hidalgo, but he is more apt to be the son of a villager. Often related to the big-house family, he was more like the European small farmer than like the mediæval serf. But the enterprising youngster may well be the grandson of the peon or even the slave. If so, he may suffer from New Mexico's brand of snobbery. A lady tickles her ego by referring to people of her surname but of humble origin as *"esos indios"* (those Indians). One politician describes his hearers as descendants of Spanish grandees and himself as son of a sheep-herder who made good. Thus he bows at once to Spanish pride and the log-cabin tradition.

Some politicians take advantage of the old reverence for the *patrón*, and are not above winning votes by arousing resentment against gringos. Though slavery ended with the Fourteenth Amendment and peonage was abolished—on paper—by suitable New Mexico legislation, the old ways clung. Ignorant people, confused by the new laws and given no chance to learn English, continued to work for the *patrón*, to do as he said, to borrow from him. Debt peonage persisted. It may still persist. It is common practice to prepay sheep-herders and other workers. It is not uncommon for a powerful politician rancher to jail workmen who have taken the advance but have failed to show up on the job. But the most un-American hangover was the persistence of the *patrón* as the political boss.

Recently a rancher who employed some sixty workers was invited to a meeting: they must know how the *patrón* wished them to vote. The rancher, innocent of our Spanish heritage, seized the opportunity to make what he thought an effective speech on the importance of the vote and the voter's independence. The men listened respectfully, but after the gringo had walked away one followed him. "Señor," he said, "you are right. That was a fine speech. But who pays us our dollar?"

It is a rare aspirant for office who refuses to take advantage of such a situation. In fact, New Mexico's political habits, so folksy and so funny, are due to the use of this handy political weapon by both parties. Nor is this a proper complaint against the gringo. He merely followed the lead and learned the techniques of the old Spanish families in dealing with their people. The Spanish word for people, *gente*, has a special connotation in New Mexico. The don's *gente* do as he says.

With the U.S. occupation, the rich dons—many of whom had already been educated in the States—easily overcame the language difficulty, intermarried with the newcomers, and merged so completely with them that strangers studying New Mexico often do not recognize them as Spanish. Such men went into politics and were clever at it. The don could deliver the county or precinct vote unfailingly, and was rewarded with a fair share of offices. But it is notable that the Spanish-speaking counties were not favored in the distribution of political plums, in spite of the fact that Spanish-speaking voters were in the majority until the middle 1930's. Perhaps the political *patrón* was not clever enough; more likely he was closer to the thinking of the aristocratic Spanish hidalgo than to the American faith in an enlightened citizenry. Even bosses from the poorer groups, as they delivered the vote and gained power, married the pretty daughter or sister of the real don and became *patrones* themselves. Such men did nothing to inculcate democratic ideas in their less fortunate neighbors and little to protect them from political or financial exploitation.

Nor did the Church, preoccupied with spiritual matters and distressed to see the Protestant churches making converts, make any unified effort to teach English. Bishop Lamy opened a school for boys in 1850, and a few others followed, but only those who could pay attended these schools. A few bright youngsters learned good English in Protestant mission schools, where it was emphasized. But both Protestant ministers and Catholic priests preached in Spanish. Many still do, though in some cases they have been forced to turn to English by young members of their congregations. So the mass of the population was left trapped in a foreign language and ideology. New Mexico's public school system dates from 1891, but for many years teachers were often political appointees who spoke English poorly or not at all. Before World War I many counties had no high schools. Consequently few students reached college, and few educated leaders with democratic ideas appeared to offset the old domination by the *patrón*.

As new *patrones* rose to power, many young dons who could not adjust to the American pattern slipped into a less favored position. Rich young men, knowing that if a storm wiped out ten thousand sheep there would be more sheep, used to finding plenty of money in the strongbox, and believing that work was degrading and close trading un-

worthy of a gentleman, were at a sad disadvantage against
frontier lawyers with a tradition of hard work, canny trading, and long saving. So the young hidalgo (literally, son of
somebody)—when his horse failed to win, or gambling debts
piled up—could easily find some son of nobody from "the
States" ready to make a loan or at least to talk business. Such
talks usually concerned the family grant.

Gringos on the make found the land-grant situation most
interesting—and profitable. The United States had guaranteed to recognize all existing valid land claims. In case of a
Spanish or Mexican grant, an act of Congress was necessary, but Congress was generally lenient and most claims
were allowed. But lands had been poorly surveyed or not
surveyed at all; often boundaries were described by such
perishable landmarks as trees, ditches, and adobe walls; not
infrequently ownership had devolved, through the years,
upon dozens—even hundreds—of heirs. Many cases were in
the courts for years, especially after 1890, when Congress
wearied of grant cases and set up the Court of Private Land
Claims. Many lawyers now became specialists in land-grant
cases. Often the attorney worked for a contingent fee, accepting part of the grant for his services. It was not unknown—if terms were not too well defined at the start or if
a case took many years—for the lawyer to end as owner of
the whole grant. Some lawyers actually ended their lives
land-poor.

Cases of community grants were the most complicated.
Here ignorance of the new laws was often decisive, especially ignorance of American tax procedure. Owners of
grants could sign a "petition for partition," which permitted
selling the grant and paying off the owners in cash. Getting
such petitions became almost a profession. Spanish-speaking
men, often briefless lawyers, would reach every heir—those
in the penitentiary and the insane asylum, as well as university professors and men doing well in the East. Then a

sale was held. The instigator of the affair might be the only bidder on the courthouse steps. One more grant would go into gringo hands, and more landowners would become seekers for day labor at low wages.

This is not ancient history; it is a recurring scene. As late as 1950 grants were still bought for 35 cents an acre when assessed valuation was $1.04 an acre for grazing land, as high as $6.00 an acre for cultivated plots. The biggest upset of recent years came through the Middle Rio Grande Conservancy District, which bonded landowners for an elaborate program of draining ditches and flood control. Many owners could not meet the payments, and their farms are now owned by gringos who work in Albuquerque.

Now and again village people have held onto their grant. Chilili in the Manzano Mountains, far in arrears on taxes, was advised by the county agricultural agent to take legal advice, and its lawyer negotiated a Farm Security Loan. Chilili then paid up its back taxes and the people owned their own grant; they then began to market the yield of their forest lands through a co-operative. Thus the United States, one hundred years late, is at long last helping its New Mexico citizens to keep their lands and help themselves.

But there are few Chililis and thousands of displaced villagers. In town they try valiantly to Americanize themselves without such aid as eastern cities offer the immigrant. An overgrown boy, guyed on the playground for his accent, turns ugly and ends in juvenile court. A girl, resentful of her old-fashioned family, evades their control, runs the streets, and comes eventually to the Welfare Home. Most parents try to help; many struggle hard to speak English at home, hoping their children will have no accent.

One mother, believing in progress but in parental control too, required her children—sons as well as daughters—to turn all their wages over to her. She administered the family budget cannily, bought plain food, and worked hard: she acquired oilcloth for the kitchen, scatter rugs and standing lamps for the living-room, better dishes, and mechanical aids —all bought on the installment plan. She could not explain her policy in English, but what she said was: "I want my children to have the best, and when they have payments to meet they do not waste their money."

Many such families, trying to get ahead, meet discrimination in getting jobs. New Mexico has a better record of fair dealing than many states, but a native daughter must admit —with shame—that even here good people are often hurt and hampered by prejudice. This is most true in counties settled by people from the southern states and those in which the evangelical churches are strongest. New Mexico is fighting a battle for decency. The question is: will the old easy tolerance of our grandfathers be blotted out by hordes of newcomers, or will there be among the newcomers enough people of good feeling to offset the prejudice of those who know no better?

Despite manifold handicaps the young Spanish-speaking citizen is forging ahead, becoming a new New Mexican. And he is doing it in the best American style, by individual initiative, courage, and brains. This is nothing new: always, in New Mexico as elsewhere, the class that seemed doomed to be forever poor and ignorant has produced a few individuals who could force themselves up and out. First they thought the only way to get ahead was through politics, so they played politics, demanding certain offices for men with Spanish names. Young lawyers, fearing they would never get the fat fees, sought political appointment. Some left the state to practice in eastern states. Few stuck it out at home, weathering the lean years as any young lawyer must expect to weather them. Business was easier. Many enterprising men, owning a village store and handling sheep as a sideline, made a comfortable living and sent their children to eastern schools. But New Mexico still had no strong middle class of Spanish heritage.

World War I made some change. Youths who had been no farther from home than Ranchos or Arroyo Hondo saw foreign lands and great cities. Many brought home medals or citations for bravery; most importantly, they brought home the realization that they were American citizens. But the burden of ignorance was still heavy. Few could speak fluent English. The real advance was to come through tragedy.

A professor of sociology said: "I'm a Republican, but I must admit that the Republican party consistently played the old *patrón* game. Their machines won elections by subsidizing local leaders to bring in the vote. But when the depression struck and people were desperate for jobs and food, the old system broke down and federal agencies took over. For the first time simple people found help in their government. Of course it made the state Democratic at one stroke; but best of all it broke the power of the bosses and developed young local leaders."

Here, at long last, was government helping the poor man, not—as one old villager said—"helping the rich to rob the poor of their meagerness." Scrawny, sullen boys grew sturdy and busy in CCC camps. Older men, shy and hesitant before a teacher, were won by a matter-of-fact approach, and enrolled in literacy classes to the number of 1,474. Fortunately the work was directed by Mrs. Adelina Otero Warren, herself a balanced product of two cultures, and she based the courses on actual vocabulary needs and taught teachers to meet their classes with old-fashioned dignity. As one result, many older men subscribed for newspapers, and five hundred unschooled youngsters were able to sign up for the draft as literates.

PWA projects provided work, reduced hazards on highways, and built many needed public buildings, as well as some buildings of a highly private nature. One privy bore the legend "PWA Project." But the WPA contributed even more to Americanization than the PWA. The WPA music project, directed by Mrs. Helen Chandler Ryan, published a *New Mexico Song and Game Book* that carried our customs far. Many choruses and orchestras earned small fame at home, and one singer of old songs became a night-club success in New York. But the most important result of the WPA program was that New Mexicans got, for the first time, the true American idea that poverty was no insurmountable handicap and no disgrace; that a man needed no *patrón*; that if presidents have come from log cabins and captains of industry from work gangs, so could presidents come from adobe huts and tycoons from sheep camps. New Mexico was beginning to develop its own valid and solid middle class.

One young man, son of a family that had lost its land grant and of a father who believed in education, found the going hard. "In high school I began to run with a gang. We all felt queer because of our accent, we wanted obscurely to get even. I might have gone bad if things hadn't got so tight at home; there really wasn't much to eat. So my brother and I stood in line and signed up for the CCC. It was a fine experience. And when they moved me out to make room for others, I got a WPA job and then a wife. . . . A Spanish wife! My mother had warned us never to marry a *gringa*; she said gringas only wanted what they could get out of a man, but a true Spanish wife would help him to get ahead. Mine certainly did. She kept her job and insisted I finish at the University. Then the war came and I worked in Relocation Centers and finally in Japan. I'm not allowed to say much about that." This veteran graduated and became a teacher. Working nights, he took an advanced degree in philosophy. He needs philosophy when ignorant and prejudiced parents protest having their children taught by him because he is an Hispano. He says he has no trouble with children, but only with parents. But even parents can learn.

One parent who protested at his son's riding in a bus driven by a Spanish-speaking man and filled with Spanish-speaking children, was referred to the school principal, our friend with the degree in philosophy. Although he looked altogether gringo, his Spanish name gave pause to the father, who demanded to see the county superintendent. But when he heard there the same Spanish name and found the superintendent a suave and amused American gentleman proud of his long Spanish ancestry, the gringo decided to accept the queer ways of this new state.

Such a superintendent has his difficulties with old style politicos too; they demand teaching posts for "our people," regardless of qualifications. One superintendent met this by outlining the qualifications of two applicants; one well-trained, the other not. "Which would you choose to teach your children?" So the one from Ohio got the job over the school board president's niece. But the pressure is great. Another superintendent offended Spanish parents when he proposed pre-school classes to teach their children English. Discrimination was the cry. But he won, to the children's great advantage. Children love to learn English. One tiny tot who had been too shy to play with English-speaking children—whose parents hoped he would swap languages with them—was their first visitor when they came home after months away. Bounding into their house with eyes shining, the little fellow cried: "How do you do, Mrs. B? How do you do, Mr. B? Welcome home! Now I can speak English."

Shyness and a proud desire to avoid discrimination often act as bars quite as effective as the occasional discrimination that undeniably exists. Some employers refuse to hire men with Spanish names; certain labor unions have barred them openly or connived to keep them overlong as apprentices. During World War II a PX at an army camp in New Mex-

ico advertised for clerks, stating: "Only Anglos need apply."
The Governor of New Mexico, showered with protests, referred them to the Commanding Officer of the military district, who had it corrected at once. But private
groups cannot be so easily controlled. On occasion, even
church groups have made Spanish converts so uncomforta-
ble that they have ceased to attend services. Apprehensive
of such slights, members of a Spanish Protestant church declined to attend a party given by an English-speaking congregation of the same faith. These are the difficulties—personal as well as social—which the new New Mexican meets.
But his problems are not as important as are the gallantry,
determination, and humor with which he is solving them.

Some New Mexicans, aided if not abetted by sentimental
sympathizers and designing politicians, make rather a profession of their woes. Too many would-be leaders, even if
they take off with *"nuestro glorioso pasado,"* pass quickly
on from "our glorious past" to a dreary present in which
our "poor people" are forever put upon. Their followers
naturally demand certain political jobs as their right, expect to pass easily through schools as some politico's appointees, and lay every failure not to their own fault but
to nasty discrimination. They are least concerned with improving their fitness.

This group is more than offset by the new New Mexican
who has no time for repining and whose pride is in himself,
not in his ancestors. So we had forebears on horseback?
Fine! So we had others that were hard put to it to eat? Not
so good, but true. But we refuse to bask in a warm nostalgic
glow over past glories or to melt into tears over our poverty,
past or present. Such young men and women squirm at being considered pitiful and helpless. They repudiate such
books as George Sanchez's *Forgotten People*, dealing with
the seamier side of life in Taos County. "Don't you believe
a word of it!" cries one of them.

These spunkier New Mexicans find several solutions. Some of them get up and get out. It may be no farther than to the nearest town, a vocational training school, or where-ever they can obtain whatever it takes to qualify as a good workman. They are found in factories, stores, business, and the professions from coast to coast, in universities in this country and other countries, and with business firms or government service in foreign lands, where their Spanish and natural suavity are great assets. These often brilliant men and women have certainly deprived New Mexico and their own villages of leadership. Others may be just as lost by staying at home to play the old-fashioned political game. Those who portend the best for the state's future are making a career of working at home. They include the best educators, and workers in public health, agriculture, and home economics. Their policy is well expressed by a few of them.

Ernesto Gutierrez, agricultural graduate and county agent, says: "Our job is to live at home, plant recommended seeds, control pests, spray and fertilize, practice rotation. Save our land, improve it, use it!" Slim and hard, in tight blue jeans, field boots, and a tall hat, he drives his own car because the county does not provide one, visits every farm, and helps everywhere. He grows enthusiastic over every evidence of sound farming; but, as the county has no demonstration agent, he is just as proud of a cellarful of canned food as of a good job of contour plowing or ditch grading. Here is a smart and snappy young American who believes in production, improvements, and self-help. He considers it his job to reduce the number of poor people by helping every one to dig his own acres and make them produce to capacity. His enthusiasm is a refreshing sight.

Such young people work hard with Parent-Teacher Associations, 4-H Clubs, co-operatives, and Soil Conservation districts, and promote rural electrification. Their protégés often win state and even national prizes. They do not favor

Spanish-speaking children, but who would not be proud when a village girl in Rio Arriba County spells down the state and goes to Washington, or a Doña Ana County girl sees her Spanish name lead for state president of the 4-H Clubs?

Many such youngsters go on to vocational schools or to college. Those who cannot, have learned the priceless lesson of self-confidence and the value of old-fashioned ways that prevailed in the villages long ago: hard work, thrift, and dependability. Like their grandfathers, they pay their bills. If they go to town they are likely to become good workmen rather than whiners.

Gilbert Lopez worked up to be foreman in a foundry and is slowly building his own home. It took three years to floor the living-room, and his wife decided on steel casement windows before a bathroom. Now she has both. They had rented out an extra room during those three years, and had saved the money for these improvements. "If I can do it," he says, "anybody can."

Joe Rivera, who ran away from home to go to school and worked his way from the age of fourteen, became an organizer in the sawmill workers' union and was elected state president of the American Federation of Labor.

The young people who get to college are most articulate about their handicaps and how they are overcoming them. As county high schools were established, more and more young people from poor families enrolled in state universities. There they met many difficulties because they spoke English with a Spanish accent and because they were poor. Few were invited to join fraternities and sororities, though young people of Spanish families of wealth and social glamor became "Greeks." The discrimination is social and snobbish. In any case, these adolescent standards have had little effect on returning GI's seeking an education.

One veteran, studying law and planning to run for county sheriff after graduation, said: "Fraternities don't bother me. I've got all the friends I need. Besides, I've got a wife and two kids and a political machine to build."

Girl students show more sensitiveness than the men. One Spanish-speaking girl, working her way through college, said: "Something that happened in high school made me realize that I might be considered not acceptable. So I didn't accept any sorority invitations. I think many Spanish girls do that." This girl, pretty, dainty, exquisitely turned out, is most successful in an exacting departmental job. Others like her take honors in class, go on to graduate work, but hold apart in quiet dignity.

Men students are preparing for the professions—education, law, pharmacy, medicine. If they contemplate business it is as a means to an end. One told a success story the equal of any. "I was born," he said, "in a tiny mountain hamlet where I never heard English. My father took us to town for school, but in high school I still had to translate every question into Spanish in my mind, think of the answer in Spanish and translate that into English. By that time some smart gringo had put up his hand and the teacher put me down as a stupid Mex. But I wasn't. I learned and I graduated tops. I was in China for four years and I tried out dozens of American and British accents before I found the one I liked best." He spoke easily with an accent more cultivated than that of most Americans.

Another veteran broke a national record as a salesman and refused a post as manager of a branch in Mexico. "I think I'll finish my law first. Then I'll take that job and make enough to live on while I build up my practice. . . . Last summer I made $3,500. That's enough."

Another, studying government, is going into politics. "My county is one of the dirtiest in the state. I think I'll clean it up. Of course, I'll have to buck some pretty ugly gringo bosses. But it'd be fun to see a Mex cleaning out the dirty gringos—now wouldn't it?"

Another, more realistic, perhaps with less humor, plans to play the game with the bosses. "It's the only way; get in and play it the way they do. . . . But I'll never play the racial game. I've already told one native I'd never vote for him; all he ever does is wave the bloody shirt. . . . Sure there's discrimination. It's harder to get ahead if you're Spanish. It's not enough to be good; you've got to be super. O.K., I'll be super."

"The racial game" is becoming more discredited with every campaign, even against the increasing flood of people from states where only certain names and heritages are considered correct. One defeated candidate stated it well. "I was getting along all right, even in that gringo precinct, when that paper came out with its blast, daring people to vote against me because of my Spanish name. That cooked my goose. Lots of people who were going to vote for me changed their minds. I don't blame 'em. We've got to take our chances like anybody."

Another candidate, campaigning in a county where prejudice is rife, related his experience with a grin. "When I walked into that meeting in the church I felt antagonism like a wave. I was Spanish; they talked about making New Mexico 'a white man's country'—even in the churches they talked like that! But I said to myself: 'Now brother, keep your shirt on. If they feel like that it is because they are ignorant. It's up to you to teach them; teach them by what you do.' So I was very quiet, but when I had a chance I matched a joke with a joke, I talked with a group of men during supper; and when they asked me to speak I told them what I hoped for New Mexico. They listened respectfully. Afterward the preacher came up and said: 'I've never voted for an Hispano, but I'm going to vote for you!' I thought if I'd won a preacher I wasn't doing so badly."

New Mexico is not out of the woods yet, that darkling forest where good people have been held back by lack of a chance to learn. But quietly and often unnoticed, we are developing leaders who, while holding to the best Spanish traditions, have accepted the best United States tradition and are coming ahead under their own power, using every advantage that a free land offers, relying on themselves, and making good. These are the new New Mexicans who will finally bring our state to its full maturity as the heir of two fine cultures.

PART THREE

Gringo

XVII

GRINGO DISCOVERERS

◧ MEXICO lost her northern provinces to a new country, whose explorers came neither for God nor glory, but for gain. They came as individuals seeking, first, furs and then trade with Mexico. That astute patriots back in Washington saw far beyond them to a frontier on the Pacific was proved by what followed. Even the first official explorer of the unknown land between Mexico and the United States appears to have been quite innocent of what his adventure might lead to. This was Zebulon Montgomery Pike, and his orders were to find the headwaters of the Arkansas, which flowed into the Mississippi in U.S. territory, and to return to Natchitoches by way of the Red River, also presumed to rise in the Rockies. This was an error of several hundred miles, but it gave Pike a chance to see a lot of Spanish territory.

Pike's expedition, in 1805–6, revealed basic differences between the homespun republic and the resplendent empire. Pike was no general, but a lieutenant who was promoted to captainship on the way. He came not in plumed helmet and glittering mail with an armored army, but with a handful of soldiers and a civilian doctor. Nobody carried the cross. Pike's detail was supplied with whisky, corn meal, pork, gunpowder, salt, and tobacco for its use, and with calico and knives for the Indian trade. The men had a few tents and blankets, and their clothes were too light. Like many later travelers, they thought they were going into warm country.

Pike saw, even rounded, the peak that bears his name, though he neither climbed nor named it. As usual with U.S. discoveries in the Southwest, the Spaniards had been there earlier. The Americans had a bitter-cold and trying January as they crossed the divide and came upon a clear rushing stream they took to be the Red River. They were actually in the Rio Grande watershed, and when Pike built a fort and raised the stars and stripes he was in Spanish territory. There he was taken into pleasant captivity by Lieutenant Don Facundo Melgares, who met him with a troop of militia mounted on white horses in stunning contrast with its officers' black steeds. In view of New Mexico's dire poverty, this was clearly an effort to impress. Pike and his captor became good friends, and the young gringo certainly saw more as a prisoner than as an explorer. Pike's own story, *The Expedition of Zebulon Montgomery Pike*, is the first of many officers' books on the new land, and, like them all, very readable and amusing for its upstage Protestantism and U.S. indignation at having to conform to Spanish law. Pike reports courteous treatment all the way.

Even before Pike, a few lone drifters from the States had appeared in Santa Fe: Baptiste Laland and James Pursley were there in 1806. But the real westward movement began after Pike's book was published. Trappers came first; then traders.

Trapping, especially for beaver for men's hats, began on the streams Lewis and Clark had followed. It produced one of our national heroes, idol of men who yearn for a hardy, womanless world—or think they do. The trapper went alone, needing only salt and gunpowder, knife, gun, and traps. He killed his food, made his clothes, got along well with Indians on the live-and-let-live principle, and wed an

Indian girl. When he had a good stack of furs he put into this or that "hole" to sell his pelts, swap tales, replenish supplies, and find the needed release of liquor, women, and the gambling that reduced him again to gun, knife, and traps. In the northern mountains trappers worked for large companies, rugged individuals enriching men of wealth sitting comfortably in officers back in St. Louis. Farther south they worked as "free trappers," men on their own. They drifted into New Mexico by way of the Colorado Rockies and worked on through the Mogollons to the Gila and Colorado rivers. Among these men were Mexican trappers, a fact that our writers have overlooked. We are likely to see things from our own point of view, and in this case we lack records. Mexican trappers left no written record, and their names do not appear on the tax rolls: only gringos had to pay for permission to trap.

Taos was the rendezvous of trappers and mountain men. Major Jacob Fowler of Kentucky, who put in there in 1821, described his visit. "A collection of men and ladys of the Spanyerds Had a fandango . . . wheare they appeered to injoy them Selves With the Prest at their head." Major Fowler, a surveyor and described as an educated man by his granddaughter, who wrote the introduction to his *Journal of Jacob Fowler*, encountered so many difficulties in his travels that he ended by misspelling "difficulties" twelve ways.

The mountain men were the real discoverers of the West. From Canada to Mexico, they trapped beaver on every creek, followed every river, crossed every divide, learned to avoid every precipice and to shelter in every cave. They knew the Rockies intimately and in detail; the maps they carried in their heads had no blank spaces. As guides, the trappers led the traders who followed soon, and as scouts they showed old moccasin-worn trails to such "pathfinders" as Frémont and Kearny. Then, as soldiers, even as officers, they proved invaluable to the country they had never considered changing for another. Perhaps the archetype of such men was New Mexico's Kit Carson, the illiterate boy who ran away from an apprenticeship in Missouri and became a legend in his lifetime.

Like the early Spanish explorers, these gringos were agog to tell their adventures, and apparently every one who could write and many who could not spell wrote books. Unfortunately, we have no account of how this invasion looked to the Mexicans. How enriched our history would be if we had such diaries and private letters as vitalize our pre-Revolutionary and pre-Civil war periods! After Don Pedro Pino's report to the King in 1812 we have no first-hand account of the natural fears and forebodings of Mexican citizens as they watched the relentless advance of the United States bringing the end of the world they knew. We need, too, their detailed picture of the interlopers. We know only from old gossip and family tradition that they were considered ignorant, boorish heretics, with only an occasional man among them with whom a gentleman could be at ease. If the *ricos* wrote anything, their confidences have disappeared into coffers in Mexico or were prudently burned when the new government took over. We have only one comment, quoted by Twitchell. Don Mariano Chaves, sending his son to a St. Louis school, said: "These heretics are going to overrun all this country. Go learn their language and come back prepared to defend your people." That lad was José Francisco Chaves, who became one of the most distinguished citizens of the territory of New Mexico and its representative in the United States Congress from 1865 to 1871.

Before the United States took over, Mexico had revolted from Spain, and New Mexico was part of the Mexican Republic. We have an amusing account of those days in General Thomas James's *Three Years Among the Mexicans and Indians*. He found Santa Fe all freshly whitewashed and the churches adorned with fine altar vessels and hangings for the celebration. Governor Melgares, who had been a friend to Pike, told General James that his Spanish passport would no longer serve, but he would be welcomed and no duties would be assessed. The general was the last trader with no complaint about duties.

As a citizen of a country experienced in celebrating independence, James was consulted. He recommended a liberty pole, a flag, and a salute to each province of the new republic. He suggested an eagle as an emblem, but the Mexicans decided on clasped hands to typify the unity of all nations.

James writes: "I informed the governor that all was ready for the raising of the flag, which honor belonged to him. 'Oh, do it yourself,' he said, 'you understand such things.' So I raised the first flag in the free and independent state of New Mexico."

Santa Fe, however, understood fiesta. A local painter had decorated a stage, on which little girls posed as Independence, Religion, and Union, and where eloquent gentlemen made stirring speeches. The general thought the handsomest people were the San Felipe Indians in their hand-woven cotton garments and coral and turquoise jewelry. "They danced with admirable harmony," he wrote. Altogether he found that the Indians acted with "more moderation and restraint than the Spaniards," who, he complained, "abandoned themselves to the most reckless dissipation and profligacy." He had never seen such gambling. Even ladies gambled away their money, then their jewels, and finally their gold-fringed shawls, leaving the tables only to find more riches to risk.

Even as the fiesta ended, word came that Navajos had attacked settlements in the Rio Abajo. James watched Melgares review his troops: "a gang of tatterdemalions . . . of all colors, some bare-headed, others bare-backed. . . . Most were armed with bows and arrows, a few had guns that looked as if they had been imported by Cortés, while others had iron hooks fastened to the end of poles which passed for lances." By the time the militia got going, the Navajos had killed all the people in several villages, destroyed what they could not take, driven off all the cattle, and swept north along the Rio Grande to raid Taos and be on their way.

This is what New Mexico's citizens faced when fourteen men of good families gathered in Santa Fe in 1851 to organize a legislature. Two of them were disqualified because they could neither read nor write. They were all inexperienced. Yet Twitchell makes a plea for proper recognition of these men in place and street names. They were our first legislators; they were earnest and generous, serving without pay; and they had good intentions. They even discussed establishing schools. But the province had no money; it would be some years before trade with the States would begin to bring in duties.

Trade was the great hope. It was profitable even when the only transportation was long trains of mules, each loaded with two hundred pounds of goods. But in 1824 Captain William Becknell daringly brought to Santa Fe 25 wagons, 81 men, 150 horses and mules. On his return he took back $180,000 in gold packed in rawhide sacks, and $10,000 worth of furs.

But the enterprising men were not all in Missouri. In 1828, just a year after Antonio Armijo's successful trek to California, twenty-six Mexicans made it to Independence and came home rich. Trade on the Santa Fe Trail was well established by 1860, when it employed ten thousand men and was estimated as worth four or five million dollars annually to the traders.

In those days, once a year a dusty caravan stopped just over the hills from Santa Fe so that the men could trim their beards and wash, don new shirts, tie new crackers to their whips, and roll into town with as much dash as could be got out of footsore beasts. "*La caravana! La caravana!*" To New Mexicans this trade meant better goods at lower prices and the excitement of dealing with gringos with their harsh speech and free ways. Conservative families held back; especially they tried to hold their daughters back. Lesser folk, including the daughters, took the newcomers to their hearts. Even the most rigid families' ramparts were breached by some diplomatic merchant from Kentucky like James Magoffin, some physician from Maryland like Henry Connelly, some engaging rascal like Richens Lacy Wootton, who ran away from one of Virginia's first families rather than go to school.

In 1824 the Bent brothers from Virginia built a trading-post on the Arkansas near where the Purgatoire (Picket Wire) River came in. This was Bent's Fort; its walls were four feet thick; at its corners were watchtowers; its court-yards could contain a small army; its storerooms could supply the whole Southwest; and its living quarters housed every traveler on the trail. William Bent, who stayed with the fort, married an Arapaho. His brother Charles settled in Taos, where he married Maria Ignacia of the rich Jaramillo family. Her sister, Josefa, became Mrs. Kit Carson. So these two men were committed to New Mexico. They made much of its history—Charles Bent as governor and Kit Carson as guide, scout, officer, and Indian agent. Perhaps their most important contribution was keeping the trust and friendship of their wives' people while remaining patriotic citizens of the United States. Kit Carson even held the admiration of Indians he defeated. He was an honorable, square-dealing gentleman, and modest withal.

When twenty-two-year-old Franz Huning took his first look at Santa Fe in 1849, he found "the branch of industry . . . most flourishing and lucrative was monte and faro. The government spent much money in those days in this territory . . . and . . . gambling places were crowded every night. . . . Every time I went to those places I saw there, and bucking, a small thin, bow-legged man of about forty." Kit Carson! Young Huning had read a book about the famous scout illustrated with a picture of a tall man with flowing beard, "clad all over in ornamental buckskins, mounted on a powerful charger. He was in the act of killing two Indians . . . one with a pistol, the other with a large Bowie knife. . . . In later years when he was a colonel . . . and was stationed with his regiment in Albuquerque . . . one day I showed him the picture. 'Why,' he exclaimed with his thin voice, 'is that me?' "

We know Santa Fe Trail days better than most eras because so many men and women, who rode those swaying wagons or prodded those heavy oxen across the rutted plains wrote about it. The classic of the trail is *The Commerce of the Prairies* by Josiah Gregg, who first crossed the plains in 1844. One hundred wagons was the usual train made up by several merchants. Oxen were to prove better draft animals than the more temperamental mules, and those slow beasts set the day's journey at ten or twelve miles. Among the wagons were a few Dearborn carriages for the ladies, many animals for replacements, and mounted men to serve as guides and hunters. The first leg of the journey was easy enough, as the trail crossed long-grass country with frequent streams and shady groves. But at Council Grove experienced men rode cautiously, alert for signs that Indians were near, and discipline was tightened. At night wagons were swung into a circle with wheels interlocked, sentinels were posted, and men rode around the grazing animals, crooning softly to calm them.

At the ford of the Arkansas there was a choice of routes, each with its special hazards: steep mountain grades on the northern trail, long waterless stretches on the southern. Today's traveler may see for himself how difficult this terrain was for wagon trains, even as he sits comfortably in a Pullman on the Santa Fe Railroad, whose tracks follow both old trails.

In a rainy season or when the grass was good, the shorter southern route was preferred. At Cimarron Crossing on the Arkansas, barrels were filled with water, animals made to drink all they would, and late in the day the train set out to cross the Staked Plains, whose flatness had so impressed Coronado's men. Here the men from the States met the Mexican *ciboleros*, buffalo hunters often more deadly with a lance than the best shot with a musket. Traders relieved the long day's drag by running buffalo or dashing after antelope or deer.

Within New Mexico's modern boundary the trail crosses a rolling prairie where grass runs forever before the wind and cloud shadows smudge its creamy bowl like smoke-stains on the creaminess of pottery. The land lies in bowls marked off by straight dark lines that are narrow canyons where cottonwoods and willows find footing and cattle always find water. For here the mountains are not far away and streams converge to form the Mora, the Red, and finally the Canadian. The motorist, speeding at seventy miles per hour over good roads, comes at times upon shallow grass-grown ruts that were cut more than a century ago by loaded wagons. Flyers see them clearly from the air. The New Mexico Historical Society has erected markers: Josiah Gregg's Route. But best of all we can follow the same landmarks the traders knew. Nobody could miss the island of dark basalt, whose outline is so like straining beasts pulling a prairie schooner, that is Wagon Mound. Here the two trails joined.

The northern route followed the Arkansas River toward the Rockies. And every wagon train stopped at Bent's Fort, where one hundred men worked as carpenters, smiths, butchers, wranglers, storekeepers, and clerks. Mountain men came in with their hides to be pressed and stored and Indians stopped to barter and to visit their close friends and relatives, the Bents. There were billiard tables, a telescope, and often a doctor. Every novelist of the Trail has made Bent's Fort the scene of a birth or a death, a seduction or an eye-gouging fight.

Bent's Fort was so closely linked with our history that New Mexico seems to have begun there. But beyond it there remained a long crawl up over the foothills of the Rockies to the pass that was the true gateway to New Mexico. The Spanish Peaks lifted ever closer to the blue, as animals labored more and more heavily in the thinning air to reach Raton Pass.

Two miles a day was good time crossing the Pass. Beasts strained and men pushed, sweated, and swore on the way up. On the other side they lashed wheels together and held back just as hard going down. Axles broke on stones, hotboxes developed, animals died, delicate ladies like Susan Magoffin trembled with fright.

Here, at a spot that the modern tourist-catcher would consider a realized dream, Richens Lacy Wootton made a road that was an engineering feat, and set up a tollgate. Doubtless his welcome was worth the fee he charged. His stone-and-adobe house was warm from a big fireplace before which the weary traveler could sit to hear tales of how the big game heads on the wall had been taken, of scouting with Kit Carson, and of trading trips with the Bents and St. Vrain. In time the tollman became "Uncle Dick Wootton" and his home a stage stop. Then the Santa Fe Railroad took over his road and left of Uncle Dick only a name on a watertower.

Beyond Raton Pass there was another choice of mountain trail or grassy track across the plains. Taos tempted some loaded wagons and many animal trains to cross the Sangre de Cristo range into that rich wheat-growing valley. The road traversed, as it still does, fertile uplands and canyons alive with game and veined with coal and precious metals, to the high Moreno valley, beyond which it dropped down into Taos. On the eastern slope lay the 1,700,000 acres of highly productive land that was to be best known as the Maxwell Land Grant. Granted by the Republic of Mexico to Charles Beaubien and Guadalupe Miranda, it came to Lucian B. Maxwell of Illinois when he married Luz Beaubien. When Maxwell failed, British capitalists and then Hollanders owned that vast empire which came finally into the hands of an Oklahoma oil magnate, who gave it to the Boy Scouts of America. There at Philmont young Americans, properly directed, may now play at pioneering and learn emasculated tales of the true pioneers. The Maxwell Land Grant has attracted many fiction writers. Its true story would reveal the actual history of New Mexico.

The trail for Santa Fe avoided the mountains and led south past Wagon Mound and toward Hermit's Peak. There lived one of New Mexico's first escapists: Juan María Augustine Anna, an Italian nobleman who came west with Don Manuel Romero in 1863. Seeking solitude, the count was too kind not to heed a call for help, and when a child he had treated was cured of smallpox his fame as a healer was set. The Italian made no claim as a healer, but sufferers came to beg his touch. The Penitentes built a shelter for him and every year placed there another cross to mark their penitential procession. Less credulous friends worried about the lonely man. Mr. Watrous at La Junta, where the Mora River and Coyote Creek join, watched nightly for a fire on Hermit's Peak. If he did not see it he would go or send aid. La Junta is called Watrous now; from there the traveler can see how clearly that flame would have shown against the sky above the peak.

The hermit, wearied at last by his fame as a healer, moved to Las Cruces and found haven in a cave in the Organ Mountains. There Sheriff Mariano Barela made with him another pact about a nightly fire. One sad night, when the fire failed, the sheriff went with assistance and found the old Italian's body thrust through by an Apache lance.

In the Santa Fe Trail days there was a settlement at the Gallinas River where Las Vegas stands, but more important was El Bado de San Miguel on the Pecos. It is off the highway now, and nobody has marked the ford where so many thousands of wagons splashed across the river on the way to Santa Fe. But beyond San Miguel, modern roads and the railroad follow the old ruts closely, especially where the old Indian trails wound through Glorieta Pass and Apache Canyon.

Franz Huning wrote that where teamsters began to dress up for arrival in the capital, final bets were laid as to whether Santa Fe was in New Mexico or New Mexico in Santa Fe, "a question that had been much in dispute all the way from Independence." So the tenderfoot might wonder. But the men of the trail, like the mountain men before them, knew well the country they traversed. After they had learned the way across the mountains, the Army had only to follow.

XVIII

THE GRINGO OCCUPATION

❧ NEW MEXICO was occupied by the United States as an incident of the war with Mexico. Texas had achieved its independence of Mexico in 1836; within ten years boundary disputes had given expansionists in Congress cause for war with the neighboring republic. Manifest Destiny was the watchword; the Pacific was the goal. New Mexico was little known, but there it was, sprawling from wherever Texas ended to wherever California began. It would have to be taken on the way to California. This was construed by the invaders as "freeing New Mexicans from oppression and making them citizens of the best of all nations." An army was recruited, mostly in the border states, and Stephen Watts Kearny was put in command.

Kearny was a veteran of the War of 1812, and he knew the West from the Yellowstone to Bent's Fort, which he had visited as colonel of the First Dragoons stationed at Leavenworth, Kansas. Kearny was no tenderfoot in 1845 when he was named brigadier general and commander of the 1,658 men who composed the Army of the West.

This was a volunteer army, the very essence of democracy, and reading about it arouses sympathy for the hardest-boiled sergeant. Among its store clerks, farmers, trappers, and ox drivers came a few lawyers and doctors who were elected officers because of prowess in court or on the political stump. The men wore no uniforms. Their long hair and beards were upkempt, and their home-made hats were adorned with souvenirs or thongs and fishhooks that might

248

come in handy. But they could handle their guns and Bowie knives, and when they reached the settlements they proved adept at raiding orchards and cornfields. They had only scorn for the regular army, and shook off discipline as lightly as fleas; they had to be urged to get up in the morning, to wear coats, to salute. Regular Army officers doubted that such a crew could ever be made into soldiers, and their reports are peppered with doubt and scorn. But the way had been prepared for this undisciplined command by the gentleman who, perhaps, did the real job of taking New Mexico away from Mexico.

This was the Kentuckian, James Magoffin, who had traded along the trail to Chihuahua, where he had served as United States consul, married Señorita María Gertrudes Valdez, and become widely popular as Don Santiago. A smooth-talking Irishman with a well-stocked mind, a genial host with a well-stocked cellar, and a sound patriot, Don Santiago was better than any invading army. Thomas H. Benton, the westward-looking senator from Missouri, had introduced James Magoffin to President Polk and to Secretary of War Marcy, and they had decided to send Mr. Magoffin west with the Army. What else was agreed history does not relate. Nor do we know what Don Santiago said to Governor Armijo in Santa Fe, or how he spent his money there. He soon went on to Chihuahua; he may have had a mission there, too. His many friends in that city seemed to think so. General Wool, who had gone into Mexico with General Zachary Taylor, was advancing on Chihuahua from the east. Even as they exchanged champagne suppers with their old friend Don Santiago, wary Mexican officials were keeping an eye on James Magoffin, whom they knew as a loyal United States citizen and an astute trader.

Then one day the Mexican judge advocate of Chihuahua handed his friend Magoffin an unopened letter addressed to him; it had been found among the papers of Dr. Henry Connelly, just captured near El Paso. On opening it, Magoffin found that it contained a letter from General Kearny commending James Magoffin for facilitating the capture of New Mexico. If the Mexican judge had read those words he would have had to arrest his good friend Don Santiago as a spy. But the Mexican gentleman bowed formally to his friend with twinkling eyes and without mentioning the letter, which Magoffin burned. He thus also destroyed proof that the United States owed him some fifty thousand dollars for service rendered and expenses incurred. Years later the Congress awarded his family thirty thousand dollars.

Manuel Armijo, Governor of the Department of New Mexico, has long figured as the villain of the piece. But it is well to remember that we know him only through the reports of his enemies, many of which lose force on further research. Most writers follow Twitchell in describing Armijo as an ignorant sheep-herder who founded his fortune on stolen sheep. But he came of the *rico* Armijo family, and his mother was one of the even richer Chavez's. Manuel was born about 1800 at Los Poblanos, still a fine hacienda near Albuquerque, and he was well enough educated to write a decent letter, as may be seen in the New Mexico archive. He was a trader on the Santa Fe Trail in partnership with Adolph Speyer. Armijo had been Governor in 1828, but he came to real power in 1837 when he put down a revolt of malcontents at Santa Cruz de la Cañada. He was then a dictator, a loyal imitator of his idol, the Mexican general and president, Antonio López de Santa Ana.

As Governor, Armijo was vigorous and stern. He faced disloyalty at home, Indians on the borders, a threatened gringo invasion, and an empty treasury. He sought money from rich men, to whom he granted vast lands; he taxed mines; and he placed an impost of five hundred dollars on every wagonload from the States, regardless of its weight. Traders countered by reloading at Pecos Pueblo to reduce the number of wagons. Richard L. Wilson, in *Short Ravelings from a Tall Yarn*, explains that they resented the duty "especially as it was . . . for the sole use and benefit of his obesity, the Governor." Doubtless, Armijo got a rake-off; it was the custom of his country. But he managed to collect a fat tariff without discouraging the traders, who were worth some million pesos per year to New Mexico. Armijo is notable as a governor of New Mexico because he never asked the central government for money.

In 1840 Armijo had warned the Mexican government against gringo encroachment, naming such outposts as Bent's Fort as "the protection of robbers, either foreigners or Mexicans." In 1846 his apprehensions were justified. From Bent's Fort, General Kearny addressed a proclamation to Governor Armijo: "I come by orders of my government to take possession of the country over part of which you are now presiding as governor." He then crossed the Arkansas River into Mexican territory. The invasion had begun.

Kearny's march into New Mexico was uneventful; it was even disappointing to a group of young soldiers who rode sixty miles in one night to catch up because they heard there was going to be a battle. There was no battle. At Las Vegas the general mounted the roof of a house on the plaza and read his proclamation. He came as a friend to bring the blessings of self-government to the people. He absolved them from allegiance to the Mexican government and Governor Armijo; he promised that "not a pepper, not an onion shall be disturbed or taken"; but he also promised dire and quick consequences to anyone who promised to be quiet and was not. "I am not a Catholic myself . . . but at least one-third of my army are Catholics, and I respect a good Catholic as much as a good Protestant."

This army had much to say about the new land and said it well. Officers' books reflect character and opinion, and many include accurate comments on geology and geography, flora and fauna, people and their ways. These books are well printed and illustrated with fine, sensitive drawings and maps of an engineer's precision. Above all, they vibrate with the joy of youth riding into an unknown country where discomforts and dangers only spiced the adventure. Among them, those gringos saw everything and they had a lot of fun.

Lieutenant J. W. Abert of the Topographical Engineers heard mockingbirds in the osage hedges, the meadow lark's liquid call, and the whirr of partridges rising. There on the prairies, grass topped the boot of a mounted man and the streams ran pebbly and clear. In the short-grass country he met long-eared jackrabbits that seemed larger than the bounding balls that were antelope. The air was fresh and clear and ever headier as he neared the mountains. They killed buffalo and saw Indians; once young Abert lay awake all night with his rifle at hand because they had seen Pawnees that day. In camp they feasted on buffalo tongue and venison, quail and doves, and now and then fish.

It was not all paradise. There were days and nights of rain, and there were dust storms. Mules proved recalcitrant, and horses got away. Men sickened from drinking puddle water. Young Abert himself was taken with a fever and had to stay at Bent's Fort while General Kearny went on. There he talked with a voyageur who knew all the mountains, saw Magoffin, met Ceran St. Vrain and "Karson." Not everybody could spell the famous scout's name, but every young man saw him. Abert wrote with awe of the mountains' grandeur and of the toughness of Raton Pass.

When the soldiers reached the settlements, their interest shifted to the people, all strange in dress and manner. Now and then they met a well-dressed and well-mounted hidalgo. Usually they saw country folk on burros: men sitting on the animals' rumps, guiding them with kicks in the ribs or whacks on the neck and "*Arre, burro!*" Sometimes a couple rode the same beast. Sometimes both walked beside four little mouse-gray legs bearing a huge circle of piñon wood or of hay trailing in the dust. Always such people spoke with heads down and eyes averted from the gringos they had been warned against.

Beyond Las Vegas there was still hope of a battle. So the troops rode on confidently, spurs jangling, guidons unfurled, guns at the ready. But there was no battle, and the brisk advance settled into a dull jog. Some captured Mexicans reported that Armijo awaited them at a defile that would prove a regular Thermopylæ; others said that he had fled. So the troops crossed the Pecos and came to the ruins of Cicuyé. West Point had rather muffed history and archæology: the young officers described the old mission as an Aztec castle or a temple where maidens were sacrificed in a perpetual fire.

Near there a fat Mexican on a burro told Kearny that General Armijo had indeed absconded. So the volunteers, deprived of a battle, rode unopposed through Apache Canyon. As any traveler can see, a handful of determined men there could have held an army larger than Kearny's. But Armijo had decamped—he turned up later in Socorro—and his army had melted away. The way to Sante Fe was open.

This defection of Armijo's and what Mexico made of it remain mysteries. Had Magoffin bought him off? Was he an arrant coward? No record of a court martial has come to light, so maybe Mexico did not consider him gravely at fault. The Mexican historian, José María Roa Barcena, quotes a letter of August 26, 1846, stating that Armijo's officers had pulled out with the auxiliaries, leaving the Governor nothing to do but retire. In any case there was no defense, and this gringo invasion has been called Occupation and not Conquest.

On August 18, 1846, General Kearny read another proclamation from the roof of the Palace of the Governors, then under its third flag, as Mexico's red, white, and green with its eagle, snake, and cactus sank before the red, white, and blue. Even that proud emblem was to be hauled down by a conqueror before the stars and stripes would fly over New Mexico forever.

General Kearny named Charles Bent Governor of New Mexico, and His Excellency entertained the officers at dinner with fine wines and appointments as correct as any in the States. The young officers mooned over dark eyes under lace mantillas and swooned at the smooth grace of the dancers.

Less formally, the young dragoons, officers and men, were making themselves at home in Santa Fe. In the market they bought fruits, cheese, bread, wine, and the fiery distillation known as Taos Lightning; they had all learned enough Spanish for that. The biggest money changed hands at Tules's place, where Palace Avenue still meets Burro Alley. Tules Barcelo, formerly Governor Armijo's *querida*, had become wholeheartedly *gringa*. Once she even lent an embarrassed colonel enough money to pay off his men, asking only that he escort her to the regimental ball—which he did, to the scandalization of the ladies of the town.

General Kearny had done well. Without firing a shot, he had taken over a vast territory. By a couple of proclamations, spoken in English to people who did not understand it, several oaths of allegiance parroted by men speaking from the heart or through clenched teeth, New Mexico was declared part of the United States and all who opposed the idea traitors to it. Then the general rode on. Like so many to follow, he could not wait to get to California. But he left officers and troops behind to keep the peace and to explore the new possession. In charge of the military government in Santa Fe he left Colonel Sterling Price, a Virginian who had come along with the Missouri Volunteers. The main body of the Missourians, under Colonel Alexander W. Doniphan, was ordered to join General Wool in Chihuahua. If James Magoffin had done as well there as he had in New Mexico, all should go well.

Kearny started west by the shortest route: down the Rio del Norte to below Socorro, westward through the mountains to the Gila, and down the Colorado to California, where he would join General Frémont. But because emigrants were anticipated even then and a wagon road would be needed, Captain Cooke was detached from the command to swing south and find a level passage.

This West Pointer's trigger-quick temper found explosive material on every hand. In Santa Fe he had been put in command of a battalion from Colorado and Utah, Mormons who had brought their families. Among the 448 people were 25 women, uncountable children, 20 laundresses, and 60 men so ill they had to be accommodated in wagons. By stern purges, Cooke reduced his command to those who could walk, though he complained to Kearny: "The numerous guides and hirelings you sent me . . . had been idle for weeks; and I found I was to venture with my wagons into a region unknown to any of them." Cooke's professional contempt for this chuckleheaded amateur war-making salts even his military reports.

Cooke's command struggled across the Jornada del Muerto and, skirting the Mimbres range, came into the Apache country, where the Indians made the friendly proposal that they should invade Mexico together: "You want the land and we want the plunder." As usual, Indians had no use for fighting people one day and protecting them the next.

It was tough going. Often Cooke had to send scouts ahead to find water holes or puddles; sometimes they had to hack their way through mesquite thickets. Rations ran low, men grew ill, wayworn, and exhausted. As they ate up the food they abandoned wagons—the first of the dry wood and rusty iron that would mark this trail to California. Once the colonel wrote his general that he had decided "to send my useless guides to give you information." When he reached the Colorado, the resourceful Cooke tried boating on it with wagon-bed pontoons "with flattering success." Thus he pioneered a waterway that was to take many travelers into those western reaches of New Mexico.

At San Diego, Cooke, characteristically, wrote Kearny: "Thus, General, whilst fortune was conducting you to battles and victories, I was fated to devote my best energies to more humble labors." But Philip St. George Cooke had crossed New Mexico from Raton Pass to California and had laid out the wagon road that was to serve many years before it became a motor highway.

The troops left behind in Santa Fe were seeing New Mexico. Abert, on reconnaissance south of Santa Fe, was surprised "by the many men and children who both read and write, but they have no books. I can only recollect to have seen a Roman Catholic catechism at Padillas." Of the *ricos*, he wrote: "We saw several who had been to Union College, St. Louis. They speak French and English and understand their own language grammatically." At Manzano he heard Don Pedro Baca, who had been to New Orleans, telling his untraveled neighbors about big steamboats on water and little steamboats running on iron roads on land. At Albuquerque the priest quizzed his guests. Did they know the square, the circle, the triangle? Satisfied, the padre then turned to "a very handsome lady who graced the establishment," and declared the officers astronomers and mathematicians. Doubtless this was the easiest examination a West Pointer ever faced!

Abert was appalled at the condition of the poor, who, he wrote, "live not one whit better than the Negroes on a plantation; and the rico, like the planter, possesses everything." Captain A. R. Johnston of the dragoons reported the poor man's distrust of the rich. Of buying horses, he wrote: "Their people have so seldom been dealt with honorably that they cannot believe anyone is dealing fairly with them."

It is only fair to set against such comment Barcena's words: "North American historians draw a somber picture of the state of barbarism to which the tyranny of Armijo and the *ricos* . . . had reduced the population, and in the next line assert . . . that Santa Fe abounded in gambling houses and saloons established by their *regeneradores* [reformers] and that the licentious conduct of the soldiers promptly aroused . . . a vicious hatred of the Americans. To this had come the new Eden that Kearny's proclamation had promised."

Kearny had proclaimed that all who wished might go to Mexico, but that those who swore loyalty to the United States and then conspired against it would be considered traitors. So the Mexican of honor faced a dilemma. If he did not like the newcomers—as many did not; or considered them heretics—as many did; if he was loath to give up his ancient privileges—and this must have been the general, however unconscious, reaction—he would prefer Mexico. But it would be hard to leave lands owned by his family for generations. He might choose to fight for his home and the life and faith he believed in.

Some brave and honorable men who chose to fight met in the dark of night in Santa Fe and planned a general uprising. They were men of the best families; among them were priests; they fully understood what they risked. Their plot was discovered. It is said that Gertrudes Barcelo, having put her money on the new regime, learned what was afoot from a lover and betrayed him to Don Donaciano Vigil, Lieutenant Governor. There is no written proof of who the conspirators were. It is told that an agreement signed by all of them was hidden between a board ceiling and an adobe roof. This has never come to light, nor have any other papers. As late as January 20, 1847, the unreconciled Mexican Inspector of Arms, Don Antonio María Trujillo, issued orders to all officers in New Mexico to call out the inhabitants "in defense of our abandoned country." The unfortunate Don Antonio was tried as a traitor and hanged.

Most of the other conspirators got away to Mexico, but were later pardoned and allowed to return. Only Colonel Manuel Chaves, who did not run away, was tried. His defense, pleaded by Captain W. Z. Angney, was that he was not a United States citizen, and that therefore his act was not treason, but patriotism toward Mexico. He was acquitted and, like the other conspirators, lived out an honorable life as a useful citizen and a gallant officer of the United States.

The fullest account of this conspiracy, in Twitchell's *Military Occupation of New Mexico,* is based on old men's tales. Here again we meet the major difficulty in writing the early history of New Mexico—the lack of private papers. Did the hidalgos or their families destroy correspondence with Mexico and with each other? In contrast with the South's glorification of its Confederate forebears, it is noteworthy that no New Mexico family boasts of an ancestor's loyalty to Mexico.

The discovery of the Santa Fe plot did not end the revolt. In Taos and in Mora it went on. Governor Bent, knowing of the discontent but trusting his friends and neighbors, went to Taos for Christmas with his family. On January 19, Indians from the pueblo and Mexicans still loyal to Mexico attacked his house and mortally wounded the Governor in the sight of his children. While he lay dying and terrified citizens took refuge in Padre Martínez's house, the insurgents started south.

Colonel Price was advancing from Santa Fe with a force that included Captain St. Vrain, whose young son had been murdered in Taos, and Manuel Chaves, who had declined a commission and was marching sturdily as a private in the ranks of the country he had chosen at last. Price defeated one insurgent band at La Cañada, another at Embudo, and advanced on Taos. On February 3 he was bombarding that pueblo, where the last stand was made. It took all day, cost the lives of fifteen men, and demolished the church, whose gaunt and empty shell still stands. But it was a victory.

The revolt at Mora was similarly and summarily suppressed at Colonel Price's order. A few sporadic outbreaks followed, but within weeks New Mexico was finally and firmly United States territory.

We have a boy's excited account of the subsequent trial in Garrard's *Wah-to-Yah*. It struck him as "a great assumption of the Americans to conquer a country and then arraign the revolting inhabitants for treason." He found the prisoners "ill-favored, half-scared, sullen fellows." Five men were found guilty of murder, one of treason. In Garrard's judgment, the sentences for murder were correct, but of the other he writes: "Treason, indeed! What did the poor fellow know about his new allegiance? I left the room sick at heart."

The unsolved puzzle of the Taos revolt is: Did Padre Martínez direct it or not? Carson and St. Vrain thought he did. Charles Bent, before he became Governor, had expressed hatred and distrust of Padre Martínez in letters to Manuel Alvarez, United States consul in Santa Fe. "The priest will spare no means to injure me, but if he will attack me fairly, publicly, and above board, I am certain he will not accomplish his end. . . . But here [in Taos] the priest can prove anything." When the Alvarez papers, in the New Mexico archive, are fully studied we may understand what really happened in Taos.

Padre Martínez is New Mexico's most brilliant and controversial figure. Born in 1793 of a *rico* family of Rio Arriba, he lost wife and child in early youth and then went to Durango to study for the priesthood. On his return to New Mexico in 1822 he was given the church at Taos, where he proved energetic, domineering, and full of ideas. He bought the press that *Licenciado* Barreiro had shipped into Santa Fe and printed church rituals, textbooks, and the newspaper, *El Crepúsculo* (The Dawn), which still appears regularly in Taos. At his own expense the padre conducted a school for girls as well as for boys. And he protested to the bishop of Durango against tithes that were impoverishing the people, and against church fees so high that many babies were left unbaptized and many couples could not afford to marry. Padre Martínez was New Mexico's first liberal and first modern. Was he also the last unreconciled Mexican?

Pedro Sánchez, in a wholly uncritical little book, quotes him: "The American government resembles a burro; but on this burro lawyers will ride, not priests." Such a man, such a priest, might well have preferred to institute reforms as a Mexican and a Catholic. Sánchez tells us that Padre Martínez, aroused by frightened people after Bent's killing, quickly dressed and took command. He assembled all the peaceful inhabitants, including Americans, posted armed men on the flat roof, sent a courier to Santa Fe, and kept everybody reassured, fed, quiet until the arrival of Price's troop.

Taos gossip prefers the other version, as Taos chuckles to

recall that Padre Martínez's vigor was not limited to good works. More than one Taos County Martínez, in these lax days, boasts of descent from the padre and one of the lovely ladies who graced his home. They also remember that he hated heretics and was outspoken in his dislike of gringos. It is hard to believe that a man so intelligent, confessor and confidant of his people, could have been ignorant of a widespread conspiracy. But the priest kept his own secret and was never openly accused. Later he served in the New Mexico territorial legislature and was its presiding officer. His people never lost confidence in him. Even when the puritanical Bishop Lamy unfrocked him in 1856 for his irregularities, Padre Martínez continued to say Mass in a private chapel, serving his parishioners until he died in 1867.

The Army of the West had thus subdued the Mexicans within a few months, but the Indians still remained. The nomadic tribes were continuing their raids on settlements and crops, though the Pueblos, after the Taos revolt, had fully accepted the new allegiance, hoping for protection and often serving with the U.S. troops.

Lieutenant Simpson, riding against recalcitrant Navajos with Colonel Washington in 1850, wrote of Pueblo soldiers with admiration and respect. Of a pass in the Tunecha Mountains he related: "Here, if anywhere, the enemy would dispute our advance. . . . Forty Pueblos . . . (Captain Dodge voluntarily offering to lead them) were pushed forward in advance. . . . I had noticed with my glass several of the enemy upon the heights . . . and it was not at all improbable that they were strongly posted on the still more commanding heights." So the U.S. officer, far enough away to need a glass, watched the Pueblos advance into what he considered certain danger. He commended them. "The Pueblo Indians having gallantly gained the heights . . . the infantry was then ordered to move forward." In those days the Pueblos were the expendables.

Despite Pueblo prowess, this Indian business was going to take longer than anticipated, and forts were established: in 1851 Fort Sumner was built on the Pecos and Fort Burgwin on the Canadian to keep an eye on the Comanches, Fort Defiance in the very center of the unsubdued Navajos. Fort Sheldon, on the Rio Grande at the edge of Apacheria, was erected in 1869 as a tribute to the growing power of the Apache chief Geronimo. The most important was Fort Union, built in 1851 on the Mora, where the old trails met and where the forage was good. As the distributing center for the whole Southwest, Fort Union was splendidly constructed of stone and adobe. It consisted of nine sets of officers' quarters, two barracks, hospital, storehouse, smokehouse, workshops, icehouse, laundry, and jail. Its ample parade ground saw many a dashing review for some of the country's most prominent officials, and the forays it sent out trained many a young lieutenant who made history later. This famous fort is now gone. The government, abandoning Fort Union in 1894, after forty years of service, left it to vandals. A few years ago one could find bits of carved wood or hand-wrought iron, but only foundations remain now. Even the military cemetery has had no care—its headstones are toppled, their names erased.

In 1851 a territorial government was set up in New Mexico and officials appointed—the Governor, district judges who sat together as the supreme court, and United States district attorneys. Self-government was lodged in the legislative assembly of two chambers, whose members were elected by the districts. Its acts could be, and on occasion were, voided by the Congress of the United States. Naturally, most members of the assembly were new to United States citizenship. They were proud and eager to be worthy, but quite unaccustomed to the democratic process and without a word of English. The interpreter became an essential part of New Mexico's legislature, as well as of its courts and political meetings. The terrifying, but often laughable confusions, frustrations, and corruptions that resulted have been well presented by three lawyers. W. W. H. Davis, a gentleman of extreme correctness, expressed his consternation well in *El Gringo*. A later period, after newcomers from the States had learned how to deal with hidalgos and maneuver land laws, is set forth in *Fabulous Frontier* by William A. Keleher. *Black Robed Justice*, by Arey Poldervaart, fills interstices in the tale.

These books show how the United States botched its first opportunity to teach self-government to people alien in language and custom. New Mexico's advance, during her century as part of the United States, from an unkempt, poverty-stricken, and neglected frontier province to a dignified state has been the work of her people without such aid in teaching the new language and customs as the United States gave other non-English-speaking peoples who entered the Union at the end of the century.

XIX

TEXANS KEEP COMING

TEXAS has always looked toward New Mexico covetously, yearning to own it as a nation, a state, or individually. For more than a century Texans have kept coming in various guises and with various projects to occupy New Mexico. Beginning in early June, traffic flows all summer in an unbroken stream from Texas to New Mexico. This flood brings dollars, free spenders, many investors, and some fine and desirable people. Unfortunately it also brings prejudices capable of lessening New Mexico's extraordinary opportunity to make of its diverse heritages a richly patterned and truly democratic community. So far, New Mexico's record of fair dealing between peoples is better than that of its neighbors. But as Texans come in, and where they dominate, bad feeling grows and discrimination is practiced.

It is true that many broad-minded people come from Texas, that many narrow, bigoted, and stupidly intolerant folk come from other states or have grown up right in New Mexico. But so many Texans come bringing that state's inability to forget the war with Mexico that New Mexico applies the term *tejanos* to all prejudiced newcomers. Back of the dislike this expresses lie history and apprehension for the future.

In 1841, the Honorable Mirabeau Bonaparte Lamar, President of the Republic of Texas, conceived the idea of sending an expedition to Santa Fe. The five-year-old republic was broke, and it might be possible to divert some lucrative trade from the Santa Fe Trail to Texas. A military force was sent along for protection and—as President Lamar worded it—"for the occupation of New Mexico in case the people desired to become members of the Texas republic." President Lamar and his more imaginative advisors expected all New Mexicans to jump at the chance.

This venture was based on Texas's claim to all land east of the Rio Grande. The treaty of 1836, recognizing Texas's independence of Mexico, established the Rio Grande as the boundary between them. Texas construed that to mean the river's entire length up through New Mexico to its headwaters in Colorado—an assumption that blandly disregarded New Mexico's more than two hundred and fifty years as a political entity. New Mexico's eastern boundary had never been determined, but it had extended well over into what is now Texas. There are two distinct histories of this claim and its fate, one taught in Texas, the other of general acceptance.

Proceeding from this untenable premise, the Texas Expedition erred in its method of approach. Its three hundred soldiers, recruited by fiery reminders of the war with Mexico, and commanded by twenty-seven-year-old Brigadier General Hugh McLeod, were too warlike and too many to pass as a guard for artless merchants seeking trade, and too few to give a good account of themselves in a fight. Moreover, they lacked experience and knowledgeable guides. This whole junket may well rank as the first appearance of the feckless tenderfoot.

The prize tenderfoot was George Wilkins Kendall, editor of the *New Orleans Picayune*, who went along to share and report a triumphant adventure. If Mr. Kendall was not the first war correspondent, he was surely the most innocent. Starting from Austin, where the command was hailed oratorically as the "Texian Invincibles," Kendall's *Narrative of the Texas-Santa Fe Expedition* shows the Texans committing every blunder that makes the dude a figure of comedy.

While still in country teeming with fish and game, the Texans butchered their animals and so faced starvation when the going got tougher. They forced needless fights with Indians; lost goods, equipment, and even lives in stampedes; and because they could not take care of themselves, were often ill. Kendall makes it plain that the Invincibles were pretty well defeated before they ever reached New Mexico.

Mexico's excellent spy system had kept the authorities informed, and Governor Armijo was waiting and watching. In September he sent out Captain Dámaso Salazar, who met the expedition, pretty hungry by now and dragging, near the pink stone town of Anton Chico on the Pecos. Captain Salazar picked up three men as spies. Of these, one was killed trying to escape, another was executed. To Kendall, believer in the trade excursion theory, this seemed infamous murder. Hubert Howe Bancroft, dean of historians of the Southwest, considers it an accepted act of war, a judgment in which other disinterested historians concur.

Later the entire command of what Bancroft calls "the filibusters" surrendered in two lots, one of them betrayed by a traitor named Lewis. Kendall maintains that they were tricked by the wily and dishonorable Mexicans into giving up their arms. Manuel Alvarez, United States consul in Santa Fe, wrote that if the Texans had shown fight they would have won: "all the most respectable people had determined not to resist."

Kendall's account is a classic of vituperation and hatred, especially of Salazar, whom he charged with starving the prisoners and either letting the weak die or shooting them and cutting off their ears as proof that they had not escaped. Bancroft offers no defense of such atrocities, but interjects the note "if they were true." He sums it up: "The Texan adventurers were, at best, engaged in a risky invasion of an enemy's territory; fortune was against them, and disaster resulted, for which they deserve but little sympathy. Armijo and his men, on the contrary, had the most wonderful good luck in defending their country, and merit but little of the obloquy that has been heaped upon them."

General Houston, then President of Texas, appealed to the world, urging all friendly powers to mediate in behalf of the Texan prisoners in Mexico. Houston could only insist that even if they had been outlaws before, the terms of their capitulation had brought them within the pale of civilized warfare. It was agreed that after the reprehensible Salazar had taken them to El Paso they were committed to the care of a well-bred hidalgo, Don Elias Gonzales, who had had them treated well. In time the survivors were returned to Texas.

Texas was not ready to give up. The expedition of 1841 had been a failure, but in 1843 Colonel Warfield, with a detachment of vengeful Texans, raided the little town of Mora on its mountain stream. The invaders were thrown out, leaving a crop of hates. In that same year one hundred and eighty Texans, under Colonel Jacob Snively, attacked the Trail caravan on the Arkansas. Captain Cooke, still the correct West Pointer among savages, turned them back. By this time Texan vindictiveness had passed beyond all control, and a gang attacked a small wagon-train, property of Don José Antonio Chaves, whose family Kendall had named as friendly and helpful to the limping captives of '41. The name Chaves Creek still marks the spot where Don José and his servants were killed. A deep scar of hatred still throbs in New Mexico at mention of that name. By lucky chance the Captain McDaniel who led that attack had killed Chaves on United States soil. McDaniel and his associates were tried in a United States court, convicted, and hanged for murder.

Official Texas was moving along more legal channels. After Kearny's occupation, Texas assumed that the United

States would acknowledge her claim to all land east of the Rio Grande. Several gentlemen in high places seemed to admit it. President Polk was quoted as referring to "the right . . . justly asserted by Texas to the whole territory east of the Rio Grande." So Texas, in 1848, appointed Spruce M. Baird as Judge of Santa Fe County, one of four New Mexico counties that Texas had laid out on paper. One of these extended well down into Chihuahua; another ran in a long panhandle up into Wyoming.

The new judge, even faced with a job of such proportions, began by exuding hope. His letters, long unknown, have been released by his family and published in *New Spain and the West*. Baird wrote; "General Armijo espouses our cause with some zeal and is decidedly the first man in that region. I bought him out lock, stock, and barrel." But Mr. Baird may not have bought as much as he thought. Before long he was reporting "the New Mexican population openly hostile," though he, an office-holder, considered them misled by Americans animated "solely by a desire to figure as public functionaries themselves." Such men, he found, had put "frightful stories in circulation among the Mexicans . . . that we would destroy their religion, confiscate their property, hang and enslave their people for former acts of rebellion."

The prevailing attitude was probably expressed by the editor of the *Santa Fe Republican*. "We would now inform our Texas friends that it is not necessary to send us a judge . . . for there is not a citizen, either American or Mexican, that will ever acknowledge themselves as citizens of Texas until it comes from a higher authority. . . . Texas should show a little sense and not have it publicly announced that Texas' smartest men were tarred and feathered."

New Mexico was still under military rule, though two parties were trying to set up civil government. One hoped for admission to the Union as a state; the other would settle for territorial status. This kept affairs in such a turmoil that nobody had time for Mr. Baird. Colonel Washington evaded him all summer, reducing the would-be judge to a state of frustration that would demand a psychiatrist today. Mr. Baird decided to retire.

Feeling easier in Independence, Missouri, Mr. Baird prepared for his government some statesmanlike thoughts. The people of New Mexico, he explained, were one fourth Pueblo Indians. Of the rest, three quarters were peons "without shirts, shoes, or hats, and not worthy to be trusted in any way. The remainder, to say the least of them, are Mexicans." Such people, "even if they desired unanimously to be incorporated with us," would be troublesome. And as "all the interest Texas has is in the territory unappropriated, the mines, etc. . . . Perhaps it would be good policy to consent to their having a territorial government, reserving to Texas the proceeds of the public lands, mines, etc. . . . We would lose nothing and get rid of a troublesome and worthless set of customers." On a rough diagram appended to his report, Mr. Baird wrote: "It is important to make our boundary above El Paso to command the trade of Chihuahua for Texas. Texas should retain the Pecos valley for it will afford one of the finest settlements in the world. The country north of Santa Fe is not worth much."

Texas's failure in 1841, hard as it was on the Texans concerned, has been good for New Mexicans. For despite fair promises of citizenship and equal rights, Texas as a state and many Texans as individuals have, during the century since then, been notably unfair to their own Spanish-speaking citizens. It was good for the United States because hatred of *tejanos* helped keep New Mexico loyal to the Union when Texas again tried invasion in 1861. Even Texas profited by the effort, if not the failure, of 1841 because its congressman prevailed upon Congress in 1850 to settle "the boundary question" by paying Texas ten million dollars as compensation.

New Mexico was naturally a prize in the national struggle between free and slave states. Mr. Baird thought that the men he did not like "would dismember our state and turn the abolitionists against us." To New Mexicans, *tejanos* advocated slavery.

Negro slavery was no question in New Mexico: in 1853 there were only seventeen Negroes in the territory, mostly "body servants" of Southern officers. But many hidalgos feared legislation that would affect their Indian slaves and peons. At the time of the Emancipation Proclamation there were some six hundred Indian slaves in the territory. The territorial legislature was not thinking only of Negroes when, in 1859, it passed an act "for the protection of slave property in the territory." And the *ricos'* real concern was manifested in an act "providing for the arrest of fugitive servants who were bound to their masters under contract." Courts were prohibited from interfering with the masters' discipline "unless such correction was in a cruel manner with clubs or stripes." To protect the time-honored and comfortable institution of peonage, many educated Spanish gentlemen were ready to throw their lots in with the Confederacy.

In an interesting study, *New Mexico and the Sectional Controversy*, Loomis Morton Ganaway relates that Texas, disregarding Spanish and Mexican land grants, had awarded veterans of its wars good acres in the Rio Grande valley above El Paso, "not specific as to location." So all during the 1850's Texans came drifting into New Mexico—long men with long rifles and long memories of the Alamo and the expedition of 1841. With ease they dispossessed simple people whose ownership went back to De Vargas, and thus added to the hates that would grow and spread.

Part of the difficulty lay in a faulty boundary. When Mexico and the United States signed the Treaty of Guadalupe Hidalgo in 1848 they used an inaccurate map. In time an international boundary commission awarded the disputed area to Mexico, thus enraging the Texans who had dispossessed the Mexicans. When protests to Santa Fe and Washington did not bring action, Texas began to show signs of starting a private war, and Uncle Sam paid off. The United States now bought from Mexico 45,000 square miles of desert and mountainous country, Apache-infested but otherwise empty. This was the Gadsden Purchase of 1853, which gave us such a straight international line. Congress added all the new territory to New Mexico, and the New Mexico legislature extended Doña Ana County to the California line.

In the fifties the scattered inhabitants of Doña Ana County were as isolated as any lost tribes of history. They had uncharted wilderness to the north of them, Mexico to the south of them, Apaches forever raiding them, and their capital at Santa Fe, far beyond the waterless Jornada del Muerto. So they petitioned Congress for a separate territory with the parallel 33° 40′ as its northern boundary. In 1860 the active leaders, meeting in Tucson, elected Lewis S. Owings of Mesilla Governor of Arizona Territory.

Arizona's first appearance as a political entity ended abruptly in February 1861, when Texas seceded from the Union and sent Philip T. Herbert up from El Paso to claim Mesilla for the Confederacy. Flags, still cherished in the little Mesilla Museum, were going up and down at a great rate.

James Magoffin, from his rambling old adobe house at Magoffinsville (now a part of El Paso), supported Mr. Herbert, as did Simeon Hart, a miller who had made a fortune supplying United States troops, but who was reported to have offered the Confederacy $300,000 for its war coffers. Sylvester Mowry, editor of the Tubac *Arizonian* and mine owner, was as active in the Tucson area. These gentlemen were not credited with wholehearted Southern sympathies, but just with a sane eye to business. A detachment of troops marching eastward from California to join the Confederacy was welcomed in Tucson and in Mesilla, the only towns the new territory could boast.

A newspaper reports a meeting in Mesilla on March 4, 1861, at which speeches rose to bombastic heights. "The hell of abolitionism glooms to the north—the Eden of liberty, equality, and right smiles upon you from the south. Choose between them." They chose the Confederacy, but with the far-sighted proviso that "Arizona become a part of the Confederacy, and not a part of any state that has seceded."

Ganaway writes: "In contrast with the participation of the natives in territorial affairs at Santa Fe . . . no such support was solicited from them at Mesilla." He quotes *The Mesilla Times:* "One good company of Texas cavalry can do more to insure their [Mexicans'] loyalty to the Confederacy than all the offices in the territory." Wiser observers suggested that this point of view would pay off for the Union. It did.

Federal officials in Santa Fe had been slow to realize what was going on. But they awoke with a jolt when Fort Bliss went over to the Confederacy in July and Lieutenant Colonel John R. Baylor occupied Mesilla. Then Governor Connelly, he who had written that incriminating letter to Magoffin, called for volunteers. His best line was that the Confederates were *tejanos* coming to seek vengeance.

Baylor easily overcame a feeble defense at Fort Fillmore. The Confederate Territory of Arizona was now a going concern, and Confederate officials set out for their remote posts among the Apaches. But time moved faster than traffic in those days. Few appointees had reached their bases when all was over.

In December, Brigadier General Henry L. Sibley set out from Fort Bliss to take over all New Mexico for the Confederacy. Sibley was well known in Albuquerque as a major in the United States Army. Old inhabitants recollected that he had sent many sturdy mules and horses south, replacing them with scrub stock. Sibley had won a few residents of the Rio Abajo to the Confederate cause; there were a few trials for treason later. But most New Mexicans remained loyal to the United States.

The first battle was near Fort Craig at Val Verde, a leafy ford on the Rio Grande. Regulars manning the fort surrendered, and Sibley's Confederates swept on north, leaving many folktales of chapels used as stables, wine casks broken, and women raped or threatened by drunken soldiers. Perhaps few of these tales could be substantiated; invaders are always so accused. But these family legends, passed down through the generations, have edged New Mexico tongues with the tone still heard in the word *tejano*.

At Albuquerque, Sibley found that the Union troops had decamped after burying three cannon in the plaza, where they were found years later. Sibley raised the stars and bars over the plaza, raided stores, took over a well-known house as headquarters, mounted his cannon where Laguna Boulevard now crosses Central Avenue, and fought a brisk engagement with the bluecoats in the sandhills. Again the Union troops retreated, leaving the way to Santa Fe undefended.

Governor Connelly and the territorial officials had left the ancient capital and were headed for Fort Union. New Mexico's few regulars and volunteers were not enough to hold the territory. The only hope was that volunteers from Colorado and California would come to stem this gray-coated tide. Sibley took Santa Fe without firing a shot, and the fourth flag floated over the old adobe Palace of the Governors. But not for long.

California, purged of its Southern sympathizers when its Confederates marched east to join the Texans, had recruited the California Column. This now came marching along Cooke's route and found Tucson abandoned; Americans had gone east, Mexicans had retired below the border. Mesilla, too, was empty, and the Californians raised the stars and stripes there again.

At the same time volunteers from Colorado, the Pikes Peakers, were marching south. Governor Connelly had had some difficulty with his recruiting, but there was a detachment of New Mexico volunteers too. With this force Colonel J. M. Chivington of the regular Army met General Sibley in Glorieta Pass, near where General Armijo had failed to stand against Kearny. Colonel Manuel Chaves, who had risen since he marched as a private with Colonel Price, proposed a plan. Knowing his men and the mountain trails, he led them over the hills at night. At dawn of March 27 he fell with a crash on the unready Confederates. This surprise led to the rout of the Confederates, who retired down the Rio Grande and back to Texas. The Daughters of the American Revolution have marked the spot where the Confederates set up a dressing station for their wounded.

Although little noted among the greater battles being fought far to the east, this skirmish was a decisive one. If the Confederacy had held New Mexico, its way would have been open to California and sorely needed gold. Instead Sibley left Santa Fe on April 8 and retreated down the valley, where he was given a final trouncing at Peralta near Albuquerque by Major Jose D. Sena with a New Mexico volunteer company. New Mexicans of Spanish blood had proved their loyalty and their worth in battle, and had saved themselves from such indignities as their cousins have suffered in Texas.

After the Civil War, Texans kept coming, but as individuals seeking to better themselves. The war left many of them with only a ragged uniform and a gun. They had courage, enterprise, and the spirit of adventure. They also had, or knew how to get, cattle. So they invaded New Mexico, seeking better range for their stock and a life untrammeled by laws. Beyond the Texas settlements stretched an enormous emptiness in which no marker indicated the New Mexico border and there was no real water until one reached the Pecos. Eastern and southern New Mexico filled up with Texans, in a manner of speaking; there must have been at least two or three to the square mile. Along with them came many Missourians: the Southern and border states were sending their young men west. Few Northerners came into southern and eastern New Mexico, and the mores and way of thinking were—and still are—strongly Southern.

Only in Little Texas, as this area is called, could a candidate for high office be refused service in a barbershop. One politician, advised by a seasoned politician to avoid *tejano* places, insisted: "Nobody is going to discriminate against me. I'm an American citizen seeking votes; they'll treat me all right." The Anglo adviser said: "When that dirty *tejano* told him to go on down the street, it just broke his heart."

This ugly un-Americanism, so at variance with all New Mexico's tradition, can be understood only by knowing the people who brought it and who maintain it. Most of them were ignorant. The sprinkling of educated Southern gentlemen was not enough to mark the mentality of the region. Nor did the cowboy's easy tolerance long prevail. The typical cowboy was unschooled. Often he had to sign with a cross, but he was essentially a decent fellow, able to work with anybody and judge him by what he did. This appears at once in old-timers' talk. They speak with the Texas drawl, but their words reflect the friendliness that "folks is folks." Their words are gentle, their judgments broad.

The cruel prejudice in which the Ku Klux Klan could be

planted came later with women and preachers bringing the crude fundamentalist cults of the Southern frontier. They had the ignoramus's distrust of strange customs and a language they could not understand. They brought the South's phobia against the Negro and the *tejano's* hatred of Mexicans. To them God was a Protestant Nordic and only their ways were His. Too often the preaching they heard only confirmed their dull provincialism. Eastern New Mexico saw a curious mingling of the fringes of two diverse but equally rich and complex civilizations. Both groups, with few exceptions, were quite unaware of the splendors of the other's past, or even of their own. And these newcomers, living far from the current of New Mexico's life, had little chance to learn better.

People coming into the Rio Grande valley, from both North and South, dealt with hidalgos quite the equal of their best in wit, education, and political acumen. *Tejanos* saw few of these people; when they went to Santa Fe as office-seekers or officials they often were not invited into the hidalgos' homes. So the gulf remained wide and deep. People of the eastern counties, instead of becoming better New Mexicans, have too often become more Texan. They have sent their children to school in Texas or farther into the South. Only lately has the University of Texas begun work in race relations, as have the most thoughtful Southerners. But this new spirit has been slow to infuse New Mexico's Little Texas. The old spirit still shows itself in ways that are puzzling and amusing or tragic and enraging.

In these *tejano* counties the phrase "a good church member" is the accolade of respectability. Yet the churches practice discrimination. A young Catholic converted to the Baptist faith was treated so rudely that he returned to the faith of his fathers. A lady, all white-gloved for Easter service, asked: "Why does Peter Hurd want to live over there amongst all those Mexicans?" Pete Hurd, besides being an artist and a polo player in cowboy boots, is a complete New Mexican who recognizes no difference between Hispano, Anglo, Jew, Negro, Nisei—or even *tejano*—until they give themselves away. Even at their best, these churches and their ministers make no concerted efforts to lead their followers to practice the Christian brotherhood they preach.

The most odious manifestation of intolerance, the Ku Klux Klan, took root in 1928 in Little Texas, with Roswell as its center. Negroes were not the main target; the American Protestant Association was pumping up hatred against Catholics and Jews. As Spanish-speaking citizens were generally Catholics, two prejudices dovetailed neatly. And a new invasion from the Southern states, described by an eyewitness as "a lot of scum," made recruiting easy. Thoughtful, educated, and generally decent Roswell people held aloof, taking too little note, though the Masons and the Elks refused the Klan a meeting-place. Within the year a thousand men had masked and sheeted themselves, six hundred women were Kamelias, a youth organization was started, and organizers were turning to the rest of the state.

Outside Roswell the Klan had scant success in New Mexico. Even in nearby Artesia and Carlsbad the klans were puny and soon died. In Clovis the leading politicians—mostly Southern Methodists and Baptists—saw to it that organizers were not welcomed. Efforts to establish the Klan in Tucumcari and Clayton aborted. Las Cruces and Socorro would have none of it.

The Klan could not cross the mountains. At an altitude it met the prevailing climate of New Mexico—Catholic—and the unargumentative, quiet tolerance of the frontier. It tried burning crosses in Albuquerque, where membership was reported at from three hundred to three thousand. But reporters, covering sheeted meetings out on the mesa, made more of the curious gapers than of what the maskers were up to. Sheriff Tony Ortiz, with a couple of deputies, rode in and ordered them to unmask. Father Mandalari, a wise old Jesuit, directed his people to do nothing that would stir up "useless dissension." And M. L. Fox, editor of the *Albuquerque Morning Journal,* advised his readers throughout the state not to be suckers.

Even in Roswell sensible men had kept control of state and town offices. Few whippings were reported. Before 1930 the Kleagle had become involved in a scandal and members had begun to fall away and to claim that they had never been members. So the Klan passed, but the fanaticism it highlighted did not. In every political campaign somebody makes a loose remark about "keeping this a white man's state," meaning a state of prejudice. So far the spreaders of prejudice have succeeded only in the peripheral counties. The amusing and the tragic appear where petty personal prejudice can operate.

It was tragic that a Roswell hotel in 1949 refused to serve a banquet to a high school graduating class because it came from a Catholic school and families that spoke Spanish. It is more deeply tragic that even the Catholic Church, proud of its tolerance, maintains two parishes in Roswell—one for Anglos, one for Hispanos. A priest, asked what the clergy were doing to fuse those two congregations, said: "Why, nothing. I never thought of it." *Tejano* mores seem stronger than the Catholic Church.

It is funny that an old lady worried when her son went to teach in a Spanish-speaking community. He had been a football star and had come home from World War II with a few wounds and a decoration. Yet she trembled lest her darling be put upon by "those dreadful Mexicans!" It is amusing that a bride of impeccable Anglo ancestry was cold-shouldered when she went to her husband's town in Little Texas because she was a brunette and had been a teacher of Spanish. Happily she could laugh until they learned the truth and then try to teach them a few basic facts of life, history, democracy, Christianity, and related topics.

Texans keep coming, Texans from many states, but *tejanos* all. Lyle Saunders, in an unpublished paper, remarks that newcomers do not arrive as babes who will mature in the New Mexico tradition; they come as adults with all their folk-beliefs intact. And they are spreading.

These newcomers, with their notions, have not been contained in the southern and eastern parts of New Mexico. Since the opening of lands to homesteading early in this century, they have spread. With the development of industry in the oil fields and at Los Alamos and Albuquerque, the center of the state is increasingly infected. Industry timidly panders to wrong feelings. Employers state that employees would refuse to work alongside whoever is under discussion. If they ask the employees or try it out, it appears —nine times out of ten—that there is no objection. A few labor unions are also at fault, though by keeping certain groups unprotected they are building up a body of scab labor. Too often unions that discriminate turn out to be dominated by Texans.

In education, where, above all, New Mexico's old-time friendly equality should prevail, *tejano* influence grows as teachers who think like *tejanos* swarm in to take advantage of New Mexico's good salaries and retirement benefits.

Efforts to educate *tejanos* are many and various; they are largely personal, but often take on a mass effect. A wise school-principal—who happened to be part Indian—noting that every fall brought on an epidemic of Anglo-Hispano fights, announced that football practice would begin a week before school opened. This brought out all the well-muscled youths, who got to be such good friends before registration day that they forgot about being Anglo or Hispano and settled down to make the team.

Even where Negroes are concerned—always a more difficult case—New Mexico is making progress. An advanced Negro student, who had brought his wife to the University summer school, was amazed to find that he was matter-of-factly assigned space in a dormitory reserved for married students. Students boycotted a barbecue stand that refused service to Negroes, and brought about a change. A football coach, recently arrived from Texas, referred a Negro who had come out for practice to the President. That New Mexican asked: "Are you a student of the University? Then go get your suit." When the New Mexico Military Institute at Roswell announced that its team would not meet one from Phoenix that included a Negro, an influential alumnus put in a long distance call. The Arizona team was received.

Like every fight for decency, New Mexico's fight is slow, often discouraging. The question is always there: will these ignorant newcomers overwhelm us before we can teach them to appreciate New Mexico's fine tradition of tolerance? As prejudice is always founded on ignorance, and as ignorance can be cured, New Mexico may succeed in eradicating the *tejano* mores and in developing along its own traditional lines.

XX

FRONTIER PEOPLE

THE MOVIES and the westerns have given us an idea of the frontier as distorted as Russia's picture of the United States as a land of gangsters and lynchings. The separate facts may be right, but the emphasis is wrong. On the frontier there were wild men and wilder women, but they formed a noisy, noisome excrescence on the workaday life of ordinary people. Pioneers were of all kinds. Some were spectacular—adventurous, dull, highly educated, rich, saintly, or evil. Most were mediocre—hard pressed by poverty, ill educated or not educated at all, and generally decent. Coming first in ones or twos and then in dribbles, the emigrants began to come in waves as word of free lands and big opportunities got back to the States and over to Europe.

These people brought a mélange of standards and beliefs which might have proved too incendiary to make fusion possible. But all pioneers met conditions so hard and so identical that they developed a tolerance readily recognizable as that of the frontier. It accepts others' beliefs, not with studied broad-mindedness, but with a humorous admission that everybody has a right to his notions, however silly or strange.

This attitude prevailed even in New Mexico, where pioneering was complicated by the Spanish frontier it met and by the fact that settlers came from both North and South, bringing their sectional hates. The people who came along the Santa Fe Trail were best fitted to adjust to New Mexico's unique pattern because many of them were Europeans who spoke at least two languages and readily learned another. Among them were Frenchmen from Louisiana, Germans leaving a fatherland already too militarized, and a sprinkling of Jews whose contribution to New Mexico's sanity has never been adequately celebrated. Both Germans and Jews were strong Unionists and hence Republicans, but they took little part in the violent political squabbles that became hotly sectional after the Civil War. To learn what really happened in a tense time in a New Mexico town, talk with the fiery Irish or the resentful Spanish citizen, the unreconciled Confederate or the stern Yankee. He will give you the color. Then drop in on the German or Jewish merchant, hotelkeeper, or editor. He will chuckle: "Oh, yes, I remember how mad they got. It was like this." His version is as objective as good reporting.

Englishmen came along the Trail seeking adventure if that was their bent, refuge if they were scapegraces whose remittance depended upon their not going home, or investment if they were rich. In the first class was George Frederick August Ruxton, who was a true mountain man, a keen observer, and an upstage British officer who never lost his attitude of condescension. In *In the Old West* he described Doniphan's Missourians as proof that "Americans never will make soldiers." The remittance men were sometimes vague and bleary from drink, but always courteous and correct of speech—gentlemen among savages.

Several of the investors wrote their own stories, notably Captain William French, Irish by birth but stiffly British officer to the backbone. His *Recollections* recall wild days in the territory's southwestern corner. He made his home, or, more properly, established his estate, on the San Francisco River, where only a few ruined walls remain to mark his bunkhouse; the mansion is gone, but legends are numerous. Mrs. Franklin Wheaton-Smith, who lives now on the Mimbres, remembers well the old English Christmas parties when she was a child at Mogollon.

Mrs. Wheaton-Smith's father was Ernest Craig, an English mining engineer who was employed in Colorado by James McKay, a Pittsburgh millionaire. There McKay's daughter Anne attracted the young engineer's notice by putting a match to a stick of dynamite in the belief that it was a candle. Young Craig grabbed the dynamite and, as his daughter puts it, "decided he'd better marry her to make sure she didn't blow them all up."

Later, Mr. Craig found his Last Chance Mine at Mogollon, a mining camp reached even now by a steep hairpin road that clings to the mountain's eyebrow, testing not only a driver's nerve, but also his ability to keep his eye on the road instead of on the lovely valley spreading out below like green plush brocaded with silver. At every turn the road makes a suicidal run out onto beetling cliffs, but whirls away just before it plunges over among the feathery firs and candle-like blue spruce. Mogollon is a ghost town now, where gaunt gray houses follow the stream's noisy course, and only Mr. Holland in the store recalls how it was. He remembers the Craig family well and how the lady posted when she rode, but the children were soundly Western. Mr. Craig, he said, "went back to England and went into politics. He got into the House of Lords, and that's the best-paying job in England."

Their daughter was educated in England but returned to New Mexico after losing her husband in World War II. Relatives in England protested, but Mrs. Wheaton-Smith, who bought the Mimbres Hot Springs near the Gila, is making on her broad New Mexico acres a life more like the life her ancestors knew than anything in present-day England. She is, besides, a convinced and loyal New Mexican.

Another Englishman who came to stay was Montague Stevens, who brought his cultivated English bride to a ranch near the San Augustine Plains. Stevens left a reputation for unvarying success; he succeeded, so they say, in failing at everything he undertook. He also is remembered as a square-shooter, a man to trust, and a mighty hunter, who bred a pack of bear dogs and made legends with his hunts. He has told his own tale well in *Meet Mr. Grizzly*, but Agnes Morley Cleaveland, in *No Life for a Lady*, gives a more amusing picture of the Stevens's home as seen by a New Mexico ranch girl. Riding seventy miles one day to call, she found the new Mrs. Stevens washing clothes: "She wore an apple-green taffeta petticoat, a rose boudoir jacket, and a huge flower-trimmed leghorn hat." The English aristocrat was proving equal to the occasion. Naturally she won the friendly respect of her caller, who offered some helpful hints.

Kearny's army had brought, from many states, a sampling of citizens of every sort. Not a few coming to conquer were conquered by the country and stayed. Among them were young men of enterprise and education who were to become leaders in business and politics and to build the territory into the state. New Mexico had a longer period of tutelage than most; it was not admitted to statehood until 1910. During the territorial days, these young lawyers and go-getters were appointed governors and judges or elected delegates to Congress. Some men, appointed in the East, came west feeling and acting like proconsuls. Even in the middle of the twentieth century, recent arrivals from the East, seeking political office in New Mexico, campaign as devoted sons of her soil. Some Easterners have represented New Mexico in Congress while retaining their Eastern interests. Such men generally move "back east" when their political careers in New Mexico come to an end. Others have stayed on to found families who still contribute richly to the state's life. Perhaps none has so long a history as the Waldo family.

A James Waldo was on the Trail in 1828, and his son or nephew, Dr. David Waldo, was a captain in Doniphan's regiment, a trader and physician in Taos. His younger brother, Lawrence, was killed at Mora in the revolt that followed the murder of Governor Bent at Taos. Lawrence's son Henry became a prominent citizen of Las Vegas, an attorney for the Santa Fe Railroad with enormous political influence, and a justice of New Mexico's supreme court. And his grandson, Waldo Rogers, ascended the district bench in Albuquerque in 1951.

William McGuinness, who was in the battle for Albuquerque when Sibley took the town, rescued a little girl's doll from the terrible *tejanos* as he helped her family to escape. In due time he married her and established the town's first newspaper. His son, an attorney, likes to recall that his father refused several acres of sandhills in payment of an overdue bill for advertising. Those sandhills now are Albuquerque's most valuable property.

The Army also left teamsters and sutlers, who turned from supplying the Army to storekeeping, and ended as merchants with whole counties in their debt. Every county has a powerful family so founded.

To such a family belonged the Sergeant brothers, who, coming west soon after the Civil War, settled on remote but rich farming and grazing lands on the Chama, where one of their sisters joined them. Among her sons was Tom Burns, charming Irishman who married Señorita Josefina Gallegos of Abiquiu. He was, as Irishmen typically were, a Democrat, and Rio Arriba County was having its one brief period of Democratic domination. But young Tom Burns ran afoul of the Democratic boss, Antonio Joseph, son of a Portuguese nobleman who had been forced to flee his country and change his name. When Burns saw voters who asked for Republican ballots tossed bodily down the courthouse steps, he became a Republican, as the Burns-

Sergeant families have been ever since. The second Tom Burns attended Notre Dame as a small boy, but at sixteen was judged competent to stay at home and run the store. Later he met and married Señorita María Luisa Ortiz Tirado, of a distinguished family of Mexico. Their son, after a period in the diplomatic service, has returned to ranching in Rio Arriba County.

Irish names dot our map, and Irishmen have had much to do with making our history. James Thomas Cassidy ran away from Ireland with peddlers, made his way across the United States, and in 1855 built a store and home in Mora, where they still stand. When he needed help he sent back to Ireland for brothers and cousins. So John Doherty came to work in Tom Cassidy's store. When he was shot at by a political rival, he moved with his wife and thirteen children to Union County, where he achieved his ambition of owning as much land as was included in the Irish Free State. His neighbors say that at his death, John Doherty left each of his thirteen children one thousand head of cattle and one million dollars.

The aftermath of the Civil War colored New Mexico politics for years with lurid lights uglier than the nostalgic blue and gray. Doña Ana County, where the new town of Las Cruces had grown up to rival Confederate Mesilla, was torn between two powerful leaders: Colonel Albert J. Fountain, a Northerner who had entered New Mexico with the California Column, and Albert Bacon Fall, whose father had ridden with Morgan's Raiders in Missouri. Fountain was a Republican and Fall a Democrat, though he later became a Republican and was best known as a member of President Harding's cabinet.

In 1894 Colonel Fountain, as attorney for the newly created New Mexico Stock Association, had secured indictments against seventeen men accused of crimes—mostly cattle-stealing—against members of the Association. At that time Lincoln Plaza, now known as Old Lincoln, was the county seat, and Colonel Fountain had a drive of one hundred and sixty miles to his home in Las Cruces. He drove a buckboard with two horses, and his nine-year-old son Henry was with him. Somewhere between La Luz and the Organ Mountains they disappeared. The buckboard was found, but no trace of either man or boy, dead or alive, has ever been located. Four years later, three men were tried for the murder of the boy. Colonel Fountain was not mentioned. Albert Bacon Fall was one of the attorneys for the defense, so the trial reflected the old political and personal rivalry of Fountain and Fall. In a brilliant defense, the three accused ranchers were cleared, but popular opinion does not yet consider the case closed. Its mention is still good for a verbal row between adherents of the two old enemies.

Less well known and even more tragic is the story of the Rascón-Beckwith-Johnson families, which involves not only North and South, but our two frontiers. The story began between 1810 and 1820 when a wealthy citizen of Chihuahua named Rascón moved to Texas with his Spanish-German wife and their two lovely daughters. Of the two girls the most beguiling was Refugio, who caught the eye of a young Virginian and ex-Confederate named Beckwith, who had forgotten nothing. In no time he and the lovely Refugio were married, and their daughters grew up to carry on the family tradition of lovely girls.

At Seven Rivers Mr. Beckwith made his home in true Virginia tradition. His large adobe house, with pitched roof extending over verandas all around, was the epitome of comfort, with plenty of servants, cottonwood shade against the sun, and fireplaces to mitigate the winter's chill. Hospitality was boundless; every passerby was welcome. So it was natural that young William Charles Johnson should be brought there by his pals after he had been wounded in a brush with Indians, probably about 1873, though William

Johnson, who tells the story, does not like to date his birth very accurately.

Young Johnson, after his discharge from the 4th Ohio, had heard from Texas: "Grass is belly deep. Come on." So he was accepted in the Beckwith home as a Texas cowboy driving cattle to Fort Bayard. But he was fated never to reach Fort Bayard. During a pleasant convalescence, the Yankee wooed and won Carmelita, widely known as the star of the Beckwith beauties. Their romance was to have a tragic ending.

The Johnsons had one son, William, and Carmelita was again "expecting" when old Beckwith, sitting on a wagon's tongue as his son-in-law rode up with a bunch of cowboys, heard in casual conversation that Johnson was an ex-Union soldier. Without hesitation the old Confederate, retired but still bellicose, drew a bead and killed the "damned Yankee." So honor was satisfied, his daughter widowed, his grandson orphaned, and he had to become a fugitive in Texas. But not before a hot-headed cowboy named Wallace Ollinger had shot at him, demolishing a handsome nose.

The widowed Carmelita Beckwith Johnson then went to live with the family of her mother's cousin, Don Nicolás Pino, a descendant of Don Pedro Pino. Don Nicolás, as William Johnson said, "owned all the sheep in the Estancia Valley" and was politically prominent, so the Johnson family lived both on the ranch at Galisteo and in the Governor's Palace in Santa Fe. But the widow had not gone alone with her children. A faithful cowboy had ridden along to guard and to serve her: the Wallace Ollinger who had ruined Beckwith's aristocratic nose, and whose brother was to come to fame by being killed by Billy the Kid. In time the widow married the cowboy and had a son who became a prominent Standard Oil man in Mexico.

Young William Johnson stayed in the West. After freighting in Colorado and punching cattle in New Mexico, he served as a Rough Rider in Cuba, did a stretch in the Philippines, and put in a restful interlude in Hawaii, where he married a New England teacher. They came finally to live in the ghost town of Kingston, where Mr. Johnson—exceedingly tall, slow-spoken, but most verbose—has won the title of "Windy" Johnson. Mrs. Johnson is bedridden; her lovely face is luminous with soul, her words are spiced with humorous understanding, her reading is Jane Austen.

Among the workers and builders of the state was a crew known as Rawhiders. Often border mountaineers who had escaped service in both Union and Confederate armies, they were known for the rawhide they used to make shoes or chaps or to splice a broken axle or spoke. The men rode scrawny horses, scorned all work, and seldom killed their own poor cattle, finding stolen meat tastier. Their women were slatterns and skilled at putting forth their ragged youngsters to appeal to ranch women's generous hearts. Rawhiders of all ages chewed tobacco. When the supply ran low, they mounted the smartest little John Wesley or Thomas Jefferson on the fastest horse and sent him to town for more.

This picture comes from James A. McKenna's *Black Range Tales*. McKenna, a Catholic, said the Rawhiders had no religion. Probably they had that debasement of the faiths of John Wesley and Roger Williams common to Southern mountaineers. In heritage they were—much as some of us hate to admit it—the true Anglos. It is pleasanter to remember that in New Mexico's clear air, and especially through intermarriage with non-Anglo elements, the descendants of those do-nothings and slatterns have produced worthy citizens.

The word "marriage," at some points in our history, was only a manner of speaking. McKenna, true frontiersman, writes of matings like those of birds in the spring. As the Catholic Church frowned upon unions with heretics, and as often there was no church at all, these easy habits were inevitable, and many a union established without legal sanction or clerical blessing resulted in families well founded in affection and responsibility.

Under the influence of men trained in the law and of women demanding respectability, the territorial legislature in 1882 passed a law providing that a man living unlawfully with more than one woman would be ineligible for public office and liable to a $500 fine and five years' imprisonment. Naturally, there ensued an amazing amount of scurrying around to find somebody qualified to perform a marriage service. Anybody. Any marriage service.

Dr. P. T. Martin of Taos told a tale that he called the first marriage in E-town (as Elizabethtown was popularly called). Once, during the 1880's, when gold production in the Moreno valley between Cimarron and Taos was at its height, a Virginia colonel, living in E-town, got himself appointed justice of the peace and announced that decency had arrived. Dr. Martin described the colonel: "He wore his pants in his boots, a plug hat, and he liked stud poker and liquor. And he could sling words!"

Dr. Martin related that one Saturday night a miner from the Mystic Mine, in town to celebrate, singled out a lady. But she was not, as usual, acquiescent. "It is different now," she said. "The only way is for you to marry me." "And how do we do that?" he asked. The lady explained about the colonel, and the miner readily agreed. So the wedding procession started, stopping at every saloon and finally reaching the one where the Justice sat, his plug hat on the back of his head, his boots on a table. Pleased with the effect of his moral crusade, the colonel righted himself at once and called for silence. But what ceremony to use? E-town had neither law book nor prayer book, nor could the officer of the law recall any suitable words. But he was dashed only momentarily. Clearing his throat, he ordered the couple to stand before him, stayed his swaying against the bar, and intoned in full Virginia accents:

"Underneath this roof in stormy weathah
This buck and squaw now come togethah
Let none but Him who rules the thundah
Set this buck and squaw asundah.

Now you're married, by God, and let's all have a drink."

So frontier New Mexico had its dismal and its comic aspects. But the people who built the state and stamped its character were the sort that figures little in the movies—families who came in covered wagons with a few head of stock, took up land, and stayed. Most of them came poor. A few made fortunes, but usually they made only good reputations and established families who continue active in the state's life.

Squire L. Barker—that was his name, not a title—drifted westward and finally settled on Sapello Creek above its junction with the Mora River. Where the valley was wide enough Squire Barker and his sons farmed; on the hills they cut timber to build stout houses and barns; on the uplands they ran cattle and bred good horses. Hard work was the daily rule. Fun consisted in riding all day to dance all night with neighbors from fifty miles away, or in hunting. The boys knew every inch of mountain and canyon from Hermit's Peak to Wheeler's. One of them, Elliott, in *The Dogs Bark Treed*, writes of that trackless wilderness as intimately as a lady describing her garden, and of his horses and dogs as personal friends.

Elliott's brother, S. Omar Barker, is one of New Mexico's best interpreters as poet, raconteur, and writer of westerns with the flavor and rhythm of absolute truth. With his writer-wife he inhabits a hideaway at the top of Sapello Canyon, where the air smells of wild mint, wild clematis, and wild raspberries in season and pine needles all the time.

All the members of that family are useful citizens carrying on in their several ways the zeal for righteousness which made their father leave his plough or his branding to preach a funeral or lead a prayer-meeting.

Such families depended largely upon the mother, and not only in sentimental ways either. The typical woman of the frontier was sturdy, hard-working, lacking perhaps the learning of books, but knowledgeable about childbirth, nursing, and simple remedies. A true helpmeet, she did her share of cattle-driving and bull-whacking, as well as of her specialties of childbearing and cooking. But however crude the life women lived, they brought amenities. Lace tidies appeared in brothels, silverware graced tables set under lean-tos, churches were set going as soon as possible. The "chippies" at Hillsboro subscribed most of the money that opened the first church in Kingston. Women opened the Deming Ladies Hospital with no money; each woman put in hours a week cleaning, cooking and scrubbing, as well as nursing.

Before there were hospitals or even doctors, women shouldered those jobs; in some places they still do so. A good type was Ma'am Jones, wife of Heiskell Jones, who had left West Virginia with his family about 1880. The nine Jones youngsters were born in various places, including New Mexico's Lincoln County, where they finally settled. On Hondo Creek they had good farmland, but mostly Pa and the boys rode the range, hiring out as hands and dealing in whatever offered. The line between law and outlawry was tenuous and wavering.

Ma'am Jones never wavered in anything. Virginia-born, she taught her children good English and proper manners. The boys rose when a lady entered the room, offered chairs, removed their hats, never swore in a lady's presence. Her eldest and probably her favorite was John. He was his mother's constant aid, even seeing her through childbirth

9 *The Billy the Kid Museum in Old Mesilla*

NEW MEXICO
STATE TOURIST
BUREAU

10 *Sadie Orchard of Hillsboro in the 1880's*

11 *The open-pit copper mine at Santa Rita and the rock that was named for the Saint*

CAPLIN AND
THOMPSON, OLD
ALBUQUERQUE

*12   Old-time
chuck wagon
on the Bell
Ranch near
Tucumcari*

13 *Marking
sheep*

CAPLIN AND
THOMPSON, OLD
ALBUQUERQUE

14 *White-faced Here-fords have replaced the Longhorns*

CAPLIN AND
THOMPSON, OLD
ALBUQUERQUE

15   *Patrocino Barela, wood sculptor of Taos*

16 One of many mountain trails

CAPLIN AND
THOMPSON, OLD
ALBUQUERQUE

once when the neighbor woman failed to come. He was a gentle-seeming boy, never loud or coarse, never pugnacious. Yet somehow John killed fourteen men before he was himself killed at twenty-six somewhere in Texas.

Ma'am Jones could cope with anything. She never raised her voice, but her quietest word was heeded. And she was beautiful, close to six feet tall, with the broad, deep-bosomed figure of the childbearing woman. Her black hair grew down to her feet and was always brushed to shining, braided smoothly, and wound round and round her queenly head. She had clear, warm skin and a friendly smile, but her eyes were sharp rather than limpid, and they reflected both spirit and a shrewd mind. Ma'am was a judge of men, and men knew it. Her house, wherever it was, whether or not it had walls or a roof, was immaculate, shining with cleanliness. "Soap and water," she used to say, "will cure most anything." The heavy hand-woven bed and table linen, brought from Virginia, was boiled and sunned to snowy whiteness; most of it was used up making bandages, for Ma'am Jones served as midwife, nurse, and doctor. She knew the herbs; her natural cleanliness doubtless forestalled many an infection, for she boiled everything she used, and her cool competence contributed that valuable therapeutic agent, confidence.

Once when the whole neighboring Casey family came down with smallpox, and Heiskell was not at home, Ma'am took what she thought would be needed, caught her easiest mare, adjured the older children to be good until Pa got home, mounted sidesaddle, and with the baby on a pillow rode off fifty miles to help. Pa followed with the other children in the wagon as soon as he got home. Living in a tent, Pa and Ma'am Jones labored day and night. They buried three Caseys, but saved the parents and the other two children. None of the Joneses caught the disease; perhaps Ma'am's constant boiling helped.

Different, but as useful in her way, was Sadie Orchard

of Hillsboro. She was a tiny, high-bosomed woman with short feet in shorter shoes, tight spitcurls, and a wicked chuckle to punctuate her obscenities and profanities. Coming from a questionable past, Sadie had achieved respectability by marriage with Harry Orchard. Together they operated a resort of many purposes in Lake Valley on the railroad and ran a stage up through Hillsboro to Kingston in the boom days of the 1880's. Later Sadie opened a hotel in Hillsboro, known to all New Mexico's lawyers for cleanliness and good food. There they stayed during court terms; her terse, unquotable comments on them were doubtless just. Forty years later, during World War I, Sadie Orchard was discovered doubling for whatever Sierra County lacked: doctor, nurse, hospital, and undertaker. She fed the family of a man serving his term in the penitentiary, shopped "for them chippies up on the hill," cut the hair of "old Tom the Chinaman," who dreaded shears. During the flu epidemic she nursed many a family until all had recovered or died, washing, cleaning, cooking, laying out the bodies, lining the board coffin, and coming home to cut the geraniums and bleeding hearts grown in her dining-room window for just such occasions. For a bad woman, Sadie was of the best.

At the other end of the social scale was Mrs. Ada McPherson Morley, whose daughter, Agnes Morley Cleaveland, has written her story too well for another to touch it. Mrs. Morley came from Iowa with her husband, William Raymond Morley, the competent engineer who surveyed the Santa Fe Railroad's route over Raton Pass. Mrs. Morley, widowed young, left an even finer monument in the family she managed to raise and educate at Princeton and Stanford while she ran cattle on the San Augustine Plains. Mrs. Morley's standards were rigid: the Presbyterian Church; the Republican Party; the WCTU, which she helped to found in New Mexico; good English. She succeeded in giving her children a sense of superiority that demanded superior standards without snobbery.

Other women whose husbands were able to protect them gave an unexpected cachet to frontier life. They were the ladies whose grand pianos are still every town's boast, who lived in large houses with servants, whose clothes came from such style centers as St. Louis and Kansas City, and who brought true sophistication as well as mannerisms and evening dinner. They, too, were found in every county, but the most revealing types were perhaps those in the lower Pecos valley.

The southeastern corner of New Mexico—all Lincoln County in its heyday—was a land that made men rich. John Chisum, who came to New Mexico in 1864, was the best-known and the most aggressive; he held more water holes, dominated more land, and hired more men than most. But there were others who conducted continuous undercover warfare for power.

Cattle rustling was not criminal, much as the victim disapproved of it. Jesse Evans, who put in a stretch with Billy the Kid, rustled for some of the best citizens. The entire Lincoln County War of 1880 began with the killing of a wealthy Englishman and involved a cultivated churchman from Philadelphia and an Irishman keeping store with a retired German officer. It was a fight between factions in which Governor Lew Wallace, representing law and order, was only a helpless bystander. Many of these men had been trained in tough border-fighting before, during, and after the Civil War. Captain J. C. Lea, whose grandson Tom was to become famous as painter and novelist, had served as a Confederate soldier in Missouri. The Coes rode with Billy the Kid's gang. Marion Turner and Heiskell Jones were proud of having run out the Mormons. Colonel Maurice Garland Fulton, deepest student of this period, sums it up: "They were men of their times; they were no archangels."

These men made money, and their wives contributed the amenities. Captain Lea's wife promoted and saw established in 1895 the New Mexico Military Institute, one of the best in the country. But the tone of Pecos valley society was set by men and women of the great world. In the Carlsbad Museum a gentle lady, who seemed to be a resident of the town, pointed to the exhibits—old photographs of stately gentlemen and ladies in bustles, pieces of good glass and china such as might be found in Eastern museums. "This town," she said proudly, "is not New Mexico of Mexicans and Indians. Our town was settled by gentlemen. They brought water from the mountains and planted trees along our streets, and they were able to invest in developing the country."

Two men had most to do, in the last decade of the nineteenth century, with the metamorphosis of the Pecos valley from cattle range to farmland. James John Hagerman was a Canadian who had prospered in Michigan and in Colorado before he became fired with the possibilities of the Pecos valley. His partner was a New Yorker, Charles B. Eddy; the county still bears his name, though the town was renamed Carlsbad when the discovery of mineral waters roused the hope that it would rival the German spa. These two men opened the valley with a railroad and pushed irrigation. At the Hagerman home on the Old Chisum ranch, Mrs. Hagerman presided over elegant silver and cultivated conversation, and Mr. Hagerman made a valuable collection of eighteenth-century books. Their son Herbert was one of New Mexico's territorial governors.

Charles DeBremond, a Swiss officer, chose the Pecos valley after searching the whole West for the most desirable spot for colonization. Using Italian workmen, who had come as immigrants to the United States and eventually to the Pecos valley, he built a stone house at Carlsbad and planted a vineyard and orchards. Later he experimented

with Karakul sheep. He also found time to drill a unit of
the New Mexico guard, which served in Mexico in 1914
and won distinction in World War I as Battery A, New
Mexico Unit. The colonel, a dashing officer with full military mustache, dressed habitually in riding breeches and
boots, carried a crop, and rode thoroughbred horses.

Quite as military and even more spectacular was Major
Etienne de Peyster Bujac, Huguenot from Baltimore, who
was tall and dark with brilliant eyes. The major wore Nor-
folk jackets, an enormous velour hat, and a turquoise-
studded belt. His boots were made by a Frenchman who
had followed him west.

Mrs. DeBremond, a rigid Presbyterian, was accustomed
to invite a priest to her home in Carlsbad to stay overnight
and say Mass for her Catholic maid. Mrs. Bujac made her
home a center of a hunting group. These homes were built
in the current mid-Victorian style, surrounded by gardens
and orchards, and served by trained people. There was no
thought of "going Western." Their effort was to maintain
the standards they had brought from home. Happily those
standards made for a smooth adjustment with the best ways
of the frontier people and of the old Spanish families. Out
of this curious mixture of types have come New Mexico's
comfortable lack of snobbery and its ability to get along
with all sorts of people.

XXI

THE MINING MAN

◖◖ THE OLDEST mine in the United States is in Los Cerrillos, the little hills twenty miles south of Santa Fe, where Indians dug out turquoise at Mount Chalchihuitl. This name, the Aztec word for Mexican jade, might well have been applied to New Mexico's sky-stone by the discoverers. Martin W. Pollock, a mining engineer working near Madrid, estimates that about one hundred thousand tons of rock had been removed from the pit that is still traceable under a growth of piñon and cedar. Indian miners knew the trick of splitting rock by heating it and then throwing water on it. Broken rubble was then carried away on human backs and so thoroughly picked over that not the tiniest bits of turquoise have been found on the dumps. Even the site worked in the eighties as the Tiffany Mine has been long abandoned. The romantic like to believe that Santo Domingo and San Felipe Indians go there at night to dig out their best stones, but mining men consider this unlikely.

The Spanish did little about the turquoise, though legend has it that a cave-in at Chalchihuitl was one cause of the Revolt of 1680. Spain was interested in gold and silver, and every explorer—not believing his predecessor's assurance that there was none—tried again. Often the lode reported just over the hill remains the shimmering lure that leads today's seeker on. The first of these was La Sierra Azul, a mountain somewhere north of Moquiland that was blue with copper and silver and perhaps with quicksilver, too.

For years explorers crawled all over those mountains and reported traces of copper, lead, alum, and sulphur, as well as silver. But the rich vein never materialized.

Coronado's men mined sulphur in the Jemez Mountains and made gunpowder at Bernalillo, giving New Mexico its first manufacturing enterprise. And lowly salt from lakes between Quemado and Zuñi, in the lower Estancia valley and near El Paso, proved worth hauling on burros to the mines in Chihuahua. Such things would not enrich a kingdom; Spain turned to missionarying. So New Mexico first played its trick of withholding the treasure sought and coming through with something else: not gold, but souls to save; not water, but oil; not oil, but potash—or nothing at all except a good yarn. The mining man never gives up, and thereby hang all the tales of picturesque failures and lucky strikes.

The earliest mine of lasting value is near Silver City. In 1800 an Apache chief showed traces of copper to his friend, Lieutenant Colonel José Manuel Carrasco, who named the place Santa Rita del Cobre. A rock standing above the site has the outlines of a kneeling woman, and a local legend has it that the colonel thought it resembled his favorite saint, Santa Rita, and therefore gave her name to the mine. In 1804 Carrasco sold out to Don Manuel Elguea, a Chihuahua banker, who began to ship long burro-trains of copper to Mexico on its way to the royal mint in Spain. Zebulon Pike reported in 1806 that those open pits were yielding twenty thousand mule loads a year. Elguea, secure in his government contract, erected rough smelting works protected by a triangular adobe fort. One of its watchtowers still stands, lost among modern mining buildings. In 1822 James Pattie and his son leased the mines for one thousand dollars a year and worked them for five years. The Patties were unique in including the Apaches in their contract, and they had no Indian troubles in the very center of Apacheria. Pattie lost out only when he entrusted thirty thousand dollars to a friend who robbed him, leaving him cleaned out. The Apaches said: "Never trust a white man."

All the other Apache tales are of hideous attacks on wagon trains and lonely ranch-houses, with men killed fighting for their women, who saw their children dashed to death and were themselves carried off into trackless mountains. J. Frank Dobie, who has the storyteller's best gift of believing what he hears, relates, in *Apache Gold and Yaqui Silver*, many an enthralling yarn of how Apaches scared off or even killed prospectors who came near their hidden mines, and how the Apaches brought in gold dust to exchange for guns and powder. "The Lost Adams Diggings" were lost, according to Adams, a prospector who reported a fabulous gold strike in 1864, because the Apaches had "made him forget" the clearly marked trail. Only Santa Rita was an Apache's gift to a white man he could trust.

Santa Rita caught New Mexico history as it passed. Kit Carson worked there as a teamster for Robert McKnight, one of Kearny's army, who made a fortune out of the mines before the Apaches cut off his supplies by stealing an eighty-mule pack train. In 1862 Confederate General Sibley made headquarters at Santa Rita before he was turned back by the California Column.

In 1873 the first U.S. patent to the Santa Rita mining property was issued after its purchase from the heirs of Elguea, who were found scattered throughout Mexico and Europe. The purchaser was a Colorado company, which then worked the mine, erected a small smelter, and shipped high-grade ore and black copper to the nearest railroad, in Colorado. Mules were still the mode of transportation, but the mine's fame was traveling faster than its copper. During the next twenty years the mine changed hands several times. One of its owners was William Randolph Hearst, who sold it in 1899 to the Santa Rita Company.

Silver City, by the turn of the century, contained all the elements of New Mexico's frontier in highest concentration: miners from Wales, southeastern Europe, Mexico, and the States; squatters on the big cattle ranches still held by cattlemen who did not hesitate to shoot; a "Chink" washee-washee conducting a brisk smuggling in opium and compatriots; merchants trying to do business and stay out of trouble; and a lurid and luxurious red-light district across the arroyo, which, in a cloudburst, rose to a roaring flood but never cut the town off from the ladies for very long. And to top the pile was a group of sophisticated Main Liners from Philadelphia, brought by mining interests or by tuberculosis to Dr. Bullock's fine Cottage Sanatorium. Such men and women gave the town a sophisticated tone during the first decades of the century, and this has marked its life ever since. Bachelors from Princeton entertained elegantly and organized theatricals. George McCreary, each day, drove his ailing wife behind a smartly caparisoned mule to the Chinese restaurant for tea. Out on the Gila, Tom Lyons, known locally as "the Lion," built a splendid hunting-lodge not long before the First World War, and furnished it with fine furniture, even a grand piano taken apart and shipped out into the mountains on pack mules. John M. Sully, graduate of the Massachusetts Institute of Technology, suspected a vast copper deposit from the lumps of pure copper he picked up on the dumps, and spent fifty thousand dollars to prove it. He then went east to interest big capital.

In 1909 the Chino Copper Company was organized, and the Santa Fe soon thereafter built west from Rincon to Silver City, and Grant County had become important in the territory. John M. Sully, manager of the Chino Copper Company, Percy Wilson, its attorney, and Tom Lyon, representing the cattle "barons," attended every session of the legislature with other interested gentlemen, who made laws without the necessity of running for office—or the danger of being retired by democratic processes. Their highest accolade is: "They kept taxes down!"

By a series of purchases lasting over several years, the Chino Copper Company was absorbed, early in the twentieth century, by the Kennecott Copper Corporation. As the Chico Mines Division, the old Santa Rita operation ranks fourth among the country's open-pit mines, with a production valued at some twenty-two million dollars annually. The region also produces considerable quantities of lead and zinc.

The Chino Mines Division manager is proud of its housing, its clubs, and its efforts to overcome certain employees' prejudices. The earlier policy of housing Mexican nationals in a separate section is breaking down as the miners maintain better homes and gardens. The kneeling figure of Santa Rita still presides over the hilly town and the vast amphitheater of the open pit, with its lovely striations of green and turquoise, yellow and rose, all under a shimmering and sunny sky.

Although California was the land of the great gold rush in 1849, the first gold strike west of the Mississippi was made in New Mexico, twenty years before the California Gold Rush and all but forgotten in that stampede. In 1828 a sheep-herder on the Juan Ortiz Grant, south of Mount Chalchihuitl, picked up a stone that resembled the gold-bearing nuggets of his native Sonora. This was the Old Placer; in 1839 the New Placer was discovered in the San Pedro Mountains. Both were dry; lack of water has always hampered mining in this area. The Mexicans once tried hauling their ore to water, but generally they panned by shaking it in hand-hewn wooden *bateas*. Even with such crude implements, Josiah Gregg estimated that they extracted between sixty and eighty thousand dollars a year. The grim and hideous life at those mines is well described by Ruth Laughlin in *The Wind Leaves No Shadow*. She imagines a forlorn youth here for her heroine, who was to become the fabulous Tules of Santa Fe.

In 1861 a group of men from the States patented the Ortiz Grant, which, perhaps by Yankee ingenuity, had been expanded from the hundred acres of Juan Ortiz's modest holding to some 69,458 acres. The new company had grandiose plans, even proposing to bring water from the Pecos River with enough force to sluice out the rock with hydraulic jets. This was never done, but the company cleared a couple of million dollars by dry washing. The placers are still dry, but the latest owner, George W. Potter, continues to explore and to confer with local inhabitants, who offer to lead him to hidden lodes—even to tons of bullion buried at low levels during the revolt of 1680. Mining men say most such dreamers are honest. The range is streaked with "stringers," thin veins of gold not worth developing without water. Among present dreams of solving that problem is a proposal to tap the subsurface waters of the dry Galisteo Creek.

The most famous effort to mine without water was made by Thomas Alva Edison, who set up an experimental works at Dolores to develop an electrostatic process for separating gold from sand. His operation, carried on in strictest secrecy, seemed to succeed, but finally it failed. The Wizard lost two million dollars in New Mexico without getting gold. He even ran true to form in missing what lay underfoot. Mr. Edison was, at that time, seeking a substance to make a heat-resistant filament for his electric globe. Doubtless he was not looking for it in New Mexico. But in 1950 Martin Pollock, idly panning along a cut Edison had dug, noticed a sluggish movement among the light and dark particles in his pan. He took the particles of ore to town for testing; he put ultraviolet rays on them. Sure enough, he had found scheelite, from which tungsten is derived. Tungsten was what Mr. Edison had needed.

The Palace Hotel, known now as the Old Rock House, was built soon after the Civil War, when Richard Rodney Green brought from Kentucky five hundred head of cattle, a string of pure-bred horses, wagons loaded with fine furniture, and a large family. At Cerrillos, he paid Cochiti Indians $1,600 to build his three-story stone mansion, and Mrs. Green made a garden whose traces still remain in fine trees, a grape arbor, and a Virginia creeper against the walls. Cerrillos, during the mining boom, was as lurid as any Western town and its roster of distinguished visitors is longer than most.

Mr. Green's store sold miners' supplies for gold dust; his stage ran full from Santa Fe; and his hotel was a center of lavish entertaining and reckless gambling. One poker game there is said to have run four days and nights. Dr. Palmer lived there, and was at hand to sew up the fight victims. Governor Lew Wallace stayed awhile with his wife during the 1880's, when he was working on *Ben-Hur*. Another Governor, less discreet, maintained a love-nest in the upstairs suite with the bay window. The Kentucky Greens politely entertained two Union generals: General Phil Sheridan, who stopped in passing, and ex-President Grant, who was losing money in a mine at Golden in the San Pedros. Sarah Bernhardt stopped at the Palace while she played at the Cerrillos Opera House. And Theodore Roosevelt was so "dee-lighted" with Calvin Green's ambidexterity with six-shooters that he took the boy along as a Rough Rider.

These tales and many more are told by Mrs. Anna Vergolio, whose husband bought the house in 1913, when Cerrillos was still expecting to become a large city. Mrs. Nellie Trigg, a later owner, is most interested in gathering stories about Mrs. Green's mystical powers and her influence with the Indians. Harold Trigg, who runs Brahma cattle, says that Indians still reverence Mrs. Green so much that they show him good springs long overgrown and lost. To a cattleman a spring is worth more than much fine gold.

With gold discoveries came the prospector, symbol of hope invincible. Staked by men in the towns, he would load his burro with a keg of water, a sack of beans, bacon and salt, his pick and pan, and his blanket or sheepskin. Months later he would show up again with evidence of a real strike, or more likely with just enough trace of gold to extract another stake from his backer. The prospector has not disappeared. Even in prosaic Albuquerque some two hundred prospectors and treasure-seekers hole up between sorties to study their ancient maps and raise money for another try. In their minds New Mexico is underlaid not only with gleaming gold, shining silver, and green copper, but with untold wealth buried by some conqueror, missionary, or *hacendado* in iron-bound chests often topped by the bones of the peons who buried it. Treasure seekers include a priest who can decipher mediæval Latin charts, sober attorneys, and widows with maps left by deceased finders of treasure now lost.

New Mexico never became a large gold producer, but during the seventies and eighties mining was the territory's leading industry, and many a newcomer made a tidy fortune by grub-staking prospectors. The precious metal occurs in many parts of the state in lodes and placers, but too often in veins that soon pinch out or where lack of water or too much water—New Mexico's twin evils—have taken the profit out of mining.

The Old Abe Gold Mine at White Oaks, in the Jicarilla Mountains, produced several million dollars before it was flooded out. The story of White Oaks has been told charmingly in *Land of Heart's Desire* by Emerson Hough, who lived there in the 1880's with a group of young bachelors who were to serve the state and nation later as a senator, a governor, a congressman, and a Secretary of the Interior.

The Aztec and Mystic mines produced much gold for the owners of the Maxwell Land Grant during the last years of the nineteenth century, when Elizabethtown, in the Moreno valley, was a roaring mining camp. During those years, bitter charges and countercharges of high-grading or stealing ore led to a series of murders, culminating in the decapitation of Arthur Manby in Taos in 1929. On July 4 of that year, Manby's body was found in his own house, fully clothed but headless, and a skull, gnawed clean, was found in the next room with Manby's police dog, maddened by lack of water. The case seemed to have a connection with older murders and disappearances at E-town. A woman named Teresa Ferguson was the daughter of one of the miners who had charged the owners of the Aztec Mine with high-grading. She was also Manby's heiress, and he had acted as her representative in a long series of litigations. As the case of Manby's death has never come to trial, it remains one of New Mexico's unsolved mysteries, an unending topic of conversation and speculation.

Bland, in the Jemez above Cochiti, lasted longer as a ghost town. Recently one could enter the hotel, see the bell marked "Ring for night clerk," and find glasses—but, alas, no bottles—still on the shelves. The Washington Mine, too, produced well until water flooded the workings. In many such cases, mining men believe that gold remains in the mines, but in quantities too small to repay the expensive operations required to keep the workings free of water. Gold is now mined only as a secondary product in New Mexico.

Silver also failed to put New Mexico among the first producers, but it, too, had its strikes and made its towns. Socorro was a wild town when the Santa Fe Railroad ended there and stages took off for White Oaks, Lincoln, and Roswell, and for the mines in the Magdalenas. Miners, track workers, gamblers, and desperadoes added their personal quarrels to the racial and religious rows already present, and so produced a hell's broth that led to a vigilante organization. In time the vigilantes became equally lawless and were, with difficulty, reduced to law and order. But Socorro was getting rich.

Silver was booming in the Magdalenas, and a mine had been discovered on the edge of Socorro. A smelter was established; hauling was big business. But the Santa Fe, which has often given and taken away, built on down to El Paso in 1882, killing Socorro at one blow. A revival began in World War I, when the Sherwin-Williams Paint Company began to work lead and zinc mines in the Magdalenas. During the second World War more life was brought to the town by the working of volcanic products to make building-blocks.

Sierra County is full of tales. Negroes continue to show up with maps of the location of the Lost Nigger Diggings, reported by Negro troops chasing Geronimo, but never found again. Its biggest thrill was in 1880 when two prospectors, following a ten-inch stringer, burst suddenly into a chamber "as big as a house," whose silver-studded walls flashed in the lantern's beam. This was the Bridal Chamber, which produced fifteen million dollars before it shrank to a stringer again.

In that same year, Jack Sheddon was run out of Lake Valley—not a puritanical place—because of his addiction to "dizzy dames and John Barleycorn." Kenny relates that Sheddon drifted up the North Percha Creek, where he fell asleep and woke to find his head pillowed on a rock that assayed almost pure silver. This was the Solitaire Mine. By Christmas, Kingston was a town of 1,800; within three years its population was six thousand and it had twenty-two saloons and three newspapers. But Kingston long remained a tent town. There was no time to build. Even the store was a tent. Only the big saloon on the gulch was a frame building. There gamblers gathered in the silver the miners dug for, and "gay ladies" made life pleasanter for all. McKenna tells that when smallpox hit the camp those Shady Lane girls offered to nurse the patients if the doctor would agree to stay sober.

The teacher was a young Irishman, with smiling blue eyes in a ruddy face, whom everybody liked. His name was Edward Doheny. Once when Doheny's beloved wife Carrie was sick, Johnny Moffet, who had just struck it rich, lent him the money to take her to El Paso. When Moffet was old and broke in California and Ed Doheny was one of the richest men in the country, he remembered and cared for his old friend. Another friend of Doheny's, then and later, was Albert Bacon Fall, who was beginning a varied career "pounding a drill up in Kingston," as Sadie Orchard said.

A useful though unglamorous mineral product is coal. Both anthracite and bituminous coal are found near Cerrillos at Madrid, one of the few places in the world where the two types occur together. Anthracite is shipped from Madrid to zinc smelters in Amarillo, Texas, and to the Kaiser steel mills in California. Bituminous is mined near Gallup and near Raton; mining men believe there are extensive coal fields not yet worked.

The first large coal development was on the Maxwell Land Grant. The Phelps-Dodge Company in 1906 purchased the mines at Dawson and, under Dr. James Douglas, made them models of safety. Influenced by Dr. Douglas, who was deeply aware of the discomforts and hazards of a miner's life underground, the Phelps-Dodge Company became one of the first to try to make that life not only safe, but also pleasant. Dawson lasted fifty-five years, and then closed down, becoming a modern ghost town in 1950.

Gallup, which advertises Navajos, is a center of large coal fields operated by the American Coal Company, whose miners are a polyglot sampling of immigrants from Europe and Asia. The town's history has been turbulent with labor troubles, Communist charges, and some latter-day vigilante violence that New Mexico has offset by decent court procedures.

Mining in New Mexico has by no means settled into routine. Mining engineers may speak lightly of the old-time prospector, but they all keep on prospecting, though with many differences. Modern prospectors—both week-enders and professionals—travel in station wagons, carry Geiger counters, belong to the New Mexico Miners and Prospectors Association, and consult its magazine's list of "critical and strategic minerals" wanted by the General Services Administration. The January 1951 list included fifty-two items, running from aluminum and antimony through cobalt, fluorspar, mica, and nickel to tin and zinc. Some of these minerals are already in profitable production in New Mexico.

Tin offers one of the most seductive and disputable of prospectors' dreams. Essential to our country in both peace and war, tin now comes from British Malaya, the Belgian Congo, and Bolivia. The U.S. Bureau of Mines and the Geological Survey have reported that reserves of tin in the United States, including Alaska, amount to no more than seven thousand short tons. This statement is met by loud disclaim in the Black range, where Robert H. Hartson says he can see more tin than that in one canyon. Mrs. Madelyn Caraway, "the tin lady," knows that New Mexico's tin is the purest in the world and in sufficient supply to free our country from foreign dependence. Therein, "the tin lady" believes, lies the difficulty: international cartels have prevented government financing of an invaluable resource lying there on top of the ground ready to be washed out by the simplest placer methods.

Bauxite was found in 1907 in the hills in Grant County, and the site was acquired by the Mellon interests, but has never been put into active production. Molybdenum has been worked for a quarter of a century in one mine east of Questa, and beryllium has been discovered near Embudo. On the Navajo reservation, near the Four Corners, helium was discovered in 1942 in quantities to justify the erection of two large plants that were later closed down.

Naturally, the greatest hope of our "atomic state" is that uranium and perhaps pitchblende may be found in quantities sufficient to relieve our country from dependence on the Belgian Congo. Even Paddy Martinez, a Navajo sheepherder, knew that canary-colored rocks might be uranium. One day he reported that he had seen some in the broken hills north of Grants. Geiger counters proved him right. Mining men offered ten-per-cent royalties for digging privileges, and the Santa Fe Railroad, which had been selling off land thereabouts, began quietly buying it back again and generously outfitted Paddy's whole family for the winter.

The area where Paddy Martinez made his find has attracted prospectors from the whole West, as well as serious investors. The Anaconda Copper Company soon began buying up land and leasing claims throughout the district.

Since Paddy Martinez made his uranium find, New Mexico has become the largest producer of uranium ore in the United States. The increase in production has amounted to as much as 61 per cent annually; and the daily milling capacity, since four new processing plants were placed in operation in 1958, has risen to about 12,000 tons. The AEC estimates the reserve of uranium ore at 54.9 million tons, and it has guaranteed the purchase of uranium oxide in concentrates from domestic ores produced and delivered from April 1, 1962, through December 31, 1966, at the price of $8.00 per pound. Exploration and development of these resources continues at an increased pace each year.

None of New Mexico's paradoxes is more amusing than the emergence into usefulness of volcanic waste. Pumice, always of some value as an abrasive, has been utilized to make building-blocks. Scoria, lava blown shaggy when it was a hot liquid, makes an even stronger block. Albuquerque supports several factories that bid fair to make our typical house volcanic instead of earthy. Perlite, a volcanic rock that pops like popcorn when heated, is being crushed and screened in a plant in Socorro and shipped for finishing into light-weight plaster and insulation. In Mora, mica, disregarded ever since glass supplanted it in windows, is being mined and shipped off to roofing factories. These developments are of great value to New Mexico, though they have not yet industrialized the state, which remains primarily a producer of raw materials. Among the few minerals that are finished in New Mexico are abrasive pumice, which is processed at a plant in Grants established in 1939; fluorspar, which occurs widely throughout the state and is shipped to steel mills and chemical plants from a factory established at Los Lunas in 1941; and barite. Barite is the latest comer, and has been produced in finished form only since 1950 at a plant near San Antonio, eleven miles south of Socorro.

Oil is also cited as a "home industry," though less than ten per cent of the state's output is processed in New Mexico. Pipelines owned by the oil compaines carry most of it to the Gulf coast and even to California. New Mexico congressmen are forever fighting for a fair division of this resource.

Oil was first discovered on the Navajo reservation, to the disgust of the Indians, who had hoped for water. Exploration then shifted to the state's southeastern corner, but the first producer was in San Juan County, after the Navajos had been persuaded that money for leases and royalties paid into the tribal coffers might prove as valuable as the water they had hoped to find. Oil wells on the reservation at Ute Dome, Hogback, and Rattlesnake, were all producing before 1924, when three drillers brought in a gusher near Artesia. All this was of minor importance if compared with the fabulous oil fields elsewhere, but in 1926 the Hobbs pool came in with a gush that brought all the biggest companies to New Mexico and shifted the state's population and its tax structure.

Oil men complain that the twenty million dollars a year they pay in royalties, lease rentals, and assorted taxes practically support the state. They fail to mention that they lease most of their land from the state at five to fifty dollars an acre while paying private owners as much as three thousand dollars. Nor do they recall that they are removing one of the state's irreplaceable resources at great profit to themselves.

Oil has brought a new invasion of Texans zooming in high-powered cars along roads that have cut the high grasslands. Raw scars mark the pipelines; tall skeletal doodlebugs have replaced windmills; and the cowboy is yielding to the doodler, that highly paid specialist who knows oil fields from Venezuela to Saudi Arabia. Haberdashers in Hobbs tempt these men with the most expensive clothes; jewelers display gemmed fraternal charms and cufflinks. There are expensive stores for women too, but Hobbs is a man's town whose men are technicians. The chamber of commerce boasts a great number of Phi Beta Kappa keys. But Hobbs, with its twenty thousand population, has no book store; a few books are hidden behind expensive office furniture and vaguely pointed out by a young woman: "There may be a best seller here somewhere."

Lea County's rapid growth has intensified the *tejano* atmosphere of eastern New Mexico. Drillers ordinarily own no property; they buy in Texas, read Texas papers. Despite state laws, Lea County maintains separate schools for Negroes. One powerful oil man offered to send to Santa Fe "the best damned state senator that money can buy." It is a recurrence, despite motors and Phi Beta Kappa keys, of the lawless days of a century ago.

A sideline of the oil business is the production of gas, which began in 1929 when the El Paso Natural Gas Company put in its first pipeline from the Hobbs field to the city of El Paso. It was buying, processing, and selling flare gas—the escaping gas that was formerly burned as waste—and giving Hobbs a weirdly hellish look. In twenty years, the El Paso Natural Gas Company has built 5,700 miles of pipelines, through which it serves large areas of New Mexico, Arizona, Texas, and California. Its longest pipeline, from Jal near Hobbs to San Francisco, is 1,200 miles. By 1950 the company had completed a pipeline from New Mexico's San Juan basin across Arizona to the California border, where it delivers gas to the Pacific Gas and Electric Company. Two hundred and eighteen miles of this line's four-hundred and fifty miles lie within the Navajo reservation. The Navajo Council, in entering into an agreement with the Company, insisted that Navajos should be employed for all work they are competent to do, and the Company finds them good workers.

New Mexico's most de luxe mining is potash, suitably located in the gentleman's town of Carlsbad. During World War I lack of potash threatened United States agriculture with disaster, as most of our supply came from Germany. Potash had been discovered near Amarillo, but as Texas had no federal lands the U.S. Bureau of Mines explored the Permian Basin farther west near Carlsbad, where a driller for oil had found potash as early as 1912. By 1929 private capital had been interested and two companies were soon in operation.

The industry has achieved the major miracle of turning Carlsbad into a mining town without destroying its gentlemanly aspect. The companies have erected pleasant houses of light-colored plaster, where miners water lawns and tend flower gardens after work.

The mines themselves are an eye-opener to one who has

seen the dark and dusty inferno of a coal mine or felt the airlessness of almost any underground operation. One enters the potash mine in a large elevator manned by men in mushrooom-shaped hats that are reminiscent of the Army's tin hats, but are made of plastic. At a depth of a thousand feet the vast, light chambers suggest the Carlsbad Caverns rather than any mine. Fresh air is pumped in, miners travel on trolleys along wide tunnels lighted by electricity and separated by heavy columns of ore left standing. There are no unsightly timbers. There is nothing unsightly. Everything is beautiful, for potash is a sparkling, rosy crystal. Chemically it is a salt, potassium and chlorine, and tastes like salt; it was laid down by the sea eons ago.

The operation consists of drilling holes into the walls of solid potash. Nobody will say how much potash may underlie New Mexico; guesses go as high as three hundred million tons. The electric drill, jiggling in a man's gloved hand, seems the only part of the whole business that a woman could not do if she could drive a car. But ramming in the explosive would be no difficulty, and from there on everything is done by levers or pushbuttons. Great machines cut out enormous chunks of soft ore that are than lifted and dropped into shuttle buggies and finally dumped into trains that carry tons of ore to the elevators. Trains above ground haul the loads to the crushers and brine tanks, where the potash is finished. Most of New Mexico's potash is shipped to the southeastern seaboard.

New Mexico's mining man has come a long way from the sheep-herder who picked up a nugget, the miner with his crude *batea*, the prospector, or even the promoter who gave no thought to the miner as a man. But he is still prospecting and still finding what he was not looking for.

XXII

THE STOCKMAN

ꞓ꞊ TIME was when a man was a cattleman or a sheep-man. The two were enemies because cattlemen believed that sheep destroyed the range for cattle. The emergence in one person of the stockman who runs both sheep and cattle indicates how indisputable facts can be disproved within a generation. During the same time the animals have changed. Long-legged, lightly fleeced sheep able to walk across several states to market have evolved into ovine balls of heavy wool and tender lamb-chops that are gently transported by rail or motor. And the thundering herds of longhorns, swimming rivers, stampeding, outrun or soothed by hard-riding, singing cowboys, have disappeared into hornless, unsexed makers of meat.

The sheepman is no longer the don in softest deerskin and wide hat with silver braid, nor is the cattleman that hero astride a pinto. The stockman is a businessman in a business suit, driving a fluid-drive car, calculating pounds of meat instead of heads of animals, and supporting several organizations for the advancement of his business and political interests. The enemy most fulminated against nowadays is the federal government.

The stockman has always used federal domain, but he never ceases to kick like a bay steer against any regulation of it, though, at bottom, he and the federal man seek the same thing: more and better meat from less land.

In New Mexico the sheep business came first. Every Spanish expedition brought cattle, pigs, and goats, as well as sheep. Sheep found themselves most at home. Mutton became the habitual diet; Navajos learned to weave; everybody wore wool; and blankets were a popular article of trade with New Spain long before the conquest was complete. In the nineteenth century, flocks were driven to markets in California and then "the States." *Ricos* became rich, and life in New Mexico was based on the flocks.

Some *ricos* owned thousands of acres of land granted them by the King of Spain and even more generously by the Mexican governors. Under old Spanish law, grazing lands were free to all. The *rico* came to control them much as the later stockman did, by simply owning more animals. This resulted in the *partido* system of running on shares. The poor man entered into a contract to care for a rich man's sheep and to return at the end of the year a specified number of rams, wethers, ewes, and lambs. Such *ricos* as the Chavezes and Oteros of Valencia County and Don José Leandro Perea of Bernalillo owned hundreds of thousands of sheep out on *partido*. Some *partidarios* became owners of considerable flocks of their own. But most of them remained dependent on the *patrón* and developed into the type of easily led voter whose psychology has so deeply marked New Mexico's political scene.

Mexicans were sheepmen, and remained so after they became American citizens. The gold rush to California opened a new market for meat; wool was for years an inconsiderable side line. Taking mutton on the hoof to California was a profitable business and a large part of life. In 1849 Don Antonio José Luna drove 10,000 wethers to California over a trail not far from the modern highway. Thereafter he, his sons, and his associates, the Oteros, made the journey regularly.

Once when Don Antonio José's son found himself pressed for money in California, he sent a message to his father. Don Antonio José called on his old friend, Marcelino Abeyta, an

Isleta Indian, who readily dug up the needed ten thousand dollars. It was literal digging; bankers said that Indians always brought in gold coins that smelled of the earth.

Another son, Don Solomon, became the archetype of the sheepman-*patrón-politico*. Invariably elected treasurer of Valencia County, he saw to it that its considerable taxes from the Santa Fe Railroad were scrupulously managed. Other offices did not interest him, but Solomon Luna's heavy figure, dark Romanesque features, and quiet force were felt in Republican councils when the state was smoothly operated by a junta of lawyers representing mines, railroads, and livestock.

After United States troops had subdued the Plains Indians, sheep lands were extended and little plazas grew up in eastern New Mexico, southern Colorado, and the Texas Panhandle. Long trains of wool wagons now crawled across the plains to Kansas City. Don Silvestre Mirabal of San Rafael made a fortune in the eighties. Wool had then supplanted meat as the trade article: gringos refused mutton— the Army never succeeded in feeding it to soldiers. Sheepgrowers in the 1930's taxed themselves for a national advertising campaign based on the slogan "Eat More Lamb." But the consumption of mutton remains low, and seventy per cent of our country's finished lamb goes to eastern markets, where English taste prevails.

The names Otero and Mirabal are still potent in the sheep business, as are Ortiz y Pino of Galisteo and various others. But nowadays New Mexico's livestock interests are dominated by gringos and by Spanish families who have disappeared under English names.

The Hubbells, whose progenitor, James L. Hubbell, came to New Mexico from Connecticut in 1848 and married a Chaves Gutierrez, still own large ranches near the Arizona border, where two brothers and the sons of one of them live. A third brother in Albuquerque manages the office with its unchanging sign: *Ocupamos hombres para las borregas* (We hire men for the sheep). And Tom Burns of Tierra Amarilla, also third generation New Mexican, has broken his family's record for marrying Spanish by bringing home a bride from Minneapolis.

The Burns and Sergeant families typify the gringos who entered the sheep business as storekeepers. Sheep being the only collateral and no banks being available, the storekeeper carried sheepmen on his books until wool was sheared or lambs were shipped. Now and again he had to take over; he was then a sheepman. Such men are found in every county. Arriving poor, but young and vigorous, they grew rich and established families still powerful. George and Frank Bond of Quebec and their friend Archibald MacArthur established stores in many towns, and finally became wool merchants as well as ranchers. Stewart MacArthur has kept both store and ranches near Wagon Mound. Germans came too. Louis Huning established a mercantile and stock business in Valencia County. Charles Ilfeld established himself in Las Vegas, and his family carries on there and in Albuquerque.

In most such families, where sons and grandsons have "stayed with the sheep," methods have not changed much. They employ men whose fathers and grandfathers worked for their fathers; the relationship between bossman and worker is a combination of humorous respect on both sides and a common devotion to the sheep. At all crises the owner is with the sheep. Wives say: "He's out lambing— or shearing—or shipping." If drought or storm menaces the herds, he may be on the job for weeks. Such work has made a type.

Ruddy of face, sturdy of body, slow of speech, and quick of eye, he covers miles of territory. Now he goes in a jeep or car, but he still sees every poisonous weed, broken wire, or droopy lamb. He stops at every sheep camp where the iron stove stands outside the tent along with the skillet and coffeepot, the water keg, and the drowsy dog. Attentively he hears and makes notes of the sheep-herder's report of encroaching pingue, which is poisonous to sheep, lowering water holes, coyotes' howls heard at night, and what is needed.

Sheep are the dumbest and most dependent of creatures, and must be fussed over every minute. They are herded along in bands of from 1,500 to 2,500 by a herder and his assistant, the *campero* who cooks, moves camp, and fetches burroloads of beans, coffee, lard, and flour for the men, of feed and salt for the sheep. Often he brings water. Both these men are overseen by the *caporal*, a mounted man often old and always dignified. He rides the rounds, sees that bands are moved as the grass dictates, and tallies sheep strayed, diseased, or attacked by wolves or coyotes. The sheep-herder never leaves his sheep.

In New Mexico the word "sheep-herder" has become one of scorn. "Just a sheep-herder," they say in derogation. But Captain Clark M. Carr, who had hired hundreds of them, said: "Where else can you entrust twenty thousand dollars of perishable property to an illiterate and be sure that he will care for it with intelligence and devotion?" Captain Carr had in mind the happy days when sheep-herders were paid thirty dollars a month, a wage that has risen with the general rise in the cost of living to one hundred dollars a month for the sheep-herder and ninety dollars for his helper. In New Mexico it is customary to employ two men for each band of sheep, but in some states one man does the entire job and is paid correspondingly. Even at the higher wage, it is difficult to find sheep-herders, as young Americans do not care for that lonely life among the bleating flocks. Consequently many ranchers have recourse to "wetbacks," Mexicans who have crossed the Rio Grande illegally. They will work for less and, above all, they have the feeling for sheep. Fred Huning said: "Not everybody can herd sheep; not one in a hundred will stay with it."

This transformation of the old peon sheep-herder into the modern New Mexican has hastened changes that were probably coming anyway as Texas stockmen bought land in New Mexico and introduced modern methods. In the eastern counties, where twelve to fourteen inches of annual rainfall make deep sod and sheep do not have to be moved from winter to summer range, ranchers began—as early as 1915—to fence their pastures with woven wire, fortified against wolves and coyotes with barbed wire underground. Here herders have been replaced by fence riders, who often ride in jeeps. But sheep are still sheep, and their needs condition the year's rhythm.

Ewes are bred in the fall, and lambing occurs from early spring to early summer, depending upon climate and altitude. Expectant mothers are gently herded to a spot chosen for good feed and water, sometimes with a man-made shelter. On the A. D. Jones ranch in Lea County the lambing sheds are only less comfortable than a hospital maternity ward.

After twenty days baby lambs can survive on tender grass, and the herders begin to move their charges to summer range in the mountains. If winter snows have been heavy, grass will be good and water holes not too far apart. Then many pounds of wool and meat are assured. Long drought may bring tragedy. Then owners scour the state, and even other states, to rent "grass"; often they load their animals on trucks or boxcars for a long haul to grass before they are too weakened to be moved. Such a year may result in heavy loss. Lambs are ready to be earmarked, as breeding stock or as animals to be shipped to market, before the fly season begins.

Sheep are shorn when the fleeces are heaviest. Expert hand shearers who formerly traveled in bands through

many states are being replaced by mechanical clippers.
Many New Mexico owners now employ professional shearers with mechanical equipment. In these cases, the shearers
tour the ranches and, with the assistance of the local sheep-
herders, push the blatting animals into corrals where they
are caught, run rapidly over by the whirring knives, and
let go, peeled to the yellow skin, often flecked with blood
and bleating piteously. The wool is tramped down in a
sack by a man muffled against the dust in a red kerchief.

The wool market is in Boston, and wool became a dependable crop when Boston buyers began to come to New
Mexico in the eighties. Las Vegas was then one of the
world's most important wool centers. Joe Taichert, still a
wool merchant there, remembers when loaded wool wagons
would back up four or five miles waiting to reach the
crowded plaza, where bidding was conducted by the lifting of a finger. Because wool was hauled up the Pecos from
the southeastern counties, where shearing began in April,
and from northern New Mexico, where it ended late in
July, Las Vegas had a long busy season. At the turn of the
century big dealers like Gross Blackwell and Charles Ilfeld
were weighing in one hundred wagons a day.

This steady demand for wool led to improved stock. The
old *churros*, descendants of the Spanish *merinos*, were good
foragers and able to defend themselves with their large
horns, but they gave only two or three pounds of wool.
When they were bred up with Rambouillet rams from
Utah, Idaho, and Montana, the clip increased, until the
average weight is now seven or eight pounds. When the
Bond-MacArthur Company began about 1900 to weigh
lambs they averaged forty pounds; thirty years later the
average was sixty-five. This Rambouillet sheep is New Mexico's preferred strain for both wool and mutton, but a new
strain has been developed.

Amos Dee Jones, ranching on the caprock near Roswell,

crossed Rambouillet, with their dense heavy wool, with the DeLaine, whose wool is longer and finer. It took him thirty years but he stabilized and registered a *Debouillet*, a strain whose rams sell all over New Mexico and are moving into other states. After Mr. Jones's death the business was carried on by Mrs. Jones, the old foreman, Dick Miller, and the Jones's sons.

Met at luncheon in Roswell, Mrs. Jones seemed the typical small-town lady in flowered hat and dainty frock. Even on her ranch, seventy-five miles southeast of Roswell, Mrs. Jones was not the newcomer's idea of how a ranchwoman should look. She did not affect fringed buckskin or cowboy boots, though her suit was practical, her shoes stout, and her hat designed for protection from the weather. At the ranch-house, with its tree-shaded pool by the pump, she got lunch: steak, fried potatoes, tomatoes, hot biscuits, jellies and pickles, pies and cakes, and a tall pot of coffee. She let the men talk. Driving over the range she deferred to her twenty-year-old son. But her gentile questions went deep.

"I see José hasn't mended that fence yet. . . . What's the matter with that ewe's hind leg? . . . Are you going to move that band soon?" She was proud of the animals' broad chests, indicating strong hearts, and the five-inch wool. A fleece, parted, shows dusty gray on top, then white, and then yellow grease above the pink skin. The guest room was piled with fleeces ready for exhibition, and the mantel was loaded with trophy cups. Mrs. Jones proposed taking her son to Australia to study methods there.

New Mexico's sheepmen are a conservative lot, but a few have ventured into exotic schemes. Colonel DeBremond's daughter and her husband, Lowry Hagerman, for example, produced Karakul lambs, whose pelts were shipped to the New York fur market as Persian lamb. Goats figure more largely than Karakul lambs in the state's economy, especially Angora goats, whose strong silky hair makes mohair and plush. Any goat, even the long-haired Angora, can climb over rocky country inaccessible to sheep, and will eat grasses sheep do not find palatable. Several ranchers in the southeastern counties have gone in for Angoras, but the romantic story is that of Mrs. Armer & Sons, a firm of Sierra County.

When Mrs. Reid was left a widow with six children in 1892, her only asset was a herd of native goats. So she fed goat milk to the children and sold what they did not need. When she married Leven Edward Armer in 1894, Mrs. Armer went in for Angoras, recently introduced into New Mexico. In 1900 she amazed the industry by paying $1,050 for a champion buck. Now her son, Robert Reid, who heads the business, has a house filled with silver cups and blue ribbons.

The Reid ranch near Hillsboro is shaded by black walnuts, and the air is warmly spiced with creosote bush. The white stucco house, with its fenced flower-garden, is completely modern and furnished throughout with mohair: upholstery and curtains, bedspreads and table covers, rugs, and a banner woven with the Eastern Star emblem presented to Mrs. Reid when she was a Worthy Matron. In pens outside, animals being groomed for the state fair were wrapped in gunny sacks to protect their long hair, for all the world like ladies in a beauty shop. In the production of mohair New Mexico is second only to Texas.

New Mexico's cattle business began when the great herds were driven north from Texas over the famous Chisum Trail and others less known. John Chisum, finding the grass deep and sweet along the Pecos, settled there. Others followed, pre-empted the water holes, and spread out. So they encountered sheep whose smell they did not like, whose meat they would not eat, and whose owners and herders were of the hated breed of Mexican.

The fallacious belief that sheep ruined the range by cropping close was due to the overgrazing that had exhausted many of the best grasses. Grama, curly mesquite, the sedges, and needle grasses had almost disappeared. Moreover, cattle refused to drink where sheep had watered, offended by the ovine smell. So the trigger-happy *tejano*, finding lowly sheep-herders on the range, made nothing of shooting. Every old sheepman can relate his father's experience, if not his own, of sheep camps destroyed and bands scattered and killed, of sheep-herders beaten or even murdered. The last range row occurred just before World War I, when Ray Morley tried to introduce Karakul on his cattle ranches in the San Augustine Plains. Both cattle and sheepmen resented it. But Morley was no man to monkey with, and he prevailed long enough to abandon Karakuls on his own volition.

With cattle came the cowboy, a national hero who had pretty well disappeared by 1900, but who has been forever embalmed in writing and resurrected in the movies. He belonged to the era of the longhorns, who made legend, but whose meat was tough and stringy. John Chisum had prophesied that beef would some day be sold by the pound instead of the head, but as late as 1906 Ray Morley was still running longhorns on the San Augustine Plains. But the broad, quiet, rosy Herefords, with their bland white faces, had already appeared; they would produce the meat and the fifty-thousand-dollar bulls. Black Angus were brought from England about 1890, but they remain the fancy of a few men and do not threaten to replace Herefords.

Cattle-growing is an important part of New Mexico's economy, and the cattleman is still an impressive figure. The New Mexico Cattle Growers Association, with over two thousand members, brings together handsome gentlemen in soft beige cords, fancy-topped boots with sloping heels, and pale hats wide enough to satisfy any Hopalong Cassidy fan.

Their talk is of improvement in range management, better grass, water, weather, and production. Always production. These men are primarily producers of beef, pounds of beef, and more beef from fewer beasts. One sold six hundred head of cattle in 1950 for more than two thousand had brought him in 1900. A calf increase of fifty per cent was then considered good; a man who does not now get calves from seventy-five per cent of the cows bred is held of no account.

At home on the range the cattleman is a charming gentleman, with the accent on gentle. Handling beasts seems to develop a quiet demeanor, unemphatic speech, and measured movement.

Such a man is Ben Floersheim, whose Las Jaritas Ranch (The Willows) in Mora County was founded by his father, a merchant gone into sheep. Ben prefers cattle: "Sheep," he says, "are too little." He owns sixty-three thousand acres of land and runs cattle on thirty-nine thousand acres of additional state land. This is the favored northwest corner of the state, where the finest grasses grow—black and blue grama, galleta, and buffalo grass. Its normal rainfall is sixteen inches, and the land's long slope from the Sangre de Cristo to the plain is cut by the Mora, the Red, and lesser streams. Driving across that rolling prairie, the motorist would never suspect the hidden canyons with wooded sides and the clear streams that spread into pools where youngsters fish and swim.

Las Jaritas headquarters, three miles from the gate, lies in a land dimple beside the willow-shaded pool that gave the place its name. Battleship order prevails in barns, stables, and tool sheds, where everything is in its place and shining. No rubbish litters the graveled courts; men driving their rounds stop for every misplaced plank, bit of wire, or blowing paper. Never did pickups so justify their name. Ben Floersheim loves his land and his animals, and he cares for both with the combination of an agricultural college training and a faith reminiscent of his Old Testament ancestors.

The Floersheim home, surrounded by a walled garden and as well equipped as a city apartment, is like many a ranch home, as Mrs. Floersheim is like the up-to-date ranchwoman. Efficient in the house, these women can pinch-hit outdoors and they find time for the League of Women Voters, the PTA, or a bridge club in town. One of them, poking her kerchiefed head into a beauty shop in Clayton, called: "I'm going to put my clothes through the laundromat and leave my list at the grocers; then I'll be back for my permanent."

Las Jaritas is not considered a large ranch in New Mexico, though the state's oversized ranches are disappearing. The last to be reduced was the Bell Ranch in San Miguel and Guadalupe counties, where the Canadian cuts through broken land as richly colored as the Navajo reservation. That ranch, named La Campana for a rocky upthrust that resembles a bell, was the Pablo Montoya Grant. In the 1850's it went into gringo hands. It then included several small ranches and two hamlets that have recently been drowned in Concha Lake. At its greatest the Bell Ranch covered two million acres, and its owners and managers led baronial lives. In 1949 it was cut into four parts and one was bought by Mrs. Thomas B. Hoover to add to her T4 Ranch.

Like Mrs. Jones of Roswell, Mrs. Hoover is accepted by stockmen as a sound businesswoman and cattle-grower. In her modern home near Tucumcari she is a gracious hostess and a solicitous grandmother, but on the range she rides like a man, directs like a man, is respected like a man. She went into business when her first husband, Harold Krohn, died, leaving her with a big ranch and a small daughter. She smiles to recall a couple of managers who picked her as easy. "But," she smiles, "I was a trained bookkeeper and I always handled my own accounts."

The headquarters ranch was bought by a Texas corporation that does business as the Bell Ranch, Inc., and continues to use the bell-shaped brand. Its manager, George Ellis, lives in the rambling old adobe house that has known its Indian fights. A day on the ranch now is probably not unlike any day within the last fifty years. Cowboys ride in to the chuck wagon for dinner; and if the chuck wagon is now a pickup truck, it is driven by the same old "hooligan," who also fetches wood and water, peels potatoes, and polices camp. His opposite, the horse-wrangler, has not been mechanized; as of old he brings up the remounts and holds them in a rope corral.

The "hands," jogging in, could qualify for the movies, but only as background, so unpretentious are their tight chaps, worn hats, and colorless clothes. Only George Ellis, Jr., sporting fine chaps of pinto horsehair, looks as though he had seen a movie.

Mrs. Ellis said that most of these young men had served in the Navy. "Cowboys are afraid that in the Army they might have to walk." They ate quietly, then each man neatly scraped his leaving into a hole half-filled with cans and potato peelings and dropped his plate and utensils into a tub. Proceeding to the rope corral, he shouted for the mount he wanted: Buster, Chigger, Runt, Badger. He then transferred his saddle from the morning's mount, swung aboard, and was ready.

The day's job was regular fall work: to brand and alter any calves missed in the spring roundup and separate those to be shipped or held for breeding. Any cow showing up without a calf had her horns tipped with huge shears that crunched like a heavy tree falling. "If she shows up again without a calf she's earned a ticket to Kansas City," Mrs. Ellis said.

Like the sheepman, the cattleman has vastly increased the production of meat. The goal is a four-hundred-pound weaner calf and a seventy-five per cent calf crop. This emphasis on meat has led to gentle handling that would have outraged the old-timer. Unnecessary roping, dragging, and bull-dogging are frowned upon. Many ranchers now keep their stock on fenced and irrigated pastures, often planted with special grasses.

In the Estancia valley, the Valley Irrigation Company began, in 1948, to pump what they hope is an inexhaustible supply of seepage from the Ortiz and Sandia mountains onto arid acres where generations of dry farmers have made only a precarious living. Walter Mayer, the enthusiastic ranch-manager, says that the 1,800 acres of planted and irrigated pastures produce 150 times as much beef per acre as does range land. The fenced acres are beautiful to see, with the soft greening of winter wheat or oats, summer alfalfa, and a varied diet of grasses. They are protected from wind by a planting of juniper, elm, Chinese elm, Russian olive, and hackthorn, which make a pyramidal wall almost as impervious as stone. Of five thousand trees planted, not one was lost. This experiment may be another step toward removing New Mexico from the position of producing only raw materials for processing in other states. These pastures are raising the grain that is needed to ready steers for the slaughter. Sheep need no supplemental feeding. In 1950 lambs one hundred days old were sold directly to the Safeway Stores, Inc., at weight eighty pounds, thus eliminating several middlemen.

The extreme of such nursing is to be seen on Winfield Morten's Rancho de Abiquiu just under the escarpment where old Abiquiu sits. On the ranch, irrigated pastures make a bucolic foreground, with fat kine knee-deep in grass and calves gamboling in the bosky. The ranch-house is as luxurious as a Hollywood set, with shaded patios and tiled verandas. Only frescoes suggest the wild days and the wild ways of raising cattle. Mr. Morten made a fortune erecting prefabricated houses at White Rock, a town on the Pajarito Plateau built for construction workers employed at the near-by city of Los Alamos, where the atomic bomb was made. Mr. Morten later went into raising blooded bulls to improve New Mexico's stock. He calls himself "a cattleman's cattleman."

Gentleman's ranching has taken in horse-raising too. Some racers from New Mexico have done well on California tracks, and the state fair in Albuquerque is maintained by the ponies. Popular as both racers and show ponies are the palominos, so named by the Spanish for the gold or creamy coat that suggests a stain. Their best breeder, Warren Shoemaker of Watrous, has won silver cups and blue ribbons, and has suffered many a disappointment. For the palomino is a biological sport; in one season Shoemaker's best mares may produce only bay, sorrel, and one white colt, and not one golden beauty with white mane and tail.

Such developments seem normal. The earth-shaking change was the union of cattle and sheep on one ranch. Captain Burton Mossman, an Arizona Ranger and courageous, tried it about 1930 on the Diamond A Ranch east of the Pecos. Others in that area followed suit. Floyd Lee, operating the old Fernandez Ranch at San Mateo as a cattle ranch, stocked part of his lands with sheep, thus reverting to the original character of the ranch when the Chavez family operated it as a sheep ranch. The Second World War, with its high prices for beef, encouraged many sheepmen to try cattle. As they did, the superstitions disappeared and the old phobias were forgotten.

Garfield Paltenghe, who lives in the New England house his grandfather built on his ranch near Wagon Mound, is convinced that sheep and cattle improve the range for each other. Sheep eat small forage that cattle scorn; cattle relish the coarser grasses that sheep will not touch. The only difficulty remaining is that cattle do not like the sheep smell and will not drink where sheep have been. On the Magdalena Stock Drive, that three-mile-wide fenced promenade through which stock walk one hundred miles to the railhead, tanks are reserved for fastidious cows; water is carried for sheep.

So the cattleman and the sheepman have become one. They maintain separate associations because many of their technical problems differ, but they meet in the New Mexico Stock Growers Association, where they air the same troubles: bad weather, noxious weeds, a market gone sour just as there is a big increase in the flocks or herds. Always some department of the federal government is attacked by one or more speakers, though the stockman, of all citizens, gets most aid from the nation.

He has always used government land. In an arid country, owning a few scattered water holes gave a man control of thousands of acres of public grazing land. When the government opened the public domain to homesteading in 1862, the stockman's rage knew no bounds. He was right in stating that in the arid West a man could not support a family on the 160 acres first allowed, nor on the 320 acres of later legislation; even the 640 acres of the stock-raising act of 1916 were too few in New Mexico, where it takes an average of about 70 acres to feed one cow, 15 acres to graze one sheep. Stockmen managed well enough by acquiring the water holes and watching the forlorn hordes who tried dry farming starve into destitution and pull out. Meanwhile the conflict between homesteaders and stockmen had precipitated a range war even more bitter than that between cattlemen and sheepmen.

Dozens of thrillers have been written about these battles between strong men who proposed to protect their own, with guns if necessary, and the misguided nesters or squatters. Perhaps Conrad Richter's *Sea of Grass* is best balanced between sympathy for the pitiful little man and appreciation for the rancher's love of his wind-blown grass. In this case, too, the stockmen came round; most of them are now irrigating and farming the range. The difference, they aver, is that they use both land and water sensibly.

The stockman's land problem has been partly solved by the Taylor Grazing Act of 1934, which leased the public domain to men already in possession of it. This act favored the stockman already entrenched; the only way to acquire range lands now is by purchasing land that has grazing rights.

Stock-growers admit that their business has been saved from financial disaster by a series of congressional acts beginning with the Farm Credit Administration and leading to the long-term, low-interest government loans they count on now. They also enjoy price supports, and they may (and often do) call on federal agencies for technical advice. What they cannot abide is supervision. Stockmen in national convention and through their powerful congressional lobby have proposed that the federal lands they use should be sold to them without competitive bidding and at their price. In New Mexico, where stockmen are a political power, they prefer state control. As New Mexico lands are leased for the benefit of schools, the state land office is concerned with revenue rather than with land management. In all these matters sheepmen and cattlemen are in happy harmony. Perhaps we are witnessing here the last stand of the old frontiersman, who resented any restraint and did his own policing and shooting. Perhaps he is too new in business to share the eastern businessman's respect for the expert.

In spite of his grousing, the stockman is primarily a producer; nobody is more important in the nation's economy. In New Mexico his endeavors bring in over one hundred million dollars annually; the state ranks high in the production of meat, and constantly improved methods may, in time, give it a higher rating.

All this shows in the stockman. Often heavy-set, always with face burned and eyes crinkled by the sun, he has neither ulcers nor a sour disposition. His humor is often sardonic, but he sees the joke on himself. He has laughed over the ending of the cattle and sheep wars in the union of sheep and cattle on the same range. He has gone in for the farming for which he damned the squatter. Perhaps we shall live to see an end to his hatred of his active partner, the federal man.

XXIII

THE FEDERAL MAN

RECENTLY a banker in Silver City said, plaintively: "I remember when the only federal employee I knew was the postmaster!" He was doubtless wrong; he knew Army officers, men in the Land Office and on Border Patrol, and immigration officers. But he knew nothing like the number of men and women now on the federal payroll in New Mexico. Nor the rate at which their numbers increase.

The government employee appears most spectacularly and expensively in the armed forces and the Atomic Energy Commission. Largely because of New Mexico's climate, three of the nation's most important air bases are here: Kirtland Air Force Base at Albuquerque, a research and development center, Hollomon Air Force Base near Alamogordo, and a less important one at Roswell, Walker Air Force Base. The AEC, in addition to Los Alamos, where the atomic bomb was first made, maintains Sandia Base at Albuquerque, the top Special Weapons Project; the White Sands Proving Ground, where the first atomic bomb was tested; and other hush-hush installations.

The Army, accustomed to requisitioning what it needs, proposed in 1948 to extend the White Sands Proving Ground by taking in some one thousand square miles of range land, thus dispossessing about fifty ranch families. "Fair compensation" was offered, but what can be fair compensation for the loss of a man's inherited home, the only way of livelihood he knows? New Mexicans protested, and the military agreed to a less extensive bombing range. But at Los Alamos the Army won.

Los Alamos (the Cottonwoods) rests on the Pajarito

Plateau where Indians lived well and where the Ramon Vigil Grant later supported large flocks and herds. In time the grant came into the hands of a Michigander, Ashley Pond, who had become a first-rate New Mexican. On a pine-grown upland above leafy canyons, he founded the Los Alamos School for Boys on a basis of outdoor living, horses, and a respect for country as well as people. As director he chose Albert Connell, a cultivated New Yorker, who had been a Forest Ranger and a Boy Scoutmaster. The school was a Boy Scout troop mounted: it maintained a fire lookout during the fire season, and its summer session consisted of camping trips into the virgin forests of the Jemez range. Its masters, from eastern universities, consistently sent well-qualified students to the country's best colleges.

Then one day in 1942 Army officers dropped in for lunch. Mr. Connell was used to guests for lunch, and paid little heed. But he attended all right when word came that the United States was buying him out. His "not for sale" was brushed aside. Uncle Sam would pay well, would buy everything down to the kitchen brushes, the inkwells, and the guest towels. Immediate possession was demanded. So said, so done. Within a few months boys and masters were gone and the very name Los Alamos disappeared from consciousness. When J. Robert Oppenheimer's daughter was born there the birth certificate read: "Rural area, Sandoval County, New Mexico."

J. Robert Oppenheimer is the adopted New Mexican and nuclear physicist who directed the Manhattan Project at Los Alamos. Tall, gangling, with big feet, out-thrust head, and dark hair cropped to a scrub brush, he has a gentle, almost timid manner that expresses the same courtesy with the janitor, the San Ildefonso Indian, or the top scientist. Only the combination of one of the best brains of all time with compassionate human understanding could mold a face of such rare beauty. From childhood "Oppie" had spent vacations in New Mexico in a mountain cabin or astride a horse. Few men have known our mountains as he knows them. There he rested from his studies in England and Germany, and from his work as professor of physics at the University of California and the California Institute of Technology. When he was called to head the work at Los Alamos, nobody doubted that the best scientist had been chosen. Surprisingly, he proved to be also a first-rate administrator and "able to explain anything to a Congressman."

No secret was ever better kept than that of Los Alamos. The schoolboys had it that they were moving out for the Ethiopian Ski Corps or the Scandinavian Camel Artillery. Santa Feans saw lights against the Jemez peaks, but knew nothing. Guesses included a submarine base, with underground channel to the Pacific, and a home for pregnant WAC's. When the Truman Committee sent a scout to Santa Fe, he was referred to the President and retired in good order. One officer who made an indiscreet remark was relieved the next morning. Only the veteran reporter, Brian Boru Dunne, dared write in the *Santa Fe New Mexican* that "buses were coming in loaded with Indians, people jabbering Spanish, and Nobel Prize winners." Robert Oppenheimer now and again rode over the divide to his cabin on the Pecos; he was attended by an armed and very saddlesore protector. And Captain William S. Parsons's sister in Albuquerque complained that his visits were spoiled by his military guard. Captain Parsons, later Rear Admiral, was the New Mexican who "armed the bomb"—gave it, just before reaching Hiroshima, the final touch to activate it.

What life on "the hill" was like has gradually come out. Only a small core of scientists knew what was going on. Others signed up for the duration-and-six-months for specific jobs as clerks, plumbers, firemen—everything required for a town of 3,500 that rapidly expanded to 7,600. The gates were not locked, and people went into Santa Fe as necessary. They accepted no social engagements, but were known in stores and restaurants. A scientist's wife said: "We must have been as marked as though we wore a scarlet A." She signed a number, not a name for her automobile license.

GI's from the entire country, offered "special assignment," volunteered in the hope of overseas pay and adventure. Arrived at Lamy, they had no idea where they were, and when they emerged from covered vans to find themselves on a New Mexico mountain most of them were indignant. Later, of course, their pride knew no bounds. A couple of soldiers stationed at Sandia Base were assigned to drive heavy trucks from Los Alamos to a place near Alamogordo. They went always at night at a fast clip, and they were supplied with passes signed by the Governor and directing state police to let them go. Such stories came out later.

At Los Alamos tension mounted steadily all through 1943, 1944, and 1945. During the spring months of 1945 it became terrific. Eddie Brooks, Fire Chief at Los Alamos, said: "You could feel the tension like a physical thing." Wives knew only that everything depended upon saying nothing and asking no questions.

In that tense mid-July, Eddie Brooks was ordered to send to Alamogordo a fire truck driven by a dependable man, ordered late at night to start at dawn. By July 15 a hundred or so men had left for Alamogordo: technicians, truckers, guards, and cooks. A full camp operation was needed at a place called "Trinity." Scientists, headed by Oppenheimer, went. Those left at Los Alamos hied themselves to lookouts on mountain peaks. Nobody knew whether the bomb would explode or not. On paper they knew, but this was to be the proof. Then, at the lowest hour before dawn, the skies were lit up by such a flare as had never been seen before. It aroused people in various parts of the state. Gallup people heard an explosion, and the *Gallup Independent* queried the Commanding Officer at Alamogordo. "Yes," he replied, "there has been an explosion. Nobody hurt. Nothing serious." A blind girl in Albuquerque saw a flash of light. Ranchers near Alamogordo thought they had seen the end of the world. But curiosity soon petered out.

The scientists who came back to Los Alamos were more than ever wordless. Haggard, bewhiskered, distraught, and weary to exhaustion, they spoke only of going to the South Pacific. Some took shots and tests for the tropics. Captain Parsons made a last visit to his sister in Albuquerque.

Then came August 6, 1945—Hiroshima. Los Alamos people got the news over the public address system. "The President announces . . ." Eddie Brooks, who had gone to Denver for a few days "to get free of strain and catch up on my sleep," heard it over the radio. The atomic bomb had all but ended the war with Japan.

Los Alamos suffered the postwar slump with the rest of the country; it was a deeper slump only because it followed a tighter wind-up. GI's wanted only to get out. "Just let me out of this and I never want to see New Mexico again." Of 1,500 released from Los Alamos, 700 came back to stay.

Scientists yearned to return to their laboratories and classrooms—above all they wanted nothing to do with politics; they hoped to evade the consequences of what they had released. Eddie Brooks said: "It was hard to hold level."

In time it was decided to maintain the laboratories at Los Alamos, but to surround them with a civilian town. In 1946, the Atomic Energy Commission succeeded the Army, and a private concern, the Zia Company, built a town north of the "restricted area" in which silvery wire mesh fences in the huge silvery laboratories that reflect the sun's rays like mirrors.

The AEC's first job was to repair the havoc that the

Army had wrought by chopping down the pines that had
sheltered the school's pleasant log and stone buildings, bull-
dozing the land into dusty desolation, and erecting hideous
barracks. The only bit of beauty left was a golf links for
officers, with greens kept verdant by sprays of New Mexico's precious water. The AEC laid out pleasant streets
among the trees left standing, built attractive double houses
with small gardens and wide windows on magnificent views.
There is a community center with stores, but only one of
each category, and no liquor store. The only place to buy
bottled cheer is at White Rock, a town built for construction workers, but almost empty because many workers—a
mobile lot—prefer to live in trailers. Los Alamos is a model
town, but far from typical. It has a higher than average IQ
owing to its scientific and technical population, and a lower
than average age. There are more children in primary than
in high school. Theoretically self-governing, it has a city
council that is often overruled by the AEC director, a civilian who has, so far, been a retired military man. It is easier
to doff a uniform than a state of mind.

The citizens of Los Alamos are a high-grade cross-section
of the nation. As newcomers to New Mexico they were uninformed but interested. They soon spread out among the
Indians, seeing dances and buying blankets and pottery for
their homes. They were cordial, if a bit curious about their
Spanish-speaking associates, and notably without prejudice.
When a rabbi asked the personnel officer for a list of Jews,
that official knew nobody as a Jew. An announcement on
the bulletin board brought together enough to found a syn-
agogue. And when barbers refused to serve the one Negro
resident, the barbers were replaced.

Los Alamos was part of Sandoval County, which had always been completely dominated by one family. When the
state switched from Republican to Democratic control, the
family changed, but not the method of political control. The
few politically uncontrolled masters up at remote Los Ala-

mos made no difference—even if their votes were counted. Now, with the appearance of thousands of gringo voters who would not take orders, disaster threatened. New Mexico first met the threat by denying them the vote as residents of a federal reservation and subject only to federal jurisdiction. Some Los Alamos people, quick to understand New Mexico's phobias, threatened to petition Texas for admission. But before Texas could come again, Los Alamos was made a county with land taken from Santa Fe, Rio Arriba, and Sandoval counties. The Governor appointed county commissioners, who chose a sheriff. His deputies were put into horizon-blue uniforms and set to man the gate, where every visitor must show a pass and declare his intentions, although in time the necessity of passes was dropped and people could come and go as they wished. The state legislature had only overlooked giving Los Alamos County representation in the legislature—an oversight easily rectified. Otherwise, the Civil Service Commission has ruled that AEC employees are subject to the Hatch Act and may hold state and local offices only if that does not involve becoming a candidate representing a political party. Only employees of the construction company may play the political game in the new county.

All this military and atomic development has changed New Mexico more in a decade than everything in the previous centuries changed it. Near Los Alamos workers earn such wages as New Mexicans cannot match; the domestic servant, the "chile picker," and the sheep-herder have all but disappeared. In 1950, the Albuquerque Chamber of Commerce gloated over an annual payroll of forty-two-million dollars, to say nothing of its related building boom and other money-makers. But politically these new citizens have upset all the dopesters. Intelligently interested, they join leagues and associations, invite speakers to address them, listen to campaigners, and have a disturbing tendency to cut across party lines. Altogether these new citizens will probably be bothersome to the politicians, but very salutary for the state.

Advantageous as this addition to the electorate is, destruction brought them here. So it is good to turn to another federal man, one who is not spraying our water away but conserving it; who asks no man to give up his ranch but only so to operate it that it will produce more bountifully; who demolishes no trees to make dusty towns, but who tries to preserve our forests forever. He knows that our national resources can be managed to improve forest and range while halting the hideous erosion that makes dust bowls and causes floods of incalculable cost in misery as well as money. If he has failed conspicuously in any regard it has been in making the public understand this.

As an individual, the conservationist is typical of our largest and most useful body of citizens. He makes the headlines neither for fabulous fortunes nor for hideous crimes. He just does his job, lives on a small income, educates his children as well as he can, and takes part, as does his wife, in community efforts. He appears ageless. Never very young, he grows old imperceptibly, and by then he has reached retirement age. Quiet and unemotional, he seldom spills over about his work, but he genuinely loves the good earth, and is dedicated to preserving it. Often he has chosen this work in preference to a more remunerative job; a few such men live useful lives in the Southwest who would be semi-invalids in a damp climate. These men believe in the ends they serve, beliefs more and more confirmed by experience. So they work steadily with conviction and meet their vicissitudes with humor. It takes humor to bear unfair criticism from men you are trying to serve and to make no boast when they finally adopt your recommendations as their own ideas.

The idea of conservation appeared during President Theodore Roosevelt's administration. Gifford Pinchot, son of a rich and cultivated Pennsylvanian, observed that bad lumbering practices were destroying our forests, and resolved to devote his life to saving them. He went abroad to study forestry because there was no school in this country. His friend Roosevelt, who knew and understood the West, shared his enthusiasms, and under the President's influence the Congress, in 1905, created the Forest Service as part of the Department of Agriculture. The Bureau of Reclamation had already been established, but that bureau's primary function was irrigation. The Forest Service was the first federal agency devoted to the intelligent use of land and water for the general good.

The Forest Service brought into the West a kind of man sure to infuriate the rancher. He was college-bred; Pinchot had seen to it that a school of forestry was established at Yale. Few ranchers had been to college then. Scientific in mind and training, the Forester was a conserver as opposed to the ruthless exploiter and gambler who was still the national idol. Moreover he succeeded the Land Office, whose primary purpose had been to get the public domain into private ownership, really to give the land away.

The Forest Service, with no control over private lands, wished to bring all public forest and watershed lands into the National Forests so that they could be properly managed. Its first concern was to lessen the destruction of our forests by fire, blight, or misuse. People who are old enough remember that our mountains used to smoke for weeks in the dry season: sheep-herders or woodcutters had let their campfires get out of hand. Forest Service regulation and education have reduced such carelessness, and the forest lookout's quick spotting of a fire and the Service's mobilization to fight it often save many thousands of acres a year in New Mexico.

On federal lands leased to private companies the Forest Service marks timber to be cut, saving immature trees for the future. On state lands overcutting is often permitted; there one company may grow rich while the forest deteriorates.

The Forest Service is mindful of watersheds as well as of timber stands. This accounts for the signs, so mirth-provoking to the visitor: "Entering such-and-such a forest," where not a tree is in sight. It also accounts for the Jornada Experiment Station between Las Cruces and the Organ Mountains.

These plains had suffered unduly from overgrazing. In the old days the only way a man could hold his land was by keeping it fully stocked. Too often that meant the overgrazing that so weakens plants that they cannot recover from drought. This happened in the bad drought year of 1912, when losses ran as high as fifty and sixty per cent of the herds. Cattlemen then petitioned the government for aid, and under President Taft two hundred thousand acres were withdrawn from use for study. The area is still administered by the Forest Service, but is leased to two cattlemen who must comply with government rulings. In spite of the "bureaucratic restrictions" decried by critics, it is noteworthy that there is a long list of applicants ready to take up the lease if the present lessees should ever relinquish it.

It is government policy to operate the Jornada Experiment Station so economically that any stockman could apply its methods; there is no extravagant use of government money. The range's remarkable productivity is owing, according to Fred Ares, the Range Conservationist, to simple, sensible methods. During the summer, cattle are kept on tobosa grass, which is palatable until the rains begin. This leaves the black grama to ripen slowly; it cures as it stands, is good all winter, and will produce twice as much beef as inferior grasses. Often redistribution of stock will help as much as reduction of herds. Cottonseed meal, used as supplemental feed, and salt are set far from water holes to

make the cows graze widely. Altogether this station has
provided the whole arid West with guidance while its
lessees are producing over four hundred thousand pounds of
beef a year.

An even more impressive demonstration of restoring misused land to usefulness was made by the Soil Conservation
Service on the Ojo del Espiritu Santo Grant in Sandoval
County. Here the infamous Rio Puerco had dug a canyon
so deep that irrigation had become impossible, and farms
and towns were left high and dry in dusty ruin. Rest and
care are actually bringing that desolated land back into productivity as though it had really been touched by a Spring
of the Holy Spirit.

The grant by that poetic name was awarded to one
Cabeza de Baca in 1743. In time it became part of the vast
holdings of Don José Leandro Perea of Bernalillo, who ran
eighty thousand sheep there, to its destruction. Finally the
grant came, as a contingent fee, into the possession of
Thomas Benton Catron, archetype of the clever lawyer
who dealt in land and politics. He served as United States
senator and died land-poor. Catron, like Perea, permitted
the abuse that made the area a perfect field for a before-and-
after demonstration. This became possible in 1935, when
the government bought several land grants both to save land
and to help small ranchers and farmers. The Ojo del Espiritu Santo Grant, enlarged to 124,000 acres, posed the most
difficult problem. Only men confident of their methods
would have tackled it. But Hugh Calkins and Eastburn
Smith of the Soil Erosion Service, later the Soil Conservation Service, jumped at the chance. One said: "There was
no book to throw at them, so we just tried out all our
ideas." Most of them worked.

If the methods were untried the men were not; they
knew soils and grasses and were experienced with this type
of land. Luck played a part: the project was given two

hundred CCC workers for two years. Rehabilitation of youth was to go along with rebuilding land. What was done there for both men and land makes one believe in universal training of youth to conserve, not to kill. (Although in the stern days of 1942 good soldiers came out of the CCC.) In 1935 drastic measures were indicated. The entire grant was heavily overgrazed. One Wyoming outfit was running thirteen thousand head; the Forest Service had set four thousand as the outside limit for safety. And the range was overrun by stock trespassing without payment.

Drive over the grant now with federal men. Roads are what they take off from; the truck, under a strong twist on the wheel, leaps the bank and goes bounding off from hillock to hillock as the men point out salient features. Often the whole party is ordered out to observe on hands and knees just how bad grasses are yielding to good. On parts of this range even poor grasses are a step in the right direction. Eastburn Smith said: "When we took over the grass wouldn't hide a prairie dog." Now there are no prairie dogs, but there is grass.

Ring grass is just better than no grass at all. As feed it is of no value, but any growth tends to nail down soil in which better grass can grow. Salt sacaton and snake weed come next; still poor, they make way for various gramas, wheat grass or blue stem, the best for stock, and even wild rice, which the Indians are glad to see come back. Happily nature, given a chance, moves from bad to better to good. Grazing was cut to a minimum; only a few permits were issued to Jemez and Zia Indians and some Spanish ranchers who had long depended on this range. Trespass stock was got rid of. Then more positive measures were undertaken.

Land had suffered deeply from flash floods; once started, arroyos grow at both ends at an alarming rate. So trenches were dug across any cut where it began, and check dams were built to spread the water before it had force enough to slash the land. All this was done economically, using only native materials, and to prove what could be done anywhere, given knowledge and labor. Borrow pits were seeded with fifteen or sixteen types of good grasses. Many of them took hold; one can see how a gash in land heals like a wound in flesh.

So much is routine and can be done wherever land has not yet been reduced to desert sands. But more could be done with CCC labor. A pipeline from the mountains filled a large pool for watering stock, and there the boys planted trees. The gray-green of Russian olive and the willow's reddish wands are massed against verdant cottonwood; and the water reflects reeds and rushes besides offering bass, blue gill, and sun perch. On the hills, cottonwoods and Chinese elms were planted, but without much hope. There they stand, however, looking incongruous, but giving full-leaved shade. Maybe the whole Southwest could be so shaded.

This project has attracted students from foreign countries in which mismanagement has reduced the good valleys of antiquity to present deserts. Few parts of the United States have gone so far; there is still time for intelligent men to save their own lands. To this end the Soil Conservation Service has worked out a democratic procedure.

Under state laws—New Mexico's dates from 1937—twenty-five landowners in any given area may petition the state for permission to organize a Soil Conservation District. Two thirds of their number may complete the organization, whose purpose is to "nail down rainfall," halt erosion, and improve and conserve both range and farm. District members go in for spreader dams and diversion of arroyos. They practice crop rotation, terracing and contour plowing, and the fall plowing called chiseling, which leaves clods too heavy to blow away as dust. Such a program depends upon the intelligent co-operation of every farmer; no one's land is safe unless his neighbor's is. "How much does it blow?"

is the question nowadays. The farmer who lets his land blow away rates rather like the old horse-thief.

The Service is often active at the start, and it always stands ready with technical advice. At the beginning the SCS lent the Districts such equipment, as bulldozers and trucks and land planes. The District charged its members for the maintenance and operation. As that equipment has worn out, the Districts have bought their own.

New Mexico is well organized; all sorts of landowners are active, though most members are small operators. Some wealthy ranchers held back, even opposed the organization, but in time most of them have joined their District.

In the lower Pecos valley cotton farmers were the leaders. On the Ruidoso, Pete Hurd, who farms and raises quarter horses when he is not painting, took time out to organize his neighborhood. His small ranch is a model. Grama grass is coming back on the hills, his polo ponies graze in the apple orchard, and when a devastating hailstorm made the arroyo rage madly, his dams protected his home. Pete had had his artist and writer friends digging there for years.

In the Cuba area John Young, a Republican scornful of anything New Dealish, was convinced and took the lead even against prominent landowners. He tells a couple of stories.

As the District's treasurer he is responsible for advancing credit for equipment. He tells of one farmer who needed help to build stock tanks; his debt was one thousand dollars. His land and stock were then valued at under four thousand dollars. Two years after his tanks were in operation he refused ten thousand dollars for his land.

Jacobo Herrera, a small operator, needed a dirt storage tank. He requested a bulldozer; the cost would be $350. Jacobo had only fifty dollars; he offered his note for three hundred dollars, agreeing to pay off in a year. John Young, always cagey, was dubious. "If you pay out in five years you'll be doing well. Don't promise more than you can do. How do I know you won't quit and go to work for the lumber company?" But he knew his man; this was pure front. Jacobo paid off his loan not in five years or even in one, but within three months, when he had sold his first crop of one hundred sacks of wheat.

This is democracy at its intelligent best. This is the federal man serving as technical adviser, at hand when called upon, never intrusive, never autocratic. Observing the conservationist at work, it is hard to understand the rancor that some ranchers register against him. Many complaints—especially those of autocratic behavior—boil down to an elderly stockman's dislike of some individual youngster "all full of theories"; often the trouble is caused by the enthusiast's wrong approach. The most diplomatic federal men have learned never to mention how many head of stock are on the range, but only to say how more beef can be produced.

A complaint that concerns the average citizen is that our many conservation services are divided between the Departments of Interior and of Agriculture, and this makes for bad feeling among them, especially in Washington, where endless rows are the rule. The Hoover Commission of 1948 recommended a reorganization to bring all agencies for the administration of public lands under one head. This could be a great money-saver as well as a breeder of harmony.

One consolidation has paid off brilliantly. The General Land Office and the Grazing Service have been united as the Bureau of Land Management, which administers about one fifth of New Mexico's land area, some fourteen million acres. This bureau has the distinction of being the only government agency that takes in more than it spends. In New

Mexico it realizes some six million dollars annually from oil and gas leases and grazing fees. Perhaps this portends the ideal solution of the problem of the federal man, that he should so educate the public to sound conservation that his job will consist only of leasing the public lands at a good fee.

XXIV

WATER

WATER is what New Mexico never has enough of—except where and when it has too much. It is drought or gully-washer. Rainfall is called "spotty": a feeble word for a range of from fifty to two hundred per cent of normal. The state's average of only fifteen inches annually is not enough to raise crops, though it serves to maintain gazing for a limited number of livestock. How to stretch this sparse supply enough to permit farming has been the preoccupation of New Mexico's peoples since records began. How they succeeded or failed is our history.

Indians lived where there was water, they danced their prayers for plenty of it, they moved when the supply failed. All this they still do.

The Spanish, knowing similar semi-arid lands, settled along the streams, plotted ditches, based their laws on the distribution of water and the sensible use of land. They, too, prayed when water failed, carrying their holy images out into thirsty fields to invoke saintly aid. They, too, still do this.

These peoples worked with nature, using carefully what God vouchsafed, certain that only supernatural powers could increase the amount. It took the gringo, traditional nonconformist, without the humility of acceptance, to try to dominate nature and produce water where there was none.

New Mexico's last hundred years have been largely a struggle to turn its range land into farms. Advertisers encourage immigration by promising irrigated farms, even while water tables sink and towns go dry every summer. The simple proposition that the population already here—or here several years ago—would be infinitely better off if no newcomers arrived is rank heresy, and its promulgator will doubtless be tried for subversive ideas.

The Spanish had dug wells for home use, but it was the United States government that offered a bonus for water in the midst of the Jornada del Muerto. A man named Martin accepted the challenge. But after months of digging, his last spadeful of sand was as dry as the first. Then one morning his eyes were dazzled by a silver flash at the bottom of his well. A living spring was there; it has flowed ever since.

Wells now became commonplace, and with the arrival of the windmill salesman in the seventies water was produced by New Mexico's one unfailing resource. Whatever may be exhausted—minerals, water, oil, sound sense, or good men—there is no indication that wind will ever fail us. So windmills came to spin mistily atop their long-legged towers and to fill the tanks where cattle drink. The windmill was only the first machine. The battle was now joined. The gringo, with all his ingenuity, defied nature's implacable, imminent resistance. Up to the mid-twentieth century odds seem about even. Nature has upset every one of man's efforts; man has thought up a new attack every time. There are battles in every drainage basin, but the war began in the Pecos.

The Pecos, rising up under the Truchas Peaks east of Santa Fe, cold as ice and clear as air, gathers itself together in a boggy place where mariposa lilies, lady's-slippers, and columbine abound, and dashes off down the canyon as a sparkling stream. The upper Pecos canyon is the perfect recreation area. Tall pines and blue spruce rise with the slopes, and alders and willows shade pools where rainbow and mountain trout defy the fisherman. Deer and even elk peer through aspen thickets, and a clumsy bear may waddle slowly up from the Forest Service road. The Pecos gains other streams good also for fishing and mountain cabins, and emerges from its canyon near ancient Cicuyé.

The Gallinas, rising on the other side of the divide, separates Old and New Las Vegas and carries its silt into the Pecos, which goes on past the old stage stops. Tecolotito is strung along the river in bright green fields separated by red sandstone houses with fresh white trim—homes commodious enough for comfortable, partriarchal living. Many old families have lost their lands or prefer life in town. The mill site is marked only by a ruined storehouse and the canal, where the wheel swished dripping to grind the wheat. At Anton Chico many old houses are empty, but one store still serves a large area mostly settled by newcomers.

Up to this point the river has proved amenable. But where country flattens out and is treeless, the Pecos seems to lose heart. Near Las Colonias, where Coronado is reputed to have forded the Pecos, the stream ducks underground. But within ten miles it bobs up again in a series of brackish springs and goes on past Santa Rosa, the largest town in Guadalupe County, which depends on cattle and the railroad to keep it busy. Puerto de Luna, said to have been called "Gate of the Moon" by Coronado's men, seems sleepily ancient in spite of a filling station and a modern school. The Pecos is slow-moving here, probably flowing more underground than above. Near Santa Rosa the Blue Hole flashes color back to the sky, but has never revealed its depth; and ranchers report stumbling on bottomless wells harboring queer antediluvian reptiles.

Below Santa Rosa the Pecos flows gently down its wide valley. It knew the cattle drives; its first towns were cow towns. But the Pecos, famous for having "no law west of," resents man's control and has found devious ways to give him his come-uppance.

The first effort to bridle the Pecos came about because Pat Garrett, between his killing of Billy the Kid in 1881 and his second notable role in the Fountain case in 1895, found his farm too high above the Hondo for irrigating. But Berrendo Creek might, he thought, be flumed across the Hondo. Then why not dam them both and irrigate many acres even as far away as Roswell? Capital would be needed, but capital was within the imagination and reach of Charles Eddy, cattleman turning capitalist. So the new pattern emerged. Big irrigation projects, financed by "foreign" capital, began to turn grazing lands into farms.

The Pecos Irrigation and Investment Company, founded by Eddy, but taken over by James John Hagerman in 1889, began to irrigate old John Chisum's range. Eddy and Hagerman were to fall out, but before they did they had built five canals and three dams on the Pecos, had tempted a railroad to build into the valley in 1890, and had seen a rush of settlers under the Homestead and Desert Entry acts of Congress.

The panic of 1893 almost wiped out the small farmers, who were saved when Hagerman dug deep into his own reserves. But the flood of 1904 wrought havoc that even his devoted faith could not surmount. The company then petitioned the government for help, and President Theodore Roosevelt, under the Reclamation Act of 1902, took over. The gringo had now enlisted his best ally against nature, government funds.

Meanwhile the Pecos valley had been granted a lavish gift of the gods. In 1891 Nathan Jaffa, digging a well, was rewarded with a rush of artesian water. For eons of time water seeping down from the Sacramentos and the caprock had sunk into the porous limestone below the topsoil. Uncapped now, it gushed up through artesian wells in seemingly exhaustless supply. Used first to beautify lawns and gardens, it was inevitably turned into irrigation ditches. Six-inch pipes poured out from 500 to 1,500 gallons per minute. Hagerman planted 600 acres in an apple orchard and by 1905, 485 wells irrigating apple trees had turned the valley into a fairylike scene scented by blossoms in spring and ripe apples in fall.

One W. T. Hamilton of Ohio offered farms on Berrendo Creek with the promise that a forty-acre orchard would be worth at least forty-thousand dollars in six years. He advertised apple country better than anything in Oregon because New Mexico was two thousand miles nearer eastern markets and its shorter haul would be an easy downhill slide with no Rockies to cross. The soil was touted as richer than that of the Nile delta. A wide range of fruit crops was as sure as sun-up. Special trains from Chicago and Ohio cities brought hordes of eager buyers. Dr. George W. Crile came —only one of many physicians and surgeons; also listed were dentists, merchants, teachers, farmers, and capitalists. Capitalists were going to be needed.

Five out of the first six Februaries produced balmy days, and streams running full of melting mountain snows brought out the blossoms in fragrant clouds of pink-touched white. But in New Mexico it often happens that if spring comes winter is not far behind. In the sixth year came frost to turn the delicate blossoms black and ugly. Even smudge-pots could not save the trees often enough to make apples a paying crop. By 1920 apple trees past maturity were being cut out and replaced by cotton.

Meanwhile nature had been quietly demonstrating that when you use up water stored through millennia there isn't any more. In 1915 the artesian wells began to dry up; by 1925 the area of flowing wells had shrunk from 663 square miles to 425. Farms were sold for seventy-five dollars with all improvements, or offered for sale with no takers. The artesian boom had burst.

Irrigation remains New Mexico's main dependence. The dams grow larger and more complicated as misuse of land and the vagaries of the rivers produce new evils that necessitate new measures of control. It was soon apparent that larger, stouter dams could do more than divert water into irrigation ditches; they could also impound run-off water for later beneficial use. This is the water that comes in summer cloudbursts to tear loose and sweep away the earth in dense brown rivulets and swirl them into arroyos that block the highways: flash floods, gone in a few hours. But soil is gone too, fields have been inundated and houses washed away, and wealth incalculable has been dumped into the river. What could be sounder practice than to catch the run-off behind dams and release it as needed?

The first big project was an effort to tame the Rio Grande. A dam at the Elephant Butte, near the Valverde Ford, was the dream of a couple of Las Cruces lawyers, who saw that the new Bureau of Reclamation might make the Mesilla valley more fabulously productive than the Pecos. By 1914 the Bureau had finished its most ambitious project up to that time: a cement dam 235 feet high had made a lake 40 miles long and 3 miles wide at its greatest extension; it would hold enough water to irrigate 145 miles of river bottom in New Mexico, Texas, and Mexico. This meant 363 miles of canals to be maintained by tax assessments against the irrigated acreage. All seemed well. Land prices rose, settlers swarmed, experienced farmers began leveling the old hummocky fields with machines; land that had become overgrown with useless salt grass was reclaimed.

Then the river took measures. Underground seepage may have been foreseen by the Reclamation engineers, but they had not provided for it. Drainage ditches were required; this meant additional mortgaging. Some small farmers not apt at learning new ways sold out. But there were few foreclosures, largely because the Federal Land Banks, established in 1916, stabilized the district. Loans were made on land, not on perishable livestock, and each borrower was required to take five per cent of his loan in bank stock. So the farmer came out owning not only his land but his stock in the bank. Most farmers were able to repay their original loans within a few years.

This development has been a success. Protected from the east winds by the rugged blue spires of the Organ Mountains, the irrigated fields make a bright green strip two miles wide along a river now well disciplined. One hundred and twenty-six miles of dikes, built by the International Boundary and Water Commission, allow a bit of meandering, but no destructive outbreak. In normal times the channel between dikes makes a pretty green pasture; in flash floods the dikes hold. The river itself is about 150 feet wide and 2 feet deep.

The largest crop is cotton, which has produced its inevitable by-product, migrant labor. Mesilla valley farmers employ Mexican nationals brought in by the U.S. Farm Bureau under contract with the Mexican government and leased to farmers. This arrangement is criticized by labor unions, but it suits both the farmers, who get labor when they want it, and the Mexicans, who work a few months and then go home with fat wages, hoping to return another year.

The Mesilla valley's early fame for the production of fine wines and brandies remains one of New Mexico's unrealized dreams. Pass wine and Pass brandy appear only in old books, and the priest who delighted Europeans with the product of his winery at Mesilla has no successors. Grapes are raised only for local use, though their flavor is exquisite. Cantaloupes, ripening later than the Arizona crop and that of Colorado, have been abandoned because of shipping and marketing uncertainties. But experiments continue. D. F. Stahmann, a Minnesotan, has put in three thousand acres of pecan trees and a plant for shelling nuts on the place. When the trees are small he raises alfalfa as a "downstairs crop" under the trees of his orchard. He gins his own cotton and runs some 1,300 sheep on his foothills. In 1949 he employed 280 Mexican laborers, housed well near a civic center with store, barbershop, and offices. For his family Mr. Stahmann has built a thirty-thousand-dollar home decorated by a Mexican artist. His neighbor Apodaca has an equally workmanlike establishment that centers in a stately mansion inherited from his uncle, a priest. According to the law, lands held under Reclamation projects are limited to 160 acres. But many large holdings were bought before the project began.

So the Rio Grande in southern New Mexico serves man well. But above Elephant Butte Dam it remains the Rio Bravo. The middle valley, centering in Albuquerque, is perennially petitioning Congress for funds to save it from the river. In seventy-five years sixteen floods have ruined farms, demolished villages, and threatened Albuquerque, which still faces a possible major catastrophe whenever the river rises a few inches. This condition was long in the making. Irrigation had waterlogged the land, and silting had aggraded the river bed until it was four feet higher than the town's busiest corner; and the valley had become a long narrow marsh where cat-tails grew, mosquitoes bred in swarms, and migrating water-fowl fed well. People were losing their farms and might lose their town. More than irrigation, the middle valley needed drainage and flood control.

Public-spirited men, failing to enlist the Bureau of Reclamation, finally incorporated under the state laws as the Middle Rio Grande Conservancy District, and set out to sell bonds. By the time their surveys were completed in 1929 they faced a depressed bond market. But the river, the ruthless, implacable river, kept right on increasing its threat. The bonds were sold, valley folk were assessed, many small owners were forced out, and politicians made capital out of big owners selling small ones down the river. But the valley was drained.

Three hundred and sixty-three miles of canals, at a cost of ten million dollars, saved 120,000 acres for farming. The original planners, alive to the danger of silting, had included a dam up on the Chama, whose muddy flood first chokes the clear Rio Grande near Española. El Vado Dam makes a lake that is kept stocked for fishing and releases water for irrigation as needed. But the river at Albuquerque continues to build up its silty bed; no company will insure Albuquerque property against flood damage.

New Mexico's third major dam is on the South Canadian, a stream that rises in the Sangre de Cristos above Raton, picks up the Mora near Las Vegas, and flows east. Approaching the plains, the South Canadian has dug deep canyons between colored mesas looking like aspiring mountains that have been sliced off. Here cattle slither down to water as did the thirsty animals on the shorter Santa Fe Trail. Always a silt-bearer, the river grew unruly in the Texas Panhandle, where farms were in constant danger of flash floods. Texas, which had done very well in the Rio Grande Compact, hoped for a generous share of the Canadian's waters. New Mexico's Senator Dennis Chavez held out until he got what he called "the first compact which fully protects New Mexico's present and future on an interstate stream."

Primarily for flood control, the Conchas Dam project was extended to water some forty-two thousand acres whose owners obligated themselves to repay the cost of some sixteen million dollars over a period of forty years. Holdings were limited to 16 acres, and except for some large family farms, most of the land still belongs to modest farmers who raise forage crops, small grains, cotton, and sugar beets.

Dams reduce flood danger and hold water for irrigation. Their evil is that they also hold silt, which masses up behind the dam to its ultimate ruination. Elephant Butte Dam still holds enough water to irrigate the district through three years of drought, but if sedimentation continues it may not do so much longer. Less ambitious projects are less subject to silt danger. A diversion dam on the Pecos River above Fort Sumner turns six thousand acres of open range into farms of alfalfa, sweet potatoes, fruits, and melons. Several dams below the Elephant Butte bring under cultivation thousands of acres in New Mexico, Texas, and Chihuahua. There are, besides, many small dams utilizing waters that would otherwise be a menace or a waste.

Waste of our scanty supply of water is overwhelming. More than ninety per cent is lost through evaporation and transpiration. In the *bosques* above Elephant Butte Dam useless salt grass, willows, cottonwoods, and tamarisks evaporate enough water—so an engineer computed—to supply ten cities the size of Albuquerque, its size at latest quotation. Careless farmers further reduce our precious life-stream by allowing their ditches to leak over the roads; Albuquerque, faced with a water shortage every summer, squanders its water by letting its park sprays turn hilly streets into streams.

New Mexico's only substantial source of additional water is in its least known river, the San Juan, which embraces nearly ten thousand square miles of New Mexico before it sweeps on toward the west. In San Juan County industrious Mormons have built small community canals that bring some thirty thousand acres under cultivation. Farmington, Fruitland, Bloomfield, Water Flow, and Flora Vista are trade centers for farmers raising small grains, forage crops, and orchards too far north to blossom unseasonably. Navajos have used the San Juan too, but not up to capacity, and their badly eroded reservation dumps into the river much of the silt that is rapidly filling up Lake Mead above Hoover Dam. New Mexico's San Juan thus becomes a menace to Los Angeles.

The San Juan brought New Mexico into the long and acrimonious dispute over the waters of the vast Colorado River drainage which affects seven of the United States and two states in Mexico. While Arizona and California continue to bicker, New Mexico has accepted as her share 11.25 per cent of the water originating above Lee's Ferry; the rest must be allowed to go on to the other states. But New Mexico still has to agree on the best use to make of its share.

According to Spanish law and usage, water belongs to him who puts it to beneficial use; first user in time is first in right. The United States made this sensible ruling the law throughout the West. New Mexico, then, must find ways to put the San Juan to beneficial use or eventually see some other state get its water. This affects the residents of San Juan County (including the Navajo Indians) immediately, and other citizens of the state more remotely.

The Indian Service, trying to help seventy thousand Navajos to make a decent living, hopes to increase their irrigated lands. Dams on the San Juan at Fruitland and Hog Back irrigate some ten thousand acres on the reservation. Others proposed at Shiprock and Monument Rocks might add seventy thousand and from thirty to forty thousand acres respectively. White citizens in San Juan County believe their arable lands might be increased also.

Eager go-getters in other parts of the state are convinced that New Mexico's share of the San Juan is some three hundred thousand acre feet a year more than can be put to economical use on the San Juan. They propose to dam that river high up in Colorado, where it is a swift mountain stream, and so divert its waters through tunnels, canals, and a series of reservoirs into the Chama River above El Vado Dam. The cost is estimated at 250 million dollars. These waterworks could irrigate some one hundred thousand additional acres in the Rio Grande drainage, develop hydroelectric power, and help scour sediment out of the stream beds. All this might save Albuquerque from the catastrophic flood that is admittedly inevitable unless presently worsening conditions are corrected.

Saving Albuquerque has become a matter of national importance since the Air Force and the Atomic Energy Commission have found it an advantageous site for vast undertakings. In 1950 the Army Corps of Engineers inaugurated the Jemez Canyon Dam to check the silt brought in by the Jemez's frequent flash floods. An earth dam, protected from upstream pressure by a stone riprap, will slow down the flow and hold the sediment. Cleared water will then be released into the Rio Grande in amounts that will not cause damage. Army engineers propose a similar settling basin on the Chama and a dredging of the Rio Grande for twenty miles above Elephant Butte. All this should straighten the main channel and help the stream to cleanse itself.

Thus engineers think of controlling an entire river system in order to save the valley. They hope they have provided for most likely disasters, but they readily admit that complete success will depend upon arresting the destruction of the upper watershed, which has steadily increased ever since man-made erosion began to upset nature's balance. "Engineers," said one of them, "can only hope to buy time by setting up a framework for future and long-range plans. And that depends finally upon what the people will do."

What the people should do is to halt erosion where it would be easiest to control, on the upper levels—a solution that the American mind shies away from. Popular discussions of reclamation and flood control picture the lake above the dam where resort owners can advertise water sports. But public interest is best caught by plans for more and larger dams, involving federal funds, fat contracts, and large payrolls. The gringo is still trying to outwit nature with ever more ingenuity and concrete, or to bypass nature's processes by pretending that they do not exist.

It is easiest to disregard nature when unseen water is in question. Pump irrigation has pointed up the struggle between advocates of conservation of natural resources for a distant future and of unthinking people who would heedlessly exhaust them to satisfy present greed. Grandsons of men whose windmills watered a few head of stock observed that motor pumps would bring up water in artesianlike flow. Why not tap "underground lakes and streams" and go into farming? The answer is that subterranean water does not always stand in vast pools or flow in dark rivers; it often inches slowly along through beds of gravel; ultimately it depends upon rainfall for renewal. And New Mexico's rainfall still averages only fifteen inches annually. Water, even hidden water, is not an inexhaustible resource. Engineers not hired by exploiting companies or chambers of commerce agree on this, and their judgment is confirmed by what has happened and is happening daily.

The lower Pecos valley first exhausted its surface water; then by reckless use of its artesian waters dried up that resource. The water level has dropped thirty-two feet in twenty-five years. In places it actually dropped two hundred feet. Farmers then turned to pump irrigation; turbine pumps could reach deeper sources of water, and in the 1920's dessicated artesian wells were brought back.

Always in New Mexico's lush times there have been voices crying of the wilderness to come. So as Pecos valley farmers set about pumping up another debacle for themselves, some far-sighted men warned that pumping the deep water would surely deplete the supply faster than rainfall could replace it, especially as erosion on the slopes of the

Sacramentos was upsetting nature's method of holding water for slow seepage.

Through the efforts of such men the New Mexico legislature passed a law to control ground water as surface water had long been controlled—by allocating it on the basis of what a certain basin can produce. This, the first ground water code in the nation, has become the model. It had to be tested in the courts because of the claim that a landowner owned "all above and below the surface" of his property. In 1930 the State Supreme Court ruled that underground waters are public waters and that later comers who infringe on former rights err just as though they emptied a ditch without regard to downstream neighbors.

Authority was vested in the state, but the law provides for the organization of water-users to work with the State Engineer. The Pecos valley farmers, having known a couple of scares, have organized successfully and formed a salutary public opinion. No man there could look his neighbor in the eye if his misuse of water were endangering the general supply.

Lands more lately irrigated still produce water-users who believe in inexhaustible supplies. The town of Portales was named for a porchlike rock that overhung a wide, clear spring known to cattle-drivers as a permanent watering place. It is dry now. But, owing partly to rural electrification, seven hundred pumps in Roosevelt County irrigate some thirty thousand acres that produce peanuts and sweet potatoes and sustain enough milch cows and chickens to make the county the state's leader in dairy produce. Portales citizens insist that their falling water table will surely come back: "Just give it time!" They blandly disregard the fact that Roosevelt County pump farmers are refused loans by the Federal Reserve Bank, which evidently does not agree that the falling water table will rise again.

Luna County, where judicious use of the underground

Mimbres River has turned the sandiest stretches of old Doña Ana County into profitable farms, has increased its irrigated area from thirteen to twenty thousand acres without danger to its water table. The Estancia valley's pale chiaroscuro plain is delighting former dry farmers with fields of wheat irrigated by pump. This, too, promises to be a sound development. These water tables are closely watched by the State Engineer and the U.S. Geological Survey.

Lea County, latest to develop, is New Mexico's richest county, with good grazing and plenty of oil at Hobbs. But war prices, sustained by government subsidy, tempted ranchers to go in for agriculture too, and during the war controls were lax. So hundreds of pumps are sucking out waters stored in Pleistocene times in the vast gravelly saucer of the High Plains. During the ages the Pecos and the Canadian, digging their canyons, have cut off the plains from the slope of the Rockies, and their only source of water now is the clouds. Rainfall is woefully inadequate to maintain the water level, which engineers say is fast sinking below the economic pumping level.

At Los Alamos, New Mexico's newest and most scientific citizens at first showed an amazing innocence of where water comes from. That atomic city certainly needed drinking- and bathing-water; it also demanded lawns and gardens, an eighteen-hole golf course, and swimming pools. As it grew larger, its engineers soon were depleting the Pajarito Plateau's surface water. It was once proposed to pipe water through the range from the Valle Grande. The director said: "There we won't be taking water from anybody." Nobody, older New Mexicans knew, except all the prior users of the western Jemez watershed, including four pueblos. The newest had met the oldest New Mexicans. So Los Alamos settled for pumps that bring water from depths as great as two thousand feet on the Rio Grande side. AEC engineers boast that they have got a permanent supply;

other engineers are not so sure. But all seems to go well, and Los Alamos is purifying its sewage water to sprinkle its golf course.

The battle for the waters never ends. Conservationists would appraise our resources and build on them. No more unpopular program could be devised. The "practical man" vastly prefers big doings, and in his dreaming nothing is too fantastic. A Lea County farmer, warned that he was pumping the High Plains dry, said: "Well when we've used it up, we'll go back to pumping stock water and raise cattle again." A Roosevelt County businessman says: "Oh, yes, we'll pump the land dry, but by that time they'll invent something to produce synthetic water." A rancher, sensible and successful, has a dreamy young scientist working on producing water from rocks, not like Moses, but like a chemist—by reducing rocks to their component parts and recombining said parts into H_2O.

Then came rainmaking. Professional rainmakers promised to produce rain by seeding the clouds, and ranchers organized to hire them. Rain fell, though not always in sufficient quantities or where it was wanted. In 1950 a flood on the Ruidoso may have been caused by rainmaking at Socorro, and a drought on the Rio Grande may have been caused by emptying the clouds over Colorado. When the Mesilla valley farmers ordered snow to fill Elephant Butte Lake, farmers in the middle valley protested that a double dose of snow—if nature should contribute her quota later—might well wash out Albuquerque. Navajos, urged to contribute to rainmaking in their district, suggested that their rain be tinted pink so they could be sure the white man was not getting all the benefit. Possibilities of litigation seemed endless. Senator Clinton P. Anderson introduced a bill in Congress to establish federal control of rainmaking. Meanwhile scientists who are conducting basic research into the matter are reserved in their claims.

Dr. E. J. Workman, president of New Mexico's School of Mines and one of the inaugurators of sound study and controlled experimentation, makes few claims. "It may prove possible to supply some of the missing ingredients necessary for rain and snow making, but one cannot get water out of the air unless the air contains water at near-saturation conditions." New Mexico's old bugaboo arises in a new form. You cannot get water unless there is water. Dr. Workman explains that even when there is water in the upper air most of it may evaporate as it falls through dry air near the surface. Every native recalls magnificent thunderstorms seen in the upper atmosphere which seemed to be caught by lower layers of clouds without letting one raindrop reach the ground. Dr. Workman concludes with the old unpopular warning: "If we expect to maintain a normal increase in the standards of people already here, we shall have to get more water or conserve our water better." New Mexico remains an arid state, above as well as below. And the ingenious gringo has not yet devised a more certain method of bringing water either from the earth or the clouds than the tried ways of the Indian dance and the Catholic procession.

XXV

ARTIST DISCOVERERS

⊂⊒ OF ALL New Mexico's discoverers the men and women of artistic perception have found the treasure most enriching to the life and spirit of the state. Being sensitive and observant people, these newcomers saw beauty in landscape that had often seemed repellent. Because they knew other cultures, they realized what a storehouse of primitive arts they had come upon. By their work they spread the news far and wide and gradually even taught New Mexicans to value what they had. This revelation came not only from painters, but also from students of the ancient peoples and their arts, and from collectors who saved many examples of the best work for the inspiration of later workers.

The first students were archæologists such as Adolph Bandelier, ethnologists such as Washington Matthews. The first propagandist to trumpet the news abroad was Charles F. Lummis. A few people had valued and collected the fine old things before the artists' arrival. Governor and Mrs. Prince had filled their home on Santa Fe's Sena Plaza with excellent blankets, baskets, and pottery. Mrs. Mary Lester Field of Albuquerque had collected embroideries and *santos*, as well as silver. James Seligman's collection finally so overflowed his house that he set up a notable shop near the Cathedral in Santa Fe. There were others, but these writers and collectors merely heralded a spring they did not make. The freshet began when painters discovered the new landscape and began to record it.

In 1897 Ernest L. Blumenschein was commissioned by

McClure's Magazine to illustrate a story about Indians. A Santa Fe ticket agent, asked where to find Indians, advised Fort Wingate. So "Blumie," whose story called for Papagos, was set down in the middle of the Navajo country in a blinding snowstorm. By good luck an Army wagon gave him a lift to the fort several miles away, and the violin he always carried made him friends. In time he learned that his Indians were hundreds of miles farther on, and he went to Phoenix. But "Blumie's" nostrils had caught the whiff of New Mexico, and the next summer he was back with his friend Bert Phillips. From Denver they drove to Taos on their way to Mexico. One sight of that pueblo's terraced mass and sheeted Indians was enough: the Taos art colony was born.

Its development was to be along highly individualistic lines. As it was almost inaccessible over difficult mountain roads or the narrow-guage Denver and Rio Grande Western Railroad (known as Dangerous and Rapidly Growing Worse), and with no comforts whatever, only an intrepid seeker would reach it and stay on. Yet Taos was to put New Mexico on the country's art map and give it such advertising as could not possibly be bought.

In 1914 six men organized the Taos Society of Artists and offered anybody anywhere group exhibitions at no charge except transportation and insurance. At a time when there were practically no art galleries west of the Mississippi, and nobody in the art world had heard of New Mexico, these men sent forth pictures that immediately attracted wide attention. Blumenschein, Walter Ufer, and Victor Higgins won coveted prizes, and their work was bought by the best galleries. They had even booked shows for Honolulu and Shanghai, but the United States's entry into World War I caused them to be canceled.

No show was now complete without an Indian in a white sheet reflecting the fire's glow or the flicker of sunlight through yellow aspens. Every artist was overwhelmed by the glory of the clear light, the magnificence of mountains, the paintability of strong Indian faces. Such things became the hallmark of New Mexico's school, if it could be called a school; the similarity was always in subject matter, never in method. Each painter used the technique he had learned in eastern or European schools, but the best of them soon outgrew the obviously picturesque and discovered subtler beauties. Blumenschein, Higgins, and Ufer turned to experiments with light on mountains and clouds. Kenneth Adams lovingly depicted the wisdom of wrinkled old women in both paintings and lithographs, and found truth in the Indian's frank approach to our angular landscape. Oscar Berninghaus and Ward Lockwood caught humor as well as beauty in Indian and Spanish life. More cautious painters continue to produce the ever salable yellow aspens, posed Indians, and chile strings against adobe walls.

Taste for these themes was trained by the Santa Fe Railroad, whose publicity man, William Haskell Simpson, was a poet who loved pictures, but who had an eye for business. Why not use paintings to advertise the country and attract tourists? Artists were given passes to come west and paint; their pictures were bought and hung in ticket offices; every year's Santa Fe calendar carried a Taos painting by Irving Couse. The Santa Fe's affiliated Harvey System was developing the taste for good crafts. Business had discovered New Mexico.

Santa Fe's art colony was of later growth and broader base. From the beginning it was linked with archæology. Edgar L. Hewitt's work at Puyé and at the Rito de los Frijoles had led the Archæological Institute of America to establish its first school in this hemisphere: the School of American Research in Santa Fe. Dr. Hewitt was blessed with the support of Frank Springer of Cimarron, an Iowa lawyer who had made a fortune on the Maxwell Land

Grant, and who was politically powerful. In 1907 the territorial legislature established the Museum of New Mexico in the Palace of the Governors. Ten years later the state built the Art Museum, modeled on old mission churches, and Mr. Springer engaged Donald Beauregard to decorate its St. Francis Auditorium with paintings of the work of the Franciscans from Yucatan to New Mexico. Other artists followed when war in Europe forced them to desert the Left Bank and seek quaintness nearer home. Santa Fe thought itself ready to lead the world in both art and archæology.

The old capital now became infused with a new and heady spirit. A new world had been discovered, a ferment was in the air. Everybody was young, eager to learn, ready to try anything. Seeing an Indian dance was not a matter of a couple of pleasant afternoon hours. Devotees like Witter Bynner stayed in a pueblo for days to witness the preliminary rites. He entertained Indian friends in his adobe house, where he had mingled Chinese and Indian art; he made of himself a walking showcase of Navajo jewelry; he reproduced Indian cadences in his poetry. Alice Corbin Henderson, from her bed at Sunmount Sanatorium, inspired younger poets and tuned her own delicate ear to the rhythms of old *alabados* and *corridos*. Jane Henderson, before she married Gus Baumann, lived for months in Santa Clara learning to sing in true Indian style.

These people were seeing what most New Mexicans had never seen before—the true art of Indian handiwork, the pageantry of Indian dances, the dignity and suitability of adobe houses, the grace of Spanish crafts. They took it all in great gulps. They bought crumbling adobe houses for a few dollars and did their own remodeling or hired neighbors to lay adobes and raise beams; furnished dirt-floored rooms with old furniture; used pottery for dishes; took to a diet of chile and beans. Willie Henderson turned from painting to making furniture with adze and wooden pins. The Cinco

Pintores made their street, El Camino del Monte Sol, an art center. Most of them were poor; living was simple, but thinking was high, wide, and handsome.

Inspired by Jane Baumann, the "colony" organized the Santa Fe Players and produced old melodramas and modern shockers. They gave his first hearings to Lynn Riggs, who was living in Sarah McComb's chicken house while he wrote *Green Grow the Lilacs,* which reached Broadway twice, the second time as *Oklahoma!* They shook up the moribund fiesta by setting up an Indian market in the old Palace's portal and by reviving old Spanish plays and dances. With the brashest humor they burlesqued the sanctified historical pageant with a "hysterical pageant" that pulled no punches. Will Shuster built a hideous monstrosity to be burned as Zozobra, Old Man Gloom, and so established a tradition that calls him away from his easel every year.

New Mexico was now the place every artist had to visit. Many distinguished names adorn the list of exhibitors. Robert Henri stayed a while. Marsden Hartley painted the high mountains. B. J. O. Nordfeldt and Russell Cowles produced in New Mexico work that enhanced well-established reputations. These men were mature and finished painters, who in turn reflected all the movements of European and American art, but who developed no new technique here. John Sloan, known in Philadelphia and New York as one of the thoroughly American "ashcan school," made a summer home on Delgado Street. But he found no ashcans in New Mexico. His paintings of pueblos, of Indian and Spanish types, are full of shimmering light and sunshine. Perhaps his greatest contribution to New Mexico life was his wife Dolly, a sixty-inch dynamo, a veteran of suffrage parades and less successful movements in New York. She now threw herself into the effort to defeat the Bursum Bill and save the Pueblos' lands; she lined up so many New York writers in a cause they had never heard of that New Mexico's Indians became front page stuff and the *Santa Fe New Mexican* was displayed on New York newsstands. Its editor, Dana Johnson, was a most effective mouthpiece; serious in his beliefs and believing always in preserving the state's beauty and distinction, he wrote with humor, versified with pungent wit, poked up the stodgy, and restored balance to the intense.

A loftier tone was contributed by Mary Austin, who had brought from California her mystical preoccupation with "Amerindian culture" and Spanish arts. Whether she was a woman of genius or an uneven performer with flashes of good writing, Mrs. Austin was certainly practical. Crowned with queenly braids, wrapped in a Spanish shawl, and enthroned on the bootblack's stand in the Chamber of Commerce, she pushed for action. Her followers laughed at her, but they loved her—and she led them. She stirred young men to physical labor on the Acoma church, making it leakproof while saving it from the tin roof that was tempting the padre. She raised money to purchase and restore the Sanctuario above Chimayo, which was then presented to the Catholic Church. She gave her blessing to the Indian Tribal Arts Association, which, headed by the Sloans and the Misses Elizabeth and Martha White, undertook to hold Indian craftsmen to their highest standards and to educate the public to appreciate the best. Defeat of the Bursum Bill led to the New Mexico Association on Indian Affairs, which enlisted the time and political skill of people of leisure who had chosen New Mexico. Led by Mrs. Margretta Dietrich, this organization has befriended Indians as individuals and as tribes, and has become a congressional lobby to be reckoned with. Its eastern associate is the Association on American Indian Affairs, whose president, Oliver La Farge, combines ability as a writer with organizational skill and knowledge of Indian problems.

Indians for the first time met respectful comprehension.

After centuries of the white man's scorn, smug superiority, or condescension, their dances were witnessed by quietly attentive people who recognized their artistry and religious content. Their handiwork was judged with artistic discrimination. Naturally Indians responded eagerly to strangers who advocated the revival of old pottery forms, old dyes in weaving, old techniques in basketry, and ancient and significant designs. Frank Applegate lived among the Hopis, found pottery clay banks that had been forgotten, revived the potters' old skills.

Indians had long been painters. Kenneth Chapman, an authority on Indian design, believes that the tradition of kiva mural painting had never been lost. In 1902 he found a Navajo drawing good landscapes on boxtops in a trading-post. When John DeHuff and Dorothy Dunn encouraged children in the Indian School at Santa Fe, they eagerly made pictures of what they knew. When the Museum was established, Indians were given space to work, and Maria Martinez's pottery soon appeared in Fifth Avenue shops. Julian and Crescencio, who painted the designs on her pottery, were given paper and watercolors and began to make paintings for sale. The Indian's precise line, balanced design, impeccable color sense, and specialized knowledge produced pictures of dances, animals, and Indian life which won plaudits from the most critical. Indian painting went into museums and collections, and was reproduced in the most expensive form. Fred Kabotie the Hopi, Velino Shije of Zia, Alfonso Roybal of San Ildefonso, and others were recognized artists.

Perhaps an even greater gift was the artists' recognition of the value of the dying Spanish culture. Shy old men, who had hidden the old plays, now had auditors who recognized a medieval folk-art. Old women, who had been ashamed of their wool embroideries, saw their *colchas* respectfully handled by artists who recognized the old patterns. *Santeros,* whose holy figures had been repudiated by the devout in favor of plaster saints from religious supply houses, found their carvings in cottonwood and their paintings with earth colors in demand by collectors. Families of woodcarvers revived their art, especially in the secluded village of Cordova.

Jose Dolores Lopez became famous for his unpainted woodcarvings; one was bought by the Museum of Modern Art. After his death in 1937, his son George carried on the family tradition. In Taos, Patricino Barela, given a start by Vernon Hunter under the WPA Art Project, has become famous for his simple, imaginative work. After his child's serious illness he made a figure of a frightened father in the hands of an all-powerful doctor.

Altogether the artists' greatest gift to New Mexico was respectful appreciation. Out of this grew the effort to save the old arts and to aid their further development. But artists were to kill the thing they loved. Even as the Philistines they deplored, artists felt the great American urge and went into business. A group of them opened the Spanish and Indian Shop in Santa Fe, and artists were now to be met in the pueblos talking a weak-willed Indian into selling ceremonial objects, or in Spanish villages tempting a family's neediest member into giving up the chest that had traveled the Chihuahua Trail. This started the craze for native crafts in household decoration, and a general buying spree ensued.

Competition grew keen. "I got all the doors in that village. I don't know what I'll do with them, but at least nobody else will get them." Such handmade bits were built into remodeled houses at Santa Fe and Taos. A village's entire economy could be upset by these new neighbors, and the farmer's water supply was often reduced to the danger point as the new residents diverted the stream not only for crop irrigation, but much more for unproductive gardens. Tragic tales are often told as funny.

"I wanted that orchard so nobody would ever cut off my

view. Jose held out; said he was the family trustee and had to keep that land for his unmarried sisters. But one day when he was drunk he signed up. He had power of attorney, you see. . . . You should have seen him next day. Battered is the word. It seems his brothers had beaten him up when they found out he'd sold out the old maid sisters. Jose wanted to revoke the sale. One sister, he said, had planted a tree when her lover died and didn't want to lose it. But I had the paper."

As roads and plumbing reached Taos, the camp followers of the artistic shock troops moved in. Bankers co-operated in the foreclosing of mortgages, and whole villages were made over. Mabel Dodge came west with Maurice Stern, whose New Mexico paintings created a furor in New York. Mabel's extensive adobe mansion swarmed with the *cognoscenti*. John Marin and Max Weber visited. Robinson Jeffers's poetry and D. H. Lawrence's prose gave a new dimension to the literature beginning to burgeon in New Mexico. Mabel herself wrote several books marked by sensitive observation, especially after her marriage with Tony Luhan gave her an in-law's view of Indian life. Willa Cather was a Taos visitor, though she wrote more of *Death Comes for the Archbishop* in Mary Austin's Casa Querida in Santa Fe, where Don Amado Chaves told her the stories that lend such verisimilitude to her novel.

In Taos, Bert and Elizabeth Harwood remodeled Cap Simpson's old home. Later Elizabeth opened there a gallery where every artist and craftsman could show. At her death she left the place to the University, which maintains it as the Harwood Foundation. Artists were now coming in on John Dunne's stage from Taos Junction; in good weather the road was open from Raton over the divide from Cimarron. Taos was an art center equal to Provincetown or Woodstock.

Andrew Dasburg moved up from Santa Fe, bringing his

almost religious love for the land. "I felt as though I had come upon the Garden of Eden; everything was pristine." His paintings of landscape, figures, still-life, all reflect this awe; his superb technique and understanding criticism have influenced many younger painters.

Among the discoverers were photographers. Ansel Adams, Edward Weston, and Ernie Knee made studies of land and people which had both artistic and documentary value. Laura Gilpin, beginning with posed Indians, developed a more revealing manner that culminated in a magnificent book, *Rio Grande, River of Destiny*. Paul Strand sought the delicate designs hidden in old adobe or in the weathered timbers of the ghost town of E-town.

With Paul Strand came his wife Becky and Georgia O'Keeffe. The two women provided sharp accents to the kaleidoscope of pueblos on dance days by appearing in long black capes and flat black hats. O'Keeffe was quite unaware of comment. She had found her land, and was soon painting white skulls in the hard desert light. Her New Mexico canvases, shown in New York by Alfred Stieglitz, won highest critical approval and established O'Keeffe as one of the greatest living women painters. Her home in Abiquiu, with its large empty adobe rooms, is a fitting workshop for O'Keeffe's paintings, so imaginatively conceived and so definitely stated with clarity of line and color.

In the late twenties, business took over. The Santa Fe Railroad pushed its advertising, and the Harvey System began hauling tourists around under the guidance of girl couriers; both tried to uphold standards of taste while commercializing the Indian arts and crafts. Bert Staples, out near Gallup, set Navajos to making flat silver, cigarette boxes, and ash trays as fine as the best New England work. The Kirk brothers at Manuelito soon joined in; others caught the fever. Navajo blankets were now sold as Navajo rugs, Chimayo weavers supported entrepreneurs in Santa Fe, woodcarvers and leatherworkers were trained. New Mexico's oldest styles of architecture became the only thing. It seemed a triumph of good taste. But the triumph was too complete.

Slowest to catch on to the money value of New Mexico's arts and its scenery was its own business community. Businessmen had consistently disregarded artists as queer ducks; they had never understood the value of the unpaid publicity artists give the state. Belatedly they woke up. Chambers of commerce began to inquire what there was in the neighborhood that tourists might like to see, and to issue lurid advertising. In 1935 the state established its Tourist Bureau and began to advertise in national magazines. Out of this flurry have come small shops, a few small factories, a considerable debasement of standards, and a blind destruction of precisely what attracts visitors. Old plazas are neonlighted; old houses are remodeled out of all grace and charm; fine trees that sheltered caravans or armies and that could still offer shady relief are cut down. Saddest of all, standards in the arts have been prostituted by tasteless middlemen and by the Indian's ingrained adaptability. Good potters began to slap out lopsided jars and to paint them with garish colors. Such atrocities are actually sold in the portal of the Museum, where the artists had set up a market dedicated to fine work.

Indian painters, while retaining their accuracy and precision, have let their themes grow stereotyped. One of them said: "All they'll buy are deer and buffalo dancers or hunters. So I make what they want." This conviction was established when the WPA used Indians to decorate government buildings, and confirmed when ticket offices and drive-in theaters ordered more of the same. More than one hundred Indians are turning out their two-dimensional figures in high colors and lively motion. Gay pictures on the wall, but an impasse for the artists.

Art teachers hope to free the Indian from this thrall, to "help him to free himself." But what white artist, himself the product of European schools, can enter into the Indian's tradition enough to do more than impose his own values? A few Indians, like Gerald Nailer and Francisco Abeyta, have experimented with contemporary styles. Both are Navajos, always successful borrowers. But the true development of an Indian art must await the Indian genius who will grow from his own deep indigenous root and not from a graft.

A promising development is Fred Kabotie's Hopi silver. Some critics disdain his exquisite jewelry and table silver as "not Indian." But Kabotie is Indian, his work is beautiful, it is giving his people a new craft. He is perhaps the first Indian artist to defy white mentors.

Art schools and art talk have naturally produced swarms of home-grown aspirants. Some are promising, some are doomed to enjoy their endeavors in private. Few Spanish names appear on any national list, though several who show in New Mexico promise well. David Gonzales sold his first painting to Cady Wells—a spirited typhoon done in deck paint on a strip of canvas while he was in the Navy. Juan Candelaria has shown his photographs widely. Two gringos figure in national magazines and galleries: Sam Smith and Peter Hurd. Tom Lea is a native of Roswell, but he lives and works in El Paso, and Texas claims him.

Sam Smith, born in Texas, was transplanted early, and is a New Mexican. He paints experimentally as a young man trying to find himself, but strongly as to color and design with a profound feeling for cloud and tree shadows and gentle villages, but for tortured Penitentes, too. His experience as an Army combat artist painting Negroes of the Gold Coast, Chinese villages, and oriental bazaars has certainly deepened his understanding of New Mexico.

New Mexico-born Peter Hurd, having studied with N. C. Wyeth and married his daughter, returned to the place he loved most—the Ruidoso Canyon, where *paisano* and cowboy meet and the landscape is dominated by sunshine. Hurd has developed his own style of painting in tempera on yeso, a technique related to his work as a muralist. Nobody catches New Mexico's light quite as Hurd does, and when he paints a water hole in the desert it is clearly an answer to prayer.

Hurd's native Roswell is generating some of the fervor of Santa Fe's most effervescent period. The Roswell Museum, under the genial leadership of Paul Horgan, is making a permanent Hurd collection. Its early director, Thomas Messer, began cleverly with a showing of Bob Crosby's rodeo trophies, followed with frontier dress, and when he offered Mestrovic's drawings ranch people came readily and enjoyed the show. Horgan helped arrange museum concerts, and Horgan has broadened his field from sympathetic and perceptive novels and stories to a study of the Rio Grande from its Colorado spring to the Texas delta.

Most artists continue to follow the old, well-worn trails to Santa Fe and Taos, and to Albuquerque whose reputation is of later growth. A few are so ungracious as to scoff at the men who made the trails they follow. Some are drifters; many stay. New Mexico has more resident artists per capita than any other state in the land. A tourist guide lists seventy "people in the arts" in Santa Fe. These include dancers, makers of ceramics and jewelry, photographers, and sculptors. Taos has not so many, but quite as wide a range, and more galleries that sell. The 1940 Fiesta Show at Santa Fe listed 269 painters; nobody is refused. A critic rated the offering as "ranging from mediocre to lousy." But it included work of many men welcomed in New York's best galleries. A show in Albuquerque listed seventy-one painters with their addresses: even the state's commercial center has its artists, though they lack a colony's cohesiveness.

New Mexico has still developed no school of painting,

though its color, light, and angular land-forms, as well as the Indian's way of simplifying them into symbols, have affected all its artists in some degree. New Mexico might have invented cubism, but did not; and the Indian influence is not comparable with that of African sculpture on Picasso and on others of the French school.

Gustave Baumann, still the discoverer after thirty years, has reproduced pictographs and used them. His wood-block prints and gay puppet figures have caught much native humor. And only Gus could have seen fat dullards, haughty dames, and querulous snoopers in gourds and, with a few lines and a deft twist in the mounting, made them into delightful figures of fun.

Agnes Sims, who studied pictographs from the Galisteo Basin, has used the lively skinny figures in painting and has incorporated Indian symbols for water, snakes, rain, and horizon into her paintings depicting Indian life.

Experimenting goes on. Pansy Stockton has named "sun paintings" the pictures she makes by pasting on boards bits of bark, leaves, moss, pine needles, and milkweed floss. For the New Mexico sky only the bluebird's feather will do, but by its clever use she makes a mere flash of blue suggest a wide empyrean.

Dorothy Stewart gathered together her arts and interests in her Galeria Mejico, where a pink entrance with iron grille leads into a high-walled studio. There she presented musicians, speakers, and pictures too esoteric for the general public. There she printed her *Hamlet*, a series of wood-block prints to illustrate a masterly selection of quotations. This was set and printed by hand in old type on an old press; its type was distributed after one hundred impressions had been sold for twenty-five dollars a copy.

Sculpture, despite statuesque models with bronze skins, has proved too costly to develop far. Bruce Saville, who lived in Santa Fe for a few years, made an excellent series of Indian dance figures. Allan Clark and George Blodgett figured in eastern shows. Eugenie Shonnard, using techniques learned from Rodin, used native cedar and sandstone to carve figures at once solid and poetic.

All the arts lag behind painting. Collections of native music remain largely untouched. Aaron Copland's ballet score, *Billy the Kid*, used frontier and cowboy songs. J. Donald Robb, Dean of Fine Arts at the University, was the first to use Spanish songs. His opera *Little Joe*, based on Robert Bright's novel *The Life and Death of Little Joe*, used twenty-five Spanish themes. It opens with a crashing dissonance that suggests the land's harshness—a theme repeated in the scenery designed by Lloyd Goff and painted by Ted Schuyler; simple village life unfolds in song and dance. Its high point is in a Penitente scene, with its underlying fear and suffering. As a first work, it lacks dramatic force, but *Little Joe* may well be a significant first in New Mexico music.

Much as New Mexico has been written about, its writers are few compared with its painters, and its best books have been the work of outsiders. Willa Cather and Conrad Richter have won widest renown with our history, Oliver La Farge and Frank Waters with the Indian. Even writers of the Westerns truest to detail and talk are often newcomers who saw cowboys at firsthand. Of the natives, Ruth Laughlin turned to her birthplace when she wrote of Doña Tules, the gambler of Santa Fe, and Harvey Fergusson has been preoccupied with the times of his pioneering grandfather. Bill Mauldin, who became one of the best-loved cartoonists of World War II, tells in *A Sort of a Saga* of his boyhood in La Luz—a sort of a Tom Sawyer. Only Fergusson has essayed the modern scene with clear-eyed realism, but even he has presented Spanish life as a dying phenomenon, typifying it in an unsuccessful hero. Sensitive people are sure to see it so. We await the novelist whose hero may start as a pitiful "Little Joe," but end as head of a department in a great university, an authority on Inter-American affairs, a successful Wall Street operator, as actor, musician, congressman, or as a success in smaller but important fields.

Painting still dominates New Mexico's art scene. Practitioners of the latest schools, like their predecessors, are excited by new beauties of light and form and moved by the Indian's symbolism. Raymond Jonson, beginning with complicated and beautiful "earth rhythms," has developed a nonrepresentational style that has deeply influenced his students at the University. Cady Wells's landscapes, often mystical and involved, reflect his deep awareness of our rectangular land masses. Only Howard Schleeter shows a direct inspiration from Indian work, especially from Mimbres pottery designs. His gemlike color and rich texture are the result of early training, but his design seems truly New Mexican. Hilaire Hiler, whose reputation was well established before he saw New Mexico, makes a point of seeking nothing here; he likes the climate. A unique contribution to the artistic presentation of New Mexico is that of Theodore Van Soelen. His first work was typical of the newcomer who saw the striking features of landscape and painted fine studies of aspens and cottonwoods, adobes and warmly glowing earth tones. Later work, both paintings and lithographs, reflects Van Soelen's wide knowledge and sensitive appreciation of the New Mexico scene. In addition, he has become one of New Mexico's best-known portraitists. Artists continue to come to New Mexico, but the days of discovery are past. However revealing the modern artist's experience may be to the individual, he is not the herald of a new scene. He lives in New Mexico, writes or paints, but he is no molder of opinion, no fighter for causes. The causes his predecessors fought for have been taken over by ladies of competence backed by maturity and wealth, and the wonders they presented to the world have become commonplace in tourist advertising.

XXVI

LAND OF ENCHANTMENT

New Mexico advertises itself as "the land of enchantment," and it has indeed something to appeal to every taste from the crudest to the most cultivated. The discriminating visitor must find his own way to what he will find rewarding. He can lift his eyes above the garish signboards to the reddish sandstone cliffs with purple shadows. Perhaps he can even smile at the signboard's blatant untruths that offer fake wonders without shame in a land whose authentic wonders have attracted students for a century. Cliff dwellings made to order, historic wells unknown to historians, fairly recent brick houses plastered over to pass as "old haciendas."

"Forty-eight-foot rattlesnake. Alive! Man-eating Mountain Lion! Tarantulas! Wild animals!" Westbound the note is one of warning. "Desert ahead! Last chance for water!" This sells desert water-bags, though filling stations are seldom more than twenty miles apart all the way to California.

Most travelers drive quickly on, intent on reaching Colorado in the summer, Arizona or California in the winter, or home again at every season's end. The average length of the tourist's stay in New Mexico is four and a half days, though even the speeders spend enough to make the tourist business the state's largest revenue-producer, topping even oil. The State Tourist Bureau estimated in 1950 that an average of $135 million a year is left by out-of-state cars, including buses; oil brings in a mere $120 million. Chambers of com-

merce, awake at last, try to hold motorists for one more
day, but their efforts are not very inspired.

People like to see things, to know what they are seeing,
to feel that it is unique. There are no Carlsbad Caverns back
home; thousands of visitors a day thrill to that underground
wonderland. Those caverns are New Mexico's only national
park, but its eight national monuments are likewise manned
by Park Service rangers who are well-informed and courteous as well as efficient guardians against vandalism. There
are, besides, five state parks and nine state monuments with
small collections that people peer at in earnest attempts to
understand prehistoric life.

Otherwise the vast human pageant that has moved across
these uplands and valleys remains hidden from the eastern
visitor, who thinks our history began in Virginia. There
are no museums except the state institutions in Santa Fe and
a few small ones of local interest. Even Albuquerque, cross-
roads of the highways and the state's largest city, is so absorbed in its desire to become a second Chicago or Los
Angeles that it makes no official effort to detain the daily
stream of visitors. "What is there to see here? . . . Oh,
well, let's go on to Santa Fe."

From the middle of May to the middle of September the
automobiles spin along the highways as though the singing
tires were held to the asphalt. But even among these speeders are a few people with ears to hear of a Pueblo Corn
Dance just a mile down the arroyo or over the hill; with
eyes to see the beauty of the tall standard fluttering above
the flat adobe roofs massed with people brightly colored,
and to feel the deep meaning behind the throbbing drums,
the deep-toned chant, and the precisely changing figures of
the dance.

These are the visitors who stay over a day or two or try
a different route on the return journey. Once felt, the New
Mexico magic has great drawing power; it pulls obliquely

away from the tried and dully safe. It could make the motorist leave the Will Rogers Highway in Arizona to angle across the Mogollon Mountains, where parklike pine forests are carpeted with grass and starred with white desert poppies, scarlet pentstemon, and purple bee balm. He may come upon an archæologist digging for a missing link or casting for a trout. He may sit rocking with a lion-hunter or a prospector, whose verbiage is as unforgettable as it is unreproducible. If he listens he will come back to stay.

Likewise the visitor to the Carlsbad Caverns, letting his eye be caught by the waxy bloom of yucca on the desert, may be lured northward to Lincoln Plaza, the Ruidoso, and the Mescalero reservation. The lovely, noisy Ruidoso has been throttled by tourist camps and the sort of gambling resorts that are invisible to state or county police. But apple orchards offer crisp and tangy fruit, and there are hidden canyons where one can relive the Lincoln County War and try to get an Apache to tell where his tribal gold mine is.

The motorist who stays on the Butterfield stage route will dip into Texas and may cross into Mexico at El Paso before continuing along Cooke's road to the sea. But there is much to linger for in Doña County. Las Cruces is marked by three crosses on a hill. There is a legend to the effect that the crosses were erected in memory of Spanish colonists who were massacred there during the early nineteenth century, though no historical date is given. When the town was laid out in 1849, it was naturally known as Las Cruces (The Crosses). In time it became a wealthy town; the Hotel Amador is still replete with the elegance of pre-gringo days. Its splendid mahogany furniture was hauled from New Orleans by the first Amador, who presumably placed over the bedroom doors those delicately lettered names of girls: Anita, Luisa, Rosa. Its wide central hall is filled with relics of Maximilian's Mexico: lace fans, old guns, letters, papers, and paintings. A wax matador in full regalia stands by the stairs, and a wax Numidian proffers a card tray to the guest on his way into the modern bar with chromium trim or to the dining patio.

Mesilla, capital of the Confederate State of Arizona, is three miles off the highway, where it drowses pleasantly under its cottonwoods. A starkly modern church dominates the plaza, but low adobe buildings surround it and its most aggressive business house is the Billy the Kid Cantina. No New Mexico character, except Kit Carson, slept in more places than the redoubtable Kid, who was once caught and convicted in Mesilla.

La Posta, where the stages drew up dusty or muddy, sometimes battle-scarred, serves excellent Mexican meals and displays Henry Griggs's uncatalogued collection of good, bad, and indifferent articles. La Posta belongs to the family of Albert Fountain, who still hope to establish the truth of the colonel's disappearance in the White Sands. The Fountain homes and others are opened to visitors on a Sunday in May. None of Mesilla's homes is very old, but they are reminiscent of the easy living before either the Union or the Confederacy took over.

An older fiesta of deeper meaning occurs on December 12, day of the Indian Virgin of Guadalupe. Celebrated throughout the Southwest, this fiesta is most Mexican in Las Tortugas, a misnomer for the villages of San Juan and Guadalupe near Las Cruces. Scores of people come from Mexico, the prevailing language is Spanish, and venders squat on the ground beside their piles of pottery or braziers of savory foods, just as they do in the neighboring republic.

The fiesta begins early on December 11, when worshippers start the long, dusty, stony climb to the Virgin's shrine on a near-by hill. In sterner days many of the devout went on their knees and all fasted. Now they walk, carrying lunch boxes or thermos bottles. But the pilgrimage remains an act of devotion or of gratitude for favors granted, and villagers tell of many miracles the Guadalupana has wrought.

At dusk of a quiet December 11, the two villages sparkled with *faroles* on the roofs, and *luminarias* of dry cactus wood flared redly toward a skyful of stars. The only sound came from the violins and drums of dancers near the church. Three groups were dancing: Los Matachines, not very expert; Los Aztecas, said to be recent arrivals from Mexico —among their costumes was one feathered headdress reminiscent of the *Danza de las Plumas* of Oaxaca; the third group, accompanied by the chanting of old men of strongly marked Indian features, consisted of women, whose black cotton dresses were cut like those of Pueblo women.

No authoritative study of these dances has been made. Las Cruces people think the Indians are Piros, refugees from the Manzano "cities that died of fear." But the Pueblo dance group is called Los Tiwas, and a woman from Isleta, where they speak Tiwa, said she could understand the old men's chant. They are altogether a curious survival of Mexican and Pueblo rites; degenerate, unexplained. Perhaps for most participants the fiesta's true significance is Catholic, not Indian, though it centers in a long adobe house called El Pueblo.

When dark had fully come, a ruby diadem suddenly gleamed on the hilltop, where the pilgrims had lit their cruciform bonfire. Then three luminous streams began to flow down the slope as the worshippers descended, each one carrying a torch or, more likely, a flashlight. It would be hours before they arrived; the dancers went to supper. At El Pueblo a few men waited and when the time was right they lit *faroles* there. People began to gather quietly, coming on foot or in cars.

As the procession came nearer it seemed to move under a white blur. Each pilgrim was carrying a sotol wand tipped with an ivory-white flower fashioned of a yucca leaf and

tied with aromatic creosote leaves. This is very Mexican—
to make a beautiful thing of wild plants artfully put together.

At El Pueblo's closed door, the pilgrims begged admit-
tance. A voice within denied them. "You are bad people,
robbers." "No, we are the devout, come to venerate Our
Lady." "Enter then," and the doors were flung open, light
streamed forth, harsh against the warm glow of the moon
laced with silver starlight. This was the fiesta's culmination,
though there was more dancing on the Guadalupe's "very
day."

Few New Mexico fiestas are so unaffected by efforts to
appeal to the tourist. Most of them, even saint's day observances, have been dressed up for tourists with a historical parade, an elected queen, a rodeo, and a noisy carnival.

San Geronimo Day at Taos has grown into a three-day
program that lists vespers in the pueblo and the sundown
dance among a score of events including a livestock show,
square dancing, a Kangaroo Kourt for those not suitably
dressed, and a costume ball. Even tourists for whom this is
done complain that "our dear old Taos is being ruined by
tourists."

Santa Fe's fiesta opens with a candlelit and very reverent
procession from the Cathedral to the Cross of the Martyrs.
Hundreds of worshippers walk slowly to the Latin chanting
of young Mexican seminarists, and the archbishop presides
over a ceremony honoring the martyred missionaries to the
Indians. The Indians take part quite calmly.

Of the artists who rescued this fiesta from its tawdry middle period, only Will Shuster still does his stint of building
Zozobra for burning, and Dorothy Stewart mobilizes a
group to paint quaint banners for the plaza. Two little
theaters offer fiesta plays. But the fiesta is most marked by
its changes.

It is fashionable now for Santa Fe residents to leave town

during fiesta or to by-pass the town as they drive from one cocktail party to another. Tourists skirt the plaza on their way from hotel bar to Museum art show or to buy the bad Indian pottery displayed in the Museum's portal. This leaves the plaza free for old people, who sit chatting in Spanish or minding babies while older youngsters ride the merry-go-round—still best known as Tio Vivo (Lively Uncle). Country people circulate among the booths, eating, shooting, hailing each other; at night they dance in the streets. Santa Fe's fiesta has come back to the people again.

Other towns feature rodeos. Las Vegas's Cowboys Reunion on the Fourth of July is the outgrowth of the first Rough Riders Reunion held there in 1899, with Colonel Teddy Roosevelt as the honored guest. Aging Rough Riders are invited to lead the parade in hacks, and every male citizen is required to raise whiskers. Whiskers are demanded at every frontier show, but other features vary. At Cimarron, where they raise fine horses, races are important. At Grants, where Navajo cowboys often win the prizes, other Navajos dance by firelight. But always the rodeo is the thing.

This most western of sports has at last received academic recognition, and riders, ropers, and bull-doggers now vie with quarterbacks for campus hero worship. New Mexico's University and Agricultural College have joined institutions in nine other states to organize the National Intercollegiate Rodeo Association, which holds meets and promulgates rigid rules. New Mexico's Aggies, right off the range, have brought home prizes. Cattlemen are delighted to help finance a sport that demands horses, cattle, trailers, and feed-lots as well as expensive equipment.

Most of New Mexico's staged festivals occur in summer, when tourists abound. The most splendid spectacle is Gallup's Inter-tribal Indian Ceremonial in August. It has expanded, in thirty years, from a get-together of a few Navajos and Zunis to a concourse of seven thousand Indians from thirty-one tribes.

The audience faces a backdrop of tepees and covered wagons, where the Indians camp, and masses of Indians in dance regalia await their turn to perform. The smooth efficiency of the management and the Indians' perfect stage-presence combine to produce a magnificent production, especially at night, when tall bonfires almost outshine the spotlights. No dance is given in its entirety: Indians wish it so, and most visitors would be bored by the complete dances. But the sampling is good. As dancers grow more professional year after year, they develop the mannerisms of stars and tend to substitute the white man's Indian love lyrics for their own strong rhythms. But the whole retains a genuine Indian flavor, and the hall of exhibits demands high standards in the Indian crafts it shows.

The people who choose to stay in New Mexico generally have tastes that make them feel at home with the country or its people, as though a strong land would welcome only its own. The true dude ranch that handles dudes along with cattle is not here. Nor is the movie star's elaborately expensive resort. Back in the nineties the railroads built a few enormous hotels, but only Cloudcroft Lodge in the Sacramentos still keeps afloat, with week-enders from military posts at El Paso and Alamogordo. At nine thousand feet there is not much one can do. Tennis, golf, even dancing are too strenuous. Guests stay indoors at card tables or huddle behind plate glass windshields on the verandas. But the drive up is magnificent; it follows the railroad's many switch-backs, revealing wide views of the pastel Tularosa Basin with a long low-lying cloud far away that turns out to be the White Sands.

New Mexico has many hot springs of tested therapeutic value: Faywood, Ojo Caliente, Truth or Consequences, and others less advertised—but they remain simple places for simple people with arthritis. No elegant spas have been developed.

The favorite resorts are in the mountains, near art colonies or pueblos, or far out on the Navajo reservation, where traders have added guest rooms or fixed up hogans with windows and running water. Many serious students who had summered happily in New Mexico studying primitive cultures were called upon for advice during World War II, when our government suddenly faced the need to deal with alien peoples.

Other visitors, not serious at all, love to poke about among ruins. The Gallina Bench Ranch advertises that it has no modern conveniences and only one mail a week, but it can show hundreds of ruined towers on Dead Man's Mesa where prehistoric men lived. The ranch is reached by a dirt road that curls around cliffs under the northern escarpment of the Jemez range, with its familiar striations of sulphur yellow, bone white, and terra cotta. Below the cliffs the Chama River prances companionably along until the road bumps into it on a damp and sandy beach. There the visitor hails the ranch and somebody comes to man the rowboat and ferry the guest across. Surely this is the only dude ranch reached by boat?

The Ghost Ranch, set against the Chama valley's northern wall, uses a cow's skull as its insigne; its ghosts were those of cattle-thieves hanged to its tall cottonwoods. There a sheep-herder was scared out of his wits by a monster that moved. Paleontologists later identified the specter as the skeleton of a phytosaur, which accommodatingly moved enough in the breeze to justify the sheep-herder's scare.

Diagonally across the state the amateur archæologist may stop at the Gila Hot Springs Ranch and visit ruins that may connect the Mogollon with the Pueblo culture. "Doc" Campbell and his wife, a granddaughter of Tom Lyons the "cattle baron," offer luxury in the famous hunting-lodge;

and riding, fishing, and hunting in a hidden paradise, accessible only on horseback.

Most guest ranches are easy to reach by motor, and they offer the softest possible "roughing it," with good beds and plumbing in log cabins, good horses and guides, and the certainty that there will be ham for dinner in case the trout fail to rise. Such places are as small and friendly as private homes, and their guests come back year after year.

Corkin's Lodge on the Brazos is so sure of its regular professors and judges that it does not advertise, but just looks for early arrivals when the Brazos Falls begin to twist over the cliffs in their two thousand feet of spray. They dry up when the snow waters have run off Brazos Mesa, but the guests stay on to fish all summer, and even into the fall for hunting.

Los Pinos, on the upper Pecos, "where the road ends and the trails begin," allows favored guests to ride to Lake Katherine—named for the ranch owner who discovered it.

Evergreen Valley, at the top of Gallinas Creek above Las Vegas, is a lush green meadow ringed with stately conifers and guarded by tall cliffs of red and blue granite. Housekeeping cabins are tucked away, almost unseen, among the spruce and fir trees.

Such places attract people who need rest, love remoteness, and can be endlessly entertained riding new trails through pine and aspen forests where shy lady's-slippers hide or one can gather armfuls of columbine or mariposa lilies. Most of them close in September, but a few stay open for the fall's hunting.

Trout fishing is New Mexico's summer sport; lakes and streams are kept stocked with brook and rainbow trout and guarded against violation. The best trout water is in the eight-hundred-foot gorge of the Rio Grande, whose swiftness over a rocky bed makes it "a tackle buster." All its tributaries, like all New Mexico's mountain streams, are trout streams. They come tumbling clear and cold from the peaks to delight true fishermen in hip boots, who whip the water with limber rods all day, and at evening fry the catch over a fire in camp. More sedentary sportsmen may prefer fishing from a boat on Eagle Nest Lake in the Moreno valley, where anybody should be able to pull in a trout of from one to three pounds, and where seven-pounders are taken now and then.

Warm-water fishing is a by-product of irrigation and flood control; every artificial lake above a dam is kept stocked with bass, crappie, and catfish. This accounts for automobiles on the highways with boats lashed on top, and for regattas on Elephant Butte and Conchas lakes.

New Mexicans are sportsmen; most fishing and hunting licenses are sold to residents of the state. The Game Protective Association of some eight thousand members includes men from the professions, from business, and from labor, who work together to see that the law protects the game and is obeyed. They train their sons to be self-reliant, to make a camp, to pack a horse, to ride, and to be wise and wary with a gun. Here persists the frontier in the easy democracy of men who judge each other by what they are and can do.

Most migratory ducks and geese feed in the valleys, where hunters in heavy coats sit in blinds to await the opalescent dawn and the whirr of the birds rising. This they still do, though draining marshes for flood control lessens the feeding grounds. Nothing has disturbed the blue quail in the foothills, and pheasants, introduced and protected as a pleasant exotic, have made very free with chickens' feed in the barnyard. The prairie chicken, so important a food on the Santa Fe Trail, was almost lost during the dust bowl era, but is coming back.

New Mexico's toughest sport is offered by the mountain lion and the bear, both of which must be run with dogs.

The grizzly has disappeared, but the smaller black bear can test any hunter's skill and endurance. The mountain lion—known also as cougar or panther—"painter" in frontier lingo—is never a man-eater as advertised. But he can give a man and his dogs a good long run and at times a dangerous clawing when, as Elliott Barker wrote, "The Dogs Bark 'Treed.' "

Six of the New Mexico life zones, as defined by C. Hart Merriam, are found in New Mexico's rise from plain to peak. On the hottest deserts of the subtropical zone, the road runner flashes through mesquite thickets and the gopher tortoise suns himself under the cactus. Up above timberline, in the subarctic zone, one may hear the whistling marmot, which sounds like a strayed member of one's party, or the pika's note, like that of a hermit thrush. Mule deer and elk are found in all brushy, timbered country, but the Virginia white tail appears only in some protected areas, and the fantail is limited to the Gila and Apache national forests.

Care is bringing back some animals the mountain man knew but that had been lost by indiscriminate killing. No open season is permitted on javelina, squirrels, or mountain sheep. This lordly animal with the heavy horns was once reduced to a few individuals, but now is found in the Guadalupe Mountains near Carlsbad and in the Sandias, where he can peer down on Albuquerque. The beaver may be taken only under special permit; his dams are considered valuable to hold water for fishing pools and as an aid to erosion control. Antelope have been hunted for several seasons; those dainty beasts had almost vanished from their native plains, but by a special technique developed by New Mexico's Game Department they have been trapped and moved to suitable range.

Autumn brings many out-of-state hunters, on the whole a self-reliant lot who know what they want and how to find it. Winter likewise brings people of special knowledge and interests. They come to see the finest of the Indian dances: the Shalako at Zuñi, one of the most elaborate masked, ancient kachina ceremonies; and Christmas dances in the pueblo mission churches which offer a dramatic union of kachina and Catholic image—"the Jesus kachina." On Twelfth Night the pueblos dance to honor the newly elected governors, and not many weeks pass without a stylized hunting dance in some pueblo. Always the Navajos are dancing when winter has made "the thunder sleep." The winter's pageantry ends only with the Holy Week observances of the Penitentes and Easter dances in the pueblos. Winter is, for many, the best time for catching echoes of our long past.

In winter, as always, most travelers drive quickly through New Mexico. The roads are black and smooth; they lead to places beyond. Such travelers see only a treeless land with funny flat-topped houses, and they hurry eagerly on to something more familiar.

Those who will find something for them in New Mexico come soon to a promontory on which to stop and breathe deeply. They look far across immense, silent emptiness, shadowed by dark rocks or river courses marked by trees, and their eyes rise to mountains massed against the overpowering sky. Looking, they feel the long thin procession of human beings which has moved slowly across this land, working and worshipping, and in passing leaving many traces of the ways they found good.

BOOKS RECOMMENDED FOR
FURTHER READING

NEW MEXICO's story has been written in several languages, especially in Spanish and English. Anthropologists have reconstructed the record of its prehistoric, pre-literate Indians from ruins and legends and have published their findings in government reports and scientific journals and books. Spanish reports covering three hundred years of history remain, to a large extent, in still unstudied archives in Spain and Mexico. A few Spanish documents have been translated into English; many have been used as bases for historical studies. Historians continue assiduously to delve into these musty archives, often discovering documents that modify previously held opinions. New Mexico's last hundred years have been recorded by travelers and traders, Army officers, government employees, and a few sober historians. The entire pageant of the three peoples has been presented in whole or in part by an endless and growing number of writers of all sorts.

A complete list of books on New Mexico would be a manifest absurdity here. Lyle Saunders's bibliography, *A Guide to Materials Bearing on Cultural Relations in New Mexico*, includes five thousand titles, of which he estimates that well over one thousand are books. The present list includes books consulted and some books readily accessible to a reader who might wish to widen or deepen his knowledge of New Mexico.

I. FIRST DISCOVERERS

Blackwelder, Eliot: *The Great Basin*
Calvin, Ross: *River of the Sun*

Hibben, Frank C.: *The Lost Americans*
Long, Haniel: *Interlinear to Cabeza de Vaca*

II. First Settlers

Lummis, Charles F: *The Cities that were Forgotten*
Walter, Paul A. F.: *The Cities that Died of Fear*
Wissler, Clark: *The American Indian; an introduction to the anthropology of the new world.*
Wormington, H. M.: *Prehistoric Indians of the Southwest*

III. The Way of the Kachinas

Bandelier, Adolph F. A.: *The Delight Makers*
Parsons, Elsie Clews: *Pueblo Indian Religion* (2 Vols.)

IV. Changing Pueblo Life

Adair, John: *Silversmiths of the Southwest*
La Farge, Oliver (ed.): *The Changing Indian*
Lummis, Charles F.: *Mesa, Canyon, and Pueblo*
Guthe, Carl E.: *Pueblo Pottery-making; a study at the village of San Ildefonso*
Parsons, Elsie Clews: *The Pueblo of Jemez*
Waters, Frank: *The Man Who Killed the Deer*

V. The Modern Pueblo

Bynner, Witter: *Indian Earth*
Grant, Blanche C.: *Taos Indians*
Henderson, Alice Corbin: *Red Earth*
Larkin, Margaret: *El Cristo* (a play)
Lawrence, D. H.: *The Woman Who Rode Away*
Marriott, Alice: *María: The Potter of San Ildefonso*
Sedgewick, Mary K.: *Acoma, the Sky City*
Underhill, Ruth M.: *First Penthouse Dwellers of America*

VI. THE TRADITIONAL NAVAJO

Amsden, Charles A.: *Navajo Weaving; its technic and history*

Coolidge, Dane and Mary: *The Navajo Indians*

Coolidge, Mary R.: *The Rainmakers, Indians of Arizona and New Mexico*

Gillmor, Frances: *Traders to the Navajo*

Haile, Berard (for the Franciscan Fathers): *An Ethnologic Vocabulary of the Navaho Language*

Haile, Berard: *Origin legend of the Navaho Enemy Way*

Kelly, Henry W.: *Franciscan Missions of New Mexico, 1740–60*

Kluckhohn, Clyde: *Beyond the Rainbow*

La Farge, Oliver: *Enemy Gods*

Matthews, Washington: *The Mountain Chant, a Navajo Ceremony*

——: *The Night Chant, a Navajo Ceremony*

Newcomb, Franc J.: *Navajo Omens and Taboos*

——: *The Navajo Shooting Chant*

——: *The Mountain Chant*

Reichard, Gladys A.: *Spider Woman; a story of Navajo weavers and chanters*

——: *Dezba, Woman of the Desert*

——: *Compulsive Prayer*

Schevill, Margaret Erwin: *Beautiful on the Earth*

Wheelwright, Mary Cabot: *Navajo Creation Myth*

VII. THE MODERN NAVAJO

Corle, Edwin: *People on the Earth*

Faunce, Hilda: *Desert Wife*

Gillmor, Frances: *Windsinger*

Haile, Berard: *The Padres Present the Navaho War Dance* (Squaw Dance)

La Farge, Oliver: *Laughing Boy*

Leighton, Alexander and Dorothea: *The Navaho Door*
Leighton, Dorothea and Kluckhohn, Clyde: *Children of the People*
Sanchez, George I.: *The People, a Study of the Navajos*
Simpson, J. H.: *Journal of a Military Reconnaissance from Santa Fe, New Mexico to the Navajo country*

VIII. THE WARLIKE APACHE

Bourke, John Gregory: *The Medicine Man of the Apaches*
Bartlett, John Russell: *Personal Narrative of Explorations*
Clum, Woodworth: *Apache Agent, the story of John P. Clum*
Davis, Britton: *The Truth about Geronimo*
Benton, Colonel C. B.: *Sgt. Neil Erickson and the Apaches, with a description of Fort Craig, N. M. (The Westerners Brand Book)*
Opler, Morris Edward: *An Apache Life-way*

IX. THE MODERN APACHE

Barrett, S. M. (ed.): *Geronimo's Story of His Life*

X. SPANISH DISCOVERERS

Bolton, Herbert E.: *Coronado and the Turquoise Trail*
Castañeda, Pedro de Nagera: *Relación de la Jornada de Cíbola*
Hallenbeck, Cleve: *The Journey of Fray Marcus de Niza*
Hammond, George P. and Rey, Agapito (trans. and eds.): *Expedition into New Mexico by Antonio de Espejo, 1582–83*
——: *Obregón's History of 16th Century Exploration in Western America entitled Chronicle*

XI. SPANISH SETTLERS

Espinosa, Gilberto (trans.): *Historia de la Nueva Mexico, by Gaspar Pérez de Villagrá*

Hammond, George P.: *Don Juan de Oñate and the founding of New Mexico*
Horgan, Paul: *Habit of Empire*
Kubler, George: *Religious Architecture in New Mexico*

XII. CHURCH AND STATE

Ayer, Mrs. Edward E. (trans.): *Memorial of Fray Alonso de Benavides*
Hackett, Charles Wilson: *Revolt of the Pueblo Indians of New Mexico in 1680*
Lummis, Charles F.: *The Land of Poco Tiempo*
Scholes, France V.: *The Supply Service of the New Mexico Missions in the 17th Century*
——: *Church and State in New Mexico, 1610–1650*
——: *Problems in the Early Ecclesiastical History of New Mexico*

XIII. RECONQUERED PROVINCE

Chapman, Charles Edward: *Colonial Hispanic America*
Chavez, Angelico: *La Conquistadora, Our Lady of the Conquest*
Kelly, Henry W.: *Franciscan Missions of New Mexico*
Kidder, Alfred Vincent: *An Introduction to Southwestern Archæology*
Leonard, Irving A. (trans.): *The Flying Mercury (El Mercurio Volante by Don Carlos de Siguenza y Góngora)*
Thomas, Alfred B.: *Forgotten Frontiers; a study of the Spanish Indian policy of Don Juan Bautista de Anza, governor of New Mexico, 1777–87*

XIV. SPANISH COLONIAL LIFE

Barker, Ruth Laughlin: *Caballeros*
Binkley, William C.: *Early Expansionist Movements in Texas*

Bustamente, Carlos: *Expedición de los Tejanos reducida a las fuerzas del General Armijo, en 1841*

Carroll, H. Bailey and Haggard, J. Villasana (trans.): *Three New Mexico Chronicles, which includes Don Pedro Pino's La Exposición sucinta y sencilla de la provincia del Nuevo Mexico*

Fergusson, Erna: *Mexican Cookbook*

Hafen, LeRoy (intro. and notes): *Antonio Armijo's Journal of 1829–30*

Jaramillo, Cleofas M.: *Shadows of the Past*

Waters, Frank: *People of the Valley*

XV. OUR SPANISH HERITAGE

Dickey, Roland F. and Goff, Lloyd Lózes: *New Mexico Village Arts*

Foreman, Grant (ed.): *A Pathfinder in the Southwest; the itinerary of Lieutenant A. W. Whipple*

Garrard, Lewis: *Wah-to-Yah and the Taos Trail*

Henderson, Alice Corbin: *Brothers of Light*

Hollen, W. Eugene: *The Lost Pathfinder; Zebulon M. Pike*

Horgan, Paul: *From a Royal City*

Lummis, Charles F.: *New Mexico David and other stories and sketches of the Southwest*

Otero-Warren, Nina: *Old Spain in Our Southwest*

Otis, Raymond: *Miguel of the Bright Mountain*

Robb, J. Donald: *Little Joe* (an opera)

Twitchell, Ralph Emerson: *Leading Facts of New Mexico History*

XVI. THE NEW NEW MEXICAN

Calvin, Ross and Walter, Paul, Jr.: *The Population of New Mexico*

Sanchez, George I.: *Forgotten People: a study of New Mexico*

Works Progress Administration; Ryan, Helen Chandler (ed.): *The Spanish American Song and Game Book*

XVII. GRINGO DISCOVERERS

Domenech, Abbé Em.: *Seven Years' Residence in the Great Deserts of North America* (2 Vols.)

Fowler, Jacob (ed. by Elliott Coues): *The Journal of Jacob Fowler*

Gregg, Josiah: *Commerce of the Prairies; the journal of a Santa Fe trader*

Pike, Zebulon Montgomery (ed. by M. M. Quaife): *Southwestern Expedition of Zebulon M. Pike*

Rister, Carl Coke: *Southwestern Frontier, 1865–81*

Vestal, Stanley: *Old Santa Fe Trail*

Webb, James Josiah: *Journal of a Santa Fe Trader*

Wislizenus, A.: *Memoir of a Tour to Northern Mexico*

XVIII. THE GRINGO OCCUPATION

Abert, Lieutenant J. W.: *Report of Lieutenant J. W. Abert of his examination of New Mexico in the years 1846–47*

Anderson, Maxwell: *Night over Taos* (a play)

Barcena, José María Roa: *Recuedos de la Invasión Norte-americana*

Benton, Thomas H.: *Thirty Years' View*

Calvin, Ross (ed.): *Lieutenant Emory Reports*

Connelley, William Elsey: *Doniphan's Expedition and the Conquest of New Mexico and California*

Cooke, Philip St. George: *The Conquest of New Mexico and California*

Davis, William Watts Hart: *El Gringo, or New Mexico and her people*

Donnelly, Thomas C.: *The Government of New Mexico*

Grant, Blanche C. (ed.): *Kit Carson's Own Story*

Hughes, John T.: *Doniphan's Expedition*

Keleher, W. A.: *The Maxwell Land Grant*

Laughlin, Ruth: *The Wind Leaves No Shadow*
Magoffin, Susan: *Down the Santa Fe Trail and into Mexico*
Robinson, Jacob S.: *A Journal of the Santa Fe Expedition under Colonel Doniphan*
Sabin, Edwin Legrand: *Kit Carson Days, 1809–1868*
Sánchez, Pedro: *Memorias del Padre José Martínez*
Thomlinson, M. H.: *The Garrison of Fort Bliss*
Twitchell, Ralph Emerson: *The history of the Military Occupation of the Territory of New Mexico from 1846 to 1851 by the Government of the United States*
Vestal, Stanley: *Kit Carson*
Wilson, Richard L.: *Short Ravelings from a Tall Yarn*

XIX. Texans Keep Coming

Crichton, Kyle: *Law and Order, Ltd.*
Ganaway, Loomis Morton: *New Mexico and the Sectional Controversy*
Kendall, George Wilkins: *Narratives of the Texan-Santa Fe Expedition*
Binkley, William Campbell (ed.): *New Spain and the West (including Spruce M. Baird's letters)*

XX. Frontier People

Cleaveland, Agnes Morley: *No Life for a Lady*
Church, Peggy Pond: *Foretaste*
——: *Family Journey*
Fergusson, Erna: *Murder and Mystery in New Mexico*
——: *Albuquerque*
Fergusson, Harvey: *Home in the West*
——: *Grant of Kingdom*
——: *Blood of the Conquerors*
French, William: *Some Recollections of a Western Ranchman, New Mexico 1883–99*
Horgan, Paul: *Figures in a Landscape*
——: *Return of the Weed*

Keleher, W. A.: *Fabulous Frontier*
McKenna, James A.: *Black Range Tales*
Otero, Miguel: *My Life on the Frontier*
Poldervaart, Arie: *Black Robed Justice*
Ruxton, George F. A.: *Wild Life in the Rocky Mountains*
———: *In the Old West*

XXI. THE MINING MAN

Dobie, J. Frank: *Apache Gold and Yaqui Silver*
———: *Coronado's Children; tales of lost mines and buried treasures of the Southwest*
Hough, Emerson: *Land of Heart's Desire*
Jones, Fayette Alexander: *The Mineral Resources of New Mexico (Bulletin 1, Mineral Resources Survey of New Mexico; New Mexico School of Mines)*
Northrop, Stuart A.: *Minerals of New Mexico (University of New Mexico bulletin)*
Wroth, James S.: *Commercial Possibilities of the Texas-New Mexico Potash Deposits (Bureau of Mines publication)*

XXII. THE STOCKMAN

Adams, Andy: *The Log of the Cowboy*
Dearing, Frank (ed.) and Dobie, J. Frank (intro.): *The Best Novels and Stories of Eugene Manlove Rhodes*
Hough, Emerson: *Story of the Cowboy*
Larkin, Margaret (collected and ed.): *Singing Cowboy*
Richter, Conrad: *Sea of Grass*
Taylor, T. U.: *The Chisholm Trail and Other Routes*
Wentworth, Edward N.: *America's Sheep Trails*
———: *Shepherd's Empire*

XXIII. THE FEDERAL MAN

Moles, Hunter Stephen: *Ranger District Number Five*
Pinchot, Gifford: *Training of a Forester*

XXIV. WATER

Bright, Robert: *The Life and Death of Little Joe*
Cather, Willa: *Death Comes for the Archbishop*
Gilpin, Laura: *Rio Grande—River of Destiny*
Luhan, Mabel Dodge: *Taos Artists*
Stewart, Dorothy: *Hamlet*

XXV. ARTIST DISCOVERERS

Austin, Mary: *The Land of Journey's Ending*
Barker, Elliott S.: *The Dogs Bark "Treed"*
Calvin, Ross: *Sky Determines*
Coan, Charles F.: *A History of New Mexico*
Fitzpatrick, George (ed.): *Pictorial New Mexico*
Fulton, Maurice G. and Horgan, Paul: *New Mexico's Own Chronicle; three races in the writings of four hundred years*
Fergusson, Erna: *Dancing Gods*
——: *Our Southwest*
Henderson, Alice Corbin: *The Turquoise Trail*
Hibben, Frank C.: *Hunting American Lions*
Luhan, Mabel Dodge: *Edge of Taos Desert; an escape to reality*
——: *Winter in Taos*
Long, Haniel: *Piñon Country*
Stevens, Montague: *Meet Mr. Grizzly*
Works Progress Administration: *Guide to New Mexico*
Waters, Frank: *Masked Gods*

GLOSSARY

acequia	an irrigation ditch
alabado	a hymn
baile	a dance or ball
batea	a large shallow pan used for washing sand to recover gold or other valuable minerals
bayeta	a kind of baize
bay steer	a reddish-brown steer. Cowmen think the Hereford steer of that color is especially vicious
Blessing Chant	a Navajo ceremony
bolson	a flat-floored desert valley
borrow pits	a bank or pit from which earth is taken for use in filling or embanking
bosque	woods
bull-roarer	a slat of wood tied to the end of a thong: used in religious rites
cabildo	a town council
cacique	a chief
campero	the man who maintains the sheep camp
caporal	an overseer on a sheep ranch
cap rock	a top layer of consolidated rock holding a steep cliff by protecting it from erosion
carreta	a cart
chile	pepper
cibolero	a buffalo hunter
colcha	coverlet
comisario	delegate
convento	monastery or nunnery

corrido	a ballad dealing usually with current events
cortés	legislature
custodio	the Director of the Franciscan missionaries in a given area, such as New Mexico was
Devil Dance	a dance of the Apaches, more properly called Crown Dance
Diné	Navajo word meaning people
doodlebug	any scientific device by which it is claimed that minerals, including petroleum, water, etc., may be located
farol	a lantern
fetich	a material object supposed to possess magical powers
gringo	among Spanish-Americans, a foreigner
gully-washer	a rain heavy enough to wash gullies into the land
hacendado	the proprietor of a hacienda
high-grading	stealing rich ore from a mine
hogan	a Navajo house
Hoop Dance	a dance done with hoops
jerky	jerked beef; a mispronunciation of the Spanish word *charqui*
kachina	a supernatural in the Pueblo mythology; the word is also applied to dolls made in the image of the supernaturals
kiva	in Pueblo architecture, a ceremonial chamber
Koshare	a clown or fun-maker in Pueblo Indian dances
Licenciado	lawyer
lightning-frame	a jointed frame, like lazy tongs or fold-

	ing lattice, used in Navajo dances to simulate the lightning
luminarias	festival lights
malpais	country underlain by dark lava, especially basalt
mano	a hand stone for grinding maize
manta	a shawl; also cotton cloth
mescal	a small cactus
metate	a stone used for grinding cereal seeds
olla	a jar
paisano	countryman, peasant
partidario	share-cropper or lessee of sheep
partido	the share of a herd of sheep turned over to a partidario on shares
patrón(a)	proprietor, boss
quarter horse	a type of horse developed on the ranges of the United States; so called from its high speed for a short distance (a quarter of a mile)
querido(a)	dear, a term of endearment
rebozo	a scarf of cotton or silk
residencia	a court held to examine into the conduct of a retiring official
riprap	loose rocks placed at the ends of a dam to prevent its eroding away
santero	a maker of religious images, especially saints
Santo	holy; a saint
shaman	a medicine man, a tribal worker of magic
sopaipilla	a sort of fritter made of tortilla dough fried in deep fat
sotol	any yucca-like plant of the southwestern United States and adjacent Mexico

spreader dam	an earth dam, thrown up on the surface of the land to spread surface water and prevent its cutting a gully
stick-kick race	a race in which runners kick sticks
tablita	a headdress worn by Pueblo Indian women in dances
talus	rock debris at the base of a cliff or slope
tápalo	a cloth worn as a scarf
tejano	Texan
tiswin	a fermented beverage made by the Apache Indians
tortilla	a thin, flat, unleavened cake, as of maize, baked on a heated iron or stone
travois	a primitive vehicle, formerly used by the Plains Indians of North America, consisting of two trailing poles serving as shafts for a dog or horse and bearing a platform or net for the load
trobador	troubadour, versifier, poet
tufa	a porous rock formed as a deposit from springs or streams
wickiup	the hut used by the nomadic Indian tribes of the western and southwestern United States
yeso	gypsum, used as plaster
Yeibechai	supernaturals in Navajo mythology. The word is also applied to a dance in which masked dancers represent the supernaturals
zaguan	a gate or entrance way into a patio

Index

Index

iii

Index
v